D1204031

Who's Whose Right?

Other Books of Interest:

DC Press

Raising Children One Day at a Time:
A Daily Survival Guide
for Committed Parents

How to Compete in the War for Talent:
A Guide to Hiring the Best

E-R: From Prevention to Triage
— How to Retain Key Employees

If It Weren't for You, We Could Get Along:
Stop Blaming and Start Living

InSync Press

Go for the Green!
Leadership Secrets from the Golf Course (the Front Nine)

366 Surefire Ways to Let Your Employees Know
They Count

Retain or Retrain:
How to Keep the Good Ones from Leaving

Who's Right? *Whose* Right?

*Seeking Answers and Dignity
in the Debate
Over the Right to Die*

edited by

Robert C. Horn, III

with Gretchen Keeler

Foreword by

C. Everett Koop, M.D., Sc.D.

Former U.S. Surgeon General

PRESS

A Division of the Diogenes Consortium

SANFORD • FLORIDA

Published by DC Press
2445 River Tree Circle
Sanford, FL 32771
http://www.focusonethics.com

This book was set in New Baskerville
Cover Design and Composition by Jonathan Pennell

Library of Congress Catalog Number: 00-103277
          Horn. Robert, C.,
Who's Right? Whose Right? Seeking Answers and Dignity in the Debate Over the Right to Die
          ISBN: 0-9708444-2-5

First DC Press Edition
10   9   8   7   6   5   4   3   2   1
Printed in the United States of America

Courage

◆

*"You're licked before you begin
but you begin anyway and you see it through
no matter what."*
—Harper Lee, To Kill a Mockingbird

Dedication

◆

*We dedicate this book to our spouses, Judy Horn and Bruce Keeler,
to our children, Jeffrey Horn, Christopher and Kristina Horn,
Laura Horn, Michael and Christy Keeler, and Krista Keeler
and to our grandchildren, present and future.*

— **Bob Horn and Gretchen Keeler**

Contents

◆

Preface

◆

By C. Everett Koop, M.D. Sc.D.

T HE HORN FAMILY AND THE KOOP FAMILY were intertwined for multiple reasons back in the 1940's and 1950's. I was a surgical resident at the hospital of the University of Pennsylvania and Dr. Robert C. Horn was the surgical pathologist. Naturally we were thrown together a lot and became not only professional colleagues but also close personal friends, as did our wives. We had our children at about the same time and it so happened that Robert Horn, Jr. was born about the same time as Allen Koop, the first child for both of us. So, I knew Robbie Horn as he was then called as a growing child who was a friend of my oldest son, Allen. Our families were together frequently until my life took me from the hospital of the University of Pennsylvania to the Children's Hospital where I became the surgeon-in-chief in 1948. Dr. Horn moved to the Henry Ford Hospital in Detroit where he was pathologist to the hospital. He died prematurely in 1976. As what frequently happens to families who meet in academia, we grew further apart geographically, and social contact was more difficult. We did manage to see each other periodically either in one another's home or at vacation spots. But in general, I didn't know much about what was going on inside the Horn family until I heard that Rob Horn had contracted Lou Gehrig's disease or amyotrophic lateral sclerosis. From that day to this, he and I have grown closer as I have come to understand him and his thinking and have learned to love and admire his family.

I am unabashedly pro-life and can argue that position from the point of view of human rights, civil rights, ethics, morals, and religion in spite of the fact that my pro-life stand delayed my confirmation as Surgeon General for eleven months. Rob Horn was the first person who made me really understand personal choice in these matters. Why? Because his choice was also mine? No. But because although he made his choice he fully believes in and supports other choices by other people in the same position. During the years of his disability, I think I detected Rob's belief in his choice to be reinforced constantly (in spite of how he feels on what he calls the bad days). There are so many things I'd like to discuss with him but the difficulty he has in his role in the conversation keeps me from it.

One question I'd like to discuss with Rob Horn is what role did the attitudes around him play in his decision. Perhaps he doesn't know because he stresses so much the role of the attitude of the afflicted on decision making. I think in pondering the situation, Rob — careful, analytical thinker that he is would have come to this conclusion: "I made my choice based on a number of things but probably underlying them all was the reality that no one around me thought I had a life not worthy to be lived."

So, you who read this book who have cognitive skills and are of sound body consider carefully your attitude about those whom you call the disabled. Do they detect by your words, your deeds, innuendo, overheard conversation, body language, that you have concluded their lives are not worthy to be lived?

This attitude is responsible for such an enormity of social ills. Expressed before WWII probably first by Binding and Hoche — a physician and a jurist in Germany — led to the progressive destruction of defective babies, the mentally ill, those with tuberculosis, those with incurable diseases, and eventually even amputees of WWI who were no longer useful to the Reich. All because they had, in the minds of Binding and Hoche, lives individually and collectively not worthy to be lived. It is probable that from these small beginnings came the Holocaust.

The attitude — of life not worth living — led to the Eugenics Movement in the United States in days gone by, fueled the early interests in physician assisted suicide, and led to the support of euthanasia, and it certainly led to the sad state of affairs in the Netherlands in regards to euthanasia during the last decade or more.

When the frail, the infirm, the disabled, the chronically ill realize that those around them think their lives are not worth living, then they become depressed, think of suicide, assisted suicide and euthanasia.

None of these remarks are to be construed as taking anything away from Rob Horn's decision. He remains the most courageous person I have ever known.

I wish everyone who contemplates a decision such as Rob had to make would read this book; even more, I wish physicians ready with the easiest and quickest way out would be compelled to read it.

Had I put this book together I would not have included a chapter by Derek Humphrey whose requirements for a life worth living are inordinately high and one whose defeatist attitude is so far from being uplifting. The fact that such a chapter is here is one more tribute to Rob Horn and his fairness and his deep understanding of choice.

My prayer for you, Rob, is that you will have the faith and courage to sustain you, that your family and close friends know in some way that they are contributing to so many who have accomplished what they thought was impossible because of your example.

—C. Everett Koop, M.D., Sc.D.

Publisher's Comment

◆

W HAT YOU ARE ABOUT TO READ is a work of love. It is the brainchild of Bob Horn, a man who has been my personal hero since he entered my life back in 1994. Bob Horn isn't anyone special; he's just an ordinary man — a man with a wife and three children, a man who taught school for a living, a man who coached soccer, a man who rode his bike before it was chic, a man who was stricken with ALS (Lou Gehrig's Disease) in 1988 and has just flat refused to give in. In 1995 I was proud to publish his first book, **How Will They Know if I'm Dead? Transcending Disability and Terminal Illness.** The writing of a book is something that is done thousands of times annually in this country; it is done hundreds of thousands of times annually around the world. It is rarely done by anyone who is totally paralyzed. But that is what this ordinary man did. And now you are about to read the fruits of his second labor of love.

Bob first shared his idea for this book back in 1995 when we met at his home in the Northridge area outside of Los Angeles. When I say he shared it, I mean he coded a message to me through his wife, Judy and his close friend and associate, Gretchen Keeler. The idea of a book that "objectively" looked at the issues surrounding one's right to die, one's right to make a decision, one's ability to be involved in their own end of life fascinated me. And on Christmas Eve 1997 I phoned Bob from my home in Florida to wish him the best for the holidays and to give him a different kind of Christmas present. Instead of an actual gift, I gave him a challenge. The challenge: "to get off his duff" (so to speak) and write me that book that he had told me about a few years earlier. The book, as I reminded him, would consist of a series of interviews with terminally ill persons and individuals who had faced terminal or chronically painful situations for which they had faced an end-of-life decision. After a few moments of silence, Bob coded his response to me through Judy: "When do we get started?"

It is now the last few months of the year 2000 and the final stages of the manuscript have been tied up. The manuscript has been completed, all articles submitted, and the results are for your scrutiny. The editors have confined themselves to correcting grammar and spelling in an effort to make all chapters understandable to the layman. the editors in no way have changed the author's meaning.

We knew from the onset that there was no way that we could produce the all time, most extensive and objective book on the subject of right to die. And for that reason we didn't set out to accomplish that. What we have done, however, is produce a work that brings together an amazing array of people from all corners of the United States and Canada who were willing to open themselves up and share their personal, often tragic stories. Sometimes the end of an article or interview isn't the way one might have hoped the story would go, but nevertheless, the end of the piece is the way the author honestly addressed the issues. In some chapters the ending is much more than some in society would wish; in some instances the individual interviewed has opted to make death their choice. And for those who requested anonymity, they received it.

Since no book can be all things to all readers — especially when covering a topic as hotly debated as this one — we decided early on that this couldn't be a definitive work. However, we did make a strong effort to make the finished product as objective as possible. And regardless of what some readers may conclude, the editors and publisher have no axes to grind in this arena. We wanted open debate and got it. We wanted critical analysis of the issues and got it. We wanted to maintain dignity and I believe we did so. Dignity was a major concern of Bob Horn and the publisher. Without dignity, is life really being lived? And at the time of death, is death without dignity something we'd wish on our worst enemies let alone our spouses, children, or best friends? Can one experience a dignified death through assisted suicide? Can one experience a dignified death while wasting away in a coma, sustained by machines? These and many more issues are raised and addressed throughout this book.

I want to thank all who took time to assist us with the compilation of original articles for this book. While not always in agreement with each other's philosophies and methodologies, there is a common, unspoken concern that all parties hold in common: their interest in the final days of another human beings' life. As a baby, one comes into this world without being asked if he or she actually wants to be part of the adventure. After spending a lifetime learning the rules, playing the game, making mistakes, and making amends, wouldn't it be wonderful if we could leave the field of play with the feeling that we had been respected — regardless of how well we had navigated the course? Dignity and respect: that is what this book is really about. It is our hope (that of the editors, authors, and publisher) that you, the reader, find a measure of it between these pages and that you can add some of what you read here to your own decision-making model.

When one thinks of terminal illness, a few standard images no doubt come to mind: Cancer, Lupus, ALS (Lou Gehrig's Disease), Parkinson's, AIDS, and Cystic Fibrosis to mention only a few. There are those who argue that MS (Multiple Sclerosis) isn't fatal and therefore doesn't fit the definition and shouldn't be considered as part of a book like this; however, most people we talked with felt differently. Certainly the quality of life that individuals with advanced MS or complicated Post-Polio Syndrome experience doesn't give anyone the impression that the illnesses are anything less than terminal for them. And so, in this book, we have included interviews with persons suffering various stages of MS. We also have the amazing story of a man who suffered and survived the most unbelievable burns a human could endure, and after nearly thirty years, he is still disappointed in the system that would not respect his requests to die at the time.

In the motion picture *The Bone Collector*, actor Denzel Washington portrays detective and author Lincoln Rhymes, a forensics expert with the New York City Police Department who became a paraplegic due to an accident on the job. Bedfast and unable to care for himself, he passes time recalling the days that were and planning just how and when he will end his life. Death to him had become an obsession. He no longer wanted to live under what he considered to be artificial surroundings, awaiting the blood clot or stroke or seizure that would surely kill him anyway. His personal friend and doctor refused to assist him and his caregiver wouldn't discuss the matter. As his character put it, "I want to make the transition on my own terms." That seems to be the message that so many of the people we talked with and heard from were giving to us. But at the same time, we heard from many people

who, in spite of their conditions, were opting for the continuance of life —
and that was also on their own terms.

C.S. Lewis, in his classic 1945 work *The Great Divorce*, wrote: "You cannot take all luggage with you on all journeys; on one journey even your right
hand and your right eye may be among the things you have to leave behind.
We are not living in a world where all roads are radii of a circle and where
all, if followed long enough, will therefore draw gradually nearer and finally
meet at the center: rather in a world where every road, after a few miles, forks
into two, and each of those into two again, and at each fork you must make
a decision." This, in many respects appears to be what many of our contributors have said in their individual articles.

In my opinion, of all the things one can possess, I suspect the greatest is
life itself. Let's face it, there is nothing else without life; nothing else would
matter, since literally there wouldn't be anything else. Intellectually we all
know, even if we don't want to think about it too often, that life inevitably
leads to death.

Few of us are prepared for the death of a loved one or close friend. The
passing of a admired person in the community or respected national leader
often shocks us, but we usually handle it easier than those close to us. The
surprising and sudden death of a spouse, parent, or child can rock our very
foundations, challenge our beliefs, raise more questions than we have answers
for, and often send us into solitude — hiding. But the one death that really
rattles the cage of our very being is our own.

Who amongst us hasn't awakened to find that the teenager inside their
body, who went to sleep the night before, has suddenly awaken in their
midlife? The once unthreatened, invincible, immortal youth has become suddenly very vulnerable. When did any of us have our first real flash that we
weren't going to come through this adventure alive? It's one thing to contemplate our own death; it's another to know for sure that it is really coming
— that it's going to be a reality. It's another thing to realize that we might
even have some control in that end and that we might even self-direct that
end. On the other hand, it is one thing to have knowledge that death is coming sooner or later (and that the final days might be less than we had planned
for ourselves), but it is another to decide to actually participate in one's own
death or that of another. And for many, the issue isn't even up for discussion;

for them the taking of one's own life or assisting in the death of another is simply something that cannot be condoned.

You will read in this book the stories of individuals who have looked death squarely in the face — not from an angle or from behind a protective barrier — but stood toe-to-toe with death. These contributors have offered us more than a tale of pain and suffering; and they surely haven't asked us for pity. You, the reader, will be permitted into a world that few of us have experienced, into a realm of uncertainty, of hope and despair, of new-found strengths and courage, and of love and respect. Whatever the individuals interviewed share between the covers of this book, they agreed to do so for no other reason than to give us all more to think about — a better understanding of an experience any of us might awake tomorrow and have to face. Some of the decisions made might not be what you would have wished for the authors, but this is where the real challenge of this book comes in: you are asked to walk paths with people who have had no choice as to the path they now find themselves walking and to reach down inside and find respect for the end-of-life decisions they have made.

Because Bob Horn, as editor of this work, wanted everything to be presented as objectively as possible, we have gone out of our way to offer up both sides of all arguments regarding end-of-life decisions, euthanasia and assisted suicide. Individuals and groups were approached and invited to participate by sharing their positions, their arguments, and their personal and organizational points of view. We are pleased with the responses that appear in this book. We were disappointed with the refusal of some to participate and the promises of participation that produced no results. Throughout it all, Bob Horn's goal was maintained: offer open-minded readers an opportunity to read, to think, to be challenged, to debate, to dig down deep into individual souls, and to decide for themselves "who's right and whose right."

In an article appearing in the **Washington Post** in 1997, staff writer William Claiborne wrote about what he called the new battleground that had just emerged as a result of the "Death with Dignity" measure that been passed in Oregon. He quoted one of the leaders in the fight against allowing doctors to help terminally ill patients to kill themselves, when he described the battle as one that "touches the soul of the nation." This so-called battle (and to some it is all-out war) has brought to the front such powerful and divergent forces as the American Medical Association and the Roman Catholic Church.

Earlier in 1994, Oregon became the only state in the nation to make it legal for doctors to help the terminally ill by prescribing self-administered lethal overdoses of medication such as barbiturates. The taint of mercy killings or euthanasia was eliminated from the referendum when the wording of the act explicitly precluded a physician or any other person from ending another person's life by lethal injection. It was this very issue that led to the defeat of similar attempts at legislation in the states of Washington (1991) and California (1992).

Arguments against euthanasia appear to be more prolific among religious groups than arguments in support of selective choice. From where I stand, as one raised in a world dominated by organized Christian groups, there are two points of view that are typically offered up as reasons why one should not use suicide or euthanasia as a solution.

The first one that comes to mind is the position that God gifted humans with life and that we — that is, each of us — are stewards of God who reap the benefits of the life that God created. We can neither start life nor, therefore, end life (be it our own or someone elses'). To end life is to commit a sin. That is one position.

The second argument is a bit more difficult to comprehend, but goes something like this: God has never sent a single experience our way that we cannot handle. Suffering is something that all humans undergo (in one form or another and to one degree or another). God supports those who suffer and for anyone to proactively seek a way to send suffering through such means as euthanasia is showing an outright lack of trust in God's promise to be with us through our suffering. This is another position.

I know that I am not alone in my confusion over these positions — especially the second. To be confused, however, often places one in the dubious position of being lumped with agnostics, atheists, humanists, new-agers, secularists, non-Christians, and others who often have difficulty with blind acceptance of theologically based arguments or positions. Certainly when I support an individual's right to choose not to use dangerous drugs or consume large quantities of alcohol or smoke, I'm lauded for my stand. At the same time, when I or anyone else discusses personal autonomy over end-of-life issues and conclude that a person who quality of life is virtually nonexistent should be respected for their decision to put an end to their perceived suffering, the challenge has been made that one is anti-God. Is relief of intolerable pain, by means as extreme as ending life, truly anti-God? This is an issue that is addressed in this book as well.

The argument over compulsory prayer in public schools has raged for years and is no less confusing. But unlike euthanasia, school prayer doesn't lead to immediate death. The question that school prayer and euthanasia do have in common, however, is that some people question whether or not, if personal choice isn't the answer, one should be forced into following the theological beliefs of the dominant religion at any given time or place? Conservative thinking typically positions itself in support of public school prayer on this basis, stating that the country was founded on Christian beliefs and morality and therefore Christian prayers in school are a fundamental right. That very well may be true, if it weren't for the fact that this country was already occupied and dominated for centuries by non-Christians (prior to European migration). If, on the other hand, this thinking isn't flawed, then perhaps the dominant religious groups) should hold sway over how and when we pray or don't pray. And in the same vain, perhaps the position(s) of these same groups should dominate when it comes to how the country should position itself when deciding issues on euthanasia. Maybe.

Conservative versus liberal. Pro-euthanasia versus anti-choice. Labels. How fair is fair? Ad when it's your life, how far do labels go to assist in dealing with pain, suffering, disability, and life-support issues? In time, many of us will actually face these questions. How will we feel about such issues in the future—when death comes knocking at our door? Will the positions we so strongly hold today remain our positions in the days when death is coming nearer?

I've found the public positions taken by organized religious groups (both Christian and non-Christian) of interest and share them with you here. Some are more supportive of an individual's right to choose. Others are far less accepting of individual choice and more supportive of the doctrine of one rule for all. Here are some examples:

Lutheran Church, Missouri Synod: condemned euthanasia in 1979 because of its use of suicide (or murder) and was seen as contrary to the laws of God. They supported the position that suffering provides each of us with the opportunity as Christians to witness and to serve.

Evangelical Lutheran Church in America: supportive of what could be called "passive euthanasia" and in 1992 stated that in all circumstances health care professionals are not obligated to use all available medical treatment at their disposal. They went on to support the notion that medical treatment may be limited in some instances and that death can be "allowed" to occur. Their position opposes active euthanasia.

Greek Orthodox Archdiocese of America: took the following position in 1996 (when the U.S. Supreme Court was hearing a case): "the Orthodox Church opposes murder, whether it be suicide, euthanasia or whatever, and regardless if its is cloaked in terms like 'death with dignity.'" It is their position that a person facing the end of life should seek God's support and strength. They cited the Book of Job in the Old Testament as a prime example of how an individual can overcome suffering of the utmost extreme and do so by focusing on God.

Roman Catholic Church: the Church relies upon The Catechism to support its position that each of us is responsible for our lives before God who created that life. "It is God who remains the sovereign Master of life. We are obliged to accept life gratefully and preserve it for His honor and the salvation our souls. We are stewards, not owners, of the life god has entrusted to us. It is not ours to dispose of."

United Church of Christ: considered by most observers to be liberal on social issues, have supported assisted suicide and gone on record in support of individual choice.

Orthodox Judaism: in a brief filed before the U.S. Supreme Court in 1997, the Union of Orthodox Jewish Congregations of America went on record with their support of laws banning physician-assisted suicide. One spokesperson for the group stated that the issue was so critical that it spanned both constitutional and moral grounds — which is in line with traditional Jewish thinking. Jews, he said, "believe that the recognition of a constitutionally recognized right to die for the terminally ill is a clear statement against the recognition and sanctity of human life...."

Christian Reformed Church in North America: this group resolved in 1971 that "mindful of the sixth commandment, condemn the wanton or arbitrary destruction of any human being at any state of its development from the point of conception to the point of death."

Salvation Army: this organization has gone on record, stating "people do not have the right to death by their own decision." It is their position that only God is sovereign over life and death and that the grace of God can sustain anyone through any ordeal or adversity.

Mennonites: in 1995 the Conference of Mennonites in Canada took the position that "pain, isolation and fear are the main factors that drive dying persons to consider suicide." [It is interesting to note here that William Toffler, of the advocacy group Physicians for Compassionate Care, has sated that it is a myth that it is common for terminally ill patients to commit suicide with horded or over-prescribed medicines. He further stated "in twenty years as a physician, I can't recall a single case like that (suicide), unless it was a depressed patient who committed suicide." This seems to support the Mennonite statement to some degree.] They do not support the state's involvement or support the facilitation of suicide, but favor controlling physical and emotional pain along with close community care for the dying.

Islam: taking a few lines from The Qur'an, the position becomes clear: "Take not life which Allah made sacred otherwise than in the course of justice." It goes on, "Do not kill (or destroy) yourselves, for verily Allah has been to you most Merciful....The concept of a life not worthy of living does not exist in Islam." Other statements by Islamic believers include the position that followers did not create themselves, therefore they do not own their own bodies. An attempt to kill oneself is a crime in Islam and a grave sin.

Presbyterians: considered by many to be liberal on some social issues and supportive of individual decision-making in cases of euthanasia, there is considerable disagreement among local congregations and among the national membership.

Episcopalian: typically liberal on social issues, they are among the supporters of individual choice in most instances.

Unitarian Universalist: this liberal group stated in 1988 its support of euthanasia and personal choice regarding assisted suicide. However, they do support this only when "proper precautions" are in place to avoid abuse.

As we go to press with Bob Horn's work of love, I look across my desk and there lies the September 18, 2000 issue of *Time* magazine (cover story:

"Dying on Their Own Terms"). One is a close-up of the face of a physician by the name of Dan Frimmer dying of cancer, who once lectured other doctors on the importance of listening to their patients and not merely provide answers for which the patient hasn't asked the question. Inside the magazine is a series of stories about people just like you and me who are facing death. Just a week earlier, journalist Bill Moyers gave **PBS** viewers an in-depth look at the issue surrounding death and dying on "On Our Own Terms: Moyers on Dying." The issues may divide us, but the issues are surely an important part of the social fabric that defines who we are. We're all involved; we're all going to have to face these issues; it's just a matter of time. It is my hope that this book achieves what Bob Horn and I both had in mind from its inception: to make you think.

—**Dennis McClellan**
Publisher

Introduction

◆

By Robert C. Horn III

WHO'S RIGHT ABOUT physician-assisted suicide and other end-of-life decisions? Like the abortion controversy, but without the intense heat (for now), opponents basically divide into two groups: those who are pro-life and those who are pro-choice.

Whose right is it to decide end-of-life questions, to choose life or death for terminally ill people? Is it the right of the judicial system, doctors, hospital ethics committees, HMOs and insurance companies, religious leaders, the patient's family or the patient himself or herself?

This book examines these and other related issues that some day we will all face. End-of-life decisions, especially doctor-assisted suicide, have rightly provoked considerable commentary and controversy of late. In this emerging national debate, we have heard from judges and lawyers, physicians and clergymen, ethicists and editorial writers, politicians and pundits, among others. The one group conspicuously absent so far from the discussion is the one most affected by its outcome: the terminally ill and those people who suffer from debilitating and painful, but not necessarily terminal, diseases. Now, you will hear from them.

This book has two fundamental purposes. One is to provide a forum for those who are terminally ill and/or in extreme pain to express their views loud and clear. The reader won't hear from some other person interpreting, often incorrectly, their opinions; they are speaking directly. The second purpose is to gather as wide a range as possible of points of view concerning end-of-life issues from a broad array of individuals and, in some cases, organizations. (It should be recognized that including everyone of the multitude of shades of opinion on the subject would create a tome that only Jesse "The Body" Ventura and his ilk could lift.)

The editors have made every effort to ensure a balanced objective and fair presentation of the issues. The book does not strive to reach a consensus and it certainly doesn't attempt to decide who is right and who is wrong. Rather, readers can draw their own conclusions based on the arguments presented here. The book consists of nine chapters with terminally ill people or people with serious and painful illnesses. Their diseases range from post-polio syndrome to severe burns to bi-polar disorder to Lou Gehrig's Disease. Each chapter is followed by two or three commentaries from varying perspectives. The book concludes with an extensive appendix, including suggestions for further reading and a list of relevant organizations.

America has an aging population. Medical technology is likely to continue to advance, giving doctors the ability to prolong our lives almost indefinitely. The combination of these two factors will make this one of the predominant social issues of the early 21st century. Passions are already running high. What is needed is a calm, rational discussion of all the different viewpoints. This book is intended to contribute to that vitally important dialogue.

Who's Right?

Section One

1

◆

The Power of Choice
The Right to Live
and the Right to Die

by Robert C. Horn III

I
T IS AMAZING TO ME HOW RAPIDLY one can plummet from the
heights of the mountaintop to the depths of the valley. Or at least how
fast I could. And did. It was virtually instantaneous. One moment life
was glorious and the next it appeared to be over.

In the spring of 1988 I felt on top of the world. My life couldn't have
been much better. The academic year was a truly outstanding one for me. It
began with the award of a sabbatical for the fall semester. I was doing research
on Soviet-Vietnamese relations in the hopes of expanding a monograph I
had written on the subject (during a recent fellowship at the RAND
Corporation) into a book. Thanks to Asian colleagues I met at a series of
seminars at the East-West Center at the University of Hawaii, I was invited
to speak and conduct interviews in several Asian countries. So my wife, Judy,
who was not about to miss out on an excursion to Asia, and I made our first
trip to China as well as return visits to Thailand, Singapore, Indonesia and,
nostalgically, Malaysia. (We had spent a year in Indonesia in 1967-68 and a

1

year with our whole family in Malaysia in 1983-84.) We saw many old friends and colleagues, met several new ones and I gathered a substantial amount of information and insights for my project. It was wonderful to be back in Asia and it was a terrific trip!

More special things happened in the spring semester. For one, our Model UN program made its long-discussed venture from the Far West regional conference to the National Conference in New York. That conference and that city have a number of advantages, obviously the actual United Nations and each country's official mission to the world body. The experience was so successful that, despite the additional fund-raising required, our program has participated in "nationals" ever since. At about the same time, I was informed that I was to be one of that year's recipients of the Distinguished Professor Award. I felt, and still feel, very honored by that award because it particularly recognizes teaching skills and success in the classroom. Finally, I spent almost two weeks in Moscow in mid-May at the invitation of the Institute of Far Eastern Studies of the USSR Academy of Sciences. I did a seminar at that institute and had discussions with numerous scholars there and from other institutes. This visit was invaluable in bringing me up-to-date on evolving Soviet policy perspectives and giving me a first hand look at the exciting and monumental, and controversial, changes taking place under Gorbachev.

Granted, I was not wealthy financially or in material terms but I considered myself rich in areas of far greater importance: family, religion and employment. Judy and I had a loving and fulfilling marriage and our children (Jeff then in his first year in college, Chris in his junior year in high school and Laura in junior high) were doing well in all respects and continued to be a source of joy to us. We were active members of a dynamic Methodist church that more than met our spiritual needs, deepened our faith, and was filled with wonderful people. Finally, we both had jobs we enjoyed, college teaching in my case and directing a pre-school in Judy's, and that we felt made a contribution to the community. Professionally, my research was going very well.

So what was next? Immediately, there was another trip to Asia. I had been asked by the United States Information Agency to embark on a three-week speaking tour in Asia that summer under their auspices. The trip would include Australia and New Zealand, where I had never been, as well as Japan and would give me the opportunity of seeing a great many friends, personal and professional. I was eagerly looking forward to it.

The "roll" I was on was about to come to a sudden and devastating halt. The ancient Greeks said that "pride goeth before the fall." I don't really think my pride caused it but I was about to learn about the fall in a far too personal, first hand and major way. I had been having spasms in my left arm. The visit to the neurologist is, unfortunately, etched indelibly on my mind. (The only thing I can't recall is the name of the doctor; I suppose I have repressed it.) After he examined me, particularly checking my muscles and reflexes, he asked me what I thought might be the problem. "I don't know," I replied, still clueless. "A pinched nerve?" Then he said, with considerably more medical accuracy than bedside manner, "Have you ever heard of Lou Gehrig's disease?"

Of course I had; Gehrig was one of my baseball heroes. Then I went numb. The blood drained from my head. I couldn't finish getting dressed, and I had to lie down. There is no good way to deliver such news but his abrupt and harsh pronouncement was awful. The only "consolation" he could offer was that he would have to do a number of tests before a diagnosis could be confirmed.

I knew what Lou Gehrig's disease meant: progressive loss of muscles, paralysis, leading to death within a few, short, agonizing years. I was never going to be normal again. And, very soon I was going to die.

A short time later, I was officially diagnosed as having amyotrophic lateral sclerosis, commonly known as Lou Gehrig's Disease. ALS is a degenerative neuromuscular disease that swiftly robs the victim of voluntary muscle control, including those necessary for breathing. The average life expectancy after diagnosis is two to five years. ALS does not affect the mind, so one is perfectly aware of his or her physical deterioration. By the end, the individual typically is unable to move, talk above a whisper, eat without choking or breathe without difficulty.

ALS is a terminal disease. It is progressive, unrelenting, merciless. Its endgame is inevitable.

Over the next several months, whenever I reached a turning point in the progression of the disease, a new obstacle, someone suddenly appeared with a solution. Every time I was confronted by a new hurdle, someone became a hurdler. God does indeed work in mysterious ways sometimes. The more I think about it, though, the more ways don't seem so mysterious because they have been so consistent. Shortly after a problem pops up, a person or a group of them with an answer will, too.

My physical deterioration was extremely difficult for me because of the new limitations it imposed almost weekly. I had been riding my bicycle to the university for almost twenty years. It was devastating to me when I had to give it up. When I could no longer drive a car, students of mine — Steve, Ram and Dan - volunteered their assistance to get me to and from the university. When hauling me in and out of a normal car became too awkward and I was pretty much confined to a wheelchair, Lew and Joyce offered to have their van converted to make it accessible for my use. When I began to lose my energy and stamina, colleagues at the university were able to find ways to lighten my teaching load. When I had trouble writing, Gretchen volunteered to be my right hand. And as my voice weakened, she came up with the alphabet chart that I still use for communicating. Gretchen's husband Bruce became the Director of Player Personnel for my fantasy baseball team — bragging, we finished first in 1995 and 1998.

Two prominent examples of the right people appearing unexpectedly on my horizon at the right time were my "computer gurus," Jan and Diane. They were exceptional. As the ALS progressed and left me too weak to raise my hands to the keyboard, along came Jan. I hate to think of how many hours he must have put in on my behalf designing, from scratch, a program that would enable me to type with my eyebrows. He was never satisfied and was constantly working to improve his original creation. Every time he came up with a new version, he would spend a whole evening with me in my study having me test it and make suggestions. Then he would go home and work on it some more. We finally settled on version six or seven! Jan's dedication, especially for someone who was volunteering his time, was just remarkable. His invention worked beautiful for three years until my weakening eyebrows made it too difficult for me to use. To say that I was discouraged would be a vast understatement. And then, voila, along came Diane, a specialist in adaptive computer equipment. She was the one who noticed my slight leg movement and then designed and installed a terrific system which utilizes that tiny movement. As a result, for the last six years I have been typing with my foot which, as a friend pointed out to me, is quite appropriate for a retired soccer coach.

When I felt I needed some sort of creative outlet, a means of communicating what I had been reading and what was in my head about the collapse of the Soviet Union and the end of the Cold War, Dave and Maria, the pastors at Northridge United Methodist Church, agreed to allow me to start writing regular articles for the church newsletter. The more than one hundred articles I have written over the past years have done absolute wonders for the self-esteem of a physically helpless and completely dependent person. It gave me the confidence and motivation to write my book, *How Will They Know If I'm Dead? Transcending Disability and Terminal Illness.*

Another example seems to be straight out of the "Twilight Zone." One day my occupational therapist came by to see how we were doing. Typically, she wandered through the house making suggestions for changes that would keep us a step ahead of the disease. This time her "only" recommendations were to enlarge the doorway from the bedroom to the study and raise the floor of the study to the level of the bedroom. No small feat! The very next day, out of the blue, our friend Bill, a contractor, dropped in for a visit. During our conversation he asked if there was anything he could do. I casually mentioned the occupational therapist's suggestion and in three days it was completed. That still gives me goose bumps.

A final example. I suspect, almost to the point of conviction, that our children have formed a conspiracy among the three of them to make sure Judy doesn't have to deal with me alone. As evidence, I submit the fact that a week before our daughter Laura, who had just graduated from college, left for Japan, her brother Chris moved back from Colorado and took up residence with us. When he married and moved out, his brother Jeff returned from Japan and lived at home. And as Jeff went off to graduate school, Laura returned. Isn't that awfully suspicious? In any case, we enjoy having them home.

ATTITUDE

In a packet from the Michigan ALS Association I found a brief article by Charles Swindoll which was excerpted from another ALS chapter's publication. It is entitled "Attitude" and it struck a responsive chord in me. It is applicable to anyone, handicapped or not. (This was confirmed by the enthusiastic reception of dozens of people when I included it in an article I wrote for our church newsletter.)

Mr. Swindoll writes: "The longer I live, the more I realize the impact of attitude on life. To me, attitude is more important than facts. It is more important than the past, than education, than money, than circumstances, than failures, than successes, than what other people think or say or do. It is more important than appearance, giftedness or skill. It will make or break a company, a church, a home.

"The remarkable thing is we have a choice every day regarding the attitude we will embrace for that day. We cannot change our past. We cannot change the fact that people will act in a certain way. We cannot change the inevitable. The only thing we can do is play on the one string we have, and that is our attitude...I am convinced that life is 10% what happens to me and 90% how I react to it."

I think he hit the nail squarely on the head. The simple fact is that we cannot control external events or forces. That is the reality. But another part of that reality is that we do have control over how we react to what happens to us. Our attitude is of enormous significance and should not be underestimated.

This is not meant to imply that attitude can alter the nature and course of disease. Or can it? There is a heated debate about this in the scientific literature. There seems to be an emerging consensus that social support, as opposed to social isolation, positively correlates to longevity in terminally ill patients. Much less agreement exists about the role of other psychological variables. Disease cannot be simply wished away by a positive attitude, but numerous recent studies have demonstrated a link between attitude and survival rates. For instance, people who are defiant and "battle" their disease have been shown to live longer than those who just give up.

One very interesting study along these lines which examined ALS patients was recently completed. It monitored the survival status of 144 volunteers for three and a half years. At the beginning researchers tested their subjects on a range of psychological variables and then divided them into three groups based on such factors as depression, hopelessness and perceived stress. The findings are instructive. Of the group with the highest degrees of these factors, the highest level of psychological distress, 82 % died within the time span of the study. In the middle group, 65 % died. In the group with the lowest level of distress, however, only 32 % died! (Another study that I found particularly intriguing suggested that just having "an attitude" is good for you. Researchers at the Johns Hopkins Medical School divided women with breast cancer into two groups based on length of survival. They discovered that the long survivors were considered less cooperative by the hospital staff. Right on!)

Even more important, I think is the impact of attitude on the quality of life. That is really the point and, on this, there is no substantial argument. The mind and body are closely intertwined. This relationship and its effect on health and quality of life are persuasively presented by Dr. David Spiegel in his book *Living Beyond Limits*. His conclusion, like Mr. Swindoll's and mine, is that a positive attitude can greatly enhance the quality of one's life.

If nothing else, as a Hallmark greeting card sent to me by my friend Rosalyn (the church secretary!) said, "A positive attitude may not solve all your problems but it will annoy enough people to make it worth the effort." That, alone, should count for something.

One thing I do know: For me, a physical disability is preferable to a mental one. In *This Far and No More*, an ALS victim, who eventually succeeded in obtaining assistance to end her life, discusses the relative "merits" of ALS and Alzheimer's. Although her internal debate remains inconclusive, she writes wistfully of a disease where you would not be aware of your steady physical decline. Not me. My progressive deterioration was frustrating and depressing in the extreme but I'll still take that over losing my capacity to reason, to analyze or to remember. For, as the remarkable Dan Quayle — remember him? — misspoke in one of his innumerable verbal gaffes, "What a waste it is to lose one's mind." Indeed!

My mind, such as it is, has been my salvation. It still is. I am no brilliant thinker but I do enjoy the world of the mind, which is only appropriate for someone who has spent his entire life in school, either studying or teaching — and always learning. I am interested in and curious about, an unceasing flow of books I am anxious to delve into and a number of topics I would like to write about. My mind is my means of setting goals and striving to achieve them.

My area of expertise and teaching responsibility as a college professor was international relations with a specialization in the Soviet Union and Soviet foreign policy. Several common themes ran through all the courses I taught.

I emphasized — ad nauseum, I am sure, to my students — one of these in particular because it is crucial to understanding how and why states in the international arena behave and interact with each other. It is also an essential consideration in policy making. At least it should be — see, for example the discussion in Robert S. McNamara's book on American policy in Vietnam, *In Retrospect: The Tragedy and Lessons of Vietnam*. It is equally important, I think, in interpersonal relations. That theme or issue is perception.

What the study of perception in world politics teaches is that so-called "objective reality" is actually the subjective perception and interpretation of situations, events, interests, and other actors by various decision makers in every state and other entity. States pursue their interests based on their particular perception or view of reality. That, in turn, is shaped by the complex interplay between a whole range of factors and considerations, including geography, economic strengths and weaknesses, history, ideology, military capabilities, the political situation, and various intangibles such as national character. All of this means that in order to understand why the old Soviet Union or the United States, or Malaysia, Israel or Ecuador, took a certain foreign policy action, you have to put yourself in "the other guy's shoes." You have to see the situation through his eyes, understand that state's perception, its perspective.

So what, you might well ask? Is this somehow relevant to the matter at hand or just some extraneous lecture pulled from a musty file? Simply put, the study of perception reminds us that there are different ways of looking at the same issue, event, problem, or situation. And this is true at all levels of life, from the global to the personal. The linkage between perception and living life is that we act on what we perceive. In other words, our perception, or perspective determines how we live. This makes the discussion relevant for my life, indeed for all of our lives.

What is my perspective, then, on my life? Not oversimplifying the question very much at all, it comes down to that old conundrum: Do I see the glass as half full or half empty? Before the diagnosis of ALS, I had always viewed the glass as half full. I was an unabashed optimist, albeit tempered with a certain degree of realism. But how about now? Admittedly, there is not much to like, and a great deal to find intolerable, about my current situation. It is difficult, to say the least, living under the sentence of a terminal disease, knowing that I will not get better, only worse. I have to try to avoid reflecting on longer-term concepts of time, such as "never" or "forever." They are psychologically painful. Physically, I'm a mess. I can't do anything for myself, have virtually no workable muscles and can't move. It is frustrating and maddening to be so absolutely helpless and so totally dependent on others. If my head lolls to one side or the other, as it often does, it stays there unless and until someone notices and props it up again. If an arm slips off the armrest of the wheelchair, it will just dangle by my side until someone retrieves it.

There is ample evidence to think the glass is now at least half empty. Well, it almost is, but not quite. There is more to life than physical ability. There are the mental, emotional and spiritual abilities or worlds to consider as well. In these worlds, I haven't changed; I am still a vibrant, healthy and independent person. I can think, reason and analyze, remember, read, write, learn and communicate. I can love, feel happiness and sadness, be enthusiastic, get angry, have highs and lows, feel joy. I can believe, hope and have faith. This adds up to an extensive list of things I can still "do" in spite of my disease.

This brings me back to the question of my overall perspective of my situation. I am convinced that what I have left is more valuable than what I have lost. I believe that the things I can do are more important than those I can't. The key for my psychological well-being is to focus on what I can do, my abilities, rather than on my disabilities and limitations. To dwell on the latter is to wallow in grief and self-pity. Such wallowing is, for me, sometimes unavoidable and occasionally even necessary. But to concentrate on the former is to invite optimism, achievement and new opportunities.

All in all, I would say that the glass has lost some of its water but it is still half full.

In the game of life, it all comes down to how you keep score. If dying is losing, then we are all losers because we are all terminal. The game makes no sense. A far more meaningful basis for scorekeeping is the quality of life. Quality rather than quantity or longevity. How do you assess quality? That very much depends on perception.

Quality is not determined by the normal bumps in the road which everyone experiences. In life, as the bumper sticker crudely but truthfully states, "Shit happens." Indeed it does! Mary Chapin Carpenter sings about the fact of life that sometimes you're the bat and sometimes you're the ball, that "sometimes you're the windshield and sometimes you're the bug." I have always liked the way Judy's brother, Don, has expressed this basic truth: "Sometimes you eat the bear and sometimes the bear eats you." If you can't deal with the naturally occurring and inevitable downs, the game of life is not for you. You have to accept the bad with the good. Most of us have learned to do that. We have also learned that, as I told the girls on my soccer teams, the test of our character is how we respond to adversity and setbacks, losses, disappointments, and defeats.

My response to ALS has run the emotional gamut. And gauntlet. I have experienced despair, fear, resignation, anger, and the dashing of unrealistic hopes, amid a torrent of emotions. Some time ago, I arrived at an acceptance of my condition and of reality. My "psychological problems" now relate not so much to my physical limitations or the fatal nature of my disease per se, but rather the additional responsibility I have caused to those closest to me.

On the other hand, I have been surrounded by so much unconditional love that it is overwhelming. Especially by Judy. But from so many others, too. My favorite passage in the Bible has long been from First Corinthians. Paul wrote to the church in Corinth, "If I speak in tongues of men and of angels, but have not love, I am a noisy gong or a clanging cymbal." Well, no gongs or cymbals here! Family and friends are the instruments and reflection of God's love and I am continuously uplifted by them. They demonstrate that, as Paul further wrote, "Love bears all things, believes all things, hopes all things, endures all things." That passage means even more to me now. It has become very personal and very real.

There have been studies which show that social support, as opposed to social isolation, positively correlates to longevity in terminally ill patients. This doesn't surprise me at all. From my own experience, I can testify that social support like Judy and I have received also positively correlates to QUALITY of life. That is even less surprising.

Where does all this leave me? Fundamentally, I believe that I am as close as I will ever be to achieving, or being granted, the serenity so eloquently expressed in the **Serenity Prayer** by Reinhold Niebuhr: "God give us the grace to accept with serenity the things that cannot be changed, the courage to change the things which should be changed, and the wisdom to distinguish one from the other."

I love that prayer! I also think it fits my situation absolutely perfectly. I HAVE to accept my disabilities if I am going to keep on living. There is no alternative, except, I suppose, insanity and I am not quite ready for that. I definitely REQUIRE the courage to do all that I am capable of in my life. Finally, I also NEED to be able to distinguish what I can change in my life from what I can't. All of this adds up to the need to focus on things I can do and not to dwell on those I can't.

CHOICE

For most of the twentieth century, and particularly during the nearly 30 years of Stalin's murderous rule, communism required Russians, even dissidents, to adapt and make compromises in order to survive. It is the same for people with disabilities. We, too, are forced to make adjustments, adaptations, and compromises to get on with life. After all, what's the choice?

In fact, people confronted with physical disability and terminal illness have, at least they SHOULD have, three basic choices: to die, to exist, or to live. I am not ready to die. And, as long as I continue to breathe, even with the aid of a machine, I will try to live life to the fullest extent possible rather than be content merely to exist. That's my choice.

Some time ago, I saw a report on CNN that left me disturbed and reflective. It was about the controversy surrounding the issue of doctor-assisted suicide in Canada, a complex and thought-provoking issue in its own right. What personalized it for me, though, was that the three people the report profiled who all wanted to end their lives were suffering from the same disease as I am, ALS. Moreover, the impact of the report was intensified by the condition of the patients. With varying difficulty, all could eat and talk and none was on a ventilator.

Since then, there have been several highly publicized cases of ALS patients seeking medical assistance to end their lives humanely and with some dignity. Most of these cases have been in Michigan, and have involved Dr. Jack Kevorkian. I have a problem with this retired Michigan pathologist. In fact, I have a lot of problems with the man appropriately nicknamed "Dr. Death" because he has assisted in more than 130 suicides. I favor a terminally ill person's right to choose. But if he or she chooses assisted suicide, I believe certain preconditions have to be met. Kevorkian has ignored most of these.

My concern stems from several sources. First, my father was a Michigan pathologist, at Detroit's Henry Ford Hospital. He was very active in his profession, nationally and internationally, and I think he would be appalled at Kevorkian's behavior. Second, although I have lived with ALS for nearly eleven years, I am still classified as terminally ill but the last thing I want is a house call from Dr. Death.

More to the point were Kevorkian's actions on the "60 Minutes" episode in November, 1998, where he injected ALS patient Thomas Youk with a lethal dose of drugs to allow him to die. What did Kevorkian provide besides his killing expertise? Psychiatric counseling to make sure Youk wasn't suffering from depression, a common condition among those who want to commit suicide but treatable by a psychiatrist? No. Any kind of counseling, including a presentation of the alternatives to death? No. Medication or exercises to alleviate Youk's unspecified pain? Again, no. Any recommendations of books or articles by or about people living productive and meaningful lives with ALS, (immodestly) such as mine? Yet again, no.

No doctor worth his Hippocratic oath would have ignored such precautions as Kevorkian did. Of course, I don't know if it happened and just wasn't shown on the program. But if it didn't happen, I support Kevorkian's conviction of second-degree murder. He did the country a service, I think, by bringing the right to die into the public debate but it is long past time for Kevorkian to sit down and shut up and keep his hands to himself.

There were options, contrary to what Youk's family said after his death. Ultimately, though, it gets down to quality of life and the patient is obviously the best judge of that. I have had a high quality of life since going on the ventilator eight years ago but the symptoms of ALS vary widely and I recognize that my decision isn't for everyone. I just don't think Dr. Jack should be part of the decision-making process.

My choice, to go on living in spite of the disease, doesn't make me "better" or more "courageous" than those who opt for alternative solutions to the challenges they face. The personal struggles of people against life-threatening illnesses do not lend themselves to facile or self-righteous judgments. These are highly individual battles that depend on many factors, from personal outlook and philosophy, to the specific situation and circumstances of the patient, and, significantly, on the nature of the illness itself.

In considering ALS specifically, there are at least three major reasons to avoid being judgmental in the evaluation of how a particular victim of the disease reacts to it. For one, its symptoms vary dramatically from patient to patient; one person's experience with the disease is no guide to someone else's. For instance, one of the women in the CNN report suffered substantial physical pain. I have had considerable discomfort but minimal pain — other than, earlier, from falls or muscle cramps in my legs and, more recently, when a caregiver turns me awkwardly or some such thing.

Second, I greatly sympathize with those people who are in the earlier stages of the disease. As I have told Judy, for me "getting this way was worse than being this way." Much, much worse. The mental stress of watching the progressive deterioration of your basic physical abilities — loss of dexterity, falling, having trouble swallowing, losing your voice — is enormous and exceptionally depressing. My situation now is relatively secure. Much, much more secure.

Finally, the decision of whether or not to go on life support is an intensely personal one. I made the right decision for me, but that is not to suggest that my choice would be the appropriate one for everyone confronted with a similar dilemma.

Compare my situation, for example, to that of Thomas Hyde. He was the man with ALS who Dr. Kevorkian helped to end his life in August 1993. While I was in my mid-forties when I was diagnosed with the disease, Mr. Hyde was in his twenties. And our occupations were also quite dissimilar: mine was indoor-focused, college teaching, and his was in the outdoors, in landscaping and construction. These major differences mean that the impact of similar physical changes on each of us would vary due to our different lifestyles. I would like to think that if I had been in his position, I still would have chosen life — but I wasn't so I can't truly know what my ultimate decision would have been.

All that said, I would still like to talk to those people who are seeking to end their lives — and would have liked to talk to those who did. What would I say? I would simply tell them that "there is life on a ventilator." They would probably respond by asking me what good could that kind of life be. Admittedly, it is often difficult. Compared to being "normal," the list of frustrations and "wants" is endless. For me, however, it is good just to be alive! The positives outweigh the negatives (although, on my periodic "bad" days, it seems not by a whole lot). I have to assess the quality of my life in slightly different terms but it is still full of opportunities, challenges, rewards and joys. There are many things I am curious about and interested in. I enjoy the richness, diversity and complexity of life. I want to see what my children do with their lives. I have retained my thirty-year fascination with Russia and with Asia, particularly Southeast Asia. There are things I want to write about and books I want to read. And, among other interests, I also want to continue to "manage" my fantasy baseball team. I suppose the bottom line is what you do after going on the ventilator. I am fortunate in that many things I love I can still do.

This doesn't mean I don't sometimes — like daily — bemoan my situation. I do (but, usually, only to myself). There are so many things I used to enjoy that I can no longer do. There are so many things I looked forward to doing that are now impossible.

In the beginning, I agonized over the "why me" question. I soon realized, however, how emotionally draining and generally unproductive that line of inquiry could prove to be. Moreover, I eventually discovered what seems to me to be the logical answer to the question: "Why not me?" I also admire the way Arthur Ashe, the late tennis great and humanitarian, dealt with the question in his struggle with AIDS. In his autobiography, *Days of Grace*, he explains that since he never asked the question when he was enjoying personal and professional success, he had no right to raise it now. This is a philosophy with which I fully concur.

I have also lamented the fact, and others have too, that "it just isn't fair." Of course it isn't. Unfortunately, as we all know, life is not "fair." I think about "fairness" when I read about children starving in Rwanda or being killed in random drive-by shootings in Los Angeles and other American cities. Compared to them and countless other examples, what reason could I possibly have to complain about "fairness"? I have a wonderful wife, three terrific children, a super daughter-in-law, Kris, a precious granddaughter, Marley, a career I found both challenging and enormously rewarding, plus I traveled widely and coached youth soccer for many years. All these things I loved and embraced enthusiastically. No regrets. And yet, I suppose it's human nature always to want more. I know I do. I feel, arrogantly I admit, short-changed, robbed of a third of my life. There are so many things I wanted to do.

Enough bemoaning what was or what might have been.

The underlying point of all this is that I had a choice. I made a conscious decision to go on the ventilator and on with my life. The decision wasn't made by a doctor or anyone else but me. I am very happy with the decision I made and I can live with the negatives, frustrations and downs because I chose. My parents taught me that I had to live with the consequences of my decisions and, for me, the benefits of living far outweigh the costs just as I had expected. Having a choice is the key and makes all the difference in the world.

Shouldn't a person with a disease such as ALS facing horrendous prospects with an all too predictable outcome have the legal right to choose whether to go on with life or end it with dignity? I imagine that most everyone who faces the debilitating and terminal nature of a disease like ALS would prefer to have such a choice. ALS victim Dennis Kaye, in his book, **Laugh, I Thought I'd Die**, writes that he does not want to go on a ventilator when it becomes necessary. Why should he have to? **In This Far and No More**, another book about ALS, Emily Bauer (a pseudonym) poignantly wrote in her diary: "I don't know how anyone with access to a normal life can expect me to accept such a limited one. That others have accepted a drastically limited life does not mean that is the right course of action for me." Who has the right to tell Emily that she doesn't have a choice?

Life is about making decisions and choices. For the terminally ill, those choices should include when to die. This doesn't mean choice by doctors or family members or ministers or counselors or any person except the patient himself. Others can and should be consulted, but the decision must be up to — in the words of the U.S. Ninth Circuit Court of Appeals — the "mentally competent adult" patient.

But the right to choose death necessarily must include the right to choose life. I was faced with that choice in February 1991. In less than three years, I had gone from a robust, physically active person to being completely disabled. I could barely squeeze out a sound, had lost more than a third of my body weight because I had trouble swallowing even mushy foods, was almost totally paralyzed and my breathing had become very labored. What to do?

I am fortunate in that I had a real choice. Two doctors separately offered me the option of ending my life painlessly. I didn't choose that option, but I deeply appreciate their compassion. I made a conscious decision to go on a ventilator and on with my life. I talked it over with several people close to me, especially my wife, who would take on the additional role of caregiver. But I alone made the decision. I chose life.

For me, having a choice is the key. No one forced me to live. No one forced me to die. I chose. Because of that, I can cope with the negatives and "downs" as well as relish the positives and "ups" that my life presents. Choice makes all the difference; it's as simple and as complicated as that.

CONCLUSION

I look on my life as a doubleheader. An unscheduled doubleheader. I am thinking of the famous statement by Ernie Banks, the great Hall of Fame shortstop for the Chicago Cubs. Ernie had outstanding skills and it was a pleasure to watch him play. In retrospect, however, what impresses me even more than his ability is his attitude. He had an unparalleled enthusiasm and love for the game. One afternoon at Wrigley Field, he said, "It's a beautiful day for baseball. Let's play two." Think of it. An unscheduled doubleheader!

I think "playing two" is a perfect analogy for my situation. I am playing the second game of an unscheduled doubleheader. I almost died in early 1991. That's when I made one of the best decisions of my life. I chose to be hooked to a ventilator. As I told my Pastor at the time, I felt re-born. Despite my limitations, it was good to be alive. It still is. I am enjoying playing my second game.

Harper Lee, in *To Kill a Mockingbird*, defines courage as knowing "you're licked before you begin but you begin anyway and you see it through no matter what." Well, ALS has licked me, just as it licks everyone it touches. But I am only physically beaten. My spirit, though battered a bit and somewhat bruised, survives and remains strong. I refuse to let ALS win that battle, too.

There is still room for hope. Many people believe that where hope exists, life can flourish. I agree but I think the converse is also true: Where there is life, there is always hope. In the meantime, I am an admirer of Don Quixote; I can identify with his willingness, as sung in "Man of La Mancha," to "fight the unbeatable foe."

2

♦

Misplaced Compassion and Illusory Choice

by Herbert Hendin, M.D.
American Foundation for Suicide Prevention

WHEN CONFRONTED WITH THE progressive paralytic effects of amyotrophic lateral sclerosis (ALS) Bob Horn was acutely aware that he had "three basic choices: to die, to exist, or to live." He says he *chose* to live life to "the fullest extent possible." In order to be able to move around, he would use a wheel chair, in order to communicate he would use his eyebrows and an alphabet board, in order to eat he would accept a gastric tube, in order to write he would learn to operate a pedal operated computer with his few remaining functioning leg muscles, and in order to breathe he would have a tracheotomy and utilize a respirator. Despite severe incapacity he has been a productive writer while maintaining a warm and loving relationship with his wife, children, and friends. Impelled by compassion for fellow sufferers, he wants to make sure that they have choices about living or dying even though their decisions may differ from his. He believes that legalizing physician-assisted suicide will further that end.

Bob Horn is not alone in feeling that compassion for those who are suffering, and respect for their right to choose when and how to die, justify the legalization of assisted suicide. Yet despite their natural appeal, compassion and choice are poor guides toward a social policy for caring for those who are chronically disabled or terminally ill.

COMPASSION

Contemporary advocacy for euthanasia is felt to have originated in compassion for patients whose suffering was considered to be incapable of relief in any other way or who wish to be protected from what they fear will be an undignified death. In the Netherlands, the only country where assisted suicide and euthanasia have long been legally sanctioned, the patient must be experiencing unbearable and unrelievable suffering before the physician can assist in a suicide.

Compassion can be misdirected, however, and is no guarantee against doing harm. Lewis Thomas, one of the deans of American medicine, wrote insightfully about the sense of failure and helplessness that physicians may experience in the face of death; such feelings may explain why they have such difficulty in discussing terminal illness with patients. These feelings may also explain both doctors' tendency to use excessive measures to maintain life and their need to make death a medical decision. By deciding when patients die, and by making death a medical decision, the physician preserves the illusion of mastery over the disease and the accompanying feelings of helplessness. Compassion for the patient can become a rationalization for the physician's own emotional discomfort.

In overburdened families, compassion that requires the death of the patient can also be self-serving. A Swedish study examined the response of relatives to the suicide attempts of elderly patients with somatic illnesses. Family members, overwhelmed by what they felt were the relentless needs of the patient, were likely to delay calling the doctor, to urge nonresuscitation of the patient, and to have expressed death wishes to the patients. Once help from social and welfare agencies was arranged, families were able to be genuinely compassionate and the patients wanted to live.

Jack Kevorkian appears to see himself as the epitome of compassion. Yet Bob Horn appropriately asks what beside his "killing expertise" did

Kevorkian provide Thomas Youk, who also suffered with amyotrophic lateral sclerosis, and to whom Kevorkian gave a lethal injection? With good reason Horn doubts if Kevorkian gave Houk any alternatives to death, suggested any medication to relieve his symptoms, or gave him any books or articles to read about people living productive lives with ALS.

Advances in medical technology that make it possible to cruelly prolong the dying process are said to necessitate legalization of euthanasia. As D. J. Bakker points out, however, "Euthanasia is then chosen as the wrong solution for a wrong development in medicine. A medical science that is in need of euthanasia has to be changed as soon as possible to a medicine that cares beyond cure."

The case that the essential moral structure of medicine requires that "doctors must not kill" has been argued vigorously by physicians who note that for centuries physicians have not participated in capital punishment because to do so would compromise their role as healers. Advocates of euthanasia do not see euthanasia as intrinsically opposed to healing. They insist that euthanasia can be considered a proper part of medical caring, justified when it prevents pain, incompetence, or undignified dying, because the prevention of suffering is a proper part of a doctor's activities. Dr. Els Borst-Eilers, the Dutch Minister of Justice has stated it explicitly: "There are situations when the best way to heal the patient is to help him die peacefully. The doctor who, in such a situation, grants the patient's request acts as the healer par excellence."

Yet justifying euthanasia by "healing" and "helping" opens the door to ending the lives of people who have never made their wishes known, but who appear to be suffering a great deal. Involuntary euthanasia while not legally sanctioned in the Netherlands is rarely punished and increasingly justified on the grounds of the need to relieve intolerable suffering on the part of those unable to choose for themselves. I was given as a justifiable example a nun whose physician ended her life a few days before she would have died because she was in great pain but her doctor believed that her religious convictions were preventing her from asking for death. Since there is no objective way of determining what is unbearable pain and suffering, when pain and suffering become all important as criteria, the decision depends on the doctor's subjective assessment.

CHOICE

Partly for these reasons advocates of legalization are increasingly not basing their argument on compassion for those who are suffering, but on the patient's right to choose. Oregon, the only state to legalize assisted suicide, while copying Dutch guidelines in many respects, did not make suffering a criterion for assisted suicide. Simply having a terminal illness, a prognosis of less than six months to live, and a wish to die is enough. How helpful are these criteria and what choice do Oregon patients really have?

When choice is the major determinant physicians are not encouraged to inquire into the source of the desperation that usually underlies most requests for assisted suicide and euthanasia, an inquiry that leads patients and physicians to have the kind of discussion that often leads to relief for patients and makes assisted suicide seem unnecessary. Nor are physicians asked or required by the Oregon law to make such an inquiry.

When their suffering is addressed by a knowledgeable and caring physician, the overwhelming number of patients requesting euthanasia change their mind. For the exceptional case sedation may be necessary to relieve suffering. If confronted with a physician who does not know how to relieve their pain and suffering and the choice is between continuing to suffer and an expedited death, the patient really has little choice.

Under the Oregon law when a terminally ill patient makes a request for assisted suicide, physicians are required to point out that palliative care and hospice care are feasible alternatives. They are not required, however, to be knowledgeable about how to relieve either physical or emotional suffering in terminally ill patients. There is no requirement in Oregon for courses in pain management, palliative care, or the evaluation of a suicidal patient for physicians wishing to practice assisted suicide or a certifying exam for physicians who believe they are already qualified. Without such knowledge, and without inquiry into the sources of the patient's desperation, the physician cannot present feasible alternatives. It would seem necessary that lacking such training a physician should be required to refer any patient requesting assisted suicide for consultation with a physician knowledgeable about palliative care. There is, however, no such requirement in the Oregon law.

Under these conditions offering a patient palliative care becomes a legal requirement to be met, rather than an integral part of an effort to relieve the patient's suffering so that a hastened death does not seem like the only alternative. How this happens is suggested by one of the few Oregon cases about which details have become publicly known. The case was publicized by Compassion in Dying, the advocacy group that shepherded 11 of the 15 reported cases during the first year of the Oregon law's operation, as a model of how well the law operates.

Helen was described as being in her mid-80s with metastatic breast cancer and in a hospice program. Her own physician had not been willing to assist in her suicide for reasons that were not specified. A second physician also refused on the grounds that she was depressed. Her husband called Compassion in Dying and was referred to a doctor willing to participate. The doctor referred Helen to a second physician and to a psychiatrist who supported the decision. Much of the information about the case came from an audiotape the physician made of an interview he had with Helen and from interviews he gave anonymously to selected members of the media. An edited version of the audiotape was played for the media by Compassion in Dying the day after the patient's death.

On the tape, said to have been made two days before she died, Helen says of her impending death "I'm looking forward to it...I will be relieved of all the stress I have."

Helen expressed concern about her autonomy, specifically about being artificially fed, a concern that suggests both vulnerability and uncertainty about her course of action.

> **HELEN:** I've seen people suffer, they give them artificial feeding and stuff, which is really not doing anything for them in the long run.

> **DOCTOR:** Can you explain how you feel about dying in a few days?

The physician recommended by Compassion in Dying does not assure her that artificial feeding need not happen in any case because she has the right to refuse it. He ignores her concerns about living and instead asks a question designed to elicit a response about her desire to die. There is no indication that this physician was trying to find any feasible alternatives to suicide. In the taped interview released to the public the physician follows the law's requirement in telling the patient that there are other choices she could make: He lists them for her in a few sentences covering hospice support, chemotherapy, and hormonal therapy:

DOCTOR: There is, of course, all sorts of hospice support that is available to you. There is, of course, chemotherapy that is available that may or may not have any effect, not in curing your cancer, but perhaps in lengthening your life to some extent. And there is also available a hormone which you were offered before by the oncologist — tamoxifen — which is not really chemotherapy but would have some possibility of slowing or stopping the course of the diseases for some period of time.

HELEN: Yes, I don't want to take that.

DOCTOR: All right, OK, that's pretty much what you need to understand.

In an interview with Oregon Public Radio the prescribing physician described his participation as an "extremely moving experience for me." He told a reporter from the Oregonian, he stated that he was struck by Helen's tenacity and determination. "It was like talking to a locomotive. It was like talking to Superman when he's going after a train."

The case raises disturbing questions. The physicians who evaluated the patient offered two contradictory sets of opinions about the appropriateness of her decision. As the decision making process progressed, it provided no mechanism for resolving the disagreement based on medical expertise, such as that which can be provided by an ethics committee that would hear the facts of the case before going forward. Instead, the opinions of the two doctors who did not support the patient's decision — one of whom knew her for some time and the other who considered that she was depressed — are essentially ignored.

The physician who assisted in Helen's suicide, who met her two weeks before doing so, admits he never contacted Helen's regular physician before his patient died. He writes "I regret this. I don't think either of the previous MD's disagreed with her qualification, but at the time I would have clarified it. Had I felt there was a disagreement among the physicians about my patient's eligibility, I would not have written the prescription." It is striking that the physician uses words like "qualification" and "eligibility" rather than discussing the appropriateness of the decision.

The persistence of the request is one of the requirements for assisted suicide in Oregon and the physician is impressed by Helen's determination to die. The fact that he describes her as like an unstoppable express train in her unwillingness to wait in hastening death even though she is not in great immediate distress should in itself give him pause. Urgency that brooks no questioning in such a matter is usually a sign that of irrational motives. Proponents of legalizing assisted suicide maintain that knowledge that they could control when they die would permit people to postpone death. This Oregonian woman had that option, and the physician is troubled by her haste, but he is unable to resist it. Nor did Helen's family seem to raise any questions as to whether anything could have been done to cause her to be less eager to end her life.

The physician subsequently wrote an article for Lancet about the case. In it he describes Helen as primarily concerned over anticipated suffering. He informs us that she was influenced by having experienced the lingering death of her husband. This is a frequent factor in the history of those who become suicidal in response to terminal illness. Careful exploration of the circumstances of the earlier death may give a physician the opportunity to relieve anxieties that are motivating the patient's desire to hasten death. There is no evidence that such an exploration was done with Helen.

In his Lancet article the physician states that he liked Helen immediately so that the thought of her dying so soon was "almost too much to bear, and only slightly less difficult was the knowledge that many very reasonable people would consider aiding her death a crime. On the other hand, I found even worse the thought of disappointing this family. If I backed out, they'd feel about me the way they felt about her previous doctor, that I had strung them along, and in a way, insulted them." Should liking Helen and needing not to disappoint her family be such significant factors in the decision to end her life? Are they a substitute for the adequate medical assessment and care that Helen does not seem to have received?

THE DUTCH EXPERIENCE

What happens in the Netherlands where both compassion for suffering patients and respect for autonomy (choice) are integral to the legal sanction given to assisted suicide and euthanasia. Bob Horn hopes that legalization of assisted suicide and euthanasia will give patients greater control over their deaths. The Dutch experience suggests that the opposite is true.

During the past three decades the Dutch have moved from considering assisted suicide to giving legal sanction to both assisted suicide and euthanasia, from euthanasia for the terminally ill to euthanasia for the chronically ill, from euthanasia for physical suffering to euthanasia for suffering that is mental. It did not seem possible to the Dutch to sanction euthanasia for the those who are terminally ill and not permit it for those who are chronically ill and have longer to suffer. Or not to permit it for those whose suffering was mental rather than physical in origin. There were also reports of the widespread practice of "involuntary euthanasia."

Even more troublesome than the extension of euthanasia to more patients is the inability to regulate the process within established guidelines which are: that the patient must make a well-considered voluntary request; the patient must be experiencing intolerable suffering that cannot be relieved; there must be consultation with a second physician; and all cases of physician-assisted suicide and euthanasia must be reported.

These guidelines have been modified and violated; they have simply failed to protect patients. Concern over charges of abuse led the Dutch government to sanction 1990 and 1995 studies of assisted suicide and euthanasia. Many of the violations are evident from these two studies.

For example, more than half of Dutch physicians feel free to suggest euthanasia to their patients which compromises the voluntariness of the process. Frightened and suffering patients are inclined to listen to suggestions made to them by physicians even when the doctor is telling them that their life is not worth living or causes them to suspect that the doctor must foresee a worse fate than they have imagined.

Consultation takes place in about 80 percent of the reported cases, but 60 percent of cases are not reported which makes regulation impossible. Interviews with physicians revealed that in only 11% of the unreported cases was there consultation with another physician. Taken together these figures indicate that there is consultation in about half of Dutch euthanasia cases.

Twenty percent of the physician's last unreported cases involved ending the lives of patients who had not requested it. When life was terminated without request from the patient, there was no consultation in 97 percent of cases.

Probably the most alarming finding in the Dutch studies was the documentation that each year several thousand patients who have not requested it are given lethal injections by physicians. One quarter of Dutch physicians admit to having done so. Misguide compassion, the motive in the case of the nun mentioned earlier whose life was ended without her request, is not the only motive in involuntary euthanasia cases. In one documented case, a Dutch woman with disseminated breast cancer who had said she did not want euthanasia had her life ended because in the physician's words, "It could have taken another week before she died. I just needed this bed."

Guidelines concerning choice (voluntariness) are violated and physicians get around them by not reporting what they are doing.

Since the government-sanctioned Dutch studies are primarily numerical and categorical, they do not examine the interaction between physicians, patients, and families that determines the decision for euthanasia. We need to look elsewhere for a fuller picture.

Other studies conducted in the Netherlands have indicated how voluntariness is compromised, alternatives not presented, and the criterion of unrelievable suffering bypassed. A few examples help to illustrate how this occurs:

A wife who no longer wished to care for her sick, elderly husband, gave him a choice between euthanasia and admission to a home for the chronically ill. The man, afraid of being left to the mercy of strangers in an unfamiliar place, chose to have his life ended; the doctor although aware of the coercion, ended the man's life. In a study done in Dutch hospitals, doctors and nurses reported that more requests for euthanasia came from families than from patients themselves. The investigator concluded that the families, the doctors, and the nurses were involved in pressuring patients to request euthanasia

A physically healthy 50 year-old woman, who lost her son recently to cancer, refused all psychiatric treatment and said she would accept only help in dying. She was assisted in suicide by a psychiatrist within four months of her son's death. The psychiatrist had told the woman that he could not make such a decision until he knew her better implying that if after time he considered her decision appropriate he would assist her. The woman saw him for a number of sessions over a two month period eventually telling him she would leave if he did not help her at which point he did. During the course of our interviews the psychiatrist told me that his patient suffered from incurable grief. Her refusal of treatment was considered by the physician and the Dutch courts to make her suffering unrelievable. The woman had told the psychiatrist that if he did not help her she would kill herself without him. He seemed on the one hand to be succumbing to emotional blackmail and on the other to be ignoring the fact that even without treatment, experience has shown that time alone was likely to have affected her wish to die.

A Dutch physician who was filmed ending the life of a patient recently diagnosed with amyotrophic lateral sclerosis says of the patient "I can give him the finest wheelchair there is, but in the end it is only a stopgap. He is going to die and he knows it." That death may be years away but a physician with this attitude may not be able to present alternatives to this patient. The patient in this case was clearly ambivalent about proceeding and wanted to put off the date for his death. This ambivalence was ignored by the doctor who was supporting the desire of the patient's wife to move forward quickly. The doctor never sees the patient alone, permits the wife to answer all questions for him about whether he wants to die, and presents an exaggerated picture of the death that awaits him without euthanasia.

Thus euthanasia, intended originally for the exceptional case, has become an accepted way of dealing with serious or terminal illness in the Netherlands. In the process palliative care has become one of the casualties, while hospice care has lagged behind that of other countries. In recent testimony before the British House of Lords, Zbigniew Zylicz, one of the few palliative care experts in the Netherlands, emphasized Dutch deficiencies in palliative care attributing them partly to the easier alternative of euthanasia. He saw the lack of hospice care in the Netherlands and the fact that there are only 70 palliative care beds in the country as reflections of this easier option. The U.S. Supreme Court cited this deficiency in particular and Dutch experience in general as evidence that it is dangerous to give legal sanction to assisted suicide.

It would seem evident that there has been an erosion of medical standards in the care of terminally ill patients in the Netherlands when, as the government sanctioned studies documented, 60% of Dutch cases of assisted suicide and euthanasia are not reported, more than 50% of Dutch doctors feel free to suggest euthanasia to their patients, and 25% admit to ending patients' lives without their consent.

The Dutch experience also provides clear evidence that practicing euthanasia and assisted suicide actually increases the power and control of doctors who can suggest it without proposing obvious alternatives, who can ignore patient ambivalence about dying, and who can even put to death patients who have not requested it.

PARALLELS

What parallels do we already see or are we likely to see in the Dutch experience to our own? Our legal system as well as our medical and ethical values would make it difficult for us to make a distinction between assisted suicide and euthanasia. Patients wanting to die usually make no such distinction and since many of them cannot swallow medication, assisted suicide is not an option.

Nor if we legalize assisted suicide and/or euthanasia would we find it easy to exclude people who are suffering but are not terminally ill. The leading medical advocates of assisted suicide in the United States have authored model proposals calling for legalization of euthanasia as well as assisted suicide for "competent patients suffering not only from terminal illness" but also for those with "incurable, debilitating disease who voluntarily request to end their lives." "Incurable debilitating disease" would include conditions like diabetes and arthritis.

In both the United States and the Netherlands, ignorance of how to relieve suffering is probably the most frequent reason doctors comply with or encourage patients' requests for assisted suicide and euthanasia, although they rationalize what they do as respecting patient autonomy. At a small, international workshop that addressed problems in the care of the terminally ill, two American cases were presented in which terminally ill patients requested assisted suicide.

In one case a man was confined to a wheel chair with advanced symptoms of AIDS that included cystic lung infection, severe pain due to inflammation of the nerves in his limbs, and marked weight loss. By the appropriate use of steroids, antidepressants, and psychological sensitivity in dealing with his fears of abandonment, he was able to gain weight, be free of his pain and his wheel chair, and live an additional ten months for which he was grateful

In another case a woman with great pain due to lung cancer that invaded her chest wall wished for assisted suicide. A nerve block relieved her pain, and she was happy to be able to leave the hospital and live her remaining months at home

I presented these cases to a number of physician advocates of euthanasia in the Netherlands and in the United States up to the point where the patient requested assisted suicide. They at first agreed that the patient with AIDS had a right to have euthanasia performed, but were not so sure after they heard the actual outcome. In the second case, aware that a nerve block could provide relief, most would not perform euthanasia.

In other words, doctors felt free to ignore patient autonomy when they knew how to help the patient. "Patient autonomy" was in essence a rationale for assisted suicide when doctors felt helpless and did not know what else to do. This seems an argument for educating physicians, not for legalizing assisted suicide.

In both the U.S. and the Netherlands, ignorance of how to relieve suffering is probably the most frequent reason for doctors complying with or encouraging patients' assisted suicide and euthanasia requests. Studies have shown that the more physicians know about palliative care, the less they favor legalization; the less they know, the more they favor it.

The published evidence suggests that the majority of physicians are not adequately trained to deal with the many factors and symptoms commonly associated with patients' requests for assisted suicide. According to the American Medical Association's report on medical education only a handful of medical schools in the United States require a course in the care of dying patients. Only a quarter of residency programs do so. Only 17 percent of over a thousand accredited residency programs surveyed offer a hospice rotation, and only half of those programs require it. In a survey conducted by the American Board of Internal Medicine only 32 percent of 1400 residents surveyed felt they had received adequate training in talking to patients who request assistance in dying or a hastened death.

Bob Horn's own experience might lead him not to be surprised at this. Although he is surrounded by people including physicians whose care and concern helped make his meaningful survival possible, he has had had experience with those who are less skilled and less sensitive. In his chapter he mentions three. The first physician, brusquely and insensitively informed him of his diagnosis. Two others separately offered him the option of ending his life painlessly. For an individual less sure of what he wanted and less determined than Bob Horn, these unsolicited opinions could have been devastating. Although he declined their offers he is overly charitable in saying that he deeply appreciates their 'compassion'

Proponents of legalization have maintained that since both assisted suicide and euthanasia are already taking place in this country, legalization would make it possible to regulate their practice. In 1998, Diane Meier and six colleagues published the results of a survey of physicians that indicated that 3.3 percent have prescribed lethal medications at least once and 4.7 percent have given lethal injections at least one time. Perhaps most disturbing about the study was the fact that in 79 percent of cases physicians who gave lethal injections to patients had received no direct request from the patient to do so.

Meier has said that the if physicians are willing to do this with the law as it now stands, the likelihood of such practices increasing with legalization and the fact that they cannot be regulated have led her to no longer favor legalization of assisted suicide and euthanasia. The Dutch experience would tend to support her conclusion.

Some areas where there is not a parallel between the U.S. and the Netherlands are also sources of concern. The United States is alone among the industrialized democracies in not guaranteeing medical care to large numbers of its population. Without such care, assisted suicide and euthanasia could become forced choices for large numbers of those who are poor, disabled, in minority groups, or elderly; many of them would be vulnerable to pressure for assisted suicide and euthanasia by family, physicians, hospitals, and nursing homes, or by the unnecessary suffering they are experiencing because they cannot obtain proper palliative care.

Some awareness of this may be responsible for the fact that in contrast to younger groups that support euthanasia — 56 percent of those in the 18-34 age group favor it — it is supported by only 37 percent of those over 65, the presumed beneficiaries of the practice. And while a slight majority of whites favor the practice, African-Americans oppose it by over two to one.

Although Bob Horn feels empathy for people with disabilities who favor legalization of assisted suicide and/or euthanasia, most of those with disabilities, and the organizations that represent them, are not only opposed to legalization but deeply concerned about its consequences. They understand that those who are disabled can become depressed and want to die; if they were not disabled that depression would be recognized and they would be treated appropriately. When they are disabled there is a tendency to assume that their depression is existential and that any request to die should be granted.

People with disabilities are also all too often acutely aware that choice consists of more than a right to refuse a respirator or to be given a lethal dose of medication. It includes the right to the kind of care that makes the choice to live possible. Bob Horn had those options. When Medicare would not cover the nursing care required to help his wife maintain him at home on a respirator, and his primary insurer was unwilling to do so, he was able to afford private nursing care. What if he could not afford this care? Most people can not. If they have amyotrophic lateral sclerosis and need a respirator they may be obliged by Medicare policy to go to a nursing home which may not be near their home. If they refuse the respirator whose choice was it — theirs or Medicare's?

THE U.S. SUPREME COURT

In its landmark 1997 ruling denying a constitutional right to assisted suicide, the U.S. Supreme Court found that states had valid and important public interests in laws "protecting vulnerable people from indifference, prejudice, and psychological and financial pressure to end their lives" and "maintaining physicians' role as their patients' healers." The Justices expressed their understanding that people who became suicidal in response to medical illness are not so different from those who otherwise become suicidal: they are usually frightened and depressed. The Court cited my work to say that suicidal, terminally ill patients "usually respond well to treatment for pain medication and depressive illness and are grateful to be alive."

The decision handed down by the Court on June 26, 1997, was first and foremost a victory for patients. More important than what the Court rejected - the notion that a "right to die" was a fundamental liberty rooted in the Constitution — was what the majority of the Justices embraced — the right of patients not to suffer. The fact that patients involved in the cases before the Courts could in their states obtain the relief they needed was a major factor in the Court decision. The Justices in essence challenged all states to provide this relief making clear their willingness to revisit the issue if such relief were not being provided.

The decision thus made a substantial contribution to the practice of medicine and the care of patients at the end of life. For example, briefs arguing against the New York and Washington laws prohibiting assisting in suicide had equated the right to withdraw from treatment that would hasten death with physician-assisted suicide, maintaining that since one was permissible the other should be also. But a patient's right to withdraw from any treatment is no different from his or her right not to initiate any treatment — no matter how life — saving it may be. It has nothing to do with a "right to hasten death" and everything to do with the fact that medical practice depends on the principle of informed consent.

The Supreme Court reaffirmed the legal foundation for informed consent and upheld that the right to refuse treatment was not based on an abstract right to hasten death, but on traditional common-law rights to protection from unwanted invasion of one's body. The Court recognized differences in intent between withdrawal of treatment — where the doctor and patient may not intend death but merely freedom from unwanted technology, medicine, or drugs — and physician-assisted suicide, where both doctor and patient have death as their specific goal. (As a consequence, when the prescription for assisted suicide fails, families or physicians usually intervene more actively). In addition, the Court recognized causative differences between a patient dying from an underlying disease after treatment withdrawal and a patient dying from a lethal dose of drugs after physician-assisted suicide.

The Court's firm recognition of the difference between withdrawal of treatment and assisted suicide is helpful to doctors and patients. Both need to understand when it is appropriate to withdraw treatment that only prolongs suffering. Confusion created by the contention that withdrawal of treatment is the same as physician-assisted suicide has made some physicians reluctant to withdraw such treatments. The Court's decision is helping to relieve this concern.

In the brief filed opposing New York's law prohibiting assisted suicide, there were disturbing descriptions of the condition of patients who chose sedation when they were close to death because their suffering could not be relieved in any other way. They were described as being in a "deathlike" state, in the "monstrous" conditions of having "their minds chemically shut down" while they were "imprisoned in their decaying bodies." If they had chosen to forgo medically administered nutrition, the brief described them as being "deliberately starved to death." In fact, most such patients die peacefully without suffering. Had the Court accepted the frightening picture of sedation presented in the brief, it would have been hard for physicians to recommend and patients to seek what is at times necessary. The Court furthered hospice and palliative care by accepting such sedation as an essential and beneficial aspect of the medical care that may be needed to help dying patients.

Although the Supreme Court decision did not preclude the states from considering the possibility of assisted suicide in their effort to care for termi-nally ill patients, the array of legal and medical reasons they gave for ruling in favor of prohibitions against assisted suicide is having an influence on state consideration of the practice.

Most states will not become involved in a struggle over legalization, but will need to address what must be done if the Court's concerns are to be met: improved education of physicians in palliative care, removing regulations that restrict the ways in which physicians can treat pain, widening the avail-ability of hospice care, fostering proper reimbursement for end-of-life care, and passing better-crafted surrogacy laws that, while protecting incompetent patients, also permit proxies to see to it that inappropriate treatments may be withdrawn from them.

THE AMERICAN FOUNDATION FOR SUICIDE PREVENTION POSITION

When the American Foundation for Suicide Prevention (AFSP) was organ-ized 12 years ago to fund research and education designed to prevent suicide, assisted suicide and euthanasia were not our concern. Public activism for assisted suicide and euthanasia changed that. We were troubled by hasty efforts to legalize assisted suicide and euthanasia before the public had a chance to understand the implications of legislation and its potential impact on people who are depressed or become so in response to serious or terminal illness. We were concerned that they would become willing victims if assisted suicide and euthanasia were given legal sanction. What I learned in the Netherlands indicated that such fears were justified.

I had assumed, however, that assisted suicide and euthanasia in the Netherlands, where there is comprehensive health insurance for everyone was surely set in a framework of providing better care for patients who were terminally ill than we were providing in the United States. I learned that not only was that not true but that the development of such care in the Netherlands was being stunted by Dutch acceptance of euthanasia as an alternative. Euthanasia, which had been proposed as an unfortunate but necessary solution in rare cases, had become an almost routine way of dealing with anxiety, depression and pain in seriously or terminally ill patients. What I have seen subsequently in this country as well as the Netherlands has persuaded me that legalization should be avoided because it would markedly worsen the care we provide to terminally ill patients.

Eventually AFSP adopted a policy opposing legalization of assisted suicide because we believe it to be bad for patients, bad for physicians, and bad for society. The assisted suicide debate is in part over whether the need to reduce suffering in those who are terminally ill requires legalizing assisted suicide and/or euthanasia. We believe that the evidence is strongly to the contrary i.e. legalization harms rather than helps the group it is intended to serve.

AFSP contributed to the preparation of the New York brief on assisted suicide submitted to U.S. Supreme Court, consulted with the American Medical Association and other organizations regarding their briefs, and filed its own *amicus curiae* brief. We were gratified that the Court in their decision rejecting a right to assisted suicide cited the findings of studies I had done on behalf of the foundation in both this country and the Netherlands.

We do not believe, however, that it is sufficient to be for or against assisted suicide. Patient's requesting it are desperate and physicians need to know how to inquire into the source of that desperation and to know how to relieve it. We see good palliative care as a major suicide prevention measure. For that reason we have worked with pain and palliative care organizations in behalf of educating physicians in the psychiatric and medical aspects of palliative care.

There is reason to be hopeful. Increasing numbers of physicians are now requesting and receiving training in palliative care. Over the past five years the American Medical Association has undertaken a major educational initiative to meet that need. Greater knowledge of palliative care and awareness of its possibilities is probably responsible for the fact that five years ago 46 percent of cent of oncologists favored legalization of assisted suicide; that number has now dropped to twenty-two percent.

WHAT CAN WE LEARN FROM BOB HORN

When Bob Horn writes of choosing life and the value of choice one wonders if he does not also mean the comfort derived from the knowledge that if life became too intolerable he could always end it by having his respirator disconnected. Many in his predicament would share the sentiment expressed by Nietzsche "The thought of suicide is a great consolation by means of which one gets successfully through many a bad night." Thousands of people hoard medications they say they intend to take to ease their dying — most of them appear to end up dying of natural causes. An oft debated Dutch proposal would give every person who reaches 75 a lethal dose of medicine they could take when and if they saw fit.

Yet what distinguishes Bob Horn's situation is not the easy option he has of ending his life but the life choices he had that provided a viable alternative. The way he is treated by his friends and family reminds us that death becomes undignified only when dying patients are not valued or treated with respect. Bob Horn's strength, however, comes not just from his family and friends or even his adaptability and courage but from something less obvious that one does not see in those who cannot tolerate living with incapacitating or terminal illness. He is able to learn to accept his need for other people and to feel grateful for their help without feeling humiliated or degraded by the experience.

Although Bob Horn says he wants patients who need mechanical ventilation to have the right to refuse it — a right they already have — he himself wants to tell them as strongly as he can that life is possible on a respirator. His message needs telling since most patients with amyotrophic lateral sclerosis do not choose the respirator, but 85% of those who do stay on it and report a quality of life comparable to those not on the respirator.

One finishes Bob Horn's story moved not toward legalizing physician-assisted suicide but inspired to provide ways of making life comfortable and meaningful for those disabled by amyotrophic lateral sclerosis as well as other serious or terminal illnesses. If we meet the challenge of providing adequate palliative care for these patients, assisted suicide and euthanasia will not seem necessary options and the issue of legalization may become irrelevant.

REFERENCES

1. Thomas L: Dying as failure? *American Political Science Review* 1984;444:1-4

2. Wasserman D: Passive euthanasia in response to attempted suicide: one form of aggression by relatives. *Acta Psychiatrica Scandinavica* 1989;79:460-467

3. Bakker DJ: Active euthanasia: is mercy killing the killing of mercy? in *Euthanasia: the good of the patient, the good of society.* Edited by Misbin RI. Frederick, Md, University Publishing Group, 1992, p92

4. Borst-Eilers E: Euthanasia in the Netherlands: brief historical review and present situation, in *Euthanasia: the good of the patient, the good of society.* Edited by Misbin RI. Frederick, Md, University Publishing Group, 1992, p68

5. Hendin H: *Seduced by death: doctors, patients, and assisted suicide.* New York, WW Norton, 1998

6. Hendin H, Foley K, White M: Physician-assisted suicide: reflections on Oregon's first case. *Issues in Law and Medicine* 1998;14:243-270

7. Foley K, Hendin H: The Oregon report: don't ask, don't tell. *Hastings Center Report* 1999;3:37-42

8. Hoover E, Hill GH: Two die using Oregon suicide law. *The Oregonian*, March 26, 1998

9. Gianelli D: Praise, criticism follow Oregon's first reported assisted suicides. *American Medical News*, April 13, 1998, pp1 & 39

10. Personal communication from Peter Reagan to Kathleen Foley and Herbert Hendin

11. Reagan P: Helen. *Lancet* 1999;353:1265-1267

12. van der Maas PJ, Van Delden JJM, Pijnenborg L: *Euthanasia and other medical decisions concerning the end of life.* New York, Elsevier Science Inc, 1992

13. van der Wal G, van der Maas PJ: *Euthanasie en andere Medische Beslissingen rond het Levenseinde.* The Hague, The Netherlands, Staatsuitgeverij, 1996

14. van der Wal G, van der Maas PJ, Bosma JM, et al.: Evaluation of the notification procedure for physician-assisted death in the Netherlands. *New England Journal of Medicine* 1996;335:1706-1711

15. Twycross R: *Where there is hope? there is life? a view from the hospice,* in *Euthanasia examined: ethical, clinical, and legal perspectives.* Edited by Keown J. New York, Cambridge University Press, 1995

16. Hendin H, Rutenfrans C, Zylicz Z: Physician-assisted suicide and euthanasia in the Netherlands: lessons from the Dutch. *Journal of the American Medical Association* 1997;277:1720-1722

17. Hendin H: Euthanasia consultants or facilitators? *Medical Journal of Australia* 1999;170:351-352

18. Quill T, Capsules CK, Meier D: Case of the hopelessly ill: proposed clinical criteria for physician-assisted suicide. *New England Journal of Medicine* 1992;327:1380-1384

19. Hendin H: Suicide, assisted suicide, and medical illness, in the Harvard Medical School guide to suicide assessment and intervention. Edited by Jacobs D. San Francisco, Jossey-Bass, 1999

20. Portenoy RK, Coyle N, Kash K et al. Determinants of the willingness to endorse assisted suicide: A survey of physicians, nurses, and social workers. *Psychosomatics* 1997; 38:277-287.

21. Foley K: Competent care for the dying instead of physician-assisted suicide. *New England Journal of Medicine* 1997;336:54-55

22. Meier DE, Emmons CA, Wallenstein S, Quill T, Morrison RS, Cassel CK: A national survey of physician-assisted suicide and euthanasia in the United States. *New England Journal of Medicine* 1998;338:1193-1201

23. A survey of voter attitudes in the United States. The Terrance Group. Houston, Texas, September 25-28, 1994

24. Washington vs. Glucksberg. 117 Supreme Court 2258, 138L Ed 2nd, 772, 1997

25. Id.

26. Vacco vs. Quill. Statement of the Case .2 Law of the State of New York. Lawrence Tribe, Counsel of Record.

27. Emanuel E: Death's door. *New Republic*, May 17, 1998, p15

28. Nietzsche F: *Beyond Good and Evil, in The Philosophy of Nietzsche*. New York, Modern Library, 1927, p 468

29. Rolland L: Assisted suicide and alternatives in amyotrophic lateral sclerosis. Editorial. *New England Journal of Medicine* 1998;339:14-16

3

◆

A World Perspective on Euthanasia

by Derek Humphry

*Derek Humphry founded the Hemlock Society in 1980 and the Euthanasia Research & Guidance Organization in 1993, both nonprofits providing information about assisted dying, and working for law reform. He has written 13 books, six of them on euthanasia, the most famous being the best seller, **Final Exit**. His web site is **www.finalexit.org.***

WITHOUT DOUBT, ONE OF THE GREAT SOCIAL debates early in the new Millennium will be over euthanasia. Is it moral? Is it necessary? Is it the ultimate civil liberty?

During the last two decades of the old century it had become plain that public opinion worldwide favors the right to choose to die when faced with unbearable terminal suffering — and to get medical help to do so. The Judeo-Christian churches reject the notion of artificially hastened death as vehemently as they oppose a woman's right to choose an abortion.

Politicians of the right generally follow the church policy, whilst those left of center tend to support legalization of cautious, voluntary, justifiable euthanasia.

So that we all know what I am talking about, let me first spell my definitions of these controversial words:

Passive euthanasia: merely means disconnecting an obviously dying person from their life-support equipment and letting nature take its course. This procedure is either legal or acceptable almost everywhere.

Voluntary euthanasia is when a patient asks for death to avoid further terminal suffering. A doctor injects lethal drugs into a vein. Only legal in the Netherlands and Japan in certain circumstances.

Physician-assisted suicide is when a dying patient asks a doctor for lethal drugs to be taken by mouth. This is legal in the Netherlands, Germany, Switzerland and the American state of Oregon.

As to whether there is a right — legally or morally — is by no means a purely American or Dutch debate, although it's in these two countries where debate is loudest and progress has been made.

It has its own peculiarities in the United States connected to the lack of homogeneity in a huge US population of 265 million, absence of universal health care, and a daunting number of states with a complex variety of laws governing the subject. And in the Netherlands social progress and reform in general is so far out in front of the rest of the world that it is not easy to use their actions as a test model.

But there are also some forty organizations around the globe fighting in their respective nations to educate and legitimize some form of aid in dying. With the exception of India, Colombia, and Zimbabwe, they are all located in highly developed countries.

A few fortunate nations do not have the problem — at least legally. Switzerland's laws have permitted assisted suicide since 1937 provided it is for the relief of terminal suffering and carried out for compassionate and altruistic motives.

The Swiss Academy of Medical Sciences opposes doctors actively helping patients to die but it nevertheless supports the principle and practice of 'double effect' — administering morphine to relieve all pain despite the risk of accelerating death. In a population of seven million, there are between 100-120 cases of assisted suicide every year in Switzerland. Doctors carry out some twenty of them; family and friends effect the rest. There has never been a prosecution.

Although discretion on this matter has been prevalent in their country for a long time, many Swiss realize that they possess a precarious right which opponents would not hesitate to strike down. Consequently, in the last twenty years two right to die organizations have sprung up; the largest, EXIT, has more than 60,000 members — three times the size of the Hemlock Society in the USA.

JAPAN

Japan is a contradiction. As most people know, in both past and present, suicide is neither forbidden nor a taboo. While the act no longer has the official and religious sanction — even glorification — which it had in ancient times, or even in World War II, the Japanese people generally understand and tolerate self-destruction by an individual. But as a society they no longer promote it. Strange as it may seem, given this tolerance, voluntary euthanasia and PAS for the terminally ill are veritable taboos. Worse, many people still are allowed to die without being told that they are terminal, although this practice is diminishing.

Overuse of life-support systems for the hopelessly ill in Japan is a major problem. For example, to the horror of much of the public, the Emperor Hirohito in 1989, at the age of 87, suffering from advanced pancreatic cancer, was kept alive by machinery and drugs for 111 days after he would have died naturally.

Every medical procedure carried out on the old man was reported in detail in the daily newspapers and on television. This protracted and macabre medical death of so highly respected a figurehead produced a national revolution in attitudes to dying: for instance, within a short time the membership of the Japan Society for Dying with Dignity leaped from 3,000 to 80,000.

Voluntary euthanasia has been legal in Japan since 1962. That year the High Court of Central Japan, located in Nagoya, issued a ruling in the 'Yamanouchi case' in which a son had killed his suffering father. The three judges ruled that death by euthanasia was lawful if these six conditions were met:

1. The patient's condition must be a terminal one (meaning incurable) with no hope of recovery and death imminent;

2. The patient is being forced to endure unbearable pain.

3. Euthanasia must have the purpose of alleviating the patient's suffering;

4. Euthanasia can only be undertaken at the request or with the permission of the patient. The patient's genuine request or permission should be provided

5. A doctor must perform the task of euthanasia;

6. The method of euthanasia must be ethically acceptable.

How often euthanasia takes place in Japan is completely unknown. Given the ethical and religious rules and taboos that govern that society, it probably happens very rarely, and then only in great secrecy. What is known from several well-publicized prosecutions is that doctors who accelerate a death **without** clear permission from the patient quickly find themselves in trouble with the law.

GERMANY

Not unlike Japan, Germany has legal procedures allowing hastened death but the taboos are so strong that they are rarely used. There has not been a law forbidding assistance in suicide in Germany, provided the motive was altruistic, for more than two hundred years. It was decriminalized by Frederick the Great in 1751 along with the conditions that the person seeking assisted death must be rational and acting out of free choice. (Direct killing by euthanasia is a crime in Germany.)

But getting PAS remains a forbidding task there. The combination of strong religious opposition and the haunting legacy of the genocidal Nazi so-called 'euthanasia program' during World War II renders it virtually unobtainable unless privately negotiated in great secrecy.

One man who tested the law was the late Professor Julius Hackethal, a cancer specialist. On several occasions he announced that he had provided cyanide to people suffering from cancer, on one occasion issuing a video of a woman dying in this manner. Attempts to stop him by German law enforcement authorities failed completely.

Elsewhere in the world, the struggle to legalize and regulate assistance in dying has so far been a stumbling, sporadic process.

AUSTRALIA

Australia has shown remarkable involvement and some progress in securing the right to choose to die. From the early 1970s — a decade before the USA and Canada — it had small but dynamic voluntary euthanasia groups struggling to educate its population with a view to law reform.

This special interest in dying apparently stems from the toughness of much of Australian family life; with huge distances in the outback separating homes and hospitals, the people have been obliged to deal themselves with the death of loved ones instead of — as so often occurs in America — shipping them off to nursing homes and hospitals to die. Secondly, the pioneering, 'handle-problems-yourself' spirit of the vast outback generated an interest in knowing how to kill oneself if terminal suffering became unbearable.

So it was no surprise to many people when Australia became the first place in the world actually to legalize euthanasia by statute, albeit in one small 'territory' which had not yet qualified to be a full state. The nation comprises a Federal Government, five full states, and three territories that will eventually become states. These territories have their own elected legislatures, and are largely self-governing, but — as the Northern Territory was to find to its chagrin — the Federal Government can override some of its decisions.

Although the Northern Territory is twice the size of Texas, its population is a mere 170,000, of which 27 percent consists of Aboriginal people. On average, death comes earlier here than the rest of the country — at age 53 for men and 64 for women — while infant mortality at 11.3 deaths per thousand live births, is nearly twice the national rate. Thus in terms of quality health care and longevity, particularly lacking for the Aborigines, it was not the ideal place to start.

As is often the case, the impetus for reform came from one person who gathered support among colleagues for a universal idea — the right to choose to die if suffering unbearably.

Marshall Perron, the chief minister of the Territory, had no personal experience of painful death to influence him when he made the first moves to change the law; he was impressed by the intellectual arguments put forward in a paper by Dr. Helga Kuhse, published by the Australian Medical Association, and entitled "Medically Assisted Dying for Competent Patients".

Perron also read the papers arguing against any form of euthanasia. The argument that impressed him most was in the paper by Prof. Kuhse, director of the Center for Bioethics at Monash University, Melbourne. Perron has said: "[It was] so compelling so absolute in its logic and good sense, it motivated me to try and do something about it," he has said.

"What is to be done?" she asked. "It seems that at least one option is open to us: to adopt a public policy approach that is based on mutual respect or autonomy. This is not a morally arbitrary approach. Personal autonomy or freedom is a very important moral value, and central to what it means to be a person and a moral agent.

"It follows from this acceptance of the value of autonomy that persons should be free to pursue their vision of 'the good life' and that it is inappropriate for the state to either adopt a paternalistic stance towards its mature citizens, or to restrict their freedom through the enforcement of a particular moral point of view. Only if one person's actions cause harm to others will it be legitimate for the state to step in, and to bring in laws that restrict individual liberty...It is inappropriate, argued Prof. Kuhse, that the law or the policies of medical associations should enshrine a particular moral point of view.

She went on: "Public policies should be based on respect for autonomy, where people who approach questions of the good life from different moral, cultural, and religious perspectives are provided with a moral space that allows them to live their lives in accordance with their values and beliefs."

The first draft of the **Rights of the Terminally Ill Act**, was released in February of 1995. A national uproar, for and against, began. I happened to be in Australia for much of the controversy. The Australian Medical Association, church groups and right to life organizations reacted strongly. Within days euthanasia became the foremost news topic in the nation, continuing as such for the next two years, although this piece of legislation applied only to the little Northern Territory.

The elected members of the Northern Territory legislature were now confronting the same dilemma as politicians all over the world when faced with a highly controversial issue: many had won their seats with a majority of a mere 30 or 50 votes which — if they supported law reform — could vanish with even a minor church boycott

When the crucial vote came to the floor of the Parliament, it was left to a conscience vote, with no party restrictions or personal loyalties involved. It narrowly passed by thirteen votes to twelve on May 25, five months after its introduction.

BOB DENT #1

The first person to request death under the new Act was Mr. Bob Dent, who had suffered from prostate cancer for five years, had undergone numerous surgeries, and was impotent, unable to urinate, and losing bowel control. Despite heavy analgesic medication he still suffered considerable pain. Dr. Philip Nitschke, a local doctor, offered to help Dent die.

Having satisfied the detailed and complex legal conditions for assisting a suicide, Dr. Nitschke then connected Dent to an apparatus comprised of a bottle of lethal drugs linked to a laptop computer. The computer asked him three questions, all restatements of the same question, "Do you know what you are doing?" This was to demonstrate that the patient was conscious and able to interact, demonstrating 'informed consent'. The last message on the little screen warned that if he or she pressed the spacebar the drugs would kick in automatically and he would die. Dent chose death.

All four individual deaths in Australia who died under the Northern Territory law became huge media events. The print and television media headlined every single statement and event as though it was a prelude to a major war.

Cardinal Edward Clancy, head of the Roman Catholic Church in Australia, said: "This first case of legalized euthanasia in all the world is an act of reckless disregard for the convictions of people around the globe, and will be widely condemned." The Territory's Catholic Bishop said it was immoral. The widow, Mrs. Dent, said it was what her husband wanted.

In the battle to get it passed, the law had undergone several changes. For instance, it allowed dying people from other parts of Australia to come to the Northern Territory to avail themselves of the procedure.

One of the arguments against the passage of the law was that, since it allowed dying people from other states to travel to the Northern Territory to die, it was in effect legislating euthanasia for all of Australia, for which, of course, it had no mandate. Sick people all over the huge nation were applying to go to the Northern Territory for help in dying.

The battle to make or break the Northern Territory's vanguard law then shifted to Canberra, where the Australian Federal Government is situated. Church groups intensified their objections, chiefly on the grounds that hastened death defiled the sanctity of life.

DR NITSCHKE

The fires of the controversy were constantly refueled by the highly publicized deaths under the Act, all carried out by one doctor, Philip Nitschke, and the pathetic stories of other people who wanted to use the law but could not for one reason or another.

Just before the debate in the national parliament, The Medical Journal of Australia published in February 1997 a paper, entitled **End-of-Life Decisions in Australian Medical Practice**. The survey's objective was to estimate the number of medical end-of-life decisions in Australia, to describe the characteristics of such decisions, and to compare these with medical end-of-life decisions in the Netherlands.

The report stated that in 30 percent of all Australian deaths, a medical decision was made with the explicit intention of ending the patient's life. Crucially, overall Australia had a higher rate of ending life than did the Netherlands. The authors' conclusions were that Australian law against it had not prevented doctors from practicing euthanasia or making medical end-of-life decisions explicitly intended to hasten the patient's death without the patient's request.

The final vote on March 25, 1997, in the Australian Federal Parliament — according to conscience, not party lines — was fairly close: 38 for repealing the Northern Territory law, and 33 wishing to keep it.

The world was once again without any statutory euthanasia laws. Dr. Nitschke confines himself to traveling advisory clinics on euthanasia.

COLOMBIA

While it was no surprise that some people in Australia legalized euthanasia, if only briefly, the biggest shock of 1997 came with the announcement that the highest court in Colombia had also approved it. On May 20 the nation's Constitutional Court announced that by a vote of 6-3 it had ruled that "no person can be held criminally responsible for taking the life of a terminally ill patient who has given clear authorization to do so."

The court defined 'terminally ill' as patient with cancer, kidney or liver failure, or AIDS, at the same time excluding patients with Lou Gehrig's, Parkinson's, or Alzheimer's Diseases. Comatose patients were specifically ruled out, as were physically healthy people. Up to that point, anyone killing a patient who was terminal had been liable to between six months' and three years' imprisonment.

Ironically, the change in the law came about because somebody went to court to try and strengthen the penalties for mercy killing. Jose Euripides Parra, a Bogota lawyer, objected to a 1980 penal code mandating lesser prison sentences for mercy killing than for murder. His argument was not so much against euthanasia as that the Constitutional Court had no right to change laws, only interpret them.

The Roman Catholic Church, to which the overwhelming number of Colombians belongs, was staggered at the court's decision. Gino Concetti, a Catholic theologian said to be close to Pope John Paul II, wrote in the Vatican's semi-official newspaper, *L'Observatore Romano*, under the headline "A Perverse Hypocrisy: Killing for Mercy" that the ruling that the freedom from prosecution applied only to dying people able to make the request did not make it any more morally acceptable. Concetti went on, "The fact that euthanasia would be carried out in a terminal stage and with consent of the patient does not change the nature of the act which is intrinsically perverse."

Carlos Gavira, the chief magistrate of the court, said that the ruling was consistent with reforms passed by the national legislature in 1991 when the constitution was altered to give individuals more freedom of choice.

Magistrate Gavira explained: "What the court did was simply to recognize what is already consecrated in the constitution: the autonomy of a person to decide whether to opt for euthanasia. What it means is that if a person has religious beliefs and regards this as reprehensible, he will have the liberty not to partake. But if the person doesn't have these kinds of beliefs, he can observe his rights legally."

The surprise court ruling triggered Colombia into suddenly discussing the rights and needs of the dying, an issue which had remained dormant in a predominantly Catholic country (pop. 36 million).

Immediately the Roman Catholic Church lodged an appeal against the decision of the court, calling it, in the words of Monsignor Dario Molina, bishop of Monteria, "an attack on life which is especially monstrous in a society where we've lost all sense of direction because of so much violence." The Bishop was referring to the long-running battles between police and drug runners, and between the army and guerrillas.

Once more, the question arises of whether a nation may decently introduce euthanasia whilst there are other, pressing problems, such as appalling violence in Colombia, lack of universal health care in America, and grinding poverty in India.

Must the dying wait for a perfect society — an ideal world — before they can obtain compassionate and lawful relief from their suffering?

Undeterred, on October 3, 1997, the Colombian Constitutional Court Magistrates, by exactly the same margin, 6-3, affirmed their earlier decision. The court directed that the law should now go to the Congress for detailed study and regulations to be adopted. But at the end of 1999 it still had not done so. So while it is still not the applied law in Colombia, it would be extremely difficult to prosecute a doctor who carried out a justifiable euthanasia.

FRANCE AND BRITAIN

All other nations retain criminal sanctions against voluntary euthanasia and PAS. The French since 1986 have even had a law forbidding the publication of literature giving advice about any form of suicide. It caused the French right to die organization, Association pour le Droit de Mourir dans la Dignite, to destroy its own literature on the subject. My book, **Final Exit**, remains on the list of banned books.

The biggest division between public opinion and Establishment power is in Britain, said to be the fountainhead of democracy, where a massive contradiction exists:

- On the one side, 82 percent of the public would like some form of lawful euthanasia to be available.

- But, on the other side, seven times in the last 60 years when presented with bills Parliament has refused to act. It makes no difference which political party is in power in Britain; the answer is always in the negative.

Timidity in tackling moral issues seems to be universal amongst politicians.

Like many other nations, the British Establishment prefers to allow assisted deaths to be carried out covertly. A survey of physicians published in the **British Medical Journal** in 1994 showed that nearly one third of the nation's doctors who had been asked for active euthanasia did administer lethal injections. A larger proportion — 46 percent — would consider taking active steps to bring about a patient's death if it were legal to do so.

The Voluntary Euthanasia Society, founded in London in 1935 and still vainly laboring to change the law, commented in its journal: "Voluntary euthanasia in Britain today takes place in a shadowy criminal world. Patients cannot always be sure they will get what they are asking for, and doctors are denied the open advice and support of their colleagues."

WHERE IT IS PRACTISED

In only two places in the world in modern times has assisted dying been accepted into the rule of law: The Netherlands and the American state of Oregon. Both places have some uniqueness in that their citizens are noted for their independent-mindedness and social progressiveness.

The Dutch have legalized prostitution; they have legalized the purchase of small amounts of recreational drugs. They are a nation of 'doers' of 'achievers' — when they have a problem they set about solving it.

For their part, Oregonians are noted for their pioneer spirit, their reluctance to be told how to live by outsiders, and they keep proudly in place the

right of the citizenry to pass laws by direct vote, not only through the elected legislature.

In both the Netherlands and Oregon, no one church is dominant over
the population. Fewer Oregonians attend religious services than any other
state in America.

OREGON'S LAW

Let me deal with Oregon's new law first:

The Death With Dignity Act, 1994, specifically bans voluntary
euthanasia. It permits only physician-assisted suicide, and sets out strict conditions that must first be obeyed.

These are the fundamental rules inherent in the law:

- The patient must be an adult in a rational state of mind. By
  'rational' is meant that the person can understand what is being
  said to him or her by the doctor.

- The patient must be terminally ill and close to death — at least
  within six months of the end.

- The doctor must offer the patient better pain management and
  the opportunity to enter a hospice program.

- The patient must first ask the doctor for lethal medications and
  14 days later ask again both verbally and in writing. The requests
  must be witnessed.

- No person who is asking for death on the grounds of old age, or
  disability or handicap, may be considered for assisted suicide.
  Advanced terminal illness is the only criteria.

- A second doctor must also agree in writing that the patient is
  end-stage terminal.

- If either of the two doctors suspects the patient is clinically
  depressed, then a psychologist must make an evaluation. If there
  is depression, the procedure cannot go ahead until it is successful
  treated.

- Three days after the last request by the dying person for lethal drugs, the doctor can ask a pharmacist to issue the drugs.

- At any point the patient can change his or her mind, and revoke the request.

- No doctor, nor pharmacist, nor any medical person is **obligated** to help in assisted suicide. Hospitals may ban the procedure on their premises if they wish. The patient is then free to seek a doctor who is willing to help.

- Residents of the state only may apply.

- Criminal sanctions in the law call for penalties for anybody using coercion, force, or fraud leading to a patient's death.

Those are the main rules of a very limited law. It does not help people who have chronic, long-term illnesses, nor cannot it help a person who has a degenerative disease like Alzheimer's because they are not competent to make an informed request.

I have some reservations about the Oregon law. The waiting period may be too lengthy. Some people discover death approaching more rapidly than they had believed, and find the 17 day waiting period too long. Some become incompetent between the first request and the time for the second, and get disqualified.

But the Oregon law is a good start. It is an intensely learning experience for a great many people and professions. Opponents predicted that there would be suicides galore but in its first full year of operation, 1998, only fifteen (15) people died while using the law, and in their own homes. Three quarters of the 15 were in hospice programs.

A survey by the state health department found that the 15 were typical, average Oregon people — neither rich nor poor, of ordinary education, and receiving normal medical care. More than half of the 15 who died this way were receiving Hospice care for their pain.

How did such a law come to pass — the only state in America so far?

The citizenry of Oregon used their century-old right to pass laws by popular vote because their elected representatives would not do so. In 1994 the electors of Oregon voted 51-49 percent for the new law, and when asked to confirm it in 1997 voted 60-40 percent in favor.

In early 1999 the Oregon Legislature got its hands on the right to die law again, but this time was afraid to nullify it. It tinkered with it, setting out the standards by which residency must be proved and clarifying that pharmacists were included in all the law's clauses. The Legislature also added wording to say that people could not use the law on the grounds of age or disability. The law's original authors had taken these two exclusions for granted, but now it was spelled out and removed any doubt.

The Oregon law is still under tremendous pressure from its opponents, particularly in the US Congress.

THE NETHERLANDS

The Dutch began practicing euthanasia openly in 1973 when a doctor was freed by a court after injecting a lethal dose of drugs into her sick and aged mother. Then began extensive debates, committees, commission of inquiries, until in 1984 the Dutch Supreme Court gave the go-ahead to both voluntary euthanasia and physician-assisted suicide. Later the Dutch Parliament approved rules by which it should be carried out. The legal principle which Dutch judges used to approve euthanasia was that of *'force majeure'* — that, given the hopeless, painful, undignified situation of the patient, the doctor had no decent alternative but to accelerate death. In other words, an action caused by necessity.

Only three percent of all those who die in the Netherlands each year do so from voluntary euthanasia or physician-assisted suicide. It is undisputed that 90 percent of the Dutch people approve of voluntary euthanasia.

As with all things ethical and medical, the Dutch have had their problems. The most controversial has been when patients have suddenly deteriorated, become incompetent, and cannot make the proper requests for euthanasia. Yet often they are suffering agonies. At a certain point there is nothing more the doctor can do.

Dutch doctors have openly admitted that in such drastic cases they sometimes bring the life to an end to avoid further suffering. So there we might have 'involuntary euthanasia', which nobody wants to legally sanction. But in such painful cases might not it be ethically justified? In some instances, the body can turn from apparently healthy to dying in a very short time.

In typical Dutch fashion, they have been setting our rules to deal with such emergencies, more guidelines, and review committees

Perhaps the biggest problem in the Netherlands has been the under-reporting of assisted dying cases. Doctors are supposed to fill out forms and send them to the government saying how they helped the patient die, and why. Then follows an inquiry to make sure that the doctor obeyed the rules.

Only about 40 percent of doctors have been reporting their euthanasia cases to the authorities. Those who do not claim they do not have the time, or they fear prosecution because, still, euthanasia — although permitted, is technically a criminal act. What the courts and the government have done so far is to 'sanction' it according to guidelines.

But the latest development is that the Dutch government in 2000 intends to change the procedures and have Parliament pass a statutory law on when and how any form of euthanasia may be practiced. This step is what many Dutch people have been asking for as it removes all criminality from the action provided it is done according to high medical and ethical standards, much the same as those in Oregon.

In November of 2000 the voters of Maine are due to be asked whether they, too, want a law permitting physician-assisted suicide. Twice their elected representatives have refused to pass such a law.

In *every* nation where there have been scientific surveys of public opinion, it has become obvious that the general **public wants action**, while the **politicians** (who actually make the laws) are either **against law reform or afraid of a religious backlash** if they follow the public's wishes.

The medical profession almost everywhere is split down the middle on the issue of euthanasia. Some doctors covertly practice euthanasia where they see it is the compassionate and appropriate thing to do. Others will not on ethical grounds. I respect that.

But would it not be better if this was out in the open, enabling doctors to discuss a request for euthanasia with other doctors, other experts, and have a shared responsibility. Until the criminal sanctions surrounding euthanasia are lifted, the supporters must act alone and in secret.

My plea is for tolerance on this issue. Surely in a free and democratic society there is room for both acceptance of euthanasia, and rejection of it. It must never be an obligation to die, but — equally — free people ought to have the right to choose to die if they wish it.

Who's
Right?

Section Two

4

◆

Mary

Dedicated to all the
"Marys — female and male"
who also suffered greatly
during the dying process

by *Judith Beay, R.N.*

M Y EVOLUTION OF EMBRACING THE CONCEPT of
physician-aid-dying began almost 40 years ago when I was a
brand-new R.N. (registered nurse). Following nurses training,
I began attending college to pursue a bachelor's degree in
nursing. I worked as a "private-duty nurse", which afforded me flexible work
hours.

I'll never forget "Mary"; one of my very first patients. Mary was in her
late 70's, dying from rectal cancer. While oozing blood constantly from her
rectum, she received continuous blood transfusions. Mary was barely conscious and was in agony. Webster defines agony as "pain so extreme as to
cause writhing or contortions of the body".

The nurses were only permitted to administer pain medication every 4
hours which provided Mary with about 1 hour of partial pain relief. Her

physician refused to increase the dosage or frequency of the pain medication because, "A higher dose would depress her respirations and kill her!

Following my morning classes, I would call the Nursing Registry to inquire if Mary had died, or did I need to work that evening? When I asked, under my breath, I was praying Mary had died and was released from her suffering.

For seven days — that's 168 hours — Mary lived in agony. The reader must understand as a private-duty nurse, I was at Mary's bedside for 8 hours continuously, except for a brief supper and bathroom break. I was helpless to relieve Mary's suffering; even gently bathing or lotioning her, increased her moans. The doctor also ordered Mary to be repositioned every 2 hours. I did this during the hour she had some pain relief, but the other repositioning occurred without the benefit of pain medication. The nurse's aide and I were so gentle and careful in repositioning Mary, but it increased her pain to the point where her moans became heart rending screams — and I would softly cry because I felt sorry for what Mary was enduring. And, some of my tears were because I felt so helpless that there was nothing I could do to relieve her suffering.

During those long hours of sitting at Mary's beside, I began to question her "medical care". I concluded the medical establishment was not providing "care", but was actually the cause of her suffering!My pleas to the supervising nurse to call Mary's doctor and demand stronger pain medication fell on deaf ears. Instead, I was accused of "unprofessional conduct" and "becoming emotionally involved" with a patient. I considered resigning from Mary's case, but decided to stay, because at the least I could give Mary the gentlest care possible.

Finally, after a week of agony, Mary breathed her last while I held her hand and tried to smooth away the deep furrows of her suffering. I thanked God for finally releasing Mary from her suffering. Mary's room was at the end of the hall and I slowly walked to the nurses station to report her death to the supervisor. As I walked back to Mary's room to prepare her body for the morgue, I heard a "Code Blue" being announced over the loudspeaker and to my utter amazement, the room number for the Code Blue was Mary's room!

The crash cart and medical team arrived at the room immediately and began trying to resuscitate Mary! I was horrified! I tried to explain Mary had been dead at least 10 minutes and, additionally was terminally ill. No one paid attention to my, "Don't do that! Mary is dead!"

The resuscitation efforts continued 20 more minutes; I heard ribs cracking; her heart was shocked with electricity and powerful drugs were injected into her veins. And then, thankfully, it was over! The resuscitation team left, bemoaning the fact they were unsuccessful in their attempt to revive her. I was emotionally drained as I washed Mary's body and removed all the various tubes before taking her body to the morgue. The supervisor came into the room and questioned why I had taken so long to report Mary's death? She asked, "Why didn't you put on the call light or use the intercom to report your patient's death rather than walking to the nurses station? You should know valuable minutes were lost before the resuscitation team arrived. It was your actions that caused the failure to successfully resuscitate her!"

I blurted out, "I'm glad they couldn't resuscitate her! Why would anyone want to resuscitate her and prolong her suffering?" The supervisor sharply rebuked me, "That's not for you to decide; it's hospital policy! Your actions will be reported!"

I went home that night with conflicting thoughts. "Did I even want to be a nurse? Did I want to be a part of a medical community that, in my opinion, tortured patients?" And yes, I was fearful the hospital would have my newly acquired RN license revoked!

I never heard anything more of this situation, but that experience planted the seed in me, to question the "care" given to dying patients. I began to express ideas of what would become known as"palliative care"decades later. Palliative care is treating patients with various means to alleviate suffering. Traditional treatment modalities often include appropriate medication to ease nausea, vomiting, constipation, breathlessness, restlessness and of course pain. Non-traditional treatments may include music, massage, visualization, acupuncture, heat or cold packs.

My professional experience for the next 20 years was in the field of long-term care. The nursing home I co-administered provided the full gamut of care. Many patients came for several weeks or months of rehabilitation following strokes, fractured hips, etc. and returned home. We also cared for long-term patients who suffered chronic illnesses from complications of aging.

Over the years, my philosophy on end-of-life issues continued to evolve with a sharp distinction between "saving lives" and "prolonging death". In my opinion, hospitals were primarily in the business of saving lives while long-term care facilities should not prolong death when the dying process began. As I began to verbalize this idea of not prolonging death to the medical community in the small town in the Midwest where we lived, I encountered deep resistance from the physicians. "What do you mean by not tube feeding patients who can no longer eat?" Or, "If a patient develops pneumonia, of course she or he should be hospitalized for aggressive treatment! It doesn't matter if the patient is 98 years old or has Alzheimers!" I countered with, "What about 'Patient's Rights' to refuse treatment?"

If the physicians' resistance wasn't enough, the State also had strict nursing home regulations regarding the issue of malnutrition and dehydration. When patients with dementia could (or would) no longer eat, most nursing homes automatically inserted feeding tubes without even asking families if the patient would want to be kept alive in this manner. They feared state officials would cite and fine them for violations.

Thank goodness, the State also had a strong "Patients' Bill of Rights" whereby patients, or, when patients were no longer competent, their surrogates had the right to refuse further treatment. I began to counsel families of incompetent patients that hospitalization and feeding tubes did not have to be automatic; patients/families could decide otherwise. I requested families to document in writing their refusals for further treatment. This was years before there were "Living Wills" or "Health Care Powers of Attorney".

As a facility, we continued to provide terminal patients with excellent care; patients were still offered food and fluids even though the amount that was eaten or drunk was inadequate to sustain life. Of course, the patient did became malnourished and dehydrated. However the State could not cite the nursing home for breaking a law, because the patient had the right to refuse treatment. Thus it was not the nursing home's "failure to provide adequate care."

It was now the mid-80's and palliative care was still in its infancy as hospice care became mainstream.I was drawn to this field of nursing like a bee is drawn to pollen! Administration was always my forté and I developed a rural hospice agency. That was when it was widely believed that a rural area could not support a certified hospice. At last, terminally ill patients could finally receive adequate pain and other symptom relief. Furthermore, if an attending physician refused to order appropriate and adequate medication, the hospice medical director could over-ride that decision and prescribe what the patient needed! Hallelujah! There would be no more "Mary's" in agony.

During those years as I worked full-time with terminally ill patients and saw adequate pain and other symptom relief for physical problems; the issue of emotional, mental and spiritual care came to the forefront in hospice care. For the first time,there were not only regulations addressing these needs, but there was actually reimbursement for providing counselors and spiritual advisors to meet these needs.

As an administrator in long-term care and now hospice care, I had always managed to have some direct patient contact. I began to hear some patients expressing their wish to die earlier rather than experience a prolonged dying process. Patients often expressed how weary they were and how there was no longer any "quality to their lives", i.e. doing or enjoying what was meaningful to them. They even expressed how they disliked being a "burden" to their loved ones and didn't want to use up financial resources that might be needed for spouses left behind, etc.

The hospice team also heard these concerns and discussed them at patient conferences. Team members had strong differences of opinions on these issues and philosophical discussions arose, such as, "Why can't a patient die 'earlier' and shorten the dying process if that is what the patient wants! Some team members countered with, "People need the dying process to work through all their issues; make peace with family, themselves, etc. Others countered, "But, if the patient has already done this work and still wants an earlier death; who are we to oppose them?" Some hospice team members, myself included, asked "Who are 'we' (the hospice team), to tell the patient that he or she can still find meaning in life, even when the patient says there is no meaning or quality to his or her life!

For myself, this was a definite shift regarding end-of-life issues. There was not only an acceptance of patients' right to refuse further treatment but also the right to shorten the dying process, and preferably, with assistance.

As I reviewed Webster's definition of agony; in addition to the physical suffering, Webster included "mental" anguish as agony. Shouldn't this include patients who no longer enjoyed life? Or disliked being a burden? Or couldn't accept illnesses that robbed them of their independence? As palliative care continued expanding and the use of morphine drips became routine,I personally wondered if there is really any difference between a morphine drip that relieved pain and often hastened death or morphine injected all at once and death occurred in minutes, rather than in hours or days?

In 1990 the abstract became personal for me. Following a sudden and severe loss imbalance, I was diagnosed with M.S. (multiple sclerosis), a chronic and degenerative disease. I was devastated by this diagnosis, as most people are. My nursing background and experiences painted a vivid and horrific picture of M.S. I was over-whelmed with images of bedridden and diapered patients who could barely speak or eat and drink without choking. I knew muscles often contracted and became spastic, often causing severe pain. Additionally, the end stage of M.S. may cause emotional problems and dementia.

Early in my disease process, I resolved that if my MS progressed to the point of being bedridden, diapered, etc., I would take steps to shorten my dying process. I became active in the Hemlock Society and read books, such as **Final Exit**, by Derek Humphry. (Derek Humphry is a noted journalist and writer in Britain and the US before launching the Hemlock Society in 1980 in California. The Society was named **HEMLOCK**, which means good death.) I asked my doctors if they would prescribe medications, as barbiturates, I could use to hasten my dying process. Both said they would prescribe what I might need, although one of my physician's said, "If I was asked I said this, I would deny it!" He went on to say "Most doctors do this, but we never discuss it among ourselves in order to protect one another in the case of a legal inquiry or a lawsuit."

After working many, many years in health care, I wasn't surprised by his answer. Upon further questioning, my doctor said, "If it were legal, not only would I prescribe lethal medication, I would even administer a lethal injection if that's what the patient wanted!"

These discussions provided me with such emotional and psychological relief. I no longer had to worry about "what if". I knew that if my disease progressed to the point where, in my opinion, there was no quality or joy in my life, I would not have to suffer! This reassurance has allowed me to fully live and enjoy life. In spite of fatigue, weakness, bladder and bowel problems, and some cognitive limitations, my life is full and satisfying.

Following an early medical retirement, I have been "blessed" in so many ways. I am available to baby sit my grand-daughters while my daughter completes her teaching degree. I tutor at our local elementary school and jail. This "work" has been "soooul" satisfying. I have the time to properly care for my body, i.e. Yoga, meditation, biking and cooking nutritious food. I have been fortunate in having my health insurance pay for one of the injectable MS medications which is very expensive. Hopefully this medication will minimize the complications of this degenerative disease.

I strongly support both terminally ill people and those who suffer from degenerative diseases which in their opinions have robbed them of the ability to live a life with meaning. People should have the right to decide when and how to shorten their dying process. This is their RIGHT! No one, including government or religious officials, should interfere with their decision or compel them to continue an existence that has become unbearable.

I would never have the audacity to compel a terminally ill person who may be in pain, bedridden, diapered, gurgling, tube fed, etc. to choose an earlier death. And by God, if I am in pain, bedridden, diapered, gurgling, etc. and choose to end my existence earlier, NO ONE should compel me to continue existing either! I further support this Right — the Right to choose an earlier death when dying — should even be expanded and be included in "Living Wills" and "Health Care Durable Power of Attorney" so that instructions to end a dying process can be carried out even if the person can no longer request or communicate their wishes.

This is especially important for people suffering from dementia. In the earlier stages of dementia, people can still enjoy satisfying and productive lives. However, there have been cases of people in the earlier stages of their disease killing themselves rather than risk not being able to decide or act at a later time, when their dementia has progressed to the point they no longer have the ability to communicate their wishes. If this provision was included in the Health Care Power of Attorney, it would give the person peace of mind knowing they would not have to exist months or years in a vegetative state.

My pragmatic side also wants to make one more point. As a society, we spend more health care dollars on dying people in their last months of life, than are spent on preventive health care or even necessary elective health care for uninsured or under-insured people. Not only does our society need to address the logic of providing futile medical care, but society needs to allow people to end their lives earlier — again, when there is no outcome except death.

From a personal viewpoint, my estate is modest and if my MS progresses to where I needed institutional care to exist a few more months or years, in addition to quality-of-life issues, I would want my children to have this money. I would not want to be forced to continue "living" because I no longer had the ability to actively take measures to end my life. This is why I believe it should be legal for physicians, who are willing, to assist dying patients, doing so when requested.

Opponents argue that physician-aid-in-dying, if legalized, may begin what is often called the "slippery slope" whereby people would be involuntarily euthanized. Opponents argue that family members may coerce a patient in requesting assistance in order to protect inheritances. Or perhaps an insurance company would encourage this practice to eliminate a "high cost" patient.

Safeguards could be instituted to prevent the above scenarios. For example, a person would have to request this assistance in writing and the request would need to be witnessed by a totally independent person who had no relationship with the patient or his or her family. Preferably, most people would do this far in advance of needing this assistance similar to what is done now in completing Health Care Power of Attorney.

There should be a provision for those who don't request this earlier.If a person is now terminally ill, or in advanced stages of debilitating diseases, and is of sound mind, he or she could still request aid-in-dying. This would be done by using a non-involved professional who can verify the person is not being coerced or does not have an underlying problem, as depression, that can be treated. If a person has done neither of these options, and is no longer of"sound mind", aid-in-dying would not be permitted! Period!

These steps should assure opponents who use the "slippery slope" issue to oppose physician-aid-in-dying, that ONLY people of sound mind have made these decisions. Government of family members would not be able to euthanize anyone!

I want to close with what I believe is the most important point in my chapter. It is my opinion that each person must have the freedom of choice in deciding how each of us wants to handle end-of-life issues, if faced with a terminal or a progressive, debilitating illness.

5

◆

Soul Choices and Spiritual Experiences

by Myrna C. Tashner, EdD.

Psychologist, Hospice Chaplain

D EATH IS A SPIRITUAL EXPERIENCE, just as life is a spiritual experience. The bridge between them is breath. In some languages breath and spirit are the same word. It isn't much of a stretch in logic to say then that: You are a spiritual being, living in a spiritual world, governed by spiritual laws, and having a human experience. Then some cases, if not all, humans will have some degree of choice in the death experience.

My experiences of death began as a child on a farm. Animals were born, lived and died. It was a natural part of the farm experience, the life cycle.

I grew up in a very religious home. From an early age, I recall being exposed to people being born and people dying. There was always a family gathering for each event. At birth families would gather at the home of the newborn. We young children would take turns holding the new arrival, but soon would give the infant to the adults in favor of more animated playmates. At a death, family would gather for the review of the body and the funeral. During church services we would pray for the deceased person and their family. I sometimes cried, like when my first grade friend died of polio a few days after her seventh birthday party. It was usually the older ones, great grand-parents, great uncles and aunts who died, and I stayed pretty detached, as death was supposed to happen to them.

Then February 26, 1967 death became real. It was a bitter cold day at college. As I walked back to the dorm after my World History class, the wind blew across the nearby frozen lake and whipped around my ears making the 2 blocks seem like 2 miles. When I finally got to the dorm, a classmate met me in the hall and told me that my mom had just called and I needed to call her back "right away". I went to the phone wondering why Mom would be calling me on a Tuesday afternoon at 3:00 p.m. But I was also remembering all of the warm feelings of their visit on previous Sunday, and the joy we shared over our new brother/son.

So I dialed the number. Mom answered. "Hello, Myrna. Come home right away! Your father is dead." "Okay" was all I could say and hung up. The shock set in, all I did was shake. From my earliest days I was a praying person, so as the tears came I heard myself say, "Oh God, help."

I had grown up in a small farm community, Catholic and Lutheran. My father's funeral was a very large one because everyone came. He was buried on a very cold winter day, bitterly cold, at age 42.

When I got back to college after the funeral, I began hearing him talking to me. "Myrna, can't you see me, I'm not dead." This seemed to go on for weeks. In the depths of grief and shock, I didn't tell anyone. This seemed very unusual as I hadn't heard of others talk about such experiences. But I knew the experience I was having was real. Unable to explain what I was hearing I turned to prayer. Eventually he stopped talking to me.

Sometime later, I met a spiritual teacher, who told me that hearing my father speak probably wasn't my imagination. She went on to say that when people experience instant unexpected deaths, initially they tend not to believe they have died. (Remember the main character in the movie, **Ghost?**) These disincarnate spirits hang around. Eventually they become aware they are without physical bodies and go on toward the Light they are able to find.

This was my first convincing experience with the truth and reality that the human being is more than their body. There is a real spiritual part of us. It seemed different than that which was conveyed at church.

With my experience of my father's death, I was convinced that human beings are more than mind and body. I began a quest to learn more about this spiritual reality that humans are capable of.

Simultaneously, because of my father's untimely death, I determined to live life in the world to the fullest measure. I was especially curious about what made other people "tick". Life itself seemed to be a dynamic energy force, not always predictable, and I was curious about this energy, too.

These curiosities eventually led me to study psychology and I immersed myself in it. At that time psychology focused on defining and exploring human behavior, cognitions and emotions, as well as maladaptive behavior. I was interested in the therapeutic techniques of listening, decoding mal-adaptive thoughts, and analyzing behaviors with the purpose of emotional healing. I was fascinated by the relationship between thought, emotions and attitudes in creating events in life. I never ceased to be amazed by the power of perceptions and emotions in shaping one's life events.

The power of positive thought and feelings were dramatically driven home in my dissertation research. I was looking at the personalities of pro-fessional women in non-traditional careers for women. I wanted to know what made them successful, and how they coped if life was stressful. The majority of the results are beyond the scope of this discussion. However, these wonderful women, almost to a person, indicated that they survived because of their spirituality. It was an answer I wasn't prepared for, primarily because in the 70s and 80s in the graduate schools I was studying in psychological research had to be statistical, quantifiable, reproducible and tangible in some way. Spirituality didn't meet these criteria. Stress managed by exercise, or a workout at the sports club, would have been an acceptable response; stress managed by a walking or sitting meditation was not acceptable, yet.

At the completion of my degree, I went into private practice. And being the curious observer of human nature, I soon became aware that the cogni-tive and behavioral approaches I had learned in graduate school would only go so far in emotional healing. And it seemed the clients didn't stay healed, nor were they able to apply the steps they had learned to other experiences and events. People seemed to lack the inner strength and power to do it for themselves.

In the meantime, I continued learning more therapeutic techniques including guided imagery, yoga and meditation. I was learning about inner strength and spirituality, but not in the academic perspective. One teacher introduced me to principles of metaphysics, spirituality, and the power of positive thought. For me, these principles became the bridge to healing emotions, feelings, thoughts, and sometimes the body.

One of the principles, "thoughts held in mind, produce after their kind" became basis to the concept of healing. With this new idea, I began to find ways to help clients unravel their emotional weaknesses.

The minister who was teaching metaphysical and spiritual principles was in the end stage of cancer. He was forever saying, "We are spiritual beings, living in a spiritual world, governed by spiritual laws, having a human experience." The concept of being a spiritual being first, fascinated me. I rationalized that if we are spiritual, then death was not what I had been taught, which was, when we die we go to a place with harps, angels and a judgment book.

I was fascinated with the mysticism in the Gospel of John 14:12, "...this you can do and more because I go to the Father." I took the Master teacher, Jesus, at his word. The biblical story of his death and resurrection, not to mention ascension, may be an allegory, or it may be true. If he could manage his energy force field called life, through death, burial and reorganize his energy force field to rise from the dead, and he stated before he did this act, that if he did it, we could to, now that would be a new and different lesson to learn.

Maybe death was more like the Native American concept, which is that this body is a coat. Our spirit takes on a body and uses it to learn lessons on the earth plane. When we have learned what we came to learn, we have the power to drop the body coat and go on. In questioning a Native American friend, I was told that this was true. But she added that her people had gotten so mesmerized with the material world, this wasn't taught much anymore.

I felt I was on sacred ground. I humbly was growing in the awareness and belief that we did have some degree of input into our death. Patiently and gently, I continued to ask my Native American friends to tell me what they did to drop the body coat. I was told that the Native looked at things differently from Western culture. And therefore, it was hard to explain because there aren't words for what they did. Eventually using my best listening and questioning techniques, I gleaned a few insights. First, the Native American believes that they are one with all life. As nature has its seasons, so does the person. You just know when it is the time.

What was not discussed, but what I already knew, was that living life was the preparation. Awareness and acceptance of feelings, and then, not holding on but releasing them so they don't get stuck in the body to poison the body or wear it down was important. Learning from each experience and being open to the movement of Great Spirit was essential. Also learning to listen to and follow the guidance of intuition was necessary. Prayer and meditation daily was needed for focus and sense of oneness with Great Spirit.

I also had experienced the Native American celebration called a give away. This becomes important at the time of death. At that time, when the elders knew it was their time to leave this earth walk, they hosted a celebration and gave away everything, except one blanket. This give away was done so that there were no ties to the earth for the elder, as it is believed that things tie the Native to this plane. This also served as a signal to the family members and friends to let go, to release the loved one so that they could go on. After the celebration was over, the elder would take that blanket and walk out into the distance. No one followed. At the right place, the elder would sit down, wrap in the blanket and leave the body. Later, the empty body coat and blanket were found.

In another tradition of teachings of the great masters, the focus was on getting to know the soul and its purpose in this life. I intuitively knew I had to get to know my soul, my I AM presence, indwelling divinity, and be in touch with what its purpose and timing was. Prayer and meditation seemed to be the logical places to start. And approached in humility, I would be led.

Though he continued to speak each Sunday, I watched as his body weakened. I listened carefully, trying to learn all I could, but also noting if I could discern if he was moving through the veil and trying to communicate to us, his congregation, that experience. I wanted to know what the crossing process was like when one knew he was dying.

The minister's wife asked me to counsel with her husband to deal with any residual emotion, which might be contributing to his disease process. The gift of this experience was that I saw him six hours before he left his body. There was little energy. I asked if he was in the Light tunnel, and he indicated that he was and said nothing more, then looked away.

I pursued studies in metaphysics and mysticism. I wanted to learn every-thing I could about spirituality and healing which included death, the ulti-mate healing. I began to use the word "transition meaning to change" for the dying process, because we are changing from one plane of energy to another.

Upon completion of my studies, I moved to the West and founded a counseling and retreat center for the purpose of using metaphysical and mys-tical principles to better deal with the emotional and mental problems of human beings. Also, I had observed that physical healing was possible when the thoughts and feelings were healed.

In my second year of this work, a friend and benefactor came to visit and retreat over the St Patrick's Day holiday. When I picked him up at the air-port, he had two large suitcases, golf clubs, and talked about getting a few strokes in, weather permitting. On the ride to the mountain retreat, besides asking all kinds of questions about my retreat and counseling business, he related that he had been in the hospital. He said he had trouble with his heart, from time to time, because it wasn't beating in rhythm. Besides the medications which took up half of one of the suitcases, his physicians had stopped and restarted his heart for the purpose of achieving a rhythmic beat. He told me that he almost wasn't released in time for this trip. Then he added that if he seemed to pass out, I shouldn't be alarmed or move him, it was only his heart rhythm and he would be okay.

When we got to the house, and he made a point of showing me all of his pills. He showed me his burned chest where the defibrillator paddles had been applied. I asked why he had agreed to the procedure. He said his kids didn't want him to die. We didn't discuss it further.

It was a blessed time touring the mountains, eating out, discussing vari-ous spiritual experiences, and having a delicious Irish dinner at an Irish pub on St. Patrick's. The next day, rather full from the previous night's dinner, we ate a light lunch and went to a movie, **Home Alone**. About the two-thirds into the movie, where the hot iron was dropped on the crook's head, my friend gave a brief sigh and seemed to pass out. Thinking this was what he had warned me about, and as the theater seats lack headrests, I placed my hand behind his head, and waited. He didn't regain consciousness, but died of a massive coronary.

Psychologically, my friend's relationship with his children, or his health, were none of my professional business. As his friend I listened to what he wanted to share. Spiritually, maybe he had given me clues as to his "real" purpose for coming, and maybe I neglected to give those words enough attention. However, I believe that at some spiritual level of his being, my friend had made his choice. He had set the stage so he could leave his body without medical intervention, away from his doctors, his children and on a spiritual retreat. Previously, we had talked about the Light tunnel. When it became apparent to me that the paramedics wouldn't be able to revive him, through my grief and shock, I began the spiritual prayer support of encouraging him to follow the Light in the tunnel.

My friend was a person who practiced prayer and meditation daily. He also had studied mind control, which is a focusing process with relaxation. Later, with some perspective, in a conversation with his daughter, it was agreed that spiritually he had made these choices in his dying process.

My work with healing, including dying, then took an interesting turn. I had the opportunity to serve as psychologist and chaplain in a hospital and hospice. I noted that medical doctors worked mainly in terms of "getting patients better to go home". Patients went through a variety of scientifically researched procedures and took many medications for that purpose. Less frequently would the physician discuss the process of dying with the patient's family, even more rarely with the patient. If the patient failed to heal and thrive, the chaplain was called.

Vividly, I remember the day I was walking through the hospital corridor on my way to do a psychological evaluation, when I heard a loud female voice instructing the doctor to leave her room. Upon inquiring, I learned that the doctor wanted to do another procedure, which the patient didn't want. When I entered her room, she asked me to get her friend, which I did. The friend later told me that when she went into the room, the patient reminded her of their promise. Apparently these two women had been prayer partners for years and had made a promise. In their promise, they agreed to be there for the one who was dying, hold the Light, and guide and direct the dying one into the Light. It sounded that simple. This friend had fulfilled her part of the promise. The other died peacefully.

The right to die was her choice, and it apparently happened with relaxation, focus and words of prayer. This incident does give support to the idea that the patient/dying person has potentially more choice and power in this process than certain authorities would indicate.

As hospice chaplain, I was called to the home of a dying patient. The patient had been lingering for days and, I was told the family was in distress. On the drive to their home, I was preparing myself mentally for what I might find. I arrived ready to say some words of comfort to the family members. However, they greeted me and rushed me to the patient's bedside. The patient would not open her eyes, wasn't able to speak, and didn't seem to be responsive. She was breathing, faintly. I leaned to her ear and spoke words of truth, reminding her that she was a child of God. I assured her of God's love and forgiveness. Then I directed her to look for the Light and allow her soul/spirit to go toward it as I recited the 23rd Psalm. I closed with a blessing. I left the patient's bedside and checked with the family members. They assured me that they had all given the patient permission to die. Together we said a prayer, and I left. The patient died early the next day.

This was another example of soul choice of a less dramatic nature.

By this point in my professional career (mid'90), I had read most of the literature on death and dying, and near death experiences. There was a book, **Final Gifts**, written by hospice workers about their experience working with the dying, which we encouraged our hospice patients and their families to read. But one important piece seemed to be missing. This was the discussion from persons who were in the dying process about the spirituality of their process. It seemed reasonable that those who were making the journey have much to tell us about it, if we can humbly ask and patiently listen. In particular what were their spiritual experiences and soul choices as they faced and worked with the dying/transition experience. With the assistance of the medical director, we put together a very short questionnaire.

It was to be a preliminary study. As you may know, hospice is a palliative care program for patients with a terminal diagnosis and 6 months to live. The subjects of the study had to be in the program, which meant they probably would live 6 months. We would see them one time a month for three months. Our patients usually had little strength, and some were nonverbal. Questions were kept very short with "yes" or "no" answers. The research team was composed of a nurse, a physician, a psychologist, a social worker and a chaplain who made one visit a month for three consecutive months, if possible. Patients were told that we were looking for information from them on their spiritual experience of the process of dying to share with future patients.

Interestingly enough, every patient was most enthusiastic to share with others what their experience was.

We asked them about the current: meaning and purpose in their life; feelings of peace with themselves and others; internal or spiritual support in dealing with their illness; sense of harmony with the Universe; experience of the presence and power of God or Higher Power; spiritual experiences with people, reading and thinking, nature, and religious activities. The medical director wanted to know if and how the spiritual experiences may be affecting the pain experience.

The results were enlightening. First, no one reported experiences like seeing an angel. In general, family members did tell us the patient seemed to talk more after we left. Some of the family members asked to share their perspective of the questions, so notes were taken on their responses. Patients looked forward to seeing us. I remember one male patient I visited was willing to answer the questions even though he was bare bottomed, on a morphine drip with just a few days to live. Overall, our subjects/patients wanted to share with those who would follow, what their experience was like.

The following summary of responses may not do these generous souls justice, but they wanted others to know what the spiritual part of their dying was like. First, all of the patients indicated their current life had meaning and purpose. One said he couldn't stay in bed all day. Another told us that knowing life had purpose kept him on track. A female told us that she had expanded from no purpose, to a life with even more purpose now.

All patients indicated that with a known time for living, they had found peace with themselves and with others. But they also had all of their feelings from anger to pleasure, impatience and confusion.

All of our subjects/patients agreed that they had a sense of internal support or spiritual strength dealing with their illness. One added that she dealt better with her illness than with her problems.

Harmony and peace with the world and Universe were not the experience for all of our patients. One told us he didn't experience it in today's world. Yet another found it when she was in her yard. A patient, who died after our second visit, told us at the time of the visit that "I've seen the end and I'd like to get it over with."

All of our subjects/patients had experienced the power of God or a Higher Power in their lives. One was clear with us that the power came from within and was not material. Another told us, possibly prophetically, that "it all goes back to the presence of God. My control of the quality of life has been taken."

Spiritual awakening had happened at different times—from gradually over the lifetime which affect the quality of life, to two days after the terminal diagnosis. One lovely person told us that she had always had the spiritual, but in the previous week "she had received calls and visits from those she had touched in her life and this gave her pause for reflections."

Most of our subjects/patients reported that their experience of God or a Higher Power had left them with a sense of humility. One summarized it by saying that because of the changes (due to the disease process) she was thinking more of her experience with God, and it was becoming a more acceptable part of the way she lived.

Two thirds of our subjects/patients found spiritual experience in relationships with others. Aptly summarized, one patient stated that the quality of life depends on relationships with other people. The majority also found spiritual experiences in what they read and thought. Fifty percent found spirituality in nature. One told us the nature was her therapy. Religious activities didn't necessarily provide spiritual experience. They told us the experience comes from within. "It all bounces back if you aren't thinking right," one said.

One patient told us, possibly prophetically, that he felt torn between now and the end he saw.

Our patients were unanimous in taking responsibility for their problems. One added that he didn't have problems, just opportunities.

Of the twenty three subjects, three shared over the three visits that their sense of spirituality and spiritual well being affected their quality of life, pain control and control of physical symptoms.

The caveat of visits came the day I phoned one of my patients to set the time for her interview. She was a retired career woman and mother. That day she could not meet at our time as she was having cataract surgery, because, she said, she would be going on a long trip. It took two months to catch up with her. I later learned that the questionnaire had brought much thought and peace to this patient and her family.

The research project stopped at this point due to lack of funding. Brief though it was, it seemed to stimulate the participants, possibly giving another purpose in their death experience, that is, to be of help to others. But other questions were not answered.

For these subjects/patients the right to die was the choice to die in dignity communicating with us what it meant to them spiritually within the boundaries of our crude questionnaire.

It is doubtful that anyone would dispute **Ecclesiastes 3**, "For everything there is a season, and a time for every matter under the heaven: a time to be born and a time to die;..." We humans have done wonders with the raw materials of the earth, which make our lives more comfortable than the lives of those who have gone before us. With the wonders of science and technology there seems little physical discomfort for the majority of us. Medically, science and technology have improved our lives and rid us of diseases and germs that killed multitudes before us. And we now live longer than our forefathers, except for some of the Biblical characters. Emotionally, we are supposed to have greater happiness as a result.

But it is interesting that the area we seem to fear the most is dying and prepare for it less, except for the inheritance. Yet we know it is inevitable. We treat it as a terrible thing and try to keep it away from life, when dying is a right, just as living is a right. As a society, with such wonderful scientific and technological advances, we probably understand little of the dying process. For example, I know it seems easier to take the latest headache medicine for a tension headache as advertised on TV, than practice deep muscle relaxation. But without sharpening our mental and spiritual skills, we will want to surrender our power over the life energy forces when we face our challenges of disease and death.

Yet, there are those who have walked through life in their body, and when done with the lessons of that body, dropped it and went on as the Native American. Their lives engaged the development of the mental and spiritual process and power to living. They have explored it for us, though they may not have left it in writing.

What would happen if we took the mystery, and maybe shame, from death. What if we were willing to practice ways of spiritual exercise throughout our lives which would prepare us for dropping the body coat. But to do that we would have to see ourselves as spiritual beings and our bodies as the vehicle we use to learn our lesson.

Maybe we identify too much with our bodies. Maybe we fall in love with our bodies and forget our heritage as spiritual beings. Maybe we get mesmerized with the body experience, and forget the spiritual one.

In summary, what am I humbly trying to relate regarding the right to die? By way of these experiences, I have come to the conclusion, and belief, that we do input into determining how we die, including possibly knowing when. But I also believe that as human beings, we have engaged, maybe to the fullest extent, mesmerization by this materialistic world. I am not saying that it is wrong to engage the physical world. We came to this life to engage the physical world to learn lessons for our soul's growth. What I am saying is that in this physical body, we have enjoyed all of the potential the Universe has to offer, and we have learned to operate the world using the best our intelligence has to offer. Possibly, we have missed part of the lesson of this life experience, which is to learn to use our mental and spiritual powers for the good and our own soul growth. Inadvertently, I believe, we have become attached to the material world, not the spiritual world, which is our home. And in consequence, we have forgotten how to love, but to detach from this world. Therefore, when the soul is done with this body coat, the detachment and subsequent death may seem long and pain-filled.

But I have found that those who have gone before have left clues to help us remember our power to die. And possibly, it is responsibility of each of us to find our own way out of this world and be in harmony with the Universe. In my journey to this point in my life, I learned and believe that if one desires to die (I like the phrase "make their transition" better) with the dignity they choose, this desire tends to include prayer and meditation. These two processes lead to focus and detachment of the mind from the outer material world, including pain. Doing good and kind deeds for others helps increase detachment from yourself, which lightens your soul/spirit. We probably cannot prepare for the kind of death we would like overnight. More likely it will involve conscious daily effort. As a Buddhist monk once told me, "Practice, practice, practice."

REFERENCES

M. Callanan, P. Kelly. *Final Gifts*. Bantam Books, 1997. Paperback.

E. Kubler-Ross, M.D., *On Death and Dying*. Collier Books, 1997. Paperback.

E. Kubler-Ross, M.D., *Death: The Final Stage of Life*. Simon & Schuster, 1997. Paperback.

E. Kubler-Ross, M.D., *Living with Death and Dying*. MacMillan Publishing Co., 1997. Paperback.

E. Kubler-Ross, M.D., *The Holy Bible*, NRSV, 1989.

6

---◆---

Assisted Death
Values and Emotion — Compassion or Killing

Edward Rivet
Legislative Director
Right to Life of Michigan

T HE POLARIZED DEBATE ABOUT assisted suicide and euthanasia (hereafter: "assisted death") has already grown well-worn. Traditional "anti-suicide" or "pro-life" advocates offer a myriad of reasons for why assisted death should not be legalized. Proponents of assisted death put forward standard arguments about personal autonomy and relieving unbearable suffering. The magnitude of the issue, a literal matter of life and death, and the seemingly compelling arguments offered by both sides has left many "average citizens" either confused or ambivalent about whether assisted death should be legally and socially sanctioned.

Implicated in the debate are core values which are rarely discussed. For example, what does upholding human dignity really require? Coloring the debate are intense emotions which are visible and undeniable. Yet rarely is there an effort to consider whether these emotions adversely affect our collective ability to reach a final resolution of this question socially and legally.

In other words, no one denies the emotions involved with the debate. We simply haven't acknowledged the impact they have on our thinking and our potential collective conclusions.

Along with the void created by ignoring these fundamental features of human dialogue and conflict resolution, is the basic level of ignorance that exists regarding assisted death. Social, legal and political positions are being staked out by many uninformed or under-informed individuals and social institutions (courts, professional associations, etc.).

So in addition to offering the traditional "pro-life" arguments against legally sanctioning assisted death, I will also attempt to discuss the importance of the core values, emotions, and lack of information which has given rise to this social debate. For it seems obvious to me, from my admittedly biased perspective, that if these factors were forthrightly addressed, the obvious conclusion would be to never legalize assisted death.

The first and most obvious pro-life argument is simply that human life is unique and sacred, and therefore, one should never take steps to purposely take a human life. I will talk bluntly hereafter about "killing" in the context of assisted death, because that is exactly what this subject is about. Supporters of assisted death have invented all sorts of phrases and euphemisms to detract from what this subject is about ("Death with dignity," "hastening death," etc.). But the truth is, it's about killing. Killing is when you take something that is alive and you make it dead. It can be a plant or an animal or a person. But when something is alive and you take an action to make it dead, you have killed it. Assisted suicide and euthanasia is killing, plan and simple.

Using this term may seem harsh or even inflammatory because of the connotations associated with such a word. Assisted death proponents usually object very strongly if you use the word "killing" in any kind of public dialogue. They get very defensive and have accused me of trying to incite rancor into the public debate.

Here is the first point on the core values and emotion factor. Words have two types of meanings: "denotation" is the strict or technical definition of a word; "connotation" is the contextual meaning of the word. The connotation of a word has the values and emotions attached. Connotations have purpose. They, in fact, give color and meaning to the words we use. By definition, connotations reflect values and emotions. Proponents of assisted death do not like the connotations associated with the properly denoted use of the word "killing." The purpose of euphemism is to hide the truthful connotations we don't like.

Assisted suicide and euthanasia really are killing. We know that. Proponents want to hide from that truth. Something in our core values tells us that killing another human being is wrong. Even if we add the motive of sympathy for a terminal patient's suffering, there is a core value that instructs us to be uncomfortable with introducing a lethal agent for the purpose of killing another human being. From a purely self-interested standpoint, we have viewed killing another as wrong to create a social expectation that we ourselves won't be killed by others. (i.e. the "Golden Rule").

This underlying value against killing another is the essential principle in opposition to assisted death. If we legalize assisted death, we will remove the fundamental "social security" that our lives will be viewed as immeasurably valued regardless of how close we are to death, or how productive society may view us or we view ourselves.

We opponents of assisted death realize that laws banning such behavior will not eliminate it. The strongly motivated and situationally-advantaged persons who want to end their lives will make the arrangements for doing so. This bespeaks one of the emotion-driven arguments that assisted death proponents make in favor of legalizing it. "Since people are going to do it anyway, we might as well make it legal and make sure it's done properly," they say. This is emotional rather than logical reasoning because laws against prostitution or shooting heroin don't stop those crimes from occurring either. But we don't generally argue that those things ought to be legalized simply because people "will do it any way." How much dignity is there in selling your body for someone else's sexual pleasure?

Beyond the self-preservation that is insured when we reject assisted death, laws prohibiting assisted death preserve the core value of protecting the more vulnerable members of our society. That is a fundamental purpose of civil law — to protect the weak from the strong — lest we live by Darwinian law. Increasing risks to the vulnerable is at the heart of opposition to assisted death. As previously noted, those of firm resolve will take their own lives, whether legally allowed or not. The effect of legalizing assisted death, however, will be to open vulnerable members of society to a threat to their very lives.

In what is generally referred to as the "slippery slope" argument, pro-lifers firmly believe that legalizing assisted death will result in disabled, elderly, mentally impaired, racial minority and poor citizens choosing assisted death more often out of circumstantial compulsion rather than free choice. This was exactly the unanimous conclusion of the New York State Task Force on Life and the Law. Though there were proponents of limited assisted death on the Task Force, it unanimously concluded that the economic, social, and health care disparities that persist in our society mean that such vulnerable groups will end up being victims, not beneficiaries, of legalized assisted death.

Support for legalized assisted death is strongest among the wealthier, more highly-educated members of our society. Theirs is a world of general economic well-being and the social connections which would facilitate a choice for assisted death on their own terms. What such supporters either don't know, or choose to ignore, is the outright lack of health care options that other people face. A number of studies have shown how women, minorities, and the poor are regularly offered less-aggressive or lower quality medical treatment, than say, a middle-class white male. University of Michigan professor of philosophy J. David Vellman has written convincingly on how giving people the legal option of assisted suicide, without equally giving them the options of complete health care and economic options, actually makes them worse off. Assisted death doesn't become a free choice, merely a least-worst option given the other undesirable choices. I think all people of good will would reject legalizing assisted death if they had this information to include in their considerations.

Disability rights groups have become increasingly vocal in opposition to assisted death as the reality of financially-based health care decision making becomes less transparent. The rationed health care plan offered in the State of Oregon is a clear example. That plan will pay to kill you, but not always pay to cure you. What sort of "choice" is that? This applies particularly to persons with disabilities who are frequently not offered aggressive treatment because their perceived "quality of life" does not "justify" the expense or effort to insure their continued existence. Bias against persons with disabilities, especially in the health care world, is every bit as pervasive as it is against racial and other minorities.

With these vulnerable individuals in mind, another core value reflected in opposing assisted death is the rejection of unjust discrimination. Like it or not, legalizing assisted death will inevitably discriminate against those least able to defend their right to adequate health care and support. We have laws against discrimination in health care. But guess what? The health care system still regularly discriminates against these people. Arguments that "safeguards" built into assisted death laws will protect against potential discrimination ring hollow in the face of this present discrimination. The decision by these individuals would still be "voluntary" under the "safeguards" of an assisted death law, but it would not be a truly free decision.

The traditional "slippery slope" argument against assisted death is not only about discrimination, nor is it only hypothetical paranoia. Involuntary euthanasia of the incompetent persons will be an inevitable result of the "narrowly defined right-to-die" prescribed in Oregon — like assisted suicide laws. It is already an open question in Oregon, where the state attorney general's office issued a letter indicating that the law may illegally restrict disabled persons' ability to avail themselves of this "right" to assisted death. In the Oregon law, a person must be able to "self-administer" the fatal medication. The attorney general letter points out that the Americans with Disabilities Act requires that accommodations must be made to allow persons with disabilities to access the same public accommodations that able-bodied persons can. Persons whose disabilities prevent them from putting the deadly pills in their mouth or feeding tube are denied access to this "right." Rest assured that a lawsuit will come to challenge the "restrictiveness" of assisted suicide-only laws.

The point of expanding such laws though would not be simply to allow disabled persons to be killed. It is a necessary step in getting death by direct injection legalized. Referendum votes in Washington and California in the early 1990's failed because the specter of lethal injections made the bills unpalatable for too many voters. Oregonian death advocates learned from this and "restricted" their proposal to "self-administered" assisted suicide only. The potential ADA challenge will be one means of opening the lethal injection door. The other means will be through court challenges that will extend the legal principle of "substituted judgment," which has already led to legally sanctioning passive euthanasia in this country.

Prior to the debate on assisted death, the 1980s and early 1990s were consumed with high-profile court cases involving incompetent patients and their families' efforts to have "life-support systems" removed. While some of

these "pulling the plug" cases did involve removing high-tech medical equipment, others including the pivotal Cruzan decision, dealt with withholding
food and fluids from non-dying patients so that they would die by dehydration and starvation. The means by which the courts granted families the ability to make these death-inducing decisions was to invent the "substituted
judgment" principle. It simply means that the relatives of the incompetent
patient are legally allowed to substitute their judgment in place of a decision
made by the patient directly. Remarkably the courts have declared that
patients are exercising their legal rights through a proxy. We don't even let
someone vote in elections through a proxy, but they can "exercise their right
to terminate themselves" by proxy?

The result of this concept imbedded in law today is that any decision
competent patients can make for themselves, can now be made on their
behalf if they become incapacitated. In Oregon, competent adults can choose
assisted suicide if they are terminally ill. There is nothing in the court-
defined right of "substituted judgment" that prohibits a proxy from making
that same decision on the patient's behalf. Once lethal injections are legit-
imized for disabled persons, the incompetence of a patient will be deemed
just another type of disability, and substituted judgment will authorize the
proxy to order the patient euthanized.

Only if this were hypothetical paranoia. The experience in the
Netherlands has already demonstrated the reality of the slippery slope.
Doctors can and regularly do euthanize patients who have not specifically
requested death. Some are not even conscious when the decision is made for
them. Likewise, physicians have euthanized disabled newborns with the consent of the parents. Though prosecutions and convictions followed in a few
such cases, the physicians never spent a day in jail for these infant homicides.
What is considered murder in our country today is passively accepted in a
society that has progressively accepted one more step in the killing for compassion march.

What makes the entire assisted death debate so disturbing is the lack of
necessity for killing any patient. Tremendous strides are being made in the
area of pain and symptom management in treating terminal and chronic illnesses. Hospice care is creating THE paradigm for addressing death and
dying. Seeing the end-of-life as a crucial phase of life is not part of our
national social mind set. Our country, probably more than any, hides death

in nursing homes and other care facilities. The whole "right-to-die" movement was spawned by the increasingly medicalized and impersonal deaths
people were experiencing. Dying peacefully at home has been almost entirely eliminated from our American death experience. Hospice and palliative
care are beginning to reverse that. What patients fear most is the loss of control that illness and dying potentially bring. Hospice care returns control of
care to the patient and the family. Patients decide when to eat or bathe, or
other basic day-to-day preferences. The desire to end one's life in the face of
terminal illness usually subsides in terminally ill patients once their needs for
comfort and control are assessed and met.

The first "report" about assisted suicide under Oregon law indicated that
only 1 of 15 suicides mentioned "fear" of pain or suffering as the motive for
choosing death. The other 14 patients cited fear of losing control or dignity
as the main reason for choosing death. Contrary to the highly emotional stories offered by assisted death proponents about patients in horrible pain,
moaning in the night, and begging for a "merciful release" from their suffering, the practical truth about assisted suicide in Oregon is that patients
choosing to kill themselves were not suffering horribly. They feared dependence and lack of control, but they were not suffering excruciating pain.

This reality, along with the reality of the slippery slope, and the threat to
vulnerable citizens all add up to the conclusion that assisted death is a
Pandora's box. Once you accept the premise that certain lives are expend-
able, the rationale for accepting that premise can be applied to so many other
situations. There is no practical way to legalize "a little bit" of killing. No
matter where you draw the line for determining who can and who cannot kill
themselves, there will always be someone on the other side of the line making an equally compelling case as to why they should be allowed to kill themselves too.

This point was driven home to me personally when I served on the
Michigan Commission of Death & Dying, appointed by the Legislature. In
one of several public hearings around the state, a man in his late 40's testi-
fied before the Commission on proposed bills to either ban or legalize assisted suicide. He suffered from a very aggressive, painful form of arthritis that
afflicted much of his body, particularly his spine. No doubt this man spent a
considerable portion of his time trying to manage the effects of this disease
and its accompanying pain. The intensity of his comments cut through to

your conscience like a knife. He basically said, "If you do take the step to legalize assisted suicide, don't you dare limit it to just those who are terminally ill. Those people know they are going to die. They can see an end to their suffering. I could easily live another 20 to 30 years. When I decide I have had enough of this, I don't want your laws telling me my suffering isn't as bad as someone who will be dying in a matter of days, weeks, or months."

For the proponents of assisted death, there is no answer to this man except to say he can kill himself too when he wishes. And the next person to come, and the next . . .

This man's argument exposes one of the major weaknesses in the case for assisted death. The major pillars of that case are: 1) placing the values of "freedom" and "choice" above the other values I have asserted, and 2) escaping terrible pain and suffering. The freedom to choose argument really boils down to having control to define, at the individual level, what human dignity means and what value one's life has. This all seems very convincing, doesn't it? After all, isn't it our right to define the value and meaning of our own lives?

This is where the debate over core values usually gets very emotional and the dialogue ceases. Rarely do we discuss whether freedom and choice are superior values to the sanctity of life or the protection of the vulnerable. Strident proponents of assisted death dismiss the threat to the vulnerable as not carrying much weight. They generally deny its reality. But as both Dr. Velleman and the New York Task Force point out, the disadvantaged in our society would not be free to choose. The freedom to choose among bad options is not much of a freedom.

And on another point about core values, "choice," or the ability to choose is not a value. Choice is morally neutral. All of us can make choices for both good and evil. In fact, it is values that must be applied to choices in order to discern when a choice is good or bad. Anyone of a few years of adult maturity can point to their own past choices that were less than ideal. Having the ultimate freedom to choose includes the freedom to choose to enslave oneself to bad outcomes from our choices. Not having the legal freedom to make some choices is not always a bad thing. We can choose to drive 125 mph on the freeway, though not legally. For in so choosing, we are not free from the incumbent risks of such a high speed. Freedom to drive fast binds us more closely to the risk of injury or death.

Creating the legal freedom to kill oneself or be killed, binds us to the negative social consequences that will inevitably come. In a broad public debate about an intensely value-laden subject, "choice" or the "ability to choose" must not be viewed as a superior or overarching value. The "rightness" or "wrongness" of a choice is independent of the ability to choose it.

The case for legalizing assisted death by granting a limited "freedom to choose" it, is further built on the myth that taking one's own life would be an individual decision. The choice is not just the individual's. If individuals are going to seek the aid of a physician to receive lethal medication to take their lives, then the physician is a decision-maker too. Will the physician agree with the patient's request? Is that person's suffering "sufficient" to warrant lethal aid? The actual power to decide whether a person will die lies with the physician who holds the means to kill. Under Oregon's law, at least two physicians must concur in the death decision. This is why the American Medical Association formally opposes legalizing assisted death. It is clear to doctors they would be in the position of making subjective judgements about the value of individual lives. One cannot consciously participate in an activity without making a value judgment about the "rightness" of that activity.

The cracks in the assisted death foundation are pretty severe. The individual freedom to choose offered by its proponents is almost an illusion. The legal freedom for the advantaged to choose will bind the vulnerable to bad choices. Choice itself is not a value, since choices can be made for good and evil. The choices that would be made are not individual, but social, with physicians and a potentially larger cast involved. And escaping terrible pain is a diversionary argument, as 14 out of 15 cases in Oregon have proven.

Everything to this point leads us perhaps to the most fundamental issues that need to be addressed. Namely what do we mean by preserving one's human dignity? Does appropriate compassion require us to allow or support others in a self-killing action? When a once vibrant individual is reduced to a mentally incoherent, crippled mass of physical deterioration, is there any human dignity left to preserve?

Now we're getting to the real stuff, aren't we?

The answers to these questions may be found in the other writings of this book, which I am not privy to as I write. Volumes have been written about this subject, and volumes more probably could be written. So my reflections here will be brief.

The technical meaning of "compassion" is "to suffer with." Our modern connotation is closer to meaning "to have empathy or sympathy" for someone. Or beyond that, to pity them. These are essentially emotions. We can talk about the value of "compassion" as a motive for supporting assisted death. But we must recognize the sympathetic emotion that drives our "compassion." When the television news displays the destruction brought by war or natural disaster, and we see the suffering caused by injury, hunger, homelessness, and death, our sympathetic emotional response is truly compassionate. We want to "suffer with" these people by offering our support and by sacrificing from our material wealth. We will give up some of our material well-being to improve the well-being of those who are afflicted. That is true compassion. With assisted death, however, our sympathy turns lethal. We kill in order to provide help.

Here compassion changes emotional colors from sympathy to pity. We justify killing the suffering or dying because we believe "they will be better of dead." This is not a trivial point. For those who believe in a life after death, there is a hope that the life to come is better. Death is an inevitability for all of us. For the terminally ill, death is even more predictable. If so many of us hold to this belief, can we not set aside the paramount value of life in the really tough cases to allow this "inevitability of death to a better life" to occur sooner, and with less suffering?

It is indeed a tempting siren's song.

Of course, this temptation would not exist if there were no suffering associated with our dying. No sympathy or pity would be evoked. In fact, if dying were easy and beautiful, we would envy, not pity, those departing from this life.

Improving the lot of those who are dying is one point of agreement that does exist between proponents and opponents of assisted death. We who oppose assisted death are striving to make the intentional killing part irrelevant. We believe, in the end, that we need not abandon the principle value of the sanctity of life in order to provide truly compassionate care to the suffering and dying. For us it is not a zero-sum, "either/or" proposition. We believe a "good death" and respect for human life is attainable. We can have both if we so choose and work hard to accomplish it. Admittedly we are not there in every circumstance and every community. There are people who are not dying well. But the solution is not to kill our failures.

This is what preserving human dignity demands. The effort to legalize assisted death embodies a pessimism and fatalism that denies the power of the human spirit to overcome adversity. All of the killing in our world today, be it war or shootings in our schools, stems from a failure to, first and foremost, respect the value of each human life. Preserving the dignity of the human person begins with respecting human life. No other aspect of respecting persons — their physical being and property, their civil rights, their religious beliefs — can happen without first respecting the value of their life.

So those of us opposed to assisted death will press on with the challenge of helping those who suffer without having them feel compelled to kill themselves. We will value human life and the protection of the vulnerable in our society above other competing values. It is a course worthy of following.

Section Three

7

◆

Interview with Dax Cowart, J.D.

Corpus Christi, Texas

December 6th, 1999

Interviewed by Dennis McClellan

Mr. Cowart was severely burned when an automobile exploded. The nature of his injuries were such that he requested assistance in dying on a number of occasions — requests that were not honored. Now, nearly thirty years after the event, Mr. Cowart is a successful litigation attorney, working with personal injury and civil rights cases. The following interview details the incident, his lengthy and difficult recovery, and his strong feelings toward an individual's right to choose.

McCLELLAN: Tell me about your accident and what happened.

COWART: I had just left the Air Force to fly in an active duty reserve unit that was located near my home town. While waiting to begin training in a new aircraft, I went to work for my father in his real estate business. That was in the summer of 1973. There was a tract of land for sale out in the country, so one afternoon after work, we drove out to take a look at it and parked the car. This was on an old bridge-like area that crossed a dry creek bed in an area that was surrounded by pine trees and thick underbrush. After we walked over the property and got back in the car, it wouldn't start. After a while, we decided to try to suction priming the carburetor. My father took out a handkerchief to protect his hand and pressed down over the carburetor while I sat behind the wheel and turned on the ignition. After a while, the car began acting like it wanted to start, then a second or two later, the whole countryside blew up. It turned out that there hadn't been anything wrong with the car. Unknowingly, we had parked the car in an ocean of invisible, odorless propane gas. It had come from a buried cross-country pipeline that had been leaking liquefied propane gas for about ten days or maybe two weeks.

After escaping from the pipeline, the liquefied propane turned into a gas and because propane is heavier than air, it gravitated down the hillside and just filled up the creek bed all up and down and settled in the other low-lying areas surrounding the creek. There were two huge explosions that came pretty close together and caused a huge fireball. It covered an elongated area that was almost a mile long at the longest point.

The explosion just rocked me over in the car seat, but I never lost consciousness. You know, I was kind of just dazed. Glass from the windshield and windows had imploded into the car. I didn't know what was happening, but righted myself up and there was no fire right there where the car was. There wasn't any fire in what was probably a ten-yard area away from the car. But past that we were surrounded by fire all the way around the car except for one small area that was up at about our eleven o'clock position. I ran about four steps towards the opening and saw that there were tons of briars with thick underbrush and stuff and fire was already burning up at the top of those trees and I just said to myself, "You'll get caught in it. You'll get caught in it and just burn slowly to death." After running about four steps in that direction, I just stopped and reversed, then went back down the road that we had driven in on. I wanted to get back to the road because at the time I was thinking that the gas tank had exploded and I felt like on the road there wouldn't be anything to get tangled up in and that other than the gas line, there wouldn't be anything to burn. I figured that would be the best way to get out. I ran through three walls of fire, got past the last one and then rolled. You know, just like the old football mucking drill where you just hit the ground rolling, then get back on your feet in one quick motion. I just got to my feet and kept on running to see if I could find help. I was just running down the road shouting for help.

McCLELLAN: Was there anyone close by?

COWART: Well, it turned out there was a man who was helping his sister or sister-in-law with a broken pipe or something at her home not too far away. He heard the explosions and heard my shouts for help. After running about a half a mile I heard him shout, "we're coming, we're coming" and he eventually came running down the road towards me.

He was a tall, strong man about 6' 6" or so and his nephew who was about ten was with him. Most of my clothes had been burned off except for my leather boots, the part of my blue jeans from the waistband to just below my hips and the yoke of my shirt. The man couldn't find anyplace to hold onto me that wasn't burned, so he reached out with hand and slid it under my belt buckle and sort of lifted me up and helped me get off the gravel road and lie down on the grassy area that ran along the side of it. The burns were unbearable. I never knew that kind of pain could even exist. The nephew had run back to his mother's house to have her call the ambulance and I asked the man to bring me a gun. He said, "Why do you want a gun?" I told him, "Can't you see I'm a dead man? I'm going to die anyway. I've got to let myself out of this misery." In a very kind and caring way, he said, "I can't do that."

MCCLELLAN: And your father? Was your father killed or did he die later?

COWART: Later. They said my father had apparently followed me out of the fire and after he had gotten through all of it, had rolled on the grass beside the gravel road. That's one thing they say is really unusual because most people don't remember that. They don't remember to roll to put out the fire. My mother had told me to do that since I was a little boy. Way back then, she had told me about one of our ranch hands whose clothes had caught on fire while he was filling a tractor up with gas. He immediately started running and none of the other ranch hands could catch him until he ran into a barbed wire fence and even then he tried to keep on running fighting the barbed wire to try to get through. You know, it sort of amazes me under those circumstances, coming out of the fire, that I remembered to roll. I remember thinking, "I don't see any flames coming from our clothes, but as bad as the burns are, as much as it am hurting, I must be on fire." So, I went ahead and rolled. It was really a hard thing to make myself do it, the thought of rolling over the sandy gravel road and my entire body was already hurting so bad from the burns. I ran almost one and a half miles down the sandy, gravel road, shouting for help. I could see everything out of the upper portion of my vision clearly, but the lower half of my vision was very blurry, a lot like trying to see under water without a facemask. Most of my clothes had been burned away, except for my leather boots, the yoke of my shirt and the part of my Levi's that would be left after you turn a pair of jeans into very short cutoffs.

Two ambulances came and took us to the emergency room of the hospital in Kilgore, Texas, a small town that was probably about ten miles away. I don't know how long we were there, maybe somewhere between thirty minutes and an hour, while Parkland Hospital in Dallas directed fluid therapy procedures over the telephone. Then they put us in one ambulance and drove us to Parkland Hospital in Dallas which was over one hundred miles away. I didn't find out until one or two days later that my father died in the accident about thirty miles into the trip.

McCLELLAN: Tell me about your hospitalization and what you had to go through there.

COWART: When I got to the Parkland Emergency Room, it seemed forever before they would give me any pain medication. They hadn't given me any in the ambulance or in the emergency room in Kilgore. I can remember lying there in the Parkland Emergency Room with everyone rushing around doing things, but there are only a few things that I can recall specifically. I kept asking them to give me something for pain, but they all seemed to be working as fast as they could. I suppose from a medical standpoint, they felt other things had to be done first.

I asked about my father and was told, "He's in very serious condition." One of the two things that I remember most clearly was someone using scissors to cut away what was left of my burned clothing. While that was going on, someone else reached down to pull off my left boot and I told him, "No, don't pull it off, cut it off". He paused and looked at me for a minute, then again started to pull off my left boot. I shouted at him then and told him the same thing, "No, don't pull it off, cut if off". He had a puzzled look on his face, but then began cutting off the boot. While I was still in high school, a boy who graduated ahead of me was trapped in his car after a bad wreck and burned to death when the car caught on fire. Someone told me that when they pulled his boot off at the funeral home, his foot came off in the boot and I couldn't stand the thought of having the same thing happen to me. I kept asking them to bring me something for pain and after what seemed like an eternity, someone told me, "We've got something on the way". I think it was pretty soon after that when someone gave me a shot and said that it would knock me out and it did. That must have been at least three or four hours after the explosion, I really don't know. But however long it was, it was the first time after getting burned that anyone had given me anything for pain.

One of the first things I remember after that was lying back on a stretcher-like thing and a tub of water and people holding onto my arms and legs. They were doing what's called a de-breeding process. It felt like I was being skinned alive. It's my understanding that brushes and a sharp scalpel-type instrument are used to do the de-breeding. That was one of the ways they went about removing dead or infected flesh. It was so painful that even being in that condition, I was strong enough to be able to overcome them where I was in an upright, seated position, but then they would push me back down into the water so that I was lying flat on the stretcher again.

McCLELLAN: What pain medication did they use on you? Do you know?

COWART: They used a number of different drugs. At times, I know they used morphine. But they had this big fear of addiction and they would start lengthening the time between shots and also giving me less. Then they would take me off the morphine and put me on Demerol. They did the same thing and took me off Demerol and put me on something that was weaker and less effective. They got me down with Talbutal, which I am told is a synthetic narcotic and it seemed to do no good at all or at least, had very little effect.

My lawyer, who was representing me in the personal injury case, would come to see me and ask me why they were leaving me in that much pain. I told him that the doctors said they were afraid that I would get hooked. He said, "It's crazy that in this modern age of medicine, (this was in 1973) "that they're letting a man suffer like you are." He would talk to the doctors and they would put me back on morphine. And then they would do the same thing all over again. They would start giving me less and less pain medication. Rex came back a number of times and after talking to the doctors, they would go back up on my pain medication, but before long, they would do the same thing all over and start decreasing it again.

McCLELLAN: And the excuse was always fear of addiction?

COWART: Addiction and their fear that giving too large of a dose would be fatal. Back then they were afraid that you could only give a certain amount without compromising safety because of things like respiratory arrest and all. During 1973, doctors and medical schools alike were relying on flawed studies that were conducted shortly after World War II. Current studies have shown that you can safely give a patient an almost infinite amount of pure opiates if you stop at the point you take care of the pain and before it begins to cause euphoria. Current studies also show that only in extremely rare instances will patients continue using opiates once they are free from pain and out of the hospital. The exceptions are primarily if there is a history of drug abuse or prior addiction.

McCLELLAN: What was the extent of your injuries?

COWART: It depends on whose figures you believe. Some of the doctors say that I was burned over 66% of my body. As I understand it, most of them were third degree burns. I recall another report saying 74% with more than 90% if collateral damage is taken into account. I also had what are sometimes called fourth degree burns. That's where the bone itself is charred. That was in my fingers.

McCLELLAN: What was the impact on your vision?

COWART: When I was running down the road, I could see clearly and perfectly out of the top half of my field of vision, but, the whole lower half was very blurry, like being underwater in a swimming pool and trying to see without goggles. They told me at the hospital early on that there would be problems fighting infection caused by the burns to my eyes. The doctor who was treating my burns did what a good doctor should do in terms of informed consent. He came to my bedside and told me what the problems were going to be. He told me there were two schools of thought.

One was that we could leave my eyelids open and if an infection set in, it could be treated quickly and aggressively. But leaving my eyelids open would make it much more likely that my eyes would become infected because of contamination from other infections that were all over my body.

He said the other school of thought was to sew my eyelids shut which would help prevent infection from other sources, but if my eyes got infected because of the burns to the eyes themselves, it would take longer to discover the infections and therefore, longer to begin treatment.

He did a very good job of informed consent. He gave me the information and I needed to make an informed choice and then allowed me to make the choice which is exactly what a doctor should do. I told him I'd like to go with the odds. If I was going to be forced to be treated and forced to live, I sure didn't want to go through life without my eyesight if I could help it. So, I asked him what he thought would give me the best odds. And I think I also asked him what he would do if he were in my position. Ultimately he told me that he thought it would be best to sew my eyelids shut, so that's what I told him to do. My eyes became infected anyway and I eventually lost all sight in both eyes.

McCLELLAN: When you were facing the pain, especially the pain I recall from the 20/20 interview, you reinforced the fact that you just wanted out of this. You didn't want this to continue. When did those thoughts begin and how did you express them to people? How did they react?

COWART: Those thoughts began before I even got to the hospital. The man who heard me shouting for help came. After I laid on the grass, I asked him for a gun. And he said why and I said, "Can't you see I'm a dead man, I'm going to die anyway. I've got to put myself out of this misery". In a very kind and compassionate voice, he said, "I can't do that".

I never even wanted to go to the hospital. All I wanted to do was end it. I was telling the doctors that from the beginning.

McCLELLAN: What did the doctors say to you? What was their rationale or reasons for not complying with your wishes?

COWART: Things like, "that's just the pain talking". They didn't think that I had the ability to see beyond the present pain to a day when I would no longer be in pain. They were wrong about that, it wasn't a problem. I felt like, "Sure, there's going to be a time when the burns are healed, but the pain I'm going through right now is much too bad to wait for that pain-free day to actually come." There's also a catch-22 situation where the doctors would say, anyone burned as badly as I was is incompetent to make their own decisions because of the pain. On the other hand, if the patient is given drugs to ease the pain, then they are incompetent because of the drugs. But, I strongly believe that the bottom line is that burn doctors are some of the most aggressive physicians there are when it comes to treating patients. I'm not using aggressive with a negative connotation. I'm just using it to say their mind set tends to be to save the patient no matter what it takes. And that usually includes saving the patient whether the patient wants to be saved or not.

There was a very good article that came out in the Journal of the American Medical Association in about 1977. It is co-authored by the Director of the University of Southern California, Los Angeles County Burn Ward and a nurse. The article was about patients who were so badly burned that there is no medical precedent of anyone in their condition having lived. They were given the choice of either being aggressively treated for the burns or foregoing treatment for the burns and simply being kept as comfortable as possible. He took the time to inform the patients of their condition, what choices were available and then allowed each patient to decide whether to accept or forego treatment for their burns. In the article, he said that usually, and I believe it's the first twenty-four hours, but I don't remember the exact time period, most burn patients are lucid and capable of making their own medical decisions.

The article created a storm of controversy both inside medical circles and out. Most doctors seemed to take the position that it didn't matter whether or not treatment was futile, they were duty-bound to treat the patient anyway. At that time, most of the general public, including most people I came in contact with, tended to think that anyone who did not choose or try to live as long as possible was crazy It didn't matter how much pain that person was in or how incapacitated they were — all that could be done was done. You know, I've seen a lot of changes. I've been speaking in 1982 and have watched public opinion shift from the "he must be crazy" mentality to "man, if I'm ever in that situation, I sure don't want to be kept alive". I think people are seeing and becoming more aware that along with the many wonderful benefits we receive from modern medical technology, there comes some really bad fallout as well. I think it took most of the public quite a while to see and to become aware of many of the quality of life issues.

McCLELLAN: Would your feelings regarding people who are burned be similar or the same for other situations due to cancer, AIDS or any other debilitating situation? Would you be supportive of the patient being involved in making a decision to end their life?

COWART: With informed consent, yes. Once the patient has been given the information necessary to make a truly informed choice, then the patient's choice should be respected. When it comes to a mentally competent adult, no one has a right to impose their will upon another human being. The right to control our own body is a right that we are born with. It's not something that we have to ask anyone else for, not the treating physician, not the government and not our next of kin. There can never be a legitimate law that takes away an individual's right to control their own body. Once we lose the right to control our own bodies, our rights guaranteed by the Constitution and the Bill of Rights tend to become pretty meaningless for the most part. I'm speaking mainly in terms of a mentally competent adult and in some cases, a mature mind. There is no legitimate authority for saying, "I don't care what you think or how you feel about it, I know better".

Traditionally, an overwhelming majority of medical doctors that tend to be extremely paternalistic. Most of the medical profession still tends to be paternalistic, but from the time in 1973 that I was burned until the present, we've made very good progress towards allowing patients to participate in and make their own choices. I'm not suggesting that as soon as a patient says, "I don't want to be treated" or as soon as a terminally ill patient says, "I want to kill myself" the doctors should just walk away or say, "Here's the gun". But, once there's some time for counseling to make sure that the patient is aware of other options that may be available in terms of treatment, pain management or other types of assistance that may not have been offered, and the patient demonstrates that they are competent and understands what is being said, then we should respect the patient's decision.

McCLELLAN: You know, in your own case, your initial wishes weren't respected. You weren't listened to. Now that you've got twenty-seven years under your belt, how do you feel about the fact that you weren't listened to? You weren't heard but here you are?

COWART: Today, I feel that it was just as wrong as I did back then. I felt that way before I ever went to the hospital. I had no idea that in the United States of America a mentally competent adult could be forcibly treated or forced to stay in a hospital. It blew my mind. I could not conceive of that kind of thing happening in this country. We talk about freedom and liberty, that's what our country was founded upon. My views haven't changed. I've always felt that the individual should have the right to decide.

McCLELLAN: Do you resent the fact that you were kept alive? Are you glad to be sitting here talking to me today or do you have mixed feelings?

COWART: I wouldn't call them mixed feelings. At different points in time, we sometimes make different choices based on the circumstances at that moment. And right now, I'm sitting here talking to you and enjoying it very much. Blindness and other disabilities can often make things that are ordinarily simple and easy for most people very difficult for me in life. I had been interested in law going back to when I was still a young kid, so after I got out of the hospital and was trying to decide what to do with the rest of my life, I remember thinking, "Well, if it's possible for someone who's blind to be a United States Supreme Court Justice, then I ought to be able to go to law school and practice law". That was one of the things that helped me.

I feel that I have a very good quality of life and I enjoy life. I guess, let me put it this way, what most people do not stop to consider that there is a very high price that I had to pay in terms of pain in order to be alive today. Some people believe the end justifies the means. All is well that ends well. But, that mentality totally ignores the unbearable pain I went through over many, many months and the better part of my life was pure hell for about seven years after I was burned in the explosion. It was like a roller coaster ride, with very few highs, but many, many very deep valleys. There is a lot of depression and feelings of total helplessness to do much of anything meaningful about it.

McCLELLAN: I'm glad you're here.

COWART: I am too. And that's very different from saying that my doctors were right in forcibly treating me. The argument that if they hadn't treated me, I wouldn't be here now to enjoy life, so therefore, the doctors were right and I was wrong ignores the pain that I had to go through to get here.

McCLELLAN: If what occurred then, occurred today, do you think as a patient you would be listened to?

COWART: Yes. Yes, better.

McCLELLAN: Would you be respected? Would you get your wishes in Texas?

COWART: Maybe.

McCLELLAN: Does Texas permit you to work with your doctors and make such informed decisions?

COWART: Yes. It's very clear now that a mentally competent adult has the right to refuse unwanted medical treatment. In the Nancy Cruzan case (1990) Chief Justice Rehnquist wrote that a mentally competent patient has a constitutionally protected liberty interest in refusing unwanted medical treatment and he extended that decision to life dispensing decisions. But, what's happening is that we have advanced directives now, healthcare proxies, natural death acts and the durable power of attorney. There are a lot of variations in what is allowed under these different types of advanced directives. But, they are basically things that people say, "Look, if I ever become incompetent or certain things happen, things like that, well, I don't want to be kept alive. I don't want to be hooked up to tubes and ventilators, things like that — artificial feed". Even so, what I'm hearing from researchers is that even when these advanced directives are in the patient's charts, a lot of times they are ignored, a lot of times the patient's wishes are still being ignored. Medical care is still very paternalistic in many ways, but we're making progress.

McCLELLAN: What do you think about people who are in persistent vegetative states who can't make informed decisions for themselves? Can the decision, or should this decision, rest with let's say, family or loved ones? Can we make that decision with good conscience?

COWART: For someone in a persisted vegetative state, yes, I think so. You know, there are a lot of ethical considerations to think about when talking about someone who, by definition, can never again be reasonably expected to even be aware that they are alive. Why do you use valuable medical resources to keep that person alive, when there are so many other people who cannot even get minimal medical care?

McCLELLAN: What about someone in a persistent vegetative state who is being kept alive by artificial means, ventilators, feeding tubes, things like that?

COWART: Personally, I don't think that person should be kept alive. If they have an advanced directive saying that they want to be kept alive under those circumstances and have the financial resources to do so, I guess that's okay so long as they're not taking up a bed that is needed by someone who's conscious and can be helped.

McCLELLAN: What are your feelings about Jack Kevorkian? What he's done and what he proposes?

COWART: Yeah. I think the individual has a right to assisted suicide if the other person is willing to assist. You know, autonomy is a two-way-street. I don't believe that a patient is the only one who should have autonomy. If I as a patient am asking my treating physician to do something that they in good conscience, cannot do, well, I don't have the right to dictate to a doctor that he or she must do it anymore than he has a right to dictate what kind of medical treatment I must receive. Autonomy is a two-way-street, but I do have the right to say, "Look, I want to go to another doctor and be allowed to do so" which is exactly what I asked to do but wasn't allowed. If I can't find another doctor, I think my treating physician has the responsibility to help put me in touch with a doctor who can.

McCLELLAN: How do you see Dr. Kevorkian as an individual — as a character? How do you view his persona? Is he a victim himself? Is he being fairly treated?

COWART: I don't know. I was on a Detroit television talk show with Dr. Kevorkian. I met him at the studio and we talked for a short time after the show. He came across to me as a very warm, caring individual. I'm not sure what to make of some of the allegations that have been made against him. It appears to me though that most of his patients had pretty well sought out and exhausted other avenues of help, either before they went to Dr. Kevorkian or before he assisted them and died. I think that he was probably a last resort for most of them. So, I think it was a good thing that he stepped up to the plate and took on an issue that might never have been taken on for another decade or possibly a number of decades. I think we need to be very cautious, but it is far better that someone like Dr. Kevorkian's first patient, Janet Atkins had someone she could go to. If Dr. Kevorkian had not helped her, she was prepared to take her own life. I don't recall for sure how she had planned to do it, but she was not going to just die from Alzheimer's. She was going to take her own life regardless. So, I think it's far better that we have a system in place so that if someone wants to end their own life they can go to someone who is trained, it doesn't necessarily have to be a medical doctor, just someone who is well trained and able to counsel with the patient to make sure that all known means of help have been exhausted. If they have not, then possibly better medical care, something not yet tried, help with depression or better pain management might very well change the patient's mind. If an individual cannot find help that will make life worth living, then it's far better that their life ends in a way that does not run the risk of leaving them brain damaged or maimed, or a quadriplegic or something like that if they are unsuccessful, which a lot of people are.

McCLELLAN: What are your thoughts on people who are not terminally ill, but suffer from extreme chronic pain such as that associated with MS, which won't kill you in and of itself, but your quality of life is greatly diminished?

COWART: From a quality of life standpoint, if the issue is physical pain, there's so much that can be done to address the pain, but for many, many reasons most physicians are not adequately doing it. One reason is a fear of prescribing opiate drugs. Doctors run the risk of being called on the carpet before state medical boards and being harassed by the Drug Enforcement Agency. A lot of doctors are very much afraid because they know Big Brother is looking over their shoulder every time they write a prescription for many types of pain relieving drugs. But, you know, I think that situation might be starting to change a little for the better. If chronic physical pain is the issue, then I believe we should do everything we can to alleviate it. Even if the person has to stay on opiate drugs or whatever type of drug they need that will allow them to have a better quality of life that is as free from pain as possible. If it is a terrible quality of life because of emotional reasons, mental reasons, and things like that kind of suffering, if we can't alleviate it and show the patient a way. I'm talking about a willing patient who wants to try to find a way, well, then, yes. If they want assistance to end their life, then they should have it. Again, I believe that it is better that they have someone to go to who may guide them, to a degree that makes a difference, and for the individual to end their own life without having lost the opportunity for help.

McCLELLAN: Is there an issue that you would like to bring up or discuss on this whole issue of a person's right to choose? What's the role of government in this? It's something we haven't touched on. Should the government even be involved? Is this an individual decision? Should there be some regulation on a national scale or is this an issue of state's rights?

COWART: An individual. It's an issue of individual rights and any government involvement should be to protect the rights of the individual. The government should do whatever it can to see that healthcare providers provide good quality healthcare to their patients and make sure that healthcare providers do not force unwanted medical treatment upon patients — to inform patients of their choices. Often there is less invasive treatment that the patient is never told about. Sometimes there are techniques and alternative types of pain treatment that patients are never told about. A patient's right to informed consent has been both a medical doctrine and a legal doctrine for many years. The government has a duty to make sure that this patient's right is upheld. Doctors, who refuse to inform patients of the potential risk and benefits of the treatment they are recommending, in a way that the patient can understand so as to make an informed choice, should not be allowed to practice. The same is true for doctors who withhold from their patients other forms of less invasive and possibly less expensive treatment.

When it comes to issues like assisted suicide, I think the government has a role to make sure that the patient has had good counseling, that the patient has been told of other possible treatments that may not have yet been tried, and that dialogue takes place to get down to what the patient's true concerns are. The patient might have concerns that nobody knows about and those concerns don't come out until the patient is ready to take his or her own life.

But, I think the government should make sure that someone who asks for assisted suicide, number one, should have good quality counsel and number two, following the counseling or after trying what may have been recommended to them, if the patient says "It's not working. This is all I can take. This is it", then that individual should be given assistance in dying.

McCLELLAN: What do you say to religious people who say that because of their beliefs, they cannot support an individual's right to make such a decision?

COWART: Well, they don't have to support it. They can make their own choices and they should make their own choices in matters that concern themselves. But they have no right to force their own religious beliefs on someone who does not agree with their views.

McCLELLAN: During your own hospitalization, were you given any support in the way of counseling by religious personnel or hospital personnel? Were you left to fend for yourself and how did your coping take place?

COWART: I don't remember talking to any hospital chaplains. I'm not saying that I didn't, but if I did I don't remember it. But, I was visited by an air force chaplain from my reserve unit and he also called to talk to me a number of times while I was in the hospital and also after I got out. Most of the chaplains I've met are very well trained. A competent chaplain is a wonderful person to have in the hospital and can give a patient the kind of support that no one else can. A good chaplain will go to the patient's bedside without bringing a personal agenda with him. They are not there telling the patient, "I'm going to do this for you", "I'm going to show you", "I want to talk to you about why you need to accept treatment", or "I want to show you the way ..." with one brand of religion or the other. Almost all the chaplains that I've encountered go to the patient's bedside with an attitude of "I'm here for you", "I'm willing just to sit and listen if that is what helps", "If you have questions, I'll do my best to answer them for you", "If there are spiritual things you would like to talk about, I'll be happy to do that", "If you don't want to talk about spiritual things, that's fine too". The most common traits that I have noticed among chaplains is that almost all of them that I've come across are very good listeners. I think they must get extensive training in how to listen with their hearts.

McCLELLAN: So, they're very respectful of the patient?

COWART: I'm not saying that every chaplain is, but I've been very impressed by most chaplains that I have met. They're wonderful, usually wonderful people.

McCLELLAN: The ones who start crossing over that boundary again, trying to influence the patient's views along their own spiritual beliefs?

COWART: Well, that crosses the line and they should not do that.

McCLELLAN: Not unless the patient asks?

COWART: Sure.

McCLELLAN: Are you constrained by any code of ethics or regulations as an attorney and how would you can counsel or instruct clients who one day might have to face similar decisions? Is there anything that prohibits you from helping them make that decision or how do you feel about that?

COWART: In refusing treatment and leading their own lives?

McCLELLAN: Right.

COWART: Well, in refusing treatment, I have a duty to talk to my clients in a way that they understand the information I am giving them so that after thinking about it they can make an informed choice. As to assisted suicide issues, I cannot tell a client to go ahead, get your friend who has offered to help, or your loved one who has agreed to help — I cannot ethically or legally advise a client to do that.

McCLELLAN: Because assisted suicide is not recognized as being legal in Texas?

COWART: The only state I'm aware of that has legalized assisted suicide is the State of Oregon, and even in Oregon it is illegal except for a pretty limited number of situations.

McCLELLAN: Where do you go from here? What kind of fantasy do you have for the future?

COWART: I don't know that I have a fantasy for the future. Right now, I'm concentrating on law, trying to be the best trial lawyer I can possibly be in representing my clients to the best of my ability. Whenever I try a case, I want to make sure that I do everything I can to get justice for my client. That's very important to me.

McCLELLAN: Who are your heroes? Yeah, Who's somebody that makes you smile? I mean, who's somebody that you really think is top stuff?

COWART: It depends on what you're talking about. If you're talking about being a trial lawyer, I've learned more from Jerry Spence than anyone else. I think highly of Jerry because of that and also because of what I've learned from him about being a person, about being a human being. Another important thing that I've learned from Jerry is that it's all right to be afraid. Fear has been passed down genetically for millions of years. Fear is a survival instinct and it can serve us very well if we pay attention to it. Jerry also taught me that it's okay to be real, to be who we really are and let our scars, warts and blemishes show. Most people try to cover them up to try to cover up their weaknesses so they don't show through. Most of us try to use some kind of a mask to cover up our blemishes and weaknesses so that we get through, but by putting on all the masks, it's not really us anymore. We allow people to see our strengths but usually try to cover up our weaknesses and that turns us into phonies. Nobody likes a phony, because a phony is a counterfeit, and counterfeits are worthless. All of us are equipped with thousands and thousands of phony detectors and they may be at the conscious or at the subconscious level, but one way or the other, we watch for it whether it's someone speaking from a stage, or just whoever we are talking to. Like you and I are talking right now, or in a courtroom, it could be the lawyer talking or a witness talking. These thousands of phony detectors are like tentacles that wrap themselves around the speaker constantly palpating for anything that doesn't quite ring true. The tone of someone's voice that doesn't sound just right, a gesture that seems contrived, trying to imitate someone else's way of doing things — stuff like that. Those are some of the important things that

I've learned from Jerry at the Trial Lawyer's College in Wyoming and the words and examples I used are pretty close to the way I learned them from him. I could name a lot of other heroes ranging from personal friends to family members, to people I work with, to people I don't even know. Competent and caring doctors and nurses and other healthcare providers, they're my heroes. People that are out there fighting for the rights of people who are underprivileged, minorities and the everyday hard working man and woman, they're my heroes. My heroes are all the people who are out there struggling to keep our earth green and beautiful, fighting to keep our air and water clean, those who are fighting to try to save animals and plants that are endangered and becoming extinct, those who are kind to children and other people, those who are kind to animals, the lovers who are truly in love with each other, the mother and the father who love their children and put their family first. I guess when you get right down to it, I can say that my real heroes are the people who are human beings first and whatever else they are, second. All my friends from the Trial Lawyer's College are my heroes. Lawyers and non-lawyers who are out there fighting for the common everyday person and the little guy who is having such a difficult time finding justice, whether it's inside or outside our courts. Chaplains are my heroes. So, I guess I have lots of heroes.

McCLELLAN: Do you consider yourself a hero?

COWART: No.

McCLELLAN: Is it that easy to say — that quickly?

COWART: Yes.

McCLELLAN: Do you think you're a good role model for kids who find themselves severely burned and have to face life? Do you think you could serve as a positive role model for them? Have you ever thought of it that way?

COWART: No. I'm not comfortable with the term role model and I'm even less comfortable with the idea of being a role model. When someone is held out as a role model, it seems to be human nature for us to begin projecting a lot of our own personally held values onto that person, then later on are disappointed when they don't quite measure up to what we expect or sometimes really not measure up to what we expect. If there is something or some things that inspires us in a way that helps to give us guidance in one way or the other, then I like the idea of learning what we can from that person.

To get back to the question you asked, if there's something that I've accomplished that has done that, helps children or others who have been burned or have other disabilities, when that accomplishment helps inspire them to hang in there, I'm fine with that.

One thing that bothers me about the concept of role modeling is that in — we look at individuals and we admire them for whatever we say that they've done and we tend to project all these other values of our own onto that person and then end up being disappointed later when we find out that they have different values and this person, this role model that — I mean, we've seen it happen thousands and thousands of times in our lifetime. We put a person on a pedestal and there should be all these other character traits and things that we value to that person without even knowing them. And, then when we find out that well, they don't believe as do about this or that or the other, or that they're not perfect or they slipped and fell, and they've done some things that we think are terrible or they didn't meet them. Well, then we tend to term them and so, for me it's not a comfortable position at all to be held up as any kind of a role model because of that.

McCLELLAN: Is there anyone else you feel are personally qualified as heroes?

COWART: Yeah, the Native American Indians. Ever since I was a little boy, further back than I can remember, I have admired so many things about them. It's not like I can just put my finger on one thing. I admire their abilities to survive, their culture, their skills and their spirituality. And do you know, their ability to do so many things that they had to do just to survive. Also, their closeness to the earth and to nature. Their respect for it.

McCLELLAN: You used the word spirituality. Are you a spiritual person?

COWART: Yes.

McCLELLAN: Were you at the time of the accident?

COWART: No. And even now my spirituality is not a religious-type spirituality that so many people think in terms of. It's a personal thing. I believe that spirituality is something that comes from within. You know, we can go places, we can talk to people and do things that can help us find spirituality. But the place where we ultimately find it is within ourselves.

McCLELLAN: What helped you get to this point?

COWART: A lot of things.

McCLELLAN: Were there people who influenced you?

COWART: People influenced me and also things I've read.

MCCLELLAN: You say you meditate?

COWART: Yes.

McCLELLAN: And that helps you in what way? What does that do for you?

COWART: It's helps me focus. It's helped me be a better listener. And I feel like it's given me just a better overall sense of well-being.

McCLELLAN: Do you still have any associated discomfort, pains and so forth related to your injuries?

COWART: Not much. There are days. There are bad days. But generally, I seem to deal with things like discomfort pretty well. I've got few complaints.

McCLELLAN: What's your opinion on having a sense of humor? Is it an important attribute to have in your case?

COWART: It's a good thing to have.

McCLELLAN: Has a sense of humor helped?

COWART: I've never thought about it, but I feel that it probably has. Including my dad, there were seven brothers and sisters on his side of the family as well as a niece who my grandparents raised from the age of two, after her mother died. Quite a big family — so, I have a lot of relatives. My grandfather was quite a character and liked to joke around. That's the way most of my dad's side of the family was, so whenever we get together there's usually a lot of good natured teasing and we'll rib each other a lot about one thing or the other.

McCLELLAN: Earlier, you also were talking about role models and you wanted to get back to that.

COWART: I'm not comfortable about the idea of role models and I'd like to tell you why.

McCLELLAN: You and Charles Barkley.

COWART: Who?

McCLELLAN: Charles Barkley, the basketball player. He's been challenged because of his somewhat anti-social behavior. They say he a role model for people and should watch what he does. But Barkley says that he does not want to be anyone's role model. He has enough trouble taking care of himself. He doesn't want to be responsible for some eight-year-old child who watches him. That's Barkley's attitude.

COWART: I share some of his reasons for not wanting to be a role model. I think that his reasons for not wanting to be a role model may go back to some of the same things as mine. The reason I'm personally uncomfortable being a role model is that no matter who you are, we're human beings and because of that, we all have faults. We all have feet that are made of clay. There are some things that I've done that I believe have helped people. If so, that's a good thing and it makes me feel good when people tell me that when they hear my story, it's helped them. I consider that something very different though from being held up as a role model because I believe that it's human nature to take someone who we admire for one or two aspects of their life, and then project many other of our own values onto the role model. I think that's usually what happens.

We project our own values onto the role model because there are some specific things we admire about that person. We didn't have unrealistic expectations for that person as far as being a role model in terms of a human being. Like you and I talked about earlier, we all have our own scars, warts and blemishes that would not be good things for other people to model themselves after.

McCLELLAN: You mentioned the support you received from people.

COWART: While I was in the hospital and ever since then as well, the support that's been given to me by my family, friend, professors and many others is one of the major things that has helped me get my feet back on the ground, put my life back together. Very few of the things that I've been able to accomplish would have happened had I not had that kind of support. For probably 90% or more of the time that I was hospitalized, my mother was there for me. Spending so much time around the hospital, one of the things she noticed was that when a patient died, it would often be when his or her family would leave to go home or had to be away from the hospital for one reason or the other. There were a lot of things she saw going on in the hospitals that were wrong and that she didn't like. If she had not been there to keep on top of things, I probably would have died. She came out of the experience feeling that it is extremely important for family members, friends, or someone close to the family to be there all the time for the patient. I'm not talking about 24 hours a day, although whenever possible, that would probably be a good thing, but as much as possible, every day or close to it.

Also, I would never be practicing law if I hadn't had the support of my family, relatives, friends, professors and people like Jerry Spence and the others at Trial Lawyer's College who had enough faith in me to give me a chance. At that time, Trial Lawyer's College only admitted 48 lawyers a year and there were many thousands of applications from all over the United States. It was at Trial Lawyer's College that I met Bob Hilliard. If Bob had not believed in me enough to ask me to join his law firm, to try cases, and to support me in the way he has, I probably wouldn't be practicing law today.

I've also had a lot of support from other people in the law firm and other people here in Corpus Christi as well.

My former wife also gave me a lot of support in speaking engagements and many day-to-day things as well.

McCLELLAN: Would you like to do more speaking? Do you enjoy it?

COWART: Yeah. I like speaking but there's a lot of travel time involved and it's extremely tiring. Then when I get back to my office, I'm usually behind. I did a lot of speaking last year and agreed to speak much more than I had actually intended. I still enjoy speaking and will continue, but I haven't been taking nearly as many lately simply because I cannot afford to spend that much time away from the office.

McCLELLAN: This whole issue of a person's right to choose and the subject of assisted suicide and the state of the country in which we live, in what direction do you see the country eventually moving? Where do you think these issues will come together and gel? Will it be a national recognition of people's individual rights, or do you see, something quite the opposite where the country will close down or put a complete abolishment, an end to anyone's individual choice on this issue?

COWART: I hope and also believe that we will probably keep moving in the direction of giving individuals more rights to decide for themselves when it comes to making medical choices. One thing that bothers me a lot though is that in other areas, the people of this country are losing more and more of their freedoms and their rights to make their own choices about matters that primarily concern themselves and also to get justice in our courts of law. It's a scary thing. Corporations, insurance companies and other types of concentrated wealth are influencing the outcome of elections and laws that affect us as individuals more and more as time goes by.

And law has already seen it in a very big way. It's the corporation and insurance companies who are at the bottom of the laws, the so-called tort reform movement and through advertising and the media, they have successfully painted a very distorted picture of what's been happening in our courts — like the McDonald's hamburger case. By an overwhelming majority, the media made it look like the case was about a little, old lady who spilled coffee on herself, filed a lawsuit, then collected millions of dollars from McDonald's for something that was her own fault. It's like, "What did McDonald's do wrong? If you're careless and spill hot coffee on yourself, you're going to get burned. Everybody knows that". You can't blame people for thinking that it was a frivolous lawsuit because that's pretty much how it was portrayed by most all of the media. What most people still don't know, even today, is that the restaurant industry itself had already adopted a recommended standard for the temperature of coffee and McDonald's chose to ignore it despite their having received several hundred complaints from customers that the coffee they were serving was too hot. Once you get above the recommended temperature, burns become much more severe and in a shorter length of time. That's why the elderly lady had third degree burns on her thighs, hips and genital area that required having to undergo skin grafts, something else that most people aren't aware of.

Another thing most people still seem to believe is that McDonald's actually had to pay her was x million dollars when the amount they actually paid was x hundred thousand dollars. Her skin graft surgery and other medical expenses were approximately x. She had to use approximately x hundred thousand dollars of that to pay for skin grafts and other medical treatment along with the high legal costs that are associated with going to trial against a major corporation like McDonald's.

A number of years before the McDonald's case, a cup of hot coffee spilled in my mother's lap. She told me that it was very painful but not bad enough to require medical treatment. It's not just the McDonald's case. The public would have a much better understanding of jury verdicts if they were told the truth about what actually happened rather than a one-sided version.

To bring it back to the healthcare industry, we're seeing cutbacks in all kinds of healthcare services. I say all kinds; we're seeing it in a multitude of them. In hospitals, the nurse-to-patient ratio has decreased greatly. Almost everywhere I go, nurses are saying that they cannot safely do what their being asked to do anymore.

I was in Illinois for a speaking engagement, it must have been four or five years ago, when it came out that an HMO was requiring radical mastectomies to be performed on an out-patient basis. There was a big uproar in Illinois about it. So, these things bother me a lot. I think people would like to have more freedom to govern their own lives. And one thing that really scares me is that we have people out there who want to govern their own lives and live their own lives the way they want to, but at the same time, tell other people how they can or cannot live theirs.

McCLELLAN: There's a lot of that going on?

COWART: There is. And that bothers me as far as the future goes. But, I think we will continue to progress in the direction of patients having the right to make their own choices when it comes to refusing unwanted medical treatment because more and more people are seeing the senseless suffering that patients are being put through. Especially in terminal cases where there's no meaning for quality of life and the patient's just lying there hooked up to all kinds of tubes and things like that. There are a lot of patients being put through agonizing pain. And, I don't think that people will continue to stand for it.

One thing that I hear from doctors all over the country is, "We're afraid that we'll get sued if we don't treat a patient, even when they ask us not to treat them". The last I knew, and I don't believe it's changed any, that there has never been a physician in the state of Texas who has been sued for failure to treat a patient when the patient's made it known that he or she does not want the treatment. On the other hand, many doctors in the state of Texas and other states as well have been sued for treating patients against their wishes. So, their concerns are very misplaced. The odds are much higher that a doctor will get sued for treating a patient who has not given consent than they are for following a patient's wishes not to be treated.

On the assisted suicide issue, it's probably quite a ways down the road, but I believe that most states will eventually legalize assisted suicide in one form or another. That's because I think the majority of people will eventually come to believe that we need to find a compassionate way to help people end their suffering. One of the good things that's happening is that when a patient is given good pain management care and other concerns they may have are being addressed properly, they will often no longer want to choose suicide. That's what seems to be working. What's happening in Oregon comes to mind.

McCLELLAN: I was just going to ask you if there was anything that you would like to cover that I didn't bring up or that we haven't talked about? Anything that would be important to put into the book, into the message?

COWART: From practicing personal injury law, I'm beginning to better understand how difficult it must be at times for a doctor to practice medicine. It's very painful to have clients come to me who have been wronged and who need help and I can't do anything to help them. Maybe it's because of something that's outside the area of law that I practice or maybe because the statute of limitations has already run on the case. It may be because the case would be so expensive to try that the damages would not even cover the expenses. Many, many reasons. Some laws are just terribly unfair and it's very difficult to tell someone who's looking to me for help that there's nothing I can do. And, I've thought about that when it comes to medical doctors and the relationship they have with their patients. Like when a medical doctor cannot save a patient's life, what that must do to him. I can also better understand what they must feel like when no matter what they do for the patient, the outcome is not going to be good. I'm not suggesting that because of this doctors should be able to force unwanted medical treatment upon their patients. But it does give me a better understanding of what they're dealing with.

What I do feel good about is that what I have done, if people can look to that for encouragement, and it helps them, then that makes me happy. But, to take any one person to call and say they've done something you admire in one area, then hold them up as a role model, you know, that's a heavy burden for that person because you can't please everybody. You know, one person may be may be Jewish, one may be Catholic, one may be Evangelical, one may be an agnostic, one may even be an atheist. And, so, we're talking about like — about like this is a suicide you know. But, one might find out that you know, have all these expectations for me and find out that you know, I feel that, you know, if everything's been done that can be done, the other person may, the quality of life is still not tolerable. There's still terrible, physical or emotional pain where their lying to you anymore. But, they should have that right within — they can take their own views. So, I just — I'd rather where people just look to me as an every day human being that had flaws and makes mistakes and isn't a man who's made who's made mistakes in the past and maybe in the future, then I'll be a role model.

McCLELLAN: Would you like to a try a case with Jerry Spence?

COWART: Not that it would ever happen, but yes, I would. I'm not sure about it, but it's my impression that as far as the actual trial goes, Jerry pretty much does it all from beginning to end. I've already used the analogy, "I don't want anyone else painting on my canvas," and that's very easy for me to understand. There is a real art form to trying a case properly. And in the courtroom, Jerry is like a Rembrandt or a Michelangelo. Who better to learn from?

McCLELLAN: The master, right?

COWART: Yeah. He has a very special approach. There are a lot of lawyers who try cases very differently than Jerry, very successful lawyers who are very good at what they do in the courtroom. For many of these lawyers it's because they found something that works good for them. But, many times, what works well for them is not something that they can teach or pass on to someone else. What we learn from Jerry, is a way to try cases that we can teach and we can pass along. That way is being real. Being you. It's not about using gimmicks or tricks, which according to Jerry, usually don't work anyway and can sometimes backfire. The most important thing that a lawyer has to offer is his or her credibility. Those types of things destroy it. We also learn not to try to be someone who we're not. Don't try to copy the way other people try cases, you know. There are certain common things we can learn, some techniques and all, but as far as the way we talk, body gestures and all, it's got to be real; it's got to be us. That's his philosophy. And I agree with him.

McCLELLAN: How do you feel about this interview? We covered the right things, didn't we? Did we get it all?

COWART: Well, we may not have it all, but I believe that we've at least touched on most of it.

McCLELLAN: Any final words? Any infomercials you want to put include here?

COWART: A couple of brief things. It's very important to have an advanced directive, I'm talking about things like a durable power of attorney which allows you to name who would like to make medical decisions for you if for some reason you become unable to communicate your own wishes. Make sure as best you can that the person you name has a clear understanding of what you would like for him or her to do and choose someone who you believe will be emotionally able to carry out what you have asked them to do.

The second thing is something I read in Monte Roberts' book **The Man Who Listens to Horses**. There's a wonderful lesson in it. Not only for medical doctors but for all of us to live by as human beings. It goes something like, to paraphrase. If the trainer opens a door that the horse wants to go through, then he has a horse that is a willing partner rather than an unwilling subject. That's what I would like to see most of all — a world in which we are willing partners and not unwilling subjects.

8

---◆---

Spirituality and End of Life Decision-Making
Thy (or my) Will Be Done?

by Elaine M. Buzzinotti, R.N., M.A., J.D.

INTRODUCTION

It is indeed an honor to be asked by Bob Horn to contribute to this work. In choosing to address the role of spirituality and end of life decision-making, I quickly became aware of what a daunting task I had undertaken. My "day job" is that of a health care attorney, hospital administrator, and ethicist. At this time in my life I am also about to embark on a spiritual journey by pursuing religious life within a Franciscan Poor Clare community. Thus, my interest is more than an academic curiosity. However, as I am not formally theologically trained, this endeavor represents relatively new territory for me. My disclaimer notwithstanding, I was from the outset, most enthusiastic about the assignment, as the subject is both one of increasing personal and also professional interest. On a nearly daily basis, I encounter patients, their families, as well as persons in my own life as they struggle with critical medical decisions, and the various factors, whether they be legal, ethical, or faith-based, which impact on end of life decision-making.

In terms of the spiritual component, the subject of this chapter, one question faced by a person of faith is that of whether the medical-legal construct of autonomous decision-making is an absolute one, and, if not, what role does or should an individual's faith play in this decisional process? My thesis is that such decision-making for a person of faith is not an absolute or purely autonomous one, involving the wishes of the "person" alone, or his or her legal surrogate, with input from other "persons", e.g., physicians and/or family. Rather, I am proposing that the process be a spiritually consultative one involving the Higher Power we know as God.[1]

The opinions set forth in this chapter are my own, unless otherwise indicated, and are intended to be consistent with the teachings of the Roman Catholic Church (hereafter "Church") in a spirit of truth-seeking, open-mindedness, and ecumenism. Consistent with the philosophy of Catholic ethicists, Benedict M. Ashley, OP, and Kevin D. O'Rourke, OP (hereafter "Ashley and O'Rourke"), I am less invested and concerned with "the conversion of others, as for a convergence of insight."[2]

When I began this chapter, it was during the season of Advent in the Church, with the sacred scriptures eloquently proclaiming this to be a time of joyful anticipation, profound hope, and an opportunity for reconciliation. In anticipation of that grandest of all birthday parties, the commemoration of our God-given new life 2000 years ago, a life given us in the form of a child of a simple maiden, who dared to risk all and say, "Yes," we are also reminded of the new life that is to come following our mortal death. Through reconciliation, another theme of the season, God enables us to be placed in a maximum state of spiritual preparedness for the celebration of the birthday of our salvation. Reconciliation also prepares us for our own mortal end and spiritual "rebirth," so that in a maximal state of God-given grace we may be vigilant and watchful for our Savior's promised return, as Christians are called upon to be, for

> "...[o]f that day and hour no one knows, neither the angels in heaven nor the Son, but the Father alone." (Matt. 24:36)

Thus, for me it is especially timely and relevant to be addressing spiritual issues related to end of life decision-making in the midst of a season, which by its very essence promotes peace, joyful anticipation, hope, and an opportunity for reconciliation.

DEFINITIONS

For purposes of clarification, I am using the term end of life decision-making, to refer to two (2) distinct types of medical circumstances. The first type concerns the time in which, in the face of an irreversibly terminal illness, that point is reached where death is deemed to be imminent, and where decisions need to be made concerning either the initiation or withdrawal of life support. Put in Christian ethics terminology, in this situation, the body no longer exhibits specific human behavior, would not be able to function humanly in the future, and no longer has even a radical capacity for human functions because it has irrevocably lost the basic structures required for human unity.[3] (Emphasis mine) Thus, in terms of the initiation of life support, such an action in this circumstance would not serve to affect the prognosis of the disease process or be restorative of human functions, but in fact would serve solely to artificially prolong life for its own sake. Similarly, under this type of medical circumstance, the maintenance of already-existing life support would serve the same purpose, i.e., the artificial prolongation of life for its own sake.

The second type of medical circumstance is very different. Also referred to as end of life decision-making, it too concerns a situation where a progressive and ultimately terminal illness reaches a point whereby life support may be initiated or withdrawn. As in the first type, the initiation of life support would not affect the prognosis of the pathophysiology of the disease process. However, the distinguishing and critical factor from the first situation is that here, the capacity for human unity exists, subject to the initiation of life support. Similarly, in this second circumstance, where the individual is already maintained on a form of life support, he or she has not irrevocably lost the capacity for human unity.

In Aristotelian terms the two situations differ in that the dominant virtuous activity of humanity, i.e., the contemplation of the Divine[4] is deemed to no longer be possible in the first situation, whereby in the second it is. Certainly, extensive consideration must be given prior to end of life actions taken in either circumstance. However, I respectfully submit that so long as the capacity for human unity or contemplation of the Divine is present, the Church's teachings on the inherent dignity of persons, as summarized below, support the prolongation of life. It is important to note that the Church does not impose a duty upon an individual to adopt heroic behavior. However, I am proposing that an individual not be denied a voluntary acceptance of suffering. For the Christian who continues to have the capacity for human unity and contemplation of the Divine, and who voluntarily and willingly chooses to prolong his or her life, he or she is provided with an opportunity to follow in the footsteps of Jesus Christ and to actively share in His passion.

THE CATHOLIC CHURCH AND
THE INHERENT DIGNITY OF ALL PERSONS

The dignity of the individual in relation to a personal God is a major tenet of the Church's teachings, as reflected by the belief that man's dignity is derived from his having been created in body and soul by God.[5] Catholic morality is indeed based upon a profound respect for man, "the only creature created by God for its own sake."[6] Further, "the human body shares in the dignity of the 'image of God'... and it is the whole human person that is intended to become, in the body of Christ, a temple of the [Holy] Spirit."[7]

The Church further instructs us that Christ is to be our moral example and Teacher. Accordingly, if in faith we believe that we are made in the image and likeness of our God, which also means sharing in His dignity, it follows that suicide and assisted suicide are inherently immoral and unjustifiable. This in fact is the position of the Church, stated in an unequivocally strong and clear manner:

> "Intentionally causing one's own death, or suicide, is equally as wrong as murder; such an act on the part of a person is to be considered as a rejection of God's sovereignty and loving pla[n]."[8]

As utilized in this chapter, suicide is defined as the willful and intentional termination of life or intentional hastening death for oneself. Similarly, assisted suicide constitutes the willful and intentional assistance by another individual in the termination of life or intentional hastening of death. The Church distinguishes between suicide/assisted suicide and the moral and legal right of a competent adult to either: (i) Refuse medical treatment (which includes the initiation or termination of life support under certain circumstances); or (ii) Make use of palliative care or other forms of aggressive pain management. This distinction is accomplished through two separate but related theories: (i) The concept of Extraordinary versus

Ordinary treatment; and (ii) The intentionality of the effect of the act, as such act relates to the initiation of life sustaining medical intervention or, conversely, its discontinuation or withdrawal.

EXTRAORDINARY VERSUS ORDINARY TREATMENT

The Church does not preclude a competent adult or, where appropriate, a legally designated surrogate or proxy, from exercising his or her legal and ethical right to refuse or discontinue medical care, when such care has been determined to be extraordinary in nature. The distinction between ordinary and extraordinary means is not a new concept in the Church.

In his *Summa Theologiae*, St. Thomas Aquinas, who was given the title "Angelic Doctor" by the Church, alluded to this distinction as early as the thirteenth century.[9] Later, in the sixteenth century, the Dominican theologian, Domingo Banez explicitly employed the present-day extraordinary/ordinary means terminology.[10] While this distinction remains a valuable one, it has become increasingly more challenging to utilize on a practical basis, as a result of major advances in medical technology over the years. For example, the medical community now views what was once considered to be an extraordinary treatment intervention, such as an amputation in the era preceding the availability of anesthesia, as relatively ordinary. Obviously, there are numerous other examples, but the point is that in order for the extraordinary/ordinary distinction to be a useful and viable methodology, it needs to keep up with medical technology. Moreover, even if such occurs, this construct is one, which by definition, is subject to interpretation. To my knowledge, the Church does not maintain a list of what procedure or intervention constitutes an ordinary versus extraordinary procedure. I would further argue that all determinations of extraordinary/ordinary means be placed in a patient-specific context, for either a medical or theological analysis. Utilizing the aforementioned example, an amputation could be determined to be extraordinary if the patient were to be so otherwise medically compromised that the procedure would be considered extraordinary by both medical and moral theological grounds, using the following criteria:

"In medicine, a means is ordinary which is: (i) scientifically established; (ii) statistically successful; and (iii) reasonably available. If any of these conditions is lacking, the means is considered to be

extraordinary. In moral theology, a means is ordinary if it is beneficial, useful or not unreasonably burdensome (physically or psychologically) to the patient."[11] (Emphasis mine)

Thus, in terms of a medical scientific analysis, an amputation in certain
situations, such as the first circumstance discussed earlier, while scientifically established and reasonably available, could be deemed to be unlikely of statistical success, in the face of an otherwise irreversible terminal illness, which
could only serve to prolong the person's life, without benefit or reversibility
of prognosis. Similarly, utilizing a moral theological analysis, the procedure
could be deemed extraordinary if it was determined to not represent a medical benefit, or be useful, or be unreasonably burdensome from both a physical and/or psychological perspective. Thus, while the Church accepts and
condones the ability of an individual to forego extraordinary treatment in
certain situations, the decision-maker must carefully weigh what constitutes
such treatment. Whether the decision rests with the patient or surrogate, certainly medical input is essential.

But so is consultation with God through prayer.

A discussion on the extraordinary/ordinary distinction of initiating or
withdrawing life-sustaining treatment would not be complete without a brief
reference to another Catholic faith-based tenet, the concept of
Disproportionate Means. While the Church's traditional teaching does not
impose a moral duty or obligation to accept extraordinary treatment, in 1980,
the Sacred Congregation for the Doctrine of the Faith, in its Declaration on
Euthanasia, modified the traditional teaching related to extraordinary treatment to one that incorporates the concept of Disproportionate Means.[12] This
construct refers to the moral legitimacy of discontinuing or not initiating
procedures in cases where such procedures would be considered to be disproportionate to the expected outcome.

The Catechism of the Catholic Church (hereafter "Catechism") clarifies
the concept further in its treatment of the issue of discontinuation of treatment by combining both the extraordinary/ordinary distinction and the theory of Disproportionate Means:

> "Discontinuing medical procedures that are burdensome, dangerous,
> extraordinary, or disproportionate to the expected outcome can be
> legitimate; it is the refusal of "over-zealous" treatment. Here one does

not will to cause death; one's inability to impede it is merely accepted. The decisions should be made by the patient if he is competent and able, or, by those legally entitled to act for the patient, whose reasonable will and legitimate interests must always be respected."[13] (Emphasis mine)

Finally, the ordinary/extraordinary concept is further distinguished in the Catechism from euthanasia by emphasizing the intrinsic value and worth of life:

"[a] decision to forego extraordinary means rests on a recognition that the means of preserving life or restoring health are being foregone because they are no longer beneficial or useful or are too burdensome. It is not a decision that the life of the patient is no longer one worthy of being lived.[14] (Emphasis mine)

INTENTIONALITY: THE PRINCIPLE OF DOUBLE EFFECT

We now come to the motivational aspect of the issue of refusal of the initiation of life sustaining treatment, its termination, and/or the initiation of palliative care or other forms of aggressive pain management. Because the resulting effect of any of the foregoing could serve to hasten an individual's death, the issue of intentionality is sometimes referred to as the Principle of Double Effect. In the Catholic ethical tradition this principle refers to "the moral permissibility of an act which has both good and bad effects."[15] Like the ordinary/extraordinary means distinction, this principle is grounded in long-standing traditional Church teachings. In order to understand the principle, one has to presuppose, as did Aristotle and Aquinas, that

"[I]f actions are undertaken precisely because the ends sought are known to be suitable and preferable, then the human being must possess something which is capable of being satisfied and completed by those ends, namely, a nature the fulfillment of which is the standard for what is truly good."[16]

The principle requires that certain criteria be met. Specifically, an act with both good and bad effects is morally permissible if:

(i) With respect to the object of the act, it is itself good or at least morally indifferent; and (ii) With respect to the intention of the act, the good effect is directly intended and the bad effect is foreseen but unintended; and (iii) With respect to the measure of the circumstances touching upon the effects and act, the good effect is not achieved by means of the bad effect; (iv) The good effect is proportionate to the bad effect; and (v) The good effect can only be achieved concomitant with, but not by means of, the bad effect."[17] (Emphasis mine)

A personal example and related analysis may serve to clarify this principle. Approximately three years ago, my father was dying of metastatic cancer. Early in the year of 1997, our family had been given a prognosis of "about three months," which proved to be remarkably accurate. Thus it was on Holy Thursday in March of 1997, that my father's status significantly worsened with accompanying severe pain. Throughout his protracted illness, he had been able to live at home, thanks to the outstanding assistance of hospice care. When the hospice nurse came to evaluate him early in the morning of Good Friday, when indeed death appeared to be imminent, after consultation with his family physician and with our informed consent, he was begun on a regimen of morphine in dosages suitable to address his severe pain. Using a Double Effect analysis, the clear object of the act of aggressive morphine administration was the alleviation of pain, certainly a moral good. With respect to the intention of the act, the positive or good effect of pain control was directly intended, and the foreseeable bad effect, i.e., the depression of respirations, alteration of level of consciousness, and concomitant hastening of death unintended. The good effect was not achieved by means of the bad effect; and it was proportionate to the bad effect, considering his prognosis.

To return for a moment to my earlier distinction between the two types of end of life decision-making, my father's situation clearly involved that of the former, i.e., a true end of life decision. Specifically, his medical circumstances were such that he had reached a point in the course of his known terminal disease where death appeared to be imminent, and where the decision for us as his surrogates was one of whether to prolong his life for the sole sake of preservation of life through the initiation of over-zealous treatment. Using Ashley and O'Rourke's analysis, in his comatose state, he no longer exhibited behaviors which were consistent with an ability to function humanly, nor was there a remote possibility that such capacity was attainable in the future. Further, utilizing an extraordinary/ordinary and disproportionate treatment paradigm, the initiation of life support would unquestionably have constituted extraordinary as well as disproportionate treatment, and would have been without question, unreasonably burdensome to him, both physically as well as psychologically.

Did the fact that our actions were compatible with the Church's teachings make it easier or provide immediate peace to us at the time? Anyone who has loved someone and who has had to engage in an end of life decision-making process as a surrogate well knows the answer. My father was a most religious man and we, I believe, took that into account at every step of this most difficult of decision-making circumstances. I recall nights of prayer during that Holy Week and throughout the Easter week-end which followed immediately prior to his death, praying that we were not in some way usurping the divine authority over life and death, but rather doing a moral, ultimately ethical and Christian good. This prayerful and truth-seeking process is what I mean by "Consultation with God."

CHRIST AS A MORAL EXAMPLE AND TEACHER

In this chapter I have set forth certain teachings of the Roman Catholic Church regarding end of life decision-making in a context of certain medical circumstances whereby an individual has either: (i) Irrevocably lost the capacity for human activity; or (ii) Has the ability to regain or sustain such activity by means of the initiation of life sustaining treatment. We know that the Church permits the refusal of life sustaining treatment when such treatment is deemed to be "extraordinary" in nature or "disproportionate" to the outcome; and that the Church places great emphasis on the moral construct of the intention or motivation of acts related to end of life decision-making.

As a final point, I return to the issue of voluntary suffering. As previously noted, another major tenet of the Church is Jesus Christ is to be our moral example and Teacher. Thus, if we are to follow Him in all ways, should we not be more willing to accept pain and suffering as He did, as a communication of ultimate love by following in His footsteps? I submit that out of the voluntary acceptance of suffering can emerge, like a butterfly, a more perfect faith and closer union with God, and that such an opportunity should not be denied to the individual who knowingly and willingly seeks it.

To comprehend such a state of mind requires an appreciation of the meaning of faith. It goes without saying that faith is a God-given grace. Those who are fortunate to be so graced, at some point in their lives come to the understanding that they can never understand God's ways, "For my thoughts are not your thoughts, nor are your ways my ways, says the Lord." (Is 55: 8). Knowing that we can never know in our mortal lifetime then ceases to be an impediment or frustration to a full and beautiful faith, but rather can enhance it. It is this faith that empowers us to accept the manifestations of God's will in the circumstances of our lives.

Why the emphasis on faith? Simply because without belief in Transcendent Reality, we cannot begin to comprehend human suffering. In his treatise on Catholic faith, **Christ Among Us**, Anthony Wilhelm eloquently depicts the movement of a Christian to turn to God in time of suffering and its theological significance:

> "The Christian revelation is sure above all of one thing: that God draws the suffering ones to Himself forever and engulfs them eternally in His love."[18]

Every day, we hear persons refer to God not being "good" or "just" in the face of innocent suffering.[19] Professor Wilhelm opines that such an attitude

> "[i]s to want a God who will conform to our notion of what is ultimately good for us."[20]

How presumptuous of us to know better than God what is good for us! Why do the innocent suffer? Why is there famine and war? The list of inexplicable tragedies is unending. The point is that the "Why" is for God to know.

His ways are not our ways. The only certainty we can have is that God is all-good and will bring good out of everything that happens to us.

Thus, if we are able, through faith, to stop asking the unanswerable question, and instead of intellectually struggling with our doubts, fears, and sufferings, accept them and place them in the hands of God, we are essentially uniting our sufferings with those of Christ. Jesus said,

"He who does not carry his cross and follow me, cannot be my disciple." (Luke 14:27)

And Peter echoes,

"For to this you have been called, because Christ also suffered for you, leaving you an example that you should follow in His footsteps." (Peter 2: 21)

Where does suffering and following in the footsteps of Jesus fit in terms of the end of life decisional process? How do Jesus' and Peter's exhortations comport with our ability to say "No" to extraordinary or disproportionate treatment interventions? Professor Wilhelm provides insight:

"When suffering comes, we should unite with Christ's sufferings, asking him to help us bear it and profit from it. Besides spreading love in the world, suffering can teach us humility, patience, tolerance, and our utter dependence on God. Many of us learn in no other way."[21]

This is not to say or imply that those who choose to forego life-sustaining treatment or to have it withdrawn under the circumstances permitted by the Church are not suffering sufficiently. In my view, the "answer" as to when or if to undertake such actions needs to be determined by each patient or their proxy through reflection and thoughtful deliberation of all of the factors. Is it fully autonomous for a person of faith? I think not. Pray. "Consult" with God.

And by all means, allow His Will to Lead and Guide.
I conclude with excerpts from Psalm 116:

"I love the Lord because he has
Heard my voice in supplication,
Because he has inclined his ear to me
The day I called.

[I] believed, even when I said,
'I am greatly afflicte[d]'

[H]ow shall I make a return to the Lord

For all the good he has done for me?
The cup of salvation I will take up,
And I will call upon the name of the Lord;
My vows to the Lord I will pay
In the presence of all his people.
Precious in the eyes of the Lord
Is the death of his faithful one[s]".22

SPECIAL THANKS

The author of this article wishes to express her gratitude to Sister Mary Francis Hone,OSC, for her input."

REFERENCES

1   Autonomous decision-making might be defined by some as incorporating a spiritual component, and I am not suggesting that such is inappropriate. I am utilizing it in this work as a purely secular process.

2   Ashley, Benedict M.; and O'Rourke, Kevin D. *Health Care Ethics: A Theological Analysis*, Washington: Georgetown University Press, 1997.

3   Ashley, Benedict M.; and O'Rourke, Kevin D., *Ethics of Health Care: An Introductory Textbook*, Washington: Georgetown University Press, 1994.

4   McInerny, Ralph, Christian *Anthropology and Happiness. Ethics & Medics*, Vol. 19, No. 8, August, 1994, p. 1.

5   Haas, John M., *The Totality and Integrity of the Body. Ethics & Medics*, Vol. 20. No. 2, February, 1995, p 1.

6   Id., citing the encyclical, Veritas Splendor of Pope John Paul II (No. 13).

7   Id., citing Catechism of the Catholic Church (No. 364).

8   Benedict and Ashley, Supra, 1997, at 413, citing the Declaration on Euthanasia (CDF), 1980.

9 ST 2a2ae 65.1

10 Smith, Russell E., STD, *Ordinary and Extraordinary Means. Ethics and Medics*, Vol. 20. No. 4, April 1995, p.1.

11 Id.

12 Id. at 2.

13 Id. citing Catechism of the Catholic Church (No. 2278).

14 Id. at 2.

15 Cataldo, Peter J., *The Principle of the Double Effect, Ethics & Medics*, Vol. 20, No. 3, March, 1995, p. 1.

16 Id.

17 Id. at 2.

18 Wilhelm, Anthony. *Christ Among Us: A Modern Presentation of the Catholic Faith, 3rd Ed.*, New York: Paulist Press, 1981.

19 Id. at 118.

20 Id.

21 Id

22 Ps 116: 1-2; 10; 12-15.

9

◆

The Oregon Death with Dignity Act
Fact versus Conjecture

by Peter Goodwin, M.D.

INTRODUCTION

The debate about physician-assisted suicide (PAS) has been intense and adversarial. An issue so important, so charged with emotion, and so at variance with long held ethical and dogmatic beliefs must continue to generate intense discussion in a democratic society such as ours. However, that part of the discussion which deals with the practical application of PAS should be factual, and based on the results of implementation of the Oregon Death with Dignity Act (The Act). We now have two years of experience since implementation, and facts should now supplant conjecture.

I intend in this essay to explain why I was in the forefront of efforts to make PAS a legal option for those terminally ill patients who qualify under the Act. I shall discuss the provisions of the Act and describe my involvement in caring for terminally ill patients who requested PAS in conformity with the Act. I shall show how that experience, supplemented by an analysis of the Oregon Health Division's report of the results after two years of implementation of the Act, confirms that the Act has been measurably successful.

PERSONAL

I have been a family physician for almost fifty years. At my medical school care of the dying had no defined place in the curriculum, and in most schools in the U S the same was true until very recently. My ignorance inevitably led to errors. They were errors of neglect and of avoidance, of inadequate treatment of symptoms, especially pain, and of failure to communicate. These errors were almost universal among my colleagues.

My first wake-up call came in the late 60's when a married couple together in my office asked me to help the husband to die. He was suffering severely from cancer that had invaded his spine, causing paralysis from the waist down, loss of bladder function and constant severe pain. The cancer was resistant to all forms of treatment. I still have a sense of desolation because of the blundering inadequacy of my response.

Years later I cared for two dying patients at home. Both had strong, close support systems. One had daily help from the religious community to which he belonged. Family members from whom he had been estranged came to assist in his care, and regained intimacy. The other had a granddaughter, a nurse, who coordinated care from devoted family members. I made frequent house calls, and observed how different the dying process was from what I observed in hospital. The contrast was startling. At home a sense of acceptance and love, in hospital usually a distancing and a loss of personhood, often with both patient and family kept in ignorance. I realized that the medical establishment was all-powerful in a hospital setting, and that physicians were often ignorant, and worse, uncaring of the needs of dying patients and their families .

The experience that finally persuaded me that dying patients needed more power to influence the way they died was in caring for a man in his late 30's with pancreatic cancer. After all treatment options had been exhausted, he asked me, with his wife present in the room, to help him to die. By then he was emaciated, vomiting frequently, and suffering unremitting pain. Later his parents came as well, to demonstrate their support for his decision. I believed that his request was entirely rational. My attempts to help him and yet remain within the law were ineffective, and he died an agonizing death. Hospice would surely have relieved much of his suffering, but he was reluctant to have hospice involved. His wife's anguish at the manner of his death and my impotence in the face of a law which then prohibited me from mobilizing all the resources that he desperately needed, impelled me to work to have PAS made legal.

I was of the opinion that the Medical profession was not ready then to deal meaningfully with requests for PAS from dying patients who desperately wanted that option. I joined the Hemlock Society, from which I have since resigned, and learned that a small group of individuals, independent of the Hemlock Society, had come together to attempt to place a citizen's initiative on the Oregon ballot to make PAS a legal option for qualified patients. I joined the group. During the next eighteen months we painstakingly drafted the proposed ballot measure, incorporating many safeguards, and reaching consensus on issues on which we initially disagreed. As an example, a minority considered the option of voluntary euthanasia, the injection by the physician of a lethal dose of medication into the dying patient's vein. I opposed this option for three reasons: firstly because of my personal discomfort with the proposal; secondly because I believed that the support of the proposed legislation by at least a substantial minority of physicians was essential, and the result of an informal poll of about thirty family physicians I conducted in Oregon showed that while half supported PAS, none supported euthanasia; lastly because I felt that the scope of the law needed to be clearly limited. The ballot measure was narrowly approved by Oregon voters in November 1997. Two years later the measure was again voted on, and this time approved by a 60% majority. Legal challenges had been rejected, and the Oregon Death with Dignity Act became law. In 1999 the Oregon legislature added several amendments to clarify definitions and rectify some ambiguities.

THE OREGON DEATH WITH DIGNITY ACT

The Act allows an adult terminally ill resident of Oregon with a life expectancy of six months or less who is mentally competent, fully informed and acting voluntarily to request from his or her attending physician a prescription for a lethal dose of medicine to end life. The physician may legally provide the prescription if all the provisions of the Act are satisfied, or may refuse the request. If the physician refuses, the only requirement of that physician under the Act is that records be transferred on request if the patient establishes care with a new attending physician.

The attending physician must ensure that the patient is indeed terminally ill, capable of making rational health care decisions and that the request is made voluntarily. The patient must be informed of the diagnosis and prognosis, and of alternative treatments, including comfort care, hospice care and pain control. The attending physician must ask the patient to involve family members and must assure the patient that he or she can withdraw the request for PAS at any time.

The attending physician then must refer the patient to a consulting physician knowledgeable about the patient's disease, who must confirm the diagnosis and prognosis, and verify that the patient is capable, is acting voluntarily, and has made an informed decision. If either physician is of the opinion that the patient's judgement may be impaired by mental illness, including depression, the patient must be referred to a psychiatrist or psychologist for determination of competence. Only if the patient is capable of understanding and making health care decisions can lethal medication be prescribed.

The patient must make two oral requests for PAS, separated by at least fifteen days. A written request must also be completed by the patient, in which the patient confirms that he or she is fully informed about the diagnosis, prognosis, the medication to be prescribed and risks associated with its use, the expected outcome, and feasible alternatives. Also, that the request is being made voluntarily, and that the patient knows that the request can be rescinded at any time. The request must be signed by the patient in the presence of two witnesses, who declare that the patient appears to be of sound mind, and not under duress, fraud or undue influence. There is a waiting period of fifteen days from the time of the first oral request, and at least two days from the date of the written request before a lethal prescription can be given to the patient. Because participation by pharmacists is voluntary, as it is with all participants, the attending physician must call the pharmacist to confirm that the prescription will be filled, and inform the pharmacist of the purpose of the prescription. The attending physician must recommend to the patient that there be a responsible individual present when the medication is taken.

All steps must be fully documented in the patient1s record, and the attending physician must include a note that all requirements of the Act have been satisfied. The attending physician who writes a prescription to end life must send to the Oregon State Health Division completed copies of the prescription, the patient's written request for medication to end life, the consulting physician's report, and the mental counselling report, if performed. In addition the attending physician must complete a special health division form detailing the documentation in the patient's record, or agree to make relevant parts of the record available for inspection by the Health Division to determine compliance with the Act.

EXPERIENCE WITH THE OREGON DEATH WITH DIGNITY ACT

A few months before the Act was implemented, Compassion in Dying of Oregon (CID) was organized. The purpose of CID is to provide counselling to patients qualified under the Act who request PAS, and to refer them to physicians in Oregon who are willing to accept PAS as an option for them. Because the Act imposes many duties and responsibilities on the attending physician, CID has prepared printed guidelines for the physician, explaining its requirements. I was the medical director of CID for the first year, and associate medical director until the present. I have been involved in the care of over thirty such patients, advising them, referring them to other physicians when that was practical, and caring for a small number personally, in special circumstances.

The Oregon Health Division recently published the second of two annual reports on the patients who received PAS, and those who were provided a lethal prescription, but died from their disease. Information provided to the Health Division by attending physicians complying with the requirements of the Act was supplemented by telephone interviews with those physicians, and with family members of the patients. Sixteen patients died from PAS in 1998, and six died from their disease. In 1999 twenty-seven died from PAS, and five died from their disease. I shall utilize information from the Health Division reports and my own experience to discuss the many concerns raised by opponents of the Act. I shall include information obtained through a recent survey of 2649 Oregon physicians performed by researchers at the

Oregon Health Sciences University, which explored their experiences with the Act. The recent Health Division report and the research survey were published in a recent issue of the New England Medical Journal.

In neither of the annual reports from the Health Division was there evidence that the poor, the uneducated or the uninsured had been victimized by the law, nor that inadequate care at the end of life influenced dying patients to choose PAS. In 1999 those who received PAS chose it most frequently for reasons of control or personal autonomy, especially control over the circumstances of their deaths, and to avoid loss of control over bodily functions. Other frequently cited reasons were loss of the ability to enjoy life, physical suffering, and concern about being a burden. When physicians believed that being a burden was one factor influencing a desire for PAS they rarely agreed to participate. All who received PAS in 1999 had medical insurance. They were generally well educated.

These findings correspond with my own experience. The patients whom I advised who wanted to explore the option of PAS were mostly college educated and financially secure. They were patients who knew their own minds, and were forthright in their requests for PAS. I have always thought that arguments that invoked the likelihood of coercion of the dying by family members unwilling to care for them or greedy to obtain an inheritance were unworthy, even insulting. Family members accepted the dying patient's request for PAS reluctantly, in my experience, and became assertive only when they felt that the request had been arbitrarily dismissed, or when they were of the opinion that the care that their loved one was receiving was inadequate. Opponents even argued that physicians would coerce patients into accepting PAS in order to save their HMO's medical expenses! I cannot imagine how that could benefit an individual physician, financially or otherwise. I can imagine the impact on an HMO that was even suspected of such behavior- it would be disastrous! My concern about the law and its effect on the disadvantaged in our society is the obverse of the concerns of the opposition. Far from being victimized, I was fearful, and remain fearful, that they will not have the power to obtain PAS however desperately they might need and desire it. The duties required of the attending physician by the Act and the extensive documentation necessary are time-consuming and stressful, and some busy physicians may find it convenient to ignore the pleas of the disadvantaged.

Concern that depression frequently triggers requests for PAS in the terminally ill, and that physicians frequently miss the diagnosis, is widespread and well-founded. Of course depression must be excluded in these patients, and the need to exclude depression which might impair judgement was uppermost in our minds as we wrote the ballot measure. I believe that physicians miss the diagnosis of depression because they are misled when patients who are depressed come complaining of symptoms such as back pain, headache and sleeplessness. In a dying patient openly requesting PAS, the need to assess the patient for depression should be obvious. Twenty percent of the patients who requested PAS from Oregon physicians were thought to be depressed, but 93 percent were considered to be competent to make health care decisions for themselves. My own experience in personally interviewing ten patients who requested PAS explains this apparent discrepancy. Sadness is understandably common among dying patients but it does not interfere with their ability to think clearly and logically.

A patient in her 80's was thought to be depressed by a physician who saw her twice. She was insulted by his opinion. She thought that it was ridiculous to label her as depressed because she wanted to die. She had not been treated for depression throughout years of self-sufficiency during which she had raised two children single-handed, after the premature death of her husband. After struggling for twenty years with breast cancer, spread of the disease to her lungs with rapidly increasing breathlessness and cough convinced her that her time to die had come, and she wanted to control the circumstances of her death. Four other physicians who saw her during her terminal illness considered her to be fully competent, yet this case has been widely publicized by opponents of PAS to support what they perceive to be a serious defect in the Act.

Many physicians worried that legalizing PAS would cause serious harm to the doctor-patient relationship. Some considered that PAS was killing. They argued that it would destroy the sanctity of life. Some argued that the concept was contrary to the Hippocratic oath that most graduating physicians swore to uphold, and which forbids the provision of poison to patients. No evidence has emerged from the experience in Oregon that these concerns about a harmful effect are real. A relationship depends on effective two-way communication. Patients are often dissatisfied with physicians' communication skills, and their unwillingness to fully acknowledge the patient's agenda.

Physicians have been slow to realize that public discontent with the nature of the doctor-patient relationship and an awareness of the relative powerlessness of dying patients to influence their treatment was an important reason for public support of PAS. When a request for PAS is accepted and the reasons for the request openly discussed, the relationship may well be strengthened, not weakened. The sources of information available, the state Health Division's report and the survey of Oregon physicians mentioned above, show that physicians prepared to participate in PAS usually do develop a close relationship with their patients. They remain attentive and involve other agencies, especially hospice, in the care of their patients. Not infrequently they are with them in their homes when they take the medication to end life. I shared the care of one such patient with a physician who stayed with the patient for the eleven hours, an unusually long interval, between the time that the patient took the medicine and the eventual peaceful death. The physician described the experience as extremely stressful, but intimate and rewarding. Other physicians with whom I have talked who have followed their patients through the process of dying have had similar reactions.

The Act defines a terminal disease as one that within reasonable medical judgement will cause death within six months. Opponents of the Act argued that the inability of physicians to accurately forecast how long patients with terminal diseases will live increases the risk that they will die from PAS prematurely. Many physicians think exclusively in terms of treating and curing, which are time limited.

They have difficulty in changing to a caring mode, which is a process in continuity. In practice the close supervision of the patient's progress by the attending physician, the caring in continuity, reassures against a premature death.

In my opinion the medical profession has not adequately considered the difficulties that patients face with prognosis, as they wrestle with the agonizing decision of when to end their lives. Some terminally ill patients do decide to end their lives because fatigue or weakness deprives them of the will to live. Others act for fear of losing competence. A man with brain cancer became demented during palliative X-ray therapy, then regained rational thought after treatment was concluded. Fearing that the inevitable growth of the tumor in the future would render him incompetent to make health care decisions for himself, he elected to end his life. The attending neurologist refused to help him, and brushed aside his concerns. Another patient who had been treated for his cancer by all available means, but had residual tumor that was increasing in size, troubled his physician by demanding the means to end his life though pain was absent, and his only troubling symptom was severe weakness. Two other patients in my experience have been demanding in their desire to die, and though they were desperate about their prognosis, their insistence was disturbing to the attending physicians. Some terminal patients who qualify under the Act and who have PAS probably do die prematurely by strictly medical standards, but it is their choice congruent with their life values and the way they assess their circumstances. Most put off the decision as long as they dare. One of the patients I attended lost competence due to the progression of her disease while she delayed. Hospital admission was necessary to care for her adequately. Her family was dismayed that she had not achieved her ardent desire to die peacefully at home.

Another dying patient who also had the medication available became progressively weaker, then confused. He died at home soon after. His family was relieved that hospitalization was avoided.

Is PAS unnecessary? Many physicians and ethicists emphasize that when dying patients who request PAS received all necessary and appropriate care, including adequate control of pain, and when they were assured that they would be cared for until they died, no more was heard from them about PAS. However,this argument is presented in circumstances where PAS is not a legal option, and usually by physicians in medical institutions where no opportunity for PAS exists. There is no doubt that effective care answers the needs of a large majority of the terminally ill. The few in whom the best of palliative care cannot relieve their symptoms can be provided terminal sedation, sedation which is maintained in a hospital setting until the patient dies. Many dying patients fear hospitalization, however, and what they perceive to be the unchecked power of high-technology medicine.

The public perception that patients and their families are powerless to influence the course of treatment is one of the major factors fueling the desire for more control. For a few determined patients a desire for control over the way they die reflects the way they have lived their lives. To deny them their wish and impose a medically-determined solution on them can be seen as a denial of their humanity. Without legalized PAS, their only option is to refuse all treatment, and all feeding. They then gain a measure of control, but their dying is often prolonged for a week or more, and may cause much suffering to them and their family members. This was the experience of one patient of mine for whom starvation was the only option. The availability of PAS gives a significant proportion of patients a sense of control, and reassurance that they have an escape hatch if their suffering becomes unbearable. I have cared for several patients who have benefited so. In fact, two of my most recent terminally ill patients, one of whom had the lethal medication in his possession, died peacefully, knowing that that option was available to them. My experience convinces me that the argument that PAS is unnecessary comes from technologically-oriented physicians, not from dying patients.

The necessity of legalized PAS is also illustrated by the tragedies that often befall terminally ill patients who attempt to end their lives because of intolerable suffering when PAS is not a legal option. Getting information about the safe use of effective medications is very difficult for them, often impossible. Physicians who might be prepared to help such patients are themselves usually ignorant of how to help because they, too, are deprived of sources of reliable information. As a consequence patients are forced to use guns or other violent means. When they do use drugs, they often fail disastrously because ineffective and often harmful drugs are used in unsuitable or dangerous doses. Not infrequently they end up in hospital emergency rooms. A published survey of Oregon emergency room physicians found that over half have had to deal with at least one of these disasters, and almost a fifth of them have seen approximately five. It is ironic that opponents of the Oregon statute claimed that the Act would lead to such events, when it was common knowledge that they already resulted from the status quo that made effective remedies impossible.

A powerful argument against PAS is that it will be the start of an inevitable slippery slope. They claim that the right to die will become a duty to die. They assert that PAS will lead to voluntary active euthanasia (the physician actively injecting a lethal dose of medication), then involuntary euthanasia, where the patient first because of mental incompetence, then perhaps because of physical disability, then old age, then poverty, is put to death with no say in the decision. They point to the example of Nazi Germany. The Act specifically outlaws all of these behaviors. The essence of the Act is that the patient must make the request voluntarily, persistently, with full knowledge of all other treatment alternatives. In practice there has been no evidence in Oregon that gives any credence to fears of a slippery slope. To the contrary, I believe that the law, by explicitly codifying what is legal, will discourage the illegal behavior that opponents fear. Opponents who blur the bright line between what is legal and what is not, run the risk of unconsciously promoting the very activities they rightly fear.

During the campaign to repeal the Act in 1997 the cornerstone of the arguments used by those in favor of repeal was their claim that the drugs recommended to cause an assisted death would often cause serious complications and would often fail to cause death. Supporters of the law maintained that these claims were false. Experience has shown that they are false. The only complication reported by the Oregon Health Division was delayed death, and that rarely. Even when delayed, each death was peaceful, and no patient regained consciousness after becoming comatose. Personal discussions I have had with physicians who attended ten patients who took the medication confirm these findings.

Holland is the only country where PAS and voluntary active euthanasia are allowed and regulated. Opponents of the Oregon Act and of PAS use statistics from Holland in their campaign, but what has happened in the past in Holland has become irrelevant to the situation in Oregon. There are fundamental differences between the legal requirements of the Oregon Act and the regulations in Holland, especially the use of voluntary euthanasia in Holland which is prohibited in Oregon. Perhaps more important. the legal practice of PAS in Oregon has been strictly regulated from the outset, whereas in Holland the process has evolved over time. Regulations were established in Holland years after PAS and voluntary euthanasia were used somewhat openly by some physicians to aid a small percentage of dying patients, and the regulations are still not supported by law. Statistics quoted from Holland are from information gathered from 1990 to 1995. Much of what opponents claim as evidence from Holland is heavily biased, often distorted, and strongly contested as being inaccurate, incomplete and selective. Such evidence may perhaps be presented between these covers.

CONCLUSIONS

The pressure to make PAS legal came from the public. In Oregon two intense political campaigns resulted in the majority of voters favoring legalization of PAS. That does not mean that they advocate PAS for the terminally ill. They accepted the need for PAS as an option in strictly controlled and limited circumstances. That is exactly how I perceive the appropriate use of PAS, and how I support it.

The care of the terminally ill in Oregon has improved significantly. There is much evidence that implementation of the Act has been one factor in achieving that goal. More dying patients in Oregon receive care from Hospice than in any other state, but one. The use of pain medication has increased dramatically. More patients in Oregon are dying at home. There is no evidence in the information available two years after the Act went into effect that the Act has led to any of the calamities or abuses forecast by its opponents. The Act has worked well. The results of early research have been positive.

Many questions still need further investigation. What is the role of depression in stimulating requests for PAS? Can physicians reliably differentiate between the sadness that is the inevitable accompaniment of terminal illness, and depression which impairs the patient1s judgement? Will increasing familiarity with PAS cause physicians to become careless in their observance of the requirements of the Act? Is there a danger of a slippery slope in the future? Though there have been no serious complications from use of the lethal prescription as yet, is it simply a matter of time before they occur?

There will always be opposition to the Act. Opponents will play an important role in watching for possible harmful effects of PAS, and publicizing them if they occur. Supporters of the law have not closed their eyes to adverse consequences, and will seek them as assiduously. Independent research is ongoing and will cast further light on the medical and social consequences of PAS.

Opposition to PAS comes from within the medical profession, from some ethicists, from a large minority of the public and from much of organized religion. Practical objections can be influenced, and perhaps overcome, by accumulated experience, and by research outcomes. Dogmatic opposition derived from religious beliefs are not likely to be influenced. A prominent religious/medical ethicist, Edmund Pelligrino, has written that pragmatic evidence will not change his opinion that PAS is the taking of human life, and will always be abhorrent. That opinion must be respected. It should not be allowed to outlaw competing dogmas and different belief systems unless they do harm. No harm has come from enactment of the Act. I argue that the suffering, and the deeply rooted belief systems of dying patients who plead for PAS, demand equal respect, and a measured response by the medical profession.

Section Four

10

To Be or Not to Be

by Helynn Hoffa

I WOKE UP TO DARKNESS and the rhythmic sound of a machine. I had no idea where I was or what was happening to me. I tried to turn but couldn't move. Fear rose up in my throat. I didn't like not knowing what was happening. I called out but got no answer and I panicked. I realized that my 60 year old body, afflicted with polio since the age of 8, was in an iron machine of some sort with only my head out resting on something.

I called out again and an authoritative voice said, "It's not morning. Go back to sleep." Bewildered, and not knowing where I was or the circumstances, I just started screaming. In no time, my room was crowded with hospital personnel. It took some time for them to calm me down. To my horror, I found I was in an iron lung and the rhythmic machine was helping me breathe.

Two weeks later, I went home in an ambulance with my iron lung on a truck. They set up the lung in the living room and mirrors were placed strategically around the head of the lung so I could see through the house from the front door to the back door and into the back yard. This vista helped to keep me from feeling penned in. I could also see the television from this angle.

The machine had port holes where a nurse could reach in and care for me. I was using the bedpan, taking bed baths and having my sheet changed through these port holes while the iron lung kept running. It was all very awkward and exhausting.

I was getting more restless as the weeks wore on. I was not in a familiar position, lying flat on my back, with my body in an iron tube, my head resting on a table outside the tube, my neck encased in a plastic sleeve creating the needed barrier to maintain the pressure I needed to breath. I hated it.

I decided to turn off the machine and get out for short periods of time trying to breathe on my own for as long as I could. This meant shutting off the machine, sliding it open, and having the bed table pulled out from the tube. Next the sleeve around my neck was loosened and my body was pulled toward the foot of the bed table so my head was pulled past the sleeve and the metal ring. Now I was fully on the bed table of the iron lung. Then I had to be turned over from my back on to my stomach so I could be propped up on my elbows. This "propped up on my elbows" posture has been familiar to me for most of my life. I didn't know if this was harming me or not but I was determined to keep it up. I had to have some feeling of being out of that machine or I thought I'd go mad.

That gave me a feeling of freedom which I wanted very badly so I'd get out of the machine for breakfast and stay out until after lunch. Then I'd get put back in and sleep the afternoon away because I was totally exhausted from the ordeal. These afternoon naps affected my night sleep cycle so I was up half the night, thinking unpleasant thoughts, remembering the dark times in my life and feeling despair haunt me.

That began the long battle between the machine and myself. For a year and a half, I wanted to die rather than to live like that. I figured it was just asking too much of me but there was nothing I could do about it. Already, the polio had left me a quadriplegic and I had spent my life in a wheelchair. Surely, this was asking too much.

It reminded me of when I first had polio and couldn't even turn my head. I'd lie upstairs in my bed listening to my friends playing outside in the summer evening. I didn't understand what had happened to me but I was determined to get out even if it was in a wheelchair. When I finally did get out, my friends were happy to see me and included me in their activities. In the fall I went to third grade. The teacher was most helpful and I could now use my right hand to do my homework. Children adjust more easily than adults. I'm not saying it was easy but it was certainly easier than getting used to the iron lung.

My parents heard about Warm Springs, Georgia as a place for treatment for polio patients because Governor Franklin D. Roosevelt of New York State had polio and he went there for treatment. We didn't have the money to send me so the Kiwanis Club offered to pay my way. That Christmas I went south to Georgia where I stayed for a year taking the treatments. The Roosevelts came down several times while I was there and I remember one morning I was seated on the steps leading into the water when President Franklin D. Roosevelt swam over and sat down beside me. I can still remember the hot Georgia sun blazing down on us and the cool air rippling the blue waters of the pool. He was a big man and I thought he was handsome. He asked me about my parents and then asked me what I wanted to do when I grew up. "I don't know. I don't guess I can do much." He looked at me and smiled and said, "If I can be elected President of the greatest country on earth even though I am in a wheelchair, you can do anything you want." "I want to be an archeologist," I said a little hesitantly. "Then do it, "he advised. Needless to say, I idolized him and his words kept me going through many a dark day but not all the dark days. Not even a hero's words could get me through some of the despair I experienced as I grew to womanhood.

When I was in my twenties, I attempted suicide. I came back to consciousness in Queens Hospital in Honolulu. I had gone to a prominent surgeon to get some work done on my right foot. My toes were curling under and made it difficult to wear high heels. He looked at me with a gleam in his eyes. With my polio, I was a surgeon's dream. I told him repeatedly, I wanted nothing else done besides my foot. When I came to, my right hand was in a cast. He had "stabilized" my thumb. My left arm was in a cast because he had operated on that elbow. I was furious, to say the least. Unable to use my right hand, which prior to the surgery was fully functional for me, I could no longer work effectively as the editor of the **Hawaiian Sportsman** magazine and sports reporter for the **Honolulu Star Bulletin**.

When the cast came off and I found my stabilized thumb unusable, I had to learn how to hold a pen all over again, and how to type without using the ineffectual thumb. My deadlines came and went and my career was at a standstill for several months all because of an over zealous doctor. I decided life wasn't worth living. I had had enough. Fortunately, I bungled a suicide attempt. When I woke up in Queen's Hospital I tried to find the words to explain my actions to my beloved Mother and Father. It was futile.

Rather than the escape which I sought, I found my life more complicated than ever. How do you tell your family you don't want to live anymore? By my attempt, I hurt a lot of people who had devoted their lives to me. They couldn't understand why I had attempted it and I had no reasonable answers for them. And now I was once again faced with another physical hardship, the iron lung, adding more anguish to my life.

Pondering this while the iron lung heaved air out of me, memories flooded me of all that I had accomplished in my life from a wheelchair. I remembered fondly the seven years I lived in Hawaii yet I never saw another person like me in a wheelchair. Yes there were plenty of disabled veterans and I knew there must be some other disabled people on the Island but I never saw another wheelchair outside of a hospital setting. I soon found out that the Orientals hide their disabled in their houses, being ashamed of having someone who is not perfect in the family; and the Portuguese believe the disabled have the evil eye and stay away from them for fear of being bewitched. It was the first time I had experienced discrimination and I remembered how it made me feel very uneasy.

In spite of this, a contingency of fishermen from Pokai came to me and asked if I would help them get a breakwater built, "The winter storms wreck our fleet every year," they said, "We need a breakwater to stop the waves." "I'll try," I said. I wrote an article outlining their problems and presented it to the Army Engineers at a meeting in City Hall. To my surprise, the breakwater was built and a small plaque put up at its entrance with my name on it. Even the drone of the iron lung couldn't take away the good feelings I still have about being able to have helped so many of the local fishermen and their families.

My parents worked for the Navy and decided to transfer to San Diego Naval Station. I would have stayed in Hawaii but I wasn't earning enough money to hire help for both the house and me so I went with them. It was not easy to leave a place where I was well known and recognized for what I did do from a wheelchair and go to a strange city where I knew no one, and was just another disabled person in a wheelchair. I became involved in Episcopal church work, becoming a member of the Franciscans. My job was to coordinate the Women's Guilds and teach junior high Sunday School. I also opened an art studio, teaching children on Saturdays and adults on weekdays.

Even though this kept me busy for quite some time, I soon began to feel like I was just spinning my wheels. Despair reared its ugly head once again and I developed a case of anorexia and got down to fifty-four pounds. My doctor despaired of me and predicted I wouldn't live beyond three months at the rate my illness was progressing. I just simply didn't know if it was that I couldn't or wouldn't eat.

The doctor suggested that Mother hire a Nurse's Aide to come in and take care of me in the afternoons. She and Dad both worked, and I was alone a lot except for a neighbor who came in to give me lunch. Mother hired a young woman named Wilma Lusk and told her it would be a temporary position.

Wilma and I have been together now for over thirty years. She and I have been through a lot together. I saw in Wilma a way to get out and about. She learned to drive and Mother bought her a little car just big enough for the two of us and she started back to college. I now have another caretaker named Karen Jasinski who has been with me for three years and we have become close friends.

Southwestern Community College was built on the urging of myself and two other ladies in Chula Vista. I feel it is one of my most important achievements. On their twenty-fifth anniversary, during graduation, they gave me a plaque and an honorary Associate of Arts degree, of which I am very proud. I was now in my forties and still living at home. I felt the need to be out on my own and grow up, so to speak. Wilma and I moved out to San Diego State where she finished her education and got a Bachelor of Arts degree in Art History. Living at the college was fun and our apartment was always crowded with youngsters. It was an exciting time to be in school during that period of social unrest in the sixties and we were in the thick of it.

I was doing fine and my health was good, so we decided to move to La Jolla and go into the printing business. I would be the bookkeeper and take care of the business end and Wilma would operate the press. That way we could earn some money and take care of ourselves. We mostly printed pamphlets and paperbound books for professors and "mouse cards" for a laboratory doing cancer research. We also did a lot of Buddhist papers for the group that Wilma belonged to.

The post polio syndrome, which I knew nothing about, crept up on me slowly. I just knew I was getting weaker. My friends said it was because I was getting older and there was some truth in that, but friends my age were not losing muscle strength at the rate I was. I knew it had to be something else and if there was anything I wanted to do I had better do it before it was too late.

So I decided I'd take one last fling and go to England. My nephew, Larry, my mother, my cousin Peggy and Wilma planned our trip. Whenever Wilma and I got a few dollars together, we'd pay for something on the trip. This is where the press came in handy. It took us a year and a half to get our part paid for and we went for five weeks doing the trip on a shoestring but having a wonderful time. We didn't all do the same thing. Larry, Wilma and I hired a camper and camped for two weeks doing our cooking and staying in farmers' fields. The one thing we all did together was the canal boat trip. With all of us sharing in the expenses, that too was reasonable.

When I returned home, I was very tired and went to a neurologist. After treating me for three months, he told me I was losing muscle power so fast that I had Amyotrophic Lateral Sclerosis and not long to live. He was well noted in this field and his diagnosis could have been correct, considering the symptoms exhibited, but he, like others, just didn't know about the post polio syndrome and how ALS and post polio syndrome appear to be similar in many respects.

For several months I put my affairs in order, expecting my life to be over shortly. And then the day came when the doctor told me I didn't have ALS but the post polio syndrome. No one had known about the post polio syndrome until it happened to a number of us as we aged. I wasn't prepared for an extended deteriorating life. After months of reviewing what I had accomplished in my long life with polio from a wheelchair, it was a severe blow to learn that now it was not coming to an abrupt end but would drag on slowly. What would I do with the rest of my life? Was this a cruel joke or a reprieve?

I read in a magazine for the disabled about a small keyboard operated by a stylus that would connect to my regular computer making it easier to operate. I ordered one. It was just the thing and now I was back to writing. I asked a friend of my nephew's, Gary Morgan, who was the journalism director of a community college, if he would help me write a book. I needed someone to look up the data because I couldn't do that. Together we co-authored the book, **Yes, You Can**. It dealt with the whole spectrum of life for the physically handicapped. It gave some purpose to my life and kept me busy. It was published by Pharos. I then decided to independently try a novel, **Golden Shores**, which was published by Paradigm.

I was so engrossed in the books I didn't realize my health was deteriorating. My right hand had weakened so much I could no longer hold the stylus. Nor had I the money in invest in a computer that could accommodate my special and diminishing capabilities. After having used an IBM electric and then a computer, I found it difficult to dictate what I wanted to write. I needed that "hands-on" feeling which is not present in dictation.

I am still writing occasionally but it goes slow and awkwardly. My latest books, memoirs of my life in a wheelchair, have not found a publisher which discourages me. I was a writer all my life for magazines and newspapers; I was editor of the **Hawaiian Sportsman**. I've had some success at writing and it is difficult to accept that my work is no longer finding an outlet.

I can do less and less for myself as the post polio syndrome advances. I can no longer feed myself or do other simple things. There are times when I am discouraged and wonder if it is worthwhile going on. But that all seems so cowardly.

I've had a full rich life in spite of my handicap. I am sure there may be more ahead of me that can be as rewarding and fun as what I have experienced in the past. For every ray of hope and optimism there is doubt and despair following close on its heels. I have found that the doubts outweigh any positiveness I can muster up, especially in the dark nights when I can't sleep and my situation seems overwhelming. When other people can't sleep, they can get up and walk around, get a drink, and read a book until they feel sleepy again. I just have to lay here staring at the ceiling surrounded by darkness, unable to move during these endless nights. It is at these times that I don't really want to go on. Why should I tolerate all this pain when I wouldn't have to?

I know there is no getting better. Each plateau I find myself on is a lower one. With post polio syndrome, exercises are of no help to build and maintain deteriorating muscles. In fact, exercise is not advised because it tires me out too quickly. However, I have found the massage which includes range of motion techniques keeps my muscles and joints from stiffening.

If only the ill effects of post polio syndrome would not continue to grind away at my body, making just plain living harder and harder, perhaps I wouldn't feel so discouraged at times. This sure progression of being able to do less and less is not easy to deal with because it takes away hope for a better future.

The lack of money exacerbates many of the problems handicapped people face. The state doesn't let us have enough to live on. The state gives a disabled person a small stipend and if we earn any extra money, the state deducts that same amount from our measly stipend, which hardly seems fair when we are trying to make a go of it. By doing this, the state perpetuates handicapped people living below the poverty level. There has to be a better way; one that would encourage the handicapped people to work and contribute when we can. This would help build self esteem and give us a feeling of earning our own way in society. To have to take hand outs, to have to fight institutions and political powers, to have to beg for everything needed for our upkeep, not only lowers our self esteem but leads to depression as well. And depression leads to suicidal thoughts and desires.

True, there are jobs a handicapped person can do depending on the disability and the availability of work. Work is often times found for the mentally challenged by the system and for the very brilliant, accommodations can be made at universities and in laboratories. But for the vast majority of us, who have just average intelligence, there isn't much emphasis on placing us in the workforce or allowing us to supplement our stipend without penalty to raise our standard of living. We are forced to work, under the table, so to speak, and we don't like having to do something illegal just to make a dollar. Something should be done about this in the legislature, but I don't know how to go about it.

I don't understand why the legislators don't see that it costs less to keep someone at home than in a skilled nursing facility. I, for one, would rather die than be warehoused. Post polio syndrome brings a lot of pain with it, as well as diminishing abilities. I have no tolerance when it comes to pain and even though I take pain medication, it never seems to be enough. I have a fear of taking too much medication to quiet the pain and slipping into a coma. Being in a coma is totally unacceptable to me. So I live with pain, some days better than others.

It would be so easy to put an end to it and then something snaps in my brain that pulls me up with a jerk and says, "Don't feel that way. There are days that are good. You have friends who would be hurt by your passing."

I noticed that people who say that suicide is a selfish act are never the ones who have contemplated it. I've also noticed that these people end up giving me a lecture on religion or the law in case I am unaware of the taboos against suicide.

There are many debates now concerning assisted suicide and people have very decided opinions on the subject. It's not easy to come to any universal conclusion because it is such an individual choice. It is not a subject to be taken lightly and I don't. Yes, there are times when I want to be dead but they are followed by times when I am glad to be alive. And so the seesaw goes on.

As it stands today, I do not choose to die but tomorrow I may. Circumstances change, sometimes abruptly, and we should have the right to terminate a life that has become intolerable.

Can an individual make this decision freely, given current societal constraints? Suicide is against most religious principles. This creates a strong ban against it in our society and makes it difficult for both the religious and the non-religious person to make a decision to end their life, regardless of the circumstances under which they are living. They feel suffering is ennobling to the soul and welcome it.

Doctors, trained to save lives, find it difficult to participate in a termination. It is against their Hippocratic Oath. So the medical field is naturally against this procedure with most doctors being reluctant to even discuss the issue. Before people make a decision about suicide, they should discuss the diagnosis and prognosis of their illness or condition with more than one doctor to clearly understand the situation they are facing. It behooves us to make sure we are not just going through a period of despondency, which we all do at times.

As long as I have my mind I want to be able to make the decision for myself. I have an over riding fear of lying in a coma and not being able to make my own decisions. I do not want to be resuscitated and live in a coma for years, so therefore I have made a legal document, stating what is to be done, if such a case should arise. I want no heroic measures taken to keep me alive.

Up until now I have been skirting the issue, avoiding the worst case scenario where the pain is unbearable and life has but a short time to be lived. When the point is reached where the pain can no longer be kept under control with a morphine pump and life is a living hell, then I think the patient has every right to ask his or her doctor to help put a merciful end to it. It serves no purpose for a person to live in agony when it can be alleviated. Death comes to all of us sooner or later. This is just bringing it a little sooner, in a merciful way ending the extreme suffering.

I had a friend, Gordon, with post polio syndrome who bought a gun and said he would take his life when it got too bad. But one morning he found he couldn't lift the gun anymore so his way out was gone. His doctor would not aid him. He said to me, "Isn't it strange that we don't let our dogs or our race horses suffer but we expect our loved ones to endure the pain." He died a long lingering death gasping for each breath.

It would be so easy for a doctor to just order an overdose of pills and it would be all over in a few compassionate minutes. I don't want what happened to Gordon to happen to me. When things get too bad, I want a doctor's assistance, so my life can end peacefully. I feel I have a right to that decision. It's my life, not someone else's and I should have some control over it and its end.

11

◆

Hospice
A Model for Living

by Sally Taylor

OB ASKED ME TO WRITE about my thoughts and personal experiences with dying persons and end of life choices. I was honored to be asked, but at the same time afraid that what I have to say would sound trivial about such an important subject. As my thoughts kept changing each day, I realized that few things can be stated with absolute certainty, but I'll give it my best shot at this particular moment. I have been a volunteer with Hospice for several years, and have also been with friends and family at the end of their lives. As I listen and observe persons making end of life choices, I have formed ideas about how we live and die, and what makes the difference between living out our days or asking for death. This observation has also forced me to face my own mortality and fears about death. I will use Hospice as the model for living because I believe in the basic tenets of Hospice, not only for the terminally ill, but also as a model for all of living whether one knows he or she is dying soon or not. What makes the difference between fear of dying and dying in peace? — or maybe more to the point — between fear of living and living life to the fullest? I apologize if there are any errors about Hospice — many of the following conclusions are my own, and reflect my own bias toward life and death. I also do not want to judge others' decisions about their own life choices. We all have our reasons for what we do or don't do, and each of us reacts differently depending on how we see life at any particular point in time.

Hospice treats the whole person — physical, social, emotional and spiritual — as well as the family, during the last six months of life. Pain and discomfort, fear and loneliness, concern about family and friends, and anxiety about what lies ahead are all addressed in the treatment. The patient is first a person with his or her individual needs, not just a disease. Hospice affirms and cherishes life, while also preparing the person to die. No discussion about death, depression or pain is ignored. There is a philosophy of caring which values the dignity of each person. Hospice is not about giving up, but it is also not about being afraid to die. The Hospice concept derives from medieval times when shelter was needed for pilgrims and injured crusaders. Modern Hospice programs began as a revolt against hospital care for the terminally ill, but it wasn't until 1974 that the first Hospice began in the United States. Today there are more that 3,000 Hospices in the U.S., and they are available in over 40 countries. Many studies show that approximately 90% of dying persons want to be at home, and Hospice offers this care with a team of professionals that help the patient feel in control, and learn how to make the most of each day. This team typically consists of doctors, nurses, social workers, chaplains, nurses aides, and volunteers — all of whom will come to the home on a regular basis. If home care is not feasible, Hospice also serves nursing homes and some parts of selected hospitals. This is a care vs. cure system.

As I said before, but want to emphasize, I believe in this model for all of life, not just for those that know they are going to die soon. One of the major functions of Hospice is to address fear. Many times these fears may kill sooner than the disease. There are many types of fear, and one of the major fears of the dying is fear of pain. In 1990 the World Health Organization set the standard for palliative care and pain control, calling it out as a priority. They also said that most patients still receive little or no effective palliative care and pain is often poorly controlled. I believe when pain is under control, depression decreases, and love of life is elevated. Let us look at the benefits of pain control and what happens without effective control.

There are all kinds of pain; among them, physical, social, mental and spiritual. Pain control determines how a person looks at life and death. By treating the total pain, the Hospice team allows the patient to want to live. Without pain control many just want help in ending their lives. I will concentrate first on physical pain, because that's what we traditionally think of when we say pain, and then look at social pain, realizing it is difficult to separate the types of pain. I visit an older lady I will call Carol who had so much physical pain that she had trouble leaving her apartment. She was also very alone, without family, and with very few friends — most of them had died. Just recently her pain lessened and she is no longer thinking that death is the answer to her pain and loneliness.

I visited Sue who was bedridden for over eight months with uncontrolled pain and, who tried to commit suicide because her doctors could not find out what was wrong, and she had given up on life. She really believed she was dying. Here was a desperate, unlistened-to woman. Her family was in denial about her pain, and did not know what to do. The chaplain from the HMO was the only one who continued to visit with her. I started visiting her once a week just to talk with her, and also to do healing touch. This is an ancient art of laying on of hands. It is a technique for comfort and well-being for anyone with physical, emotional, or spiritual needs. Over the weeks, Sue said she was pain-free when she relaxed and allowed me to gently touch her. At the same time she went to a pain clinic and began taking an appropriate medication that helped relieve her pain. She also found a doctor who listened to her symptoms, and reassured her that she did indeed have a physical ailment. Now she could begin living again — she had found new hope. After being bedridden for so long, not able to sit at all, today she is driving and is a whole person trying to help other desperate souls who suffer like she did. Her pain was so great that it cut her off from the rest of the world. Indeed she had both physical and emotional pain, and until that could be treated Sue believed that she was going to die. The fear of pain increases pain by geometric proportions. The person enters its world of horror and hopelessness that can end only in death — I can't take this pain anymore — help me die. Hospice listens to the patient's perception of pain. Hospice neither prolongs or shortens life, but does attempt to control pain, and then the person can live and concentrate on life rather than pain. There is another dimension to Hospice and to the healing of Sue. She regained her life, not only through effective physical pain control, but from support of her friends, and finally a doctor who listened to her. There is no underestimating the power of physical pain control, and additionally the support of a crying community. Social and mental pain can be just as important as physical pain.

Isolation=depression=wanting a way out. I realize this is a very simplistic formula, but many times this is true. Even at the end of life, growth can take place by bringing friends and family together. Memories are developed, and family business is taken care of. I don't feel any of us want to be abandoned at any time, let alone at the end of life. When we do feel alone, then we look for a way out of our aloneness. It may sound trite to say that good company is sometimes the best medicine, but I believe this is often the case for people seriously ill. As I sit with people in the last days of their lives, I see the tears in their eyes as they share about their family and life in general. One man comes to mind who did very little talking about his feelings, but in the days before death he cried when I talked about his family and the contribution he made to their well-being. We all want to feel that our lives have made a difference. I saw a video of the play **Mortal Coil** about several Hospice patients. The one person who wanted to die "right now" was not in physical pain, but had no connection to others. He could not accept affection from family or former students because he felt he didn't deserve it. He had never connected with others in a meaningful way and he wasn't about to start now — he just wanted to die. As we age, more and more of our lives can be lived in our hearts and minds instead of our bodies. It is enough just to "be". There can be a healing of the heart — a letting go of past resentments. The opposite of love is anger and depression — no one cares about me. Hospice and the art of healing touch say I care about you. Love can heal the heart and allow forgiveness, and life rather than death is important. Through reaching out and committing yourself to dialogue with others, you can transcend your individual existence, and through a lifetime of such commitment you can face your final end knowing you have lived your life well. Another aspect of this caring comes from the spiritual community.

Doctor Puchalski, at the Center to Improve the Care of the Dying at George Washington University said, "Wouldn't it be wonderful if spiritually assisted death was just as common as physically assisted birth?" No matter what your belief system, there is a holiness about life. Hospice addresses this holiness and centeredness that is more than a gesture of love. Many times fears can be put in words — does God really love me? What happens now? Here is an ultimate connection with a higher power. In the "Living Until

Death Program" in Park Ridge, Illinois (1974) every patient received a chaplain's visit. Elizabeth Kubler-Ross describes the importance of this program in her book, **Death, The Final Stage of Growth**. She believes this is important in helping the patient live each day as joyfully and peacefully as possible. Of course, we must value each person's belief system, and there are times a person may reject this help. The important thing is that it is offered.

Living or dying our last days is up to each of us. We all handle pain and isolation in different ways. Perhaps how we looked at life before illness affects how we see life after illness. Health is not always equated with happiness. Bob Horn is a good example of this. He led a full meaningful life before ALS, and he is doing a remarkable job of living with ALS. Once he asked the rhetorical question "Do you think I'm a lucky person?" His answer was an unqualified "YES I'm a lucky man." Even with the debilitating disease like ALS, he felt life was well worth living and that he had many things to be thankful for. Many people in his same place would not be able to say that. I'm not sure myself how I would handle a disease like ALS. Most persons choose not to go on a ventilator, but Bob had more life to live. He has a wonderful and supportive wife and family. He has full time care in his home, many friends, and is one of the most spiritual persons I know. Bob is able to reach out and embrace life even with all his limitations. Another friend Faye had cancer, and went into her bedroom not wanting anyone to see her. She found it hard to reach out to others, both before and during her illness. She had trouble accepting help or friendship until the day before she died. What a contrast to the life Bob lives! Faye was dying before death, not living until she died. She would not accept Hospice and all the help it offers. Hers was a very sad death. I believe in the triumphant death that the Hospice model offers. One doesn't have to officially be on Hospice (it may not be available or appropriate), but the mode of caring, pain control, and meaning for life can still be applied. Death can then be seen as a part of the normal process of living, and the focus is on remaining life. Hospice is about meaningful experiences and emphasizing life by helping the patient live each day to the fullest. Most people are afraid of the dying process, not of dying. I think most of us would like to die in our sleep after we have lived a full and useful life — wouldn't that be nice, but life doesn't always accommodate us like that. There are often harder choices for us to make. We can hope that the end of life is more than a medical experience. We can hope that we will reach out to others. Norman Cousins believes that death is not the ultimate tragedy, but depersonalization is. We acknowledge death, but celebrate life.

I have described an ideal Hospice model for living until death, and we all know that life is not perfect, and that all the pieces don't easily fall into place. There are times when physical pain cannot be controlled and isolation from others is a reality. But I do believe that the greater the amount of pain control, the greater the support of a community of caring persons and the more meaning in life, there is less likelihood of a person wanting to end life prematurely. I have to say that if I had a terminal illness, I do not know what I would choose. I can hope that I would choose life, but it would depend on so many unknown factors, and my thoughts today might appear to me then as simply an exercise in academic thinking. That is the reason I would never judge anyone else's decision when making end of life choices. In closing I would like to quote from the Hospice brochure at Providence Holy Cross Hospital (Mission Hills, CA).

"A terminal illness is limited. It cannot cripple love. It need not corrode faith. It cannot silence courage. It need not invade the spirit. It cannot lesson the power of caring."

REFERENCES:

Callanan, Maggie and Kelly, Patricia. *Final Gifts*. New York, Bantam Books 1993.

Kubler-Ross, Elizabeth. Death, *The Final Stage of Growth*. New Jersey, Prentice-Hall, 1975.

Kubler-Ross, Elizabeth. *On Death and Dying*. New York, Macmillan Co., 1969.

Levine, Stephen. *Healing Into Life and Death*. New York, Double Day, 1997.

National Hospice Organization. *About Hospice*. Deerfield, VA., Channing L. Bete, 1985.

Stoddard, Sandol. *The Hospice Movement*. New York, Vintage Books, 1978.

12

♦

Choosing to Live
or Choosing to Die
Psychological Perspectives

by Thomas L. Horn, M.D.

NOBODY GETS OUT OF LIFE ALIVE. In the long run, we're all dead. All of us are terminal. Given this stark, and uncomfortable fact, what makes the possibility of choosing to die different for someone with a terminal illness than for the rest of us? In some ways it isn't different, and that's why the issue of the right to die is so interesting and provocative to so many people: the topic touches us all. But in some ways, of course, the right to die is a very different issue for a person with a terminal illness and/or permanent severe disability. First, the diagnosis of a terminal illness punctures — or at least challenges — the denial of one's own death that we all use to help us move through our lives and develop meaning. This denial of death (really an ignoring of the reality of death) is a steady and comforting companion for most of us and the diagnosis of a terminal illness threatens and disturbs us deeply. But also the reality of a terminal illness alters a person's prospects for his or her future, especially when the illness creates severe disability and/or pain. These altered prospects often have profound psychological effects.

In examining the right to die in this context, we need to consider terminal illnesses and permanent severe disability, which are often linked, but not always. The ways in which the right to die is discussed in terminal illness without severe disability tend to be either as a response to uncontrolled pain if and when it occurs or as an alternative to waiting for the end, a way to seize control. Those readers old enough may remember the television program called **Run for Your Life**, in which the viewer followed a character played by the actor Ben Gazzara, a character with a diagnosis of an unnamed terminal illness but no apparent ill effects of that disease except having only a year to live. Outside of television, however, such disability-free terminal illnesses are hard to find. More commonly, an illness that is expected to be terminal will also carry with it some degree of disability. And here, the issue of the right to die usually comes up around the matter of whether to live with a severe disability and/or uncontrolled pain. Examples of illnesses that may be terminal, and when they are so are likely to include substantial disability, are some cancers (a very large and varied category), certain courses of multiple sclerosis (a disease with an especially wide range of severity) and amyotrophic lateral sclerosis (ALS, or Lou Gehrig's Disease). So the most common situation in which the discussion of a right to die comes up is one in which the degree of disability and/or pain raises the question of whether that life is worth living for the sufferer. Consideration of choosing to die is made more approachable by the fact that the illness is expected to shorten life, so arranging one's own death is only hastening the inevitable. But, as already noted, we're all terminal, so it is really the disability that raises the question, not the fact of a terminal illness by itself. Consider also that some permanent severe disabilities are not the result of a progressive fatal disease, but perhaps of an accident. The question of right to die is no less pressing because of the absence of a lethal disease.

This chapter will address primarily the matter of psychological issues that have an important bearing on how a sufferer assesses whether to end his or her life. It is not my intent to argue either for or against the concept that each person has the right to choose to continue living or to end his or her life, but rather to point out some psychological considerations to keep in mind when someone is considering whether or not to exercise such a right. My discussion only makes sense against a backdrop of the existence of this right, since I will be discussing how psychological and emotional issues may distort the perspective of the person considering exercising this right. I don't intend to be exhaustive in my list, but rather to highlight some important concepts and experiences.

In the interests of disclosure of what has shaped the views expressed in this chapter, I should comment on my "credentials" to write about this. I am a psychiatrist, with considerable clinical experience in consulting with patients with medical problems and with their doctors and other caregivers. But I now work primarily in an administrative capacity and I do not consider myself a sub-specialist expert in the psychology of death and dying. My professional perspective on this issue is formed significantly by my clinical work over the years with people with a variety of problems including serious medical illnesses and disabilities, sometimes as a consultant and sometimes working independently with these people. The other important influence on my view of this issue is a result of a family experience. My brother is the editor of this book, and has had ALS for over 10 years now, with as complete a physical disability as I can imagine. He is my older brother and I learned a great deal from him as I was growing up; I continue to learn from him — and from his family — about how disabled individuals and their families cope, in ways that enrich me personally and professionally. These professional and personal "credentials" having been stated, I should add that I strongly support this book's effort to emphasize the voices of the sufferers themselves in the discussion of right to die. Those of us not in their shoes should remain humble when opining on what they should do.

So what are the psychological issues raised by the prospect of permanent severe disability that are important to keep in mind when considering the right to die? The first of these is the experience of loss. This is probably the most profound and pervasive aspect of such a disability. To use typical losses encountered with ALS as an example, one loses muscle strength, coordination, the ability to swallow food or drink, the capacity to walk or stand or sit up. One becomes unable to shake a hand, pat a back or hug a loved one. Typically, a person with ALS loses the ability to speak, and so can't talk with others, engage in rapid back and forth conversation, hear his own voice, command attention vocally or interrupt. Eventually, he can't write a check, dial a telephone, lift a fork, turn a page or press a button on a TV remote control. And these losses of abilities and activities don't occur all at once, followed by time to adjust. They occur one after another, serially, relentlessly. As one is struggling to cope emotionally and physically with one lost competence, along comes the next. The decline proceeds relentlessly, in the case of ALS, until all the functions requiring voluntary muscle activity are lost. Only then is there a period of "stability" during which the person can expect to be more or less the same from one month to the next, and the experience of continuing accumulating loss can be replaced by the process of adjustment to the new self, a profoundly altered self. This is what the editor of this book expresses so well in saying, "Getting this way (completely physically disabled) was worse than being this way." With other illnesses, the losses may be more abrupt and less spread out and serial, but the impact of loss and the need to adjust in the losses remain critical.

The particular losses referred to above and the others like them often lead to another, more abstract loss: the loss of one's role. We all have multiple roles we play in the dramas of our own lives. The list of important roles for one person might include: Husband, father, partner in planning his family's future, breadwinner, and member of a group of friends who often go out together to shows or ball games. Such roles are very important parts of how we all find meaning, significance and pleasure in our lives, and how we develop a sense of comfort and confidence about ourselves. Severe permanent disability may affect every important role a person has developed, eliminating some and requiring major adjustments in others.

How a person adjusts to losses like the ones I've described has an enormous impact on how that person views the possibility of choosing to die. What do I mean by "adjusting" to losses? I mean the process that is often summed up by the term "grief work." A simplified and condensed description of grief work would be: acknowledging the reality of the loss; experiencing the sadness, anger and other feelings that come with that acknowledgment; and then re-kindling hope as one develops altered or new roles and restores a sense of meaning and value to one's life. This process takes time, certainly many months for important losses of the kind we are discussing, and often longer. What comes out of this process is a redefinition of one's roles and a revision of how one carries out those roles. One may still be a husband, but in a different way. One may not be a breadwinner any longer, but may remain an important part of family life. One may lose employment but still retain the interests of his profession or occupation. The development of roles that are meaningful and important, and validated by others, is a critical component of successful adaptation to permanent severe disability.

Another important psychological issue raised by permanent severe disability and the question of choosing to die is dependency. These disabilities typically mean that others must do for a person many of the things the person used to do for him/herself. Some of these are simple and basic, like turning a book page or putting on reading glasses or washing. Some are more complex, like managing the family finances or arranging social events or responding to health problems in the extended family (there are those role changes again!). For many people, the change from fending for oneself to depending on others for so much is a very difficult and distressing challenge. Some manage the change well. Some remain guilty about their imposition on others. Some find the dependency a deeply troubling aspect of their condition. Some allow themselves to become even more dependent than their disability requires.

The behavior and attitudes of family and friends have a great deal to do with how a person copes with permanent severe disability. Obviously, it is exceptionally valuable to have a loving family and caring friends, who express concern and support in various ways. It helps greatly if they are not made so uncomfortable by the illness and the disability that they avoid the disabled person, however unintentionally or subtly. But it is also important that family and friends see more than the disability when they look at a disabled person. The more they can see and relate to the parts of the disabled person that still work, that still function, that still contribute to fulfilling meaningful roles, then the more the disabled person can experience himself as valuable and contributing and more than a collection of lost capabilities. A cancer patient I once saw for a psychiatric consultation commented as I came into her hospital room for a second visit, "I'll be glad to talk with you again as long as it's not just about my cancer. There's a lot more to me than that, you know." She understood well the importance of attending to the many still functional and quite competent parts of her (and taught me about it too). Family and friends can be enormously helpful to the disabled person by validating the person's new and altered roles, by participating with the person in the carrying out of these roles.

Sometimes family and friends deal with a disabled person with kid gloves, so to speak. Everything is kept nice and light. This impulse may be understandable, but it has the effect of not taking the disabled person seriously. It turns him into a one-dimensional figure, a caricature. If a disabled person is quite capable of having important roles to play and contributions to make, he's also capable of being part of a serious conversation, of being part of a disagreement or argument, and even of behaving like a jerk. (Neither being disabled nor being the family or friend of a disabled person confers immunity from the very human shortcoming of behaving badly.) Successfully dealing with a disabled person's dependency needs means doing things for him when he cannot do them himself, but also not treating him as special and needy in other ways.

Persistent pain is all too often a companion of permanent severe disability. The management of such pain, by both doctor and patient, is a critical part of dealing with the disability. If pain cannot be successfully managed, by treatment of the illness, by pain medication, by physical therapy, by hypnosis and similar techniques, by immersion in activities, or by other means, it can take over a person's world, crowding out everything else, including meaning. Severe pain that is not successfully managed not only wears people down by the direct distress it creates, but it also robs us of the ability to attend to the important aspects of our lives.

I will leave to others the discussion of the role spirituality can play in coping with disability and assessing a possible decision to end one's life because of the disability. Its importance should not be underestimated.

In addition to the psychological issues I've raised that can distort a disabled person's assessment of choosing to live or choosing to die, we should consider a psychiatric disorder that frequently occurs as a complication of disability: depression. People often use this word, "depression", in a non-clinical way, to describe a very common state of sadness or feeling "down in the dumps", usually fairly brief (a few hours, a few days, a week or two) and fairly mild, and often after an identifiable loss. In this colloquial use of the term, it would be safe to say that everyone who experiences a permanent severe disability feels "depressed" about it to some degree at some point.

But there is a more clinical way the word "depressed" is used. For this I'll use the diagnostic term, major depressive disorder or major depression, to keep things clear. Major depressive disorder is a common psychiatric illness, happening to about 10% of people at least once in their lifetime, but it is even more common in people with disabling medical illnesses. It is characterized by low mood (sadness or absence of feelings), loss of enjoyment and interest in things, a sense of worthlessness, low energy, disturbances of sleep (either sleeplessness or oversleeping) and appetite (usually, but not always a decrease), and sometimes thoughts of suicide. It can severely affect a person's work life, home life and relationships. If left untreated, it is likely to go on for many months, even years, and sometimes indefinitely. Since it robs life of the experience of pleasure, makes its sufferers pessimistic about the future and often leads to thoughts (and acts) of suicide, and especially since it is highly treatable, it is a very important consideration when discussing the right to die of someone with a terminal illness or severe permanent disability. Someone experiencing an episode of major depression is not in a position to make a decision to decide to hasten death. The major depression needs to be recognized and properly treated. Once this is accomplished, the disabled person is again able to make a better decision about possibly exercising a right to die.

Consider the following example, which does not represent an actual particular person, but is an illustration of the impact of major depressive disorder. A 55 year old man develops ALS. The course of his illness is all too typical: gradual, then accelerating, deterioration of his physical capabilities, while his intellectual powers are left unharmed. He experiences loss after loss, never having the time to adjust to one before the next one comes along. He finds himself brooding about the changes he's experienced and worrying about what is to come. He is understandably sad and angry about what has befallen him, but then his low mood takes on a different cast. He develops a major depressive disorder, with its attendant sleeplessness, low appetite, low energy, unrelenting sadness, and complete loss of the ability to experience pleasure even from things that ordinarily make him smile and laugh. He is pessimistic about his future, seeing himself only as a dependent "vegetable", dragging down those around him. His family and friends and physicians see his reaction as understandable, not as a major depression, and support the decision he eventually makes not to go on the ventilator when his ability to breathe on his own is gone. All involved brace themselves for that time and an atmosphere of gloom descends on everyone. The time comes, the decision not to use the vent is honored, the man dies, and everyone grieves but takes comfort in the knowledge that the sufferer made his own choice.

But did he make his own choice? Not if the choice was made while he was experiencing a major depression. Psychiatrists routinely urge people in such a state not to make decisions about changing jobs, let alone about ending one's life. Had he been treated for his depression, he might well have developed a different sense about life's possibilities for him, however altered and limited, and about the potential for a meaningful life. On the other hand, he might still have made the decision not to go on the vent but would have done so for the right reasons, not because major depression distorted his ability to consider the options clearly.

The same kind of analysis can be applied to the other psychological issues I have raised. People with permanent severe disability may stumble over any of these and thereby have a distorted and limited vision of how life with their disability could be. Their assessment of the "facts" of a life with a serious disability may be inaccurate, which means that a decision about ending life may be inaccurate. The better they are able to address these issues as they arise, the better they will accurately assess the pros and cons of a life with disability, and conversely the pros and cons of ending that life. This is not an argument against the right to choose to die, but simply recognizes that given the irreversibility of ending a life, it is important to consider all the things that may distort the ability to make that decision in one's own best interests.

Section Five

13

◆

Depression and Suicide
The Search for a Way Out

by Robert Galbreath

THIS ACCOUNT IS AN ATTEMPT to describe the place of death in one life, mine. The life I will describe has frequently been confused and uncertain. Even in those instances where there was constancy of purpose and commitment to larger goals, things rarely have gone as planned.

The one true constant in my life has been the dominating influence of thoughts of death. Death and the release from pain which it presumably offers have always been somewhere in my thoughts. At times of particular distress, it has often had the dominant place.

Reading the previous lines, I get the sense that the author is someone who is afraid to confront the pain which life brings to us all. My account does not attempt to ascribe any particular values or to draw any special conclusions about people or events although one may detect an overriding air of cynicism. It is an attempt to depict my efforts to cope with events and situations which impacted so powerfully on my life.

I came to a consciousness of death at a relatively early age with the passing of my mother at her own hand. It was her third attempt to gain the release of dying. One summer night, while my father, sister and I lay asleep in our beds above, Mother closed herself into our cellar garage, started the family sedan and asphyxiated herself.

I have carried with me a fantasy image of that lady, lying by herself on the front seat of that old car, quietly inhaling the toxic fumes that would finally end her tortured life. In purely objective terms, Mother had earned this release. She was only the most recent victim of a genetic predisposition toward bipolar depression (manic-depression) which had devastated her family for generations. Not many years before, her father had shot himself to death, shortly after the death of her mother.

Medical science had been able to do almost nothing for Mother. They had provided a few drugs thought to be helpful for depressives, but they had done nothing to prevent her slide into ever deeper cycles of despondency. (She was about 7 years too early to benefit from the discovery of the remarkable relief which lithium salts held for manic-depressives.)

The doctors had concluded that the only therapy offering any hope of success was Electro-Convulsive Therapy (ECT). ECT was in its early years and physicians tended to err on the side of excessive current being sent through the patient's brain. Mother hated it and begged to be spared additional torment. Nonetheless, Mother's psychiatrist observed that, following her final dose of ECT at Shadyside Hospital in Pittsburgh, Pennsylvania, she was in much better spirits than the morose person who had originally been brought to them.

As is often the case with suicidal patients, the temporary infusion of new energy from ECT may have been just what Mother needed to give her the strength to carry out her third and final attempt on her life. Inhaling the poisonous fumes of the car exhaust must have been infinitely more calming and reassuring than the trauma of intense electrical shock to her brain. She was finally free of all that.

It is very difficult to explain (or even to understand myself) the impact that this single event has had on my life — how I viewed myself and my life. When it happened, I was just a small child, a few months short of my fourth birthday. I never got to know my mother very well as she spent too much of my early life in and out of care and treatment facilities. She was very much in the grips of the cycles of bipolar depression. (A cousin of Mother's believing that he was going mad, went into the woods and stabbed himself to death.)

Although I could never know Mother fully, I adored her. To me she was something like an angel, a shining presence whom I could only view from afar in her bed of illness at the sanitarium. Although I was only a small child, I sensed that there was something seriously wrong with Mother. It was my fondest hope that I could keep Mother there at home with me where I would be able to protect her against the things that tried to hurt her. I would be her little soldier, her security. I did not have much faith in my father to do this job.

Mother's suicide was an act of remarkable courage, determination and, probably, desperation. She clearly was aware that doctors could do nothing for her to resolve her dilemma. Her death made perfectly good sense in view of her rapid mental deterioration. It shattered my world, however. The person I loved the most, whom I had promised myself I would save and defend, was torn from me abruptly and cruelly.

I carry with me a number of memories of those terrible days. Although these images may be more the product of a severely distressed imagination of a little boy, they hold a great reality for me. I would not and could not give them up, whatever their factual basis. They are a very important part of the emotional bond that will always tie me to my dead mother and the way she suffered. To sacrifice them would be to abandon the one great love of my life which is something I would not do.

The most vivid image which I have of those agonized days was a confrontation on the front lawn of our home, talking to my older sister. She had been delegated the responsibility of informing me that we were not being allowed to attend our mother's funeral. I stamped the ground and raged in total frustration and fury that I was being excluded in this manner.

This event would establish a consistent theme in my life. I would experience myself as an observer, one for whom decisions are made by external agents, not one whose opinions and desires are respected, or even considered. In various situations, I came to feel that I was irrelevant to my own life.

As a small boy, I felt that I counted for nothing when major decisions were made to exclude me from important events. My father did not even show me the consideration of telling me himself. He did not take the trouble of explaining to me exactly why he was denying me my last chance to be with

Mother before she was gone beyond any chance to bring her back. My heart was dying with Mother, but no one cared.

I was devastated. All of my hopes that I could save Mother from the evil forces that tormented her had been dashed. She had spurned me, probably because I had been a bad boy and had done very bad things. Now, there was no way to go back to try to make it up to her. They were going to put her away where I could never reach her.

I was disgraced and very much ashamed that my own mother would not stay with me. She knew, I felt, that I loved her more than anything and that I would be lost without her. Now she was gone and all the adult world stood against any chances I might have of touching her again.

My response to my loss was to turn inward, keep away from people who could not be trusted. My sister said later that many people would have liked to hug me, if I had allowed them.

No one said much about why those awful things had happened. Our father reminded us that it was not his fault: Mother had drugged his coffee so that he would not waken to prevent her actions. My paternal grandfather tried to give me his best explanation to soften the blow of Mother's self-destruction: she felt bad about being so independent on other people, etc. I thought he said she had some kind of eye disease.

I loved my grandfather a lot but I said nothing. I did not believe him for a moment. It would have been disgraceful to tell him just how cynical I felt over his attempt to rationalize these events and make me feel better.

No one ever asked about my opinions of these awful developments. It appears obvious that, as a small child, any thoughts I might have had would be foolish and not worthy of discussion. My Dad was enmeshed in his own emotional conflict. In retrospect, it must have been a considerable relief to be rid of a spouse who had dominated his life with her constant need for special treatment. This relief probably heightened his feelings of guilt over his role in her illness and ultimate death.

As things happened, I had very little memory of my father during this time and nothing that indicated his concern for my feelings. Left to myself, I could nurture my own fantasies about these evil events and why they really happened. The adult world and its pretenses were irrelevant to me. I knew that I had failed and that Mother had punished me for that failure.

Not long after Mother's suicide, our father bought me an Irish Setter puppy. Unfortunately, while I was out sledding with friends, a car hit the puppy. We ate dinner that night listening to the puppy crying in the cellar. After dinner, my father and another man went down into the cellar and put the puppy in a sack. As I watched silently, they brought the puppy upstairs, took it out in the back yard, and shot it to death.

The puppy probably was to have provided me some sort of solace for a dead mother. Now, however, it was only death on top of death, this time more graphic yet. Like the first death, when Mother took her life, I was just a spectator once again. My desires did not matter to anyone. No one asked what I thought should be done with the puppy or explained why they did what they did. It probably was a money-saving decision.

Left to my own devices for coping with all this trauma, I elaborated my own explanation for everything with myself at the center. Mother had been the center of my life and my universe. She had been my reason for living and it must have been the same for her, I reasoned. Her decision to die and to abandon me without a word of farewell could only have been a statement of her bitterness and probably hatred toward me.

She knew how I would suffer with her loss, but she did not care. I must have done something terribly wrong. My pledge to save Mother from the evil influences around her had been shown to be false. Now I would have to suffer in her place. I had been a bad boy and my mother had shown me that she did not love me. Somehow I had to redeem myself with her.

Probably as a means of softening the devastation of her death, I dreamed of how things might have been so much better. Yearning for any sort of physical contact with her, I imagined her, on that night, awakening me and leading me with her down the cellar stairs. Opening the car door, she would gently offer me the opportunity to get up in the front seat where she would die.

I would respond happily, climbing up with joy. I would snuggle against her as she started the engine. We would sit close together, inhaling the same poisonous fumes. Finally, we would die, held in each others arms. This was the most wish-fulfilling scenario available to me at that time.

If Mother had only asked! But she never did.

In one form or another, the conviction that I had somehow contributed to the death of the one person I loved most in all the world stayed with me well into my adult life. I attempted to counter the awful responsibility of this notion with the belief that, in some magical way, I could bring Mother back to me if only I could prove to her that now I was a Good Boy rather than the Bad Boy she had hated. It was just too awful to think that I did not matter in her decision and she was gone forever. There had to be some way to win her back to me.

My efforts to prove to Mother that I was really not that Bad Boy went all the way from winning a Sunday School award to being awarded Social Work Order, Second Class by the Government of Vietnam to the award of a Ph.D. at Tufts University nearly 25 years later. Hope that somehow I might bring about a miracle through my good deeds alternated with rage that the miracle never came.

No one in my family came to join in celebrating my final academic achievement at Tufts University. (My grandmother had chosen to die at this inconvenient time.) This was hurtful to me but it helped confirm my suspicion that my struggle for redemption and justification through these various achievements was meaningless and futile. Mother was not coming back and I would have to learn to live without this hope. I never believed that these awards meant much in any case. If they were being given to me, they could not mean very much.

After Mother's death, our father entered into long-term psychological counseling to help him cope with the depression and feelings of responsibility that tormented him. It did not seem to occur to him or to anyone else that her children might be carrying any psychological baggage at this time. Psychological therapy was something for adults, it seems. The existing viewpoint seemed to be: "Kids are just kids and they bounce back." Nothing much to be done about it.

I went on to live a relatively ordinary childhood. Mother's suicide became a non-subject, something of which no one spoke or, hopefully, ever thought. It was as if she had simply disappeared from our lives. My father brought in a new lady to replace Mother and be my new mother. Louise showered her love and affection on me to the degree that it sometimes was embarrassing.

Unfortunately, right at the beginning, my new mother made a serious mistake. She did not like my name, Robert, and so she changed it to Rob, the nickname of her father. Typical of adults, she did not bother to ask me my opinion of my new name. I abhorred it. In my situation, I could not break away from this unwanted appellation until I had left home and it pursues me still.

This unthinking action, ignoring any feelings I might have about my name, confirmed my cynical attitude toward my place in the world. I would never fully trust anyone, always looking for the hidden motivation in others and suspecting that people always wanted to use me. I did not have the courage to declare my objection to this name, even when I grew older. I did change my name to "Bob" when I left home but this made no impression on the folks at home.

I was an untrusting person and this was especially true as concerned women. I feared that I wanted them too much which made me extremely vulnerable to be damaged. Better to limit any involvement with them to limit their ability to hurt me. It would be so easy for them to make a fool of me.

It was difficult for me to accept any positive initiatives from other persons. My most gratifying time was in my Freshman year at college when I took the role of leader of a bunch of Hell-raisers on campus. I was called in by the Dean of Students who threatened me with various consequences if I did not quiet down. I took that as a compliment — he actually thought I was important enough to merit serious punishment.

My sociability did not last. I joined a fraternity dominated by football players (mostly for their rebelliousness) but I never felt that I was part of the group. When the team quarterback congratulated me on one occasion for getting straight A's, I was startled and hardly knew how to respond. I thanked him but, in the back of my head, I was thinking, "You're just happy because I kept your fraternity off probation." I was and am embarrassed that I was so cold in response to his overture. I never knew how to respond to kindness.

As I grew older, I became more aware of how much illness, death and misery there was in my life. My grandfather, whom I had made into a substitute father, died without allowing me to visit him to say goodbye. Our father explained that Granddaddy did not want us to remember him ravaged by the effects of stomach cancer. In my view, that was another adult excuse for spitting in my face. Although I was just about to enter college, I still looked on myself as a child, almost an infant. Adults were hostile parties, just as in the days after Mother's death.

Shortly after Granddaddy died, "Fuzz" Eagleson, the high school basketball coach where I had served as his manager, died of a heart attack. I went to pay my respects at the funeral home. "Fuzz" was a sweet guy, probably too sweet to be a successful coach, and he never had a chance to live a full life. It was very painful to me. I wished I could have done something to change the way things happened.

I hoped to find a way to insulate myself from all of this distress. Since I was doing well in school, I decided that I should pursue the life of the pure scholar. I would spend my hours in libraries and live in the rarified world of ideas. This did not work out as something inside me rejected the possibility. Going into a library gave me a feeling of heaviness, so much information that I could never hope to absorb.

Ultimately, I took advantage of the developments in American policy toward Vietnam to leave graduate school and embark on the life of action and participation in major events as a Rural Development Specialist for the U.S. Agency for International Development in the rural pacification program in South Vietnam. I was also regaining contact with death since I assumed that possibilities for violence and dying would be an important part of my life as a rural development advisor in that tortured country.

To some degree, I was disappointed that everything seemed so ordinary and hum drum in the province where I first worked. I wanted to be part of historic events and I expected that to mean violence. When violence did strike our city and the U.S. military compound in particular, I was eager to run over to the hospital and report on the scenes blood and injury that sickened me.

My tour of service in Vietnam did bring me into closer contact with death, but not in the way I anticipated or would have wished. In my early months there, I was very careless about my own security. I did things that put my life at risk and was criticized for my careless behavior on several occasions. I seemed to be saying that I really did not care about my life. Nor did I take all of this very seriously as the threat of the Viet Cong uprising seemed very remote in the area of the Mekong Delta where I worked. If I died, so be it.

This equation changed when I became good friends with a young U.S. Army lieutenant, a graduate of Yale Law School, who had been assigned to work with our team in rural pacification. He was a warm and energetic person who seemed to win the affection of everyone he met, even when he could speak only a few words of their language. Most remarkably, he liked me.

Thus, setting aside my usual tactic of distant friendliness toward my fellow team members, I returned at least some of the warmth and happiness Ken showed. This friendship, which seemed to come almost out of nowhere, was the one truly valuable thing I had in my life in those days. In retrospect, it seems that I should have been more careful about my enthusiasm. Later I came to believe that one should never go too high since he will inevitably fall down just as far.

The fall was not long in coming. About three months after Ken joined our team, the Tet uprising struck our province with force. While I slept, Ken was in an Army helicopter sent out to monitor and interdict V.C. movements in our province. A rocket pod on Ken's gunship exploded killing everyone on board.

The next morning, as I entered the Vietnamese Army Headquarters, Col. Wallace, our team leader, approached me with the news of Ken's death. I immediately asked where his craft went down as I imagined, somehow that I might save him. The reply from Col. Wallace made it clear that there was no chance. I went cold, overwhelmed by the old feeling of impotence. There was nothing I could do. All was lost and I was left alone.

A few days later, I learned that another friend from school, an Army captain serving in I Corps, with whom I had kept up correspondence, had died in a freak vehicular accident in a northern province just about the same time Ken was killed. I also learned that Ken should not have been riding the doomed gunship that night. Only mechanical problems with his command helicopter had forced him into this exposed position. Thus, I saw two deaths that were travesties, destroying two valuable individuals for no reason.

As with many survivors, I wished fervently that somehow I might have exchanged my life for theirs. Both of my friends seemed to me to be individuals of great promise. It was wrong that they should die and I be left to slog along with a large empty spot in my heart feeling ashamed that I suffered not even a scratch.

Living in a chaotic time with violence all around me, I was very stimulated. I continued my pattern of showing little regard for my personal safety. When violence and possible death confronted me directly, however, I did not wait to die. I did my best to get on the floor and out of the road of any flying objects as small-arms fire erupted late at night near my apartment.

I stayed on in Vietnam for nine more months after the Tet debacle. I was deeply demoralized and was mostly serving out my time. I was very angry that I was left there to carry on some pretense of a rural development program without Ken or Tom to share my disillusionment.

Returning to finish my doctorate at Tufts, I adopted a solitary lifestyle. I was angry at everyone who had not lost as much as I had and I was sure that none of them would understand. I started finding myself more and more in conflict with other people, often for little reason. Life did not seem very good.

With the help of a friend, I was able to find a job upon finishing my doctorate. I would be coming to California to teach, fulfilling a fantasy of mine to live the glamorous life. Ironically, despite the help of old graduate school friends, I plunged deeper into isolation and depression during these first months in the place I had dreamed of.

My bitterness and suspicion of people made my first semester teaching American history at a community college into a trial for me. I suspected that all of my students were hostile toward me. They probably were justified, I felt, given the lousy job of teaching I was doing. One student showed my lack of knowledge on a relatively minor point before the class and I remember the scene to this day. I was mortified.

It was during this time that my thoughts of destroying myself became particularly intense. I took a large number of pills and proceeded to embarrass myself by calling the police who sent out a rather irritated officer to look around. I finally decided to shoot myself and ordered a pistol from a local store. I was very impatient for the background check to be completed so that I could finally have it in my hands.

That night I loaded the pistol and took it to bed with me. (I apparently wanted to die in comfort.) I pointed the barrel at my head and held it there with my finger on the trigger. I began to think of my family and the kind of impact such a death has on them. Finally, I put the weapon aside and decided to abandon my thoughts of self-destruction.

During this time, I was searching for some kind of help for the physical and mental problems that I experienced. For my insomnia, a doctor gave me valium which did no good. Another doctor did a complete physical examination which showed that there was nothing wrong with me. It is always very embarrassing to hear that nothing is wrong with you when you feel lousy.

Through a friend at my first college, I was referred to a psychologist who brought me into his group therapy program with the promise, "Try it; you'll like it." I hated it. In one early visit another group member asked me if I had any friends at all.

Group therapy completely overlooked the very strong probability that I was in the active stages of bipolar depression. Nothing was ever done to diagnose me. We were mostly told that our problems were of our own making and that we better get our s___ together. Knowing nothing better, I stuck with this program for 12 years.

During these twelve long years of group meetings — and listening to others tell me of my failings, I was able to get in better touch with various of the feelings I had suppressed for all these years. Any problems I might have only showed that I was f_____-up.

Attending group did not keep me from developing an increasingly troublesome dependence on alcohol. This became especially true after I had turned in my resignation from my teaching position, at least partly due to encouragement I received in group to "Be yourself." I might have been "being myself", but I was scared witless. I had no idea where I would go from there.

My Mexican girlfriend announced that she was going back to her home in Sinaloa, and I was feeling very much alone. I felt that I was Mother's true successor and that suicide was the appropriate way to follow in her path. I was useless just as she was useless in her mind. This time I purchased some strong rope and fashioned a noose. After some searching, I climbed up on the branch of a tree and sat there. Again, I decided against attempting death. When I told the therapist in group, he said I probably would have screwed it up, in any case.

Binge drinking provided a substitute for suicide. It was a small death in which a limited part of my life would be destroyed. Normally, I would wake up early in the morning around 4:00 a.m. I would try various ways to get back to sleep, but nothing usually worked. I would wait until just before 6:00 a.m. when I would drive to the liquor store I knew opened earliest in town. There I purchased only a few drinks and did this throughout the day.

This necessitated my going back and forth to liquor stores until I had bought enough alcohol to put me under, at least for some hours. I would not confront the reality of the situation and buy a large bottle sufficient to knock me out. Instead, I subjected myself to a kind of torture, getting out of bed to go from one liquor store to another. I went to all the different liquor stores in town in the foolish hope that no one would realize what a boozer I was.

This pattern recurred time and again. I never recognized how I was kidding myself. I would start out in the morning with two king-size beers that would ease the pain in my mind. I would always promise myself that these would be the only ones. Of course, they never were. Once started, I seemed incapable of calling a halt, to give up the temporary solace I was able to find in alcohol for those few hours.

I would proceed to try to drink enough to blot out all that day and, possibly the night, too. Sometimes I drank enough to blot out several days and nights. The longer it went, the heavier the price in guilt, fear and depression when I finally was forced to dry out. I punished myself even more because I was living in a lovely location on the beach where everyone else was glad to enjoy themselves, I believed.

The fact was, however, that my greatest wish as the start of that day began was to anesthetize myself against all the feelings that were flooding over me. These events came in cycles, probably a reflection of the patterns of bipolar depression. In between, I drank with no problems. I always knew the binges would be back, however. Our group therapist did not seem to be particularly concerned by all this. He mostly belittled me when I came in drunk or hung over.

Some years after leaving group therapy, I decided to attend A.A. — against my will as I did not believe that I was an alcoholic. I stayed with A.A. for two years, ultimately quitting because I was tired of hearing the same self-congratulatory speeches repeated. I do thank the movement as it helped me find strength in a troubled time. I got off alcohol and largely stayed off.

I was blessed that my internist finally recognized what various psychotherapists had not: I suffer from the same manic-depressive syndrome that afflicted Mother. I was able to obtain the psychiatric account of her last days of hospitalization which made chilling reading. It also confirmed my doctor's evaluation of me.

When I left A.A. and began lithium therapy, I gave up a significant part of my social world. I did not feel a part of their community anymore as I was not an alcoholic. My medical regimen has grown significantly and prohibits my taking more than small amounts of a glass of wine. I miss that.

The sophisticated medication I take each day, along with the basic lithium pills, provides me great help. It does not provide a magic solution to my distress, however. That has required long hours of taxing work with a sensitive therapist to try to get a handle on many troublesome parts of my life.

I have a medical power of attorney from Harvard Medical College. I do not expect that it will have much significance for me. There still are times when I wish that my life could be ended cleanly and simply so I would not have to deal with the sources of my distress anymore.

I know now that self-destruction is no longer an acceptable option, however appealing it might seem. I could never do such a thing, knowing what a burden it would inflict on my wife and, especially, my grandchildren. Sometimes I feel trapped and angry that I am caught this way, but I know that this is the reality.

14

◆

Asking the Right Questions

by Maureen Kramlinger

Hospice Chaplain

L IFE IS FILLED WITH QUESTIONS. Some concern everyday matters. "Where did I leave my keys?" or "What time is dinner?" Some concern matters of practical planning, "When should we replace the carpet in the living room?" Others touch on deeper and more intimate issues. "Shall we have a child? When is the right time?" Deeper still are the haunting personal questions, "What really matters to me?" The deepest questions are the *ultimate* ones, "Where have I come from? Where am I going? How am I doing? How do I know?" The way we answer the ultimate questions grounds our approach to all others.

Questions about the end of life can be approached from this perspective of levels. If we consider them only at the level of "practical planning," our answers will be superficial. Actions taken as a result of answers to superficial questions may be premature and yield far less meaning than we might otherwise gain.

The question, "Who has the right to determine the time and way of death?" addresses matters of ultimate significance, but seems to do so from the perspective of practical planning. I prefer to address questions that concern death from a deeper level of questioning. My concern is less with the details of when/how and more with the meaning of the event. To me, the real question is, "How shall I find meaning in the experience of death?"

My position on this comes from the deepest place inside me. It is grounded in a conviction that took root in me as a child, one that has deepened and been confirmed over time. Three experiences in particular shaped my conviction.

A CALL INTO A FULLNESS OF BEING

The first occurred when I was a child learning the content of my faith tradition. I was expected to learn and "know by heart" the answers to questions posed in the catechism. What the learning experience lacked in creativity was offset by my satisfaction in knowing I was learning "important stuff." That the questions were not ones I raised was immaterial. What mattered was that I was being introduced to the *important* questions, I was learning the answers, and invited to care about their significance.

To my best recollection, the first key questions were:

Who made me? *God made me.* Who is God? *God is the Supreme Being who made all things.* Why did God make me? *God made me to know, love and serve Him in this life, and to be supremely happy with Him in the next.*

When I first heard these questions, I was a little kid all too often in trouble for talking. I had a lot of ideas and an eagerness to share them with anyone who would listen. Unfortunately, my unbridled enthusiasm was not convenient for the persons in charge, and I was frequently "corrected" for talking. The scolding I received probably dampened my spirit a bit, but I took seriously what I was learning about who made me, and why, and for what.

I caught the happy implication that I mattered — *God made me.* What God makes is good, so that meant I was good (even if I did talk too much!). I took comfort and hope from knowing that I was made for good — to do good, to be good and to enjoy good. Even at that early age, I began to understand that the same was true for everybody. We all matter. We are created by God, known by God. We have a present that matters, and a future to look forward to.

That early learning carries direct implication for my response today to questions about "whose right." God always creates life. *Therefore*, life is a gift of God. It is not ours to take. Life belongs to God. We didn't make our life, so it isn't given to us to take our life. Life is entrusted to us and our job is to protect life. We are commissioned to take care of ourselves and of one another, to do the best we can with whatever life we have to work with.

Questions about the end of life are in every sense ultimate questions. They are questions about the "big picture." My understanding of the big picture is rooted in the catechism dialogue of my youth. I don't know exactly how the big picture works, but I believe that I am not my own idea. I know I did not create myself. I am sustained in being. My part is to be engaged with life, to enhance the quality of life for others, to participate in creating beauty, to companion others in good times and bad, and to hope for good to come, a good utterly beyond my ability to invent.

TUNING THE BELL

Early in my twenty's a second experience enhanced this understanding of life and its possibilities. I found a remarkable image, in a book whose author and title I can no longer remember, for God's creative work as an on-going process.

The author compared God's creative process to the work of a bell-maker. A bell-maker, he said, doesn't just "cast a bell." The project requires many steps. First, the craftsman imagines a bell, sees the possibility for a new and precious bell. Then he shapes a mold, gathers metal stock, fires it to liquid and pours it into the mold. He allows the material time to set and when the bell has formed, the bell-maker removes the mold. To the eye of the unknowing beholder the bell is finished, but the bell-maker knows better.

What the bell-maker envisions and brings into being is not merely the marriage of matter and form. The essence of the bell is expressed in the *sound* it yields when struck. In conceiving of the bell, the bell-maker imagined not only how it would look, but the unique and precious sound it would give off as well. To this end, the bell-maker continues to work on the bell, to refine its density, to "tune the bell." This work of filing and sounding, filing and sounding, takes time, attention, commitment and love.

So it is, the author said, with creating human beings. God does not simply envision the person at conception and deliver the completed product at birth. As the bell-maker sounds the bell, listens closely and refines the bell intentionally, sometimes determinedly, to tune the bell gradually to its authentic sound, so does God faithfully and creatively attend to the developing person. The tool God uses is life — everything that happens, especially "the rough edges." Through transforming presence in the midst of refining life experiences, God lovingly "tunes" the person to deliver a unique, authentic and beautiful sound.

This bell-maker image touched me deeply because it proclaimed that each human being and the coming to be of each person is a work so rich, so worthy of effort that it claims God's attention over a whole lifetime. It assured me the process of becoming oneself embraces all the odds and ends of life — the sweet and sorrowful, mundane and terrible — and incorporates them into a meaningful whole. Seeing life as "bell making" has helped me trust that every experience is pregnant with possibility whether I can see and value it or not. This image has given me a way to understand the entire span of life. It articulates a unifying theme that holds together all the seemingly unconnected or disparate elements of my life. Further, it gives me a simple way to describe the purpose of my life. By the time I die, I want to give off *exactly* the sound my Bell-Maker wants to hear. I'm not totally clear what that sound is. I imagine it to be some mixture of love, trust, compassion, courage and God knows what else. Whatever it is, I *really* want to give off that sound just right for me.

The bell and bell-maker motif affects how I answer the question about rights. I believe all of life can contribute to tuning the bell. Not only the days of vigor and beauty, youth and passion, productivity and abundance matter. Every single moment, every single experience can help a wondrous beauty come to be — including the moments leading up to death.

For ten years I watched my mother decline into Alzheimer's disease. At first she felt only the mild annoyance of "not being able to remember" this or that. Over time, she moved through feelings of sadness ("Isn't it awful to be cheated of these memories?") and terror ("Oh, Mosey, what will become of me?") into anger ("Why don't I have the checkbook — I've paid the bills all our life!") and finally into the need for, and non-anxious acceptance of, a protective environment.

On the surface, her seven years walking around a nursing home with head held high, bestowing gracious smiles, looked like a waste. At a deeper level, I believe a mystery of bell-making was being played out. Upset by the alcoholism of loved ones, my mother had prayed all her life for peace of mind. Once she entered the fog of dementia, her spirit became sweeter, her smile lovelier and the peace that surrounded her more palpable. Of course, I missed her old self and mourned that she couldn't share daily life with us, but the developments I saw convinced me that her life, just as it was, was precious and meaningful. Sitting with her filled me with a quiet joy. I believe she was a beautiful work of art, hidden and slow in the making — right up to the end.

With respect to making decisions about end of life, how are *we* to know when "the bell is finished"? If we are God's work of art, God holds the vision of the finished product. If we don't know what God has in mind, what God is creating, how can we presume to decide that the work is finished? Ending a life before God has completed it would be like inducing labor to delivering a baby prematurely. What might we risk not developing? How do we know what is being accomplished in our soul or in another's soul through the very circumstances we might deem worthless, meaningless, or inhumane?

ANOTHER WAY TO MANAGE ONE'S DEATH

The third influence that has confirmed my perspective on death is six years experience as a chaplain in hospice care. I've had the privilege of companioning countless people as they journeyed to the end of life. I have been awed watching people grow even as their bodies succumb to the claims of a terminal condition.

Ray Clarke faced his diagnosis and prognosis head on.[*] Prior to admission to hospice, he had given up his apartment and moved in with his parents. At our first meeting, he said he wanted someone to speak about him personally at his funeral service. He didn't want his parents' minister or his sister's pastor to bury him. He wanted a minister of his own choosing, one he could trust to do the job right. After our first conversation, he "hired me". His parents weren't too happy about any of this at first. They felt hurt that he didn't trust them to plan his funeral, that he didn't want their pastor, and they weren't too sure about me. In our subsequent meetings Ray's agenda was "preparing

---

[*] I am grateful to his parents who honored his wishes by granting permission to use his name.

his funeral." Working on that, he covered a lot of ground about his life, what mattered to him, what he had accomplished, what his disappointments were, who he loved, what he was proud of. His folks warmed up to me, but his dad still shook his head. "I never saw anyone plan their own funeral before," he said.

Ray was not happy to leave life early, but as he accepted what was happening in his body, he began to figure out a new way to take charge. He decided as the first one in his family to face death, he would do it with dignity and peace to "pave the way and make it easier" for his family members when their time came. He thought of leaving legacies to touch loved ones beyond his death so they'd remember he loved them. He took two of us from hospice on a field trip to show us his favorite places at the state park so we'd enjoy them after he was gone. He ordered subscriptions of **National Geographic** for his nieces, prepared gifts for friends, sat for a professional photograph for his parents, got a computer buddy to create and frame expressions of his "Last Dying Wish" for individual loved ones, including me.

Ray got anxious sometimes. He told his nurse about his fear of pain. He didn't want to suffer, didn't want his mother to have to watch him suffer. Gradually, this man who was so used to taking charge of things, who believed, "If you want something done right, do it yourself," began to trust that the nurse would help him be comfortable. Gradually, discussions about his funeral evolved from "how he wanted it" and "doing it right" to consideration of how things worked with God, what he might hope for. He began to open his heart, became able to say he was grateful for the good things he'd enjoyed in life, sorry for some things, sad about others, mad about some. Somewhere along the way he came to see that a funeral was also to comfort the living and he invited his parents' and his sister's pastors to visit him and to participate in the funeral. He began to be *really* sorry he was going to miss his funeral, because he thought it would be great!

A few days before Ray's death, he was weak, confined to bed, not able to sustain conversation. I told him it looked like the time was drawing near. I said I pictured at death that the soul opens up to be flooded with God's light and love, and that clogs of old unresolved things might impede the flow a bit. I asked would he mind if I checked with him for possible "blocks." He did fine until I asked if he held any grudges against anyone. He sure did—against his mother in law whom he held responsible for the break-up of his marriage, a major life disappointment. Letting go of that grudge felt impossible for him. He'd harbored it for years and didn't want to let her win by letting go of it, but he didn't want it to hurt him. I invited him to talk with God about it and ask God's help to resolve this. Two days later, he was much weaker, barely able to talk. I said, "I just need to ask you about one thing. What about your mother-in-law?" He waved his hand and said, "No problem."

The family kept vigil and Ray let go very peacefully. Despite their sorrow that he was gone, his parents felt amazement and great joy at what happened in him those last months. His funeral *was* great, joyful and inclusive. Ray had grown beyond planning his funeral as a practical question to celebrating it as an answer to his ultimate concern.

OVERCOMING FEAR THAT CHEATS US

What binds people to practical questions and keeps them from approaching death as ultimate concern? I think fear is the culprit. Fear compels one to focus on death as a practical event to plan, a personal right to claim, a legal right to promote. Fear presents itself in many forms — fear of pain, fear of burdening others, fear of abandonment, fear of dependency, fear of loss of control, fear of financial ruin, fear of loss of dignity, fear of the unknown. It does not seem to be fear of death itself, but fear of what one might experience *before* death that terrifies and compels some to seek a shortcut to death. Ray had many fears, but he also had Hospice. The presence and practical help he received from the nurse, chaplain and social worker allowed him to get past his fears so he could face ultimate questions, and ease into choices that meant so much to him and his family.

In six years of hospice work I have seen pain, unpleasant symptoms, social, emotional and spiritual distress. I know these sufferings occur not only in hospice patients, but in the general population as well. The *big difference* is that patients receiving hospice care get help to address and resolve distress. With the benefit of hospice, patients generally become less anxious and fearful, more confident and hopeful. They are less likely to focus on "rights" and more likely to concern themselves with living as well as they can.

A PRACTICAL ANSWER TO THE ULTIMATE QUESTIONS

*If offered early enough for maximum benefit,*** hospice care allows patients the opportunity to surface concerns, make plans and solve problems, reconcile with people and the events of life, reflect on their life and savor the blessings and challenges their life has offered. Hospice patients can have help to raise spiritual questions, to say and hear the things their hearts yearn for. They have an opportunity to complete personal business, to come to peace, and to prepare to hand themselves in trust to their Creator — or whatever they hope for in light of their beliefs. They are supported in hoping the best for their loved ones and themselves. They know that even after they have made their passage through death, bereavement care will be available for loved ones. They get "practical answers" and a multitude of effective interventions while they deal with the whole of life, including the ultimate questions.

With hospice care, people get to spend the end of their lives, "getting their cup filled," so that when the time is right, they flow over the edge. Not only do patients get filled by the love and care of their family and friends. In some mysterious way, those who are "filling the patient's cup" find their own cup filled in the process. One consolation for the family later is to be able to say, "We loved him well right up to the end. We did all we could for her. He was comfortable and at peace. It was her time." Convictions such as these are of immeasurable help in coming to resolution of grief.

In light of my belief about Who made us and to Whom we belong, my understanding of each life as the focus of God's creative attention, and my hospice experience of witnessing amazing development in patients and families living through the final days of an illness, I think the right to determine the end of life belongs to God — not as a "legal right" but as something inherently suitable and right. It is right that God as the one who calls human persons into life and into unimaginable fullness of life choose the time and way of this transition.

Having said that, I acknowledge that living creatively up to and through death is not easy. Every situation bears unique challenges. Some decisions call for exquisitely sensitive discernment of what's best. Terminally ill or declining chronically ill people have a right to all their questions. However,

---

** Hospice is available to people with a prognosis of six months or less. Unfortunately, many patients are not referred (or do not accept a referral) to Hospice until shortly before their death.

I think they are best served when we help them get past their fears and sup-port them to ask the right questions.

How do we know what *are* "the right questions"? I believe they're the ones that help people live up to and through death. I believe they're the ones that help people become their full and completed selves: "How shall I find meaning in the experience of death? How shall I use even this event to ring out the beautiful, authentic sound just right for me?"

15

◆

Euthanasia — Considering Death Over Life
A Psychologist's Perspective
by David R. Cox, Ph.D., ABPP

BEEP..BEEP..BEEP..BEEP.." My pager was sounding and lit up with a telephone number followed by the code 911. Emergency. I got up from the Board of Directors meeting into which I had just settled and reached for my phone.

"You've got to come quick. They say my father burst an aneurysm and may not make it. I need you..." I received calls like this before, especially when working full-time in hospital settings. However, this time, it was different. This time, I was responding to a call from my wife...

Jumping on the next plane, we flew to New York and rushed to the hospital. My father-in-law had been a walking time bomb. For years, he had cardiovascular problems as well as an abdominal aortic aneurysm. It was amazing that he had not passed away within five minutes of the burst aneurysm. Somehow, emergency medical technicians had gotten on the scene rapidly enough to keep him alive. When we arrived at the hospital, he was in emergency surgery. The hours and days that followed took me through an experience with my own family quite similar to those that I had been through on numerous occasions before with others.

The fact that this occurred the week I had promised this chapter was especially uncanny.

The 72 hours that ensued following my being paged took myself and the rest of our family through the gamut of emotion — anxiety, fear, fantasy, depression, prayer and eventual resolve that I have seen on numerous occasions. This time, though, I wasn't there simply as an outsider — a relatively detached professional — but, rather, as a family member with the mixed blessing of understanding all of the medical and psychological issues with which we were all trying to deal. This time, very personal feelings had to be weighed in with what usually was provided as a compassionate, yet objective professional opinion.

END OF LIFE ISSUES AND EUTHANASIA

Euthanasia. These days the term, and act, is at least openly discussed. Most of us in the medical professions know that for years it was not spoken of even though the act certainly occurred. Euthanasia as a concept and act has significant implications to many individuals and families. It may be perceived by some as the act of an irrational individual, by others as rational suicide and by yet others as murder (when it is assisted).

It is not my intention to sway the reader in one direction or the other with respect to "right or wrong". In fact, I'm not entirely certain that I yet have a firm stance on this. I see "both sides" of this issue in my professional work and understand the perspective from which persons argue pro and con. I understand the multitude of reasons that a person might consider ending life, decline medical care, or go the other direction and decide to fight a condition "against all odds". These are not easy problems with which we grapple, regardless of the decision that is made after careful consideration. And hopefully, one does give such a weighty issue careful consideration. My hope is that by sharing some of the issues that I have had occasion to help patients and loved ones consider, and now dealt with from a much more personal perspective, the reader will understand the very difficult thought process that is required of a person, their loved ones, and the medical professionals, taking a considered approach to life versus death.

As stated, this thought process is not required solely of the individual who is ill or injured. It is also required of the healthy loved ones and medical professionals in that person's life — for they must deal with the topic even if they are given no significant say in the matter. They may have to live with the decision, though the decider of fate has since passed away. Or they may be forced to take a more active role, whether through emotional pleadings from others or medical/legal requests or mandates.

Why a Psychologist?

The work of a psychologist is commonly misunderstood. Mention that I am a psychologist and many people respond by "Oh, I could use your advice" or "Oh, no...I'm not crazy, am I?". But psychologists do much more in our health care system (and elsewhere, for that matter) than many people realize. My work as a psychologist has not been limited to helping people with "difficulties in living", as might be portrayed to the public on the television show *Fraser* or the older *Bob Newhart Show*. Neither has it concentrated solely on those with severe mental illness as depicted publicly in popular films like *One Flew Over the Cuckoo's Nest*. Rather, in addition to my office, my work has taken me from intensive care unit to locked psychiatric unit, to jails to pediatric wards and elsewhere. Patients with a variety of problems, to a large degree directly related to medical illness as opposed to a purely "mental illness", have either been referred to me or sought out my assistance. Although many of life's difficulties do not require medical attention, relatively few serious illnesses or injuries are free from psychological difficulties. It is with those people who have emotional and physical ailing that I have worked most.

Within this realm, I have had many occasions to interact with people debating the decision of life versus death. The issue of death has come up in a variety of ways. Suicide is not an uncommon issue of discussion in my line of work. In fact, most of the patients that I have evaluated and/or treated have struggled with this at one time or another. They may be desperately emotionally stressed and see suicide as their best, or at least seemingly simplest, solution or escape. Many survivors of traumatic injury or serious illness wonder, "Would I be better off dead?" Some other patients are not struggling with whether to bring on their own death, but have already faced death acutely through heart-stopping cardiopulmonary arrest or severe brain trauma from an automobile accident. Yet others have to face death on a daily basis as they fight life-threatening cancer or autoimmune disease. They all confront death, their mortality and the very real and practical issues that exist in deciding if life is worth living. "Would my family be better off without me?", "You call *this* living?", and other such struggles are voiced silently or out loud as they try to make sense out of their current condition, their future (if they decide to have one) and the stresses of living with terminal illness, chronic disability or presumed ineffectiveness and unimportance.

The "Mind-Body" Dichotomy

Over the years my work with a variety of patients has ranged from those with severe problems such as schizophrenia and other conditions traditionally viewed as "mental illness" to others whose primary diagnosis is traumatic brain injury or a cancerous brain tumor — conditions generally viewed as "physical illness". I have come to firmly believe that the distinction between mental and physical illness is a false one. Not only is it false, but it is also misleading and seriously detrimental to individuals as well as society as a whole. It has led to a perception that there is a dissociation between physical and emotional well being, and in so doing has led to a socially acceptable denial of the responsibility one has in regard to how one's behavior and emotion effects one's physical health. As well, it has led to neglect, within society and the medical community, of the serious effects that physical ailments can have on one's emotional and behavioral well being.

This is not to deny that there are issues that are psychological (mental) processes relatively (or perhaps entirely) free from physical "illness", but rather the two are inexorably intertwined and therefore to *totally* separate them is a critical mistake. Mental processes are not predetermined, biologically-driven events over which we have no control — and therefore need claim no responsibility. The physical and mental interact and are interdependent. Just as an automobile engine requires both gasoline and an engine to operate, the human body requires both mental and physiological processes to "operate" as we know it. The problem comes in measuring whether or not these aspects — mental processes and physiological processes — are functioning, and functioning properly.

What of the Spirit?

Let's make this scenario more complicated yet.

In addition to the physical and emotional status of an individual, I believe that the spiritual well being is equally, if not more, important in one's life. Spiritual issues almost invariably come up in my practice, as people either struggle to find meaning in life or explain their faith as one reason they are able to go on living despite exceedingly difficult circumstances. It is common for me to hear from my patients with brain tumors that their faith keeps them fighting the cancer. It is also common to hear from survivors of traumatic brain injury, or others with chronically disabling conditions, that the injury or illness has left them with a new-found positive perspective in life — with a renewed and revised sense of the priorities in life. They frequently indicate to me how they now see the importance and value of things previously minimized or dismissed (such as relationships and time with people) and the relative unimportance of "worldly" material items. I give thanks to my patients in this regard, as they are constant reminders to me of the priorities in life that are so easily overlooked or taken for granted by those of us who are relatively "well".

People familiar with the writings of Victor Frankl, the psychiatrist, founder of Logotherapy and survivor of Nazi concentration camps, recognize this theme. Those not familiar with his writings owe it to themselves and their loved ones to read his book **Man's Search for Meaning**. Professionals dealing with these issues will hopefully be familiar with that as well as his book **The Doctor and the Soul**. Dr. Frankl is one of many authors to write about overcoming tremendous odds, severely depressing environments, and ghastly horrors to see the strength of the human soul and the tremendous significance of personal meaning as a reason for being.

Again, Why a Psychologist?

Now, need we still ask? If so, consider the following...

The Operation was a "Success" but...

Most of us have heard the line "The operation was a success but the patient died." Dark, "MASH-style" humor has increasingly crept into our lives as technology has brought new and better ways to save lives and heal many ailments. But, at times, the person we are left with reminds us little of the person who was.

We have come to a point in our society where we believe we can measure life and death. We rely heavily on instrumentation such as electrocardiograms and electroencephalograms to "tell" us if the heart and brain are functioning, respectively. It has long been taken for fact (and I am not necessarily disputing this) that if the heart is not beating for an extended period of time a person may be pronounced dead. The advent of improved emergency medical care has resulted in inventions that can keep a person's heart beating, keep a person breathing, and essentially keep a person "alive" in a situation that, without such medical devices, would otherwise result in death.

Years ago, I worked at a top-rank university medical training hospital and Level I trauma center (where the most serious emergency injuries are treated). Despite being one of the nation's leaders in trauma care for persons who had sustained serious brain injury, it was not until the mid 1980s that the medical center established, through the work of the Medical Ethics Committee and others, a policy on "brain death". Part of the struggle was that (for example) patients would be flown into the hospital and could be kept "alive" from a cardiopulmonary standpoint, yet may have no apparent brain activity — there was a "flat line" on the electroencephalogram. This could be interpreted to indicate that some patients might be determined to be "dead" except for the equipment keeping them alive. Our task was to address this issue, and help establish some guidelines for evaluation and treatment of such patients. Should they continue to be aggressively treated for infection, etc? Or were the doctors treating what, but for the presence of life-support machinery, was essentially a cadaver? When is a person "brain dead?" This is but one example of how our scientific advances have resulted in medical-ethical dilemmas.

In such a situation, where a patient is for all practical purposes dead (or likely would be without life-sustaining equipment), who makes the decision to treat or not, withhold or withdraw treatment, or even potentially provide medications that may hasten death? In cases of cancer, it is not uncommon to provide narcotic medication for much-needed pain relief, knowing that the medication has as a side effect a tendency to hasten death. Assuming you can agree that such pain relief treatment is acceptable (and you may or may not believe it is), would it also be acceptable to provide such "treatment" for a patient in a coma, who can not complain of pain? What about in a conscious individual who can not communicate to us his/her pain, but we truly believe is in significant pain? When are these types of decisions acceptable, and who makes them? I do not know that there are clear answers to these questions. Indeed, I know that there are *not* clear answers — I have helped too many medical teams and families try to reach an accord on these emotionally-laden and complex issues.

Consider the case of my father-in-law. After his surgery, he was on a respirator that helped him breath. His kidneys were failing and he was going to require dialysis — something that he had vehemently expressed he did not want prior to this incident, and continued to insist that he did not want after his surgery. On top of this, he had a cardiac pacemaker that had been implanted several years previously. With all of this technological assistance, there was no way that he was going to die in the traditional sense so long as the electricity was available to run the equipment. Sustaining life was guaranteed. He did, however, have brain activity and could communicate. Despite his ability to communicate his wishes, the decision to discontinue the use of technological equipment that was keeping him alive was an emotional struggle for most all of us.

Quantity is not Quality

In our daily life, we have surely all heard that our kids need our quality time, not just a quantity of time. How do we know if the time we spend with them is quality, not just quantity? We know that the term "quality" is open to various interpretations, and probably quite justly so. What is quality time for one parent and/or child may not be considered quality by another, and vice versa, because what is reinforcing and rewarding varies from person to person.

Similarly, our current medical technology tends to measure only the presumed presence or absence of life. Is "life" there or not? What about cases where "life" is measured to be present (cardiopulmonary activity and brain activity are present, even if supported by equipment), but there appears to be no "quality of life"? How do we measure "quality" of life? What of the circumstances where someone in a coma for an extended period of time later recovers? I have had occasion to work with many such individuals and their families. More than once, I have prepared a family for the death of their loved one, and the patient surprised us all by not only surviving but recovering dramatically! As one can then readily see, quality life might be presumed to either be present or laying dormant, awaiting revival, in such persons.

Assessing the quality of life of a person in coma ("What quality?", one may ask) or with severe cognitive or physical deficits is not necessarily more simple than establishing "quality" determinations with an individual who can provide self-report of his/her feelings and experiences. For example, a person living with chronic pain may complain of a very poor quality of life. Is that person's quality of life better or worse than the other person — who lies in a coma? I can not answer that question. This is such a subjective issue that to believe that anyone other than the individual can truly answer such a question is to believe that we are privy to the innermost thoughts and experiences of that person. What if the person has "let her wishes be known" such as in the case of a living will? Then, at least, we have some directive from the individual, though it was prepared at a different time than it is being carried out. That certainly seems to help — and I wish to emphasize *seems* because it may make those who carry out the person's previously stated wishes feel better. Yet it does not truly address the quality issue at the moment of decision. We simply do not know the person's internal experience at that time unless they are able to express it to us. This type of scenario raises the issue of competency to make decisions, sanity, pressure etc. It is at these times that a psychologist is frequently consulted.

Competency to Decide

When competency issues are raised (or even when they are not) one must consider the effects of a number of variables on the individual. Are the effects of pain so difficult to stand that the person is making a poor decision solely to escape what might be medicated away? Are the effects of the medications clouding the person's reasoning, memory, and perhaps even will?

So, in considering life or death, I feel compelled to address the physical, mental and spiritual issues involved — as well as the obligatory medical-legal issues. Legal issues are frequently the entry into such cases, as the issue of competency of an individual to make decisions often is referred to a psychologist. Competency is an interesting area of our work, as it is, in many cases, not clear cut at all. As well, there are various types of competency — competency to manage funds, competency to make medical decisions, competency to stand trial. The issues and factors involved in evaluation of a person's competency are considered in light of the circumstances for which the determination is being made. Strictly speaking, *competency* becomes a legal determination that is based, at least in part, on the person's *capability* to engage in rational decision making.

Can one who is competent choose death? Some, many of my professional colleagues among them, would suggest that an individual who makes such a decision may be incompetent by default — the very act of choosing to die being the defining act of incompetence. Don't you have to be crazy to elect death over life? Isn't such an act suicide — and isn't suicide in and of itself simply an act of desperation, poor decision making or mental illness — in other words, the result of incompetence?

Such is not, strictly by definition, the case. This becomes an argument for the philosophers, medical ethicists, priests and ministers. One's spiritual and religious beliefs weigh heavily in this type of decision — laying the groundwork for heated debate, emotional controversy, and potentially family discord.

We were blessed to have my father-in-law regain consciousness sufficiently to be able to clearly communicate "yes" and "no" responses in various ways despite not being able to speak to us. This allowed us to be quite certain that he understood us and the doctors and was expressing his will. This potentially saved us tremendous difficulty in making decisions for him, as it was clear that he was capable and competent to make his own decisions. It was also becoming quite clear that if he was not able to make his decisions there may be some rift between members of the family.

THE CONTINUUM OF LIFE'S MARCH TOWARD DEATH:
Are Bad Habits Suicide? Is Euthanasia Suicide, Murder, or What?

As has been pointed out to most of us,"The only two sure things are death and taxes." However, I have heard of people who have avoided taxes. Death, on the other hand, is a certain eventuality. It is absolutely inevitable. At least in reference to death of the biological entity that we refer to as our body here on earth. Certainly, many people believe in the eternal life of the soul, and that spiritual issue is one which will be addressed somewhat later in this chapter, as it is a critical factor in the decision making process of many people as they contemplate death. But it is rarely argued that our biological beings cease to function at some point. We call that death. We can hasten it, and we can even postpone it, but we can not deny it.

When do bad habits like excessive smoking, alcohol or drug abuse, or even eating become suicide? We know that many of these behaviors contribute significantly to medical conditions that hasten death. The relatively recent book, **How We Die: Reflections on Life's Final Chapter**, points out well some of the patterns of our lives that bring us closer to death on a daily, and often habitual, basis.

Everyone, I believe without exception, engages in some activity or activities that *could* hasten their death. Simply crossing the street is indeed a risk (and in some cities, at certain spots, perhaps it could be considered by some attempted suicide!) Cigarette smoking has been well proven to increase the likelihood of cancer, heart disease, stroke and other illnesses that can lead to death. Playing "Russian Roulette", while not something in which most of us would engage, does not necessarily lead to death — so is it an attempt to hasten death or merely an exciting, albeit risky, game? Is it a suicide attempt? If so, what of smoking or dashing across a busy street? Parachuting? Riding a motorcycle without a helmet? Are they behaviors with an associated risk factor, or are they "suicide with a long fuse" or "a suicide attempt with a lower risk of actual death"?

Psychologists and other mental health professionals are very familiar with persons who make suicidal "gestures". These are incidents of taking an overdose of a non-lethal medication, for example, or of superficially wounding one's wrist with plastic knife. This occurs in a number of persons who are distressed and is often viewed and interpreted as a "cry for help". This type of behavior is important in the context of considering euthanasia as a concept, because it might be that the request to end one's life is a "cry for help" that is not truly intended to result in the act of euthanasia.

Passive Death by Refusal of Intervention versus Active Euthanasia

Most of us can more readily understand a choice that a person may make to let one's life go versus take one's life. Choosing to let the course of an illness or injury continue with limited or no medical intervention seems inherently different than choosing to hasten death. It is frequently, but not always, at this point that most of us "get stuck" on this issue of euthanasia and end-of-life issues. Many people, though, also have difficulty with refusal of intervention.

A decision of — or even the initiation of discussion of — taking one's life in an active fashion can bring about heated and emotional conversation. In others, it can lead to a refusal to have conversation. "We wont' even consider such absurdity" or "How can you even say such a thing?" are not atypical responses from some when this topic arises. Communication is essential in resolving emotional conflict among persons, yet we so often refuse to communicate about the very issues over which we are conflicted. This inevitably leads to discord and upset among family members, often resulting in painful and prolonged legal battles over estates and such.

The various authors in this compilation address the issue of active euthanasia quite well. There is no need to reiterate thoughts provided eloquently elsewhere. I leave you with one notion from the standpoint of a psychologist who has been involved — both as an outsider and an insider — in this area. Communicate your wishes clearly in advance of the need to do so, and understand and respect the wishes of others regarding whom you may need to make decisions.

Remember, physicians take the Hippocratic Oath, an oath to protect and sustain life, and the concept of not doing everything possible to sustain life may be a dilemma for a physician. Most have adopted personal/professional attitudes that include some level of decision making regarding when it might be appropriate to discontinue care. The continuum, however, can vary greatly from doctor to doctor. When possible, having a discussion with your physician about end of life issues prior to needing to make decisions is important — although it is recognized that circumstances do not always permit this in advance of need. Your physician and family members should know your desires in advance of the time when critical decisions need be made. If need be, consult a psychologist in advance to help work through difficult aspects of this complex decision making — and do it before you need to page him or her emergently...

REFERENCES

Frankl, Victor E., *Man's Search for Meaning: An Introduction to Logotherapy*. Beacon Press, Boston, 1959.

Frankl, Victor E., *The Doctor and the Soul: From Psychotherapy to Logotherapy*. Second, expanded edition. Alfred A. Knopf, New York, 1965.

Nuland, Sherwin B., *How We Die: Reflections on Life's Final Chapter*. Alfred A. Knopf, New York, 1994.

Section Six

16

---◆---

What We Should Do Besides Killing People

by Barry Eliot Cole, M.D., M.P.A.
Administrator, National Pain Data Bank and Pain Program Accreditation,
American Academy of Pain Management
Sonora, CA

I MUST NOT GET IT!

Since when is killing someone who might be nearing the end of life appropriate? Why is killing someone who is suffering from a serious medical illness or even a terminal condition the best that we can offer? What about all of the wonderful technology that now exists? What about all of the new medications that keep coming out on the market? What about the changes in state laws that make strong pain relieving medications more available and lessen the risk for physicians prescribing them?

What has happened to our society and to us that we would enthusiastically look to euthanasia and physician-assisted suicide as the best solutions for the medically ill? With all of the wonderful techniques, skills and medications available for relieving pain, physical symptoms and suffering, the increasing interest in and provision of hospice care, and a desire by most people to put an end to violence, how ironic that we would even consider euthanasia as the best option.

One of the core principles of the Judeo-Christian tradition deals directly with murder. According to these teachings and beliefs we shall not commit murder. "Shall not" is the same as "no," and "do not do this." What part of "no" is not clear? Murdering people is wrong and euthanasia is just another form of murder. Deliberately taking any life is murder regardless of the underlying motivations. To clean up the fact that murder is somehow not wrong when we perform acts of euthanasia we rationalize what is being done by claiming that "merciful killing" is beneficial. Merciful killing is beneficial for whom? Is it beneficial for the people suffering from unpleasant illnesses or for those who watch loved ones suffering?

I am not naive. As a psychiatrist for two decades it is clear to me that those wanting to die do not need my help in any way. They are perfectly able to jump from high places, cut their wrists, put guns in their mouths, hang themselves, drive their cars into immovable objects and take any number of different household poisons. Physicians have little to offer those bound on self-destruction considering the wide range of readily available means that are highly effective in the community. Physicians and other health care professionals are only able to help those who are ambivalent about dying and desire help. Practitioners cannot be everywhere and importantly cannot be all things to all people all of the time.

Are there other options for the potentially terminally ill beyond killing them? I believe that there are many options available and none of them involve the deliberate taking of life. What drives the desire for an early demise may be the fear that the system is not able to deal with end-of-life care? That when we become too ill we will be abandoned by our loved ones and caregivers, left with broken bodies and in terrible pain that cannot be relieved. Are these the reasons that leave so many people sadly believing that suicide and euthanasia are their best and only options?

LESSONS FROM THE EDUCATION FOR PHYSICIANS ON END-OF-LIFE CARE (EPEC) CURRICULUM

The Institute for Ethics of the American Medical Association developed the Education for Physicians on End-of-life Care (EPEC) curriculum in 1999 with a grant from the Robert Wood Johnson Foundation to educate 750,000 American physicians about palliative care for the terminally ill. While not the only curriculum dealing with the care needs of the terminally ill, the EPEC curriculum has become the most widely publicized and universally distributed program. Many of my ideas come from the EPEC curriculum.

Physician-assisted suicide and euthanasia are ancient medical issues. We have not just stumbled on to these topics in recent times. Physician-assisted suicide involves the aiding or causing of a suffering person's death whereby the physician provides the means to commit suicide, but the patient performs the act of self-destruction. Euthanasia involves the physician performing the life ending intervention, with or without the permission of the patient. It is thought that most physicians receive requests for assistance with dying and such requests are usually signs of patient crises.

For practitioners there are serious legal and ethical concerns about assisting people to commit suicide or actively taking their lives. Practitioners have an obligation to relieve pain and suffering, and to respect decisions to forgo life-sustaining treatment. Rather than rushing to extinguish life, the EPEC curriculum provides a logical approach for responding to requests for assistance with suicide.

Although the United States Supreme Court has recognized that there is no fundamental right to assistance with suicide it has turned the debate over to the individual states to resolve. While the legal status of physician-assisted suicide can possibly differ from state to state, only Oregon has made such assistance legal as of 1999.

WHY DO PATIENTS ASK THEIR HEALTH CARE PRACTITIONERS FOR ASSISTANCE COMMITTING SUICIDE?

Some patients suffer a crisis of confidence about the goals of their treatment or the management of their many physical and psychological problems. Others have profound fears about possibly suffering with their conditions and they develop concerns about potentially losing control or becoming burdensome for others. Those who experience depression or high levels of pain may become likely to seek professional assistance in ending their lives. Because of this desperation, professional caregivers must be able to work with seriously ill people and to help them find alternatives other than assisted-suicide.

Many physicians sadly believe that they are not adequately trained to address end-of-life issues. Others are just too busy to provide the comprehensive care necessary to manage patients with serious and life-threatening illnesses. The lack of reimbursement and the need to see large numbers of people in managed care environments causes many physicians to just not address requests for suicide in any way.

What is first needed when practitioners are faced with requests for assistance committing suicide is for these practitioners to clarify what the requesters desire. What are the requesters actually trying to achieve? Not every request for assistance must be acted upon. Not every requester is actually making a direct request for immediate death. There may be many other issues to resolve.

Requests must be examined carefully and critically to determine the underlying root causes. These requests involve the provision of education about the legal and ethical alternatives for symptom control, the ability to limit the scope and duration of selected treatments, along with promoting greater levels of physical and psychological comfort.

To thoroughly clarify requests for assistance with suicide practitioners must demonstrate their immediate concern and compassion. These are not the "problems" that are adequately explored in the hallway or in five-minute office visits. Practitioners must determine if requesters are motivated to kill themselves because of underlying thoughts (ideation) regarding suicide, direct disease effects, medication toxicity or other issues. For safety reasons practitioners must be able to determine if their patients are imminently prepared to act upon well formulated plans (intent to act) that are likely to be successful. Practitioners must be aware of any personal biases they may have about suicide, about people asking them for help committing suicide, and their potential to respond negatively toward requesters (counter-transference). If practitioners will not address these issues they cannot effectively care for their patients.

To fully determine the underlying causes behind requests for suicide, practitioners should consider four major dimensions of suffering motivating people to end their lives prematurely: physical, psychological, social and spiritual. Practitioners must focus on the fears of requesters about the future and their potential for underlying depression and anxiety. To do this there must always be an assessment made for clinical depression. Serious depression is too often under-diagnosed and under-treated despite the availability of potent and effective medications. Depression may be the single most significant source of suffering and the greatest barrier for sufferers to have a "good death" without having to commit suicide.

While diagnosing depression in the setting of serious medical illnesses may initially appear challenging for practitioners, because physically ill people have overlapping symptoms with those having depression, making the depression diagnosis does not have to be difficult at all. In the absence of physical symptoms, especially in the face of complaints about significant preoccupation with themes of helplessness, hopelessness and worthlessness, the diagnosis is essentially self-evident. There are no special laboratory tests to confirm the diagnosis of depression. Depression is a clinical diagnosis. Failing to make the depression diagnosis condemns patients to early deaths. With the modern and very safe medications available for the treatment of depression there are no valid reasons to withhold these remarkable therapeutic agents.

Often the motivation for life termination involves intense psychosocial suffering related to very practical concerns. The sick may have elements of shame about their underlying illnesses or the circumstances by which they came to have these conditions. Many people may not feel particularly needed or wanted any longer as they develop progressive debilities. They may experience difficulties coping with their duties, responsibilities and activities of living. Some may experience losses of bodily function, self-image, decision-making control and independence. Already difficult and strained relationships become further disrupted because of these and other issues eventually leading to increasing isolation, abandonment and despair. Concerns about who will serve as caregivers, how domestic chores will be accomplished, and who will care for dependents and cherished pets may all exacerbate the emotional distress of seriously ill people contemplating self-annihilation.

Physical suffering is very difficult for most people to handle under the best of circumstances. The infliction of pain serves as the basis for torture. The sick and their caregivers may both wish for life ending strategies when pain becomes severe. Being in pain is awful for all of us. The sick have to deal with pain and so many other issues. Caregivers feel helpless standing by while loved ones are in agony.

Physical symptoms such as breathlessness from progressive lung disease, wasting from anorexia, progressive weakness and fatigue cause many sick people to consider suicide. Nausea and vomiting, massive swelling (edema), loss of bowel and bladder control (incontinence) producing foul odors in addition to the pain and other physical problems collectively contribute to questions about the meaning, value and purpose of life.

It is not unusual to encounter tragically afflicted people who believe that God has personally abandoned them in their hours of need or that God is punishing them for past their transgressions. Sadly, many believe that only through purification by pain and punishment can they be redeemed. These issues causing spiritual suffering may be more painful and difficult to handle than the physical and psychological aspects of being illness. When these people doubt their own self worth and question their underlying faith traditions it is likely that they will become angry and profoundly depressed with little belief that there are any reasons to seek help. Skillful and experienced clinicians must be able to reach out to these people and bring them back from their suicidal desperation.

People are rather vain. None wants to imagine a future without self-efficacy, decision-making capacity and independence. The aged in our country know best what it is like to survive their cherished friends and family members. They know too well what it is like to become abandoned, forgotten and alone in the world due to their progressive debilitation to the point where they are no longer able to even minimally care for themselves. These are very frightening prospects for most of people, but these are usually resolvable problems and not valid reasons just to kill the ill!

TREATMENT CHOICES BEYOND ASSISTED-SUICIDE

As professional caregivers we must affirm our commitment to care for all of our patients. We must learn to listen to what is said and to acknowledge the feelings and fears that our patients bring to their appointments. Practitioners must clarify and expand their role in caring for their seriously ill patients to address the psychosocial needs. Practitioners must become committed to finding solutions, exploring current concerns and addressing the roots causes for suicide requests.

Addressing the root causes necessitates professional competence in withholding and withdrawing medical care, aggressively providing comfort measures, following palliative care principles and utilizing the services of local palliative care programs. Doing these things does much to allay suffering and fear.

Practitioners must carefully treat depression, anxiety and delirium whenever it exists. Without first controlling and relieving these serious problems it is never possible to fully respond to requests for assistance with suicide. Some requesters may benefit from individual or group therapy and have an opportunity to talk about their troubled feelings and worries. Others need assurances about the care of their loved ones. They may be comforted working with a professional to bring their legal affairs to order or to have some ability to determine the scope, location and duration of treatment.

Treatment choices for serious depression, underlying requests made for assistance with suicide, depend upon the time available for therapeutic response. The most rapidly acting medications are not traditional antidepressants but the faster-acting psychostimulants. When time is plentiful and the requester is less fragile more traditional therapeutic agents include the newer selective serotonin reuptake inhibitors (SSRIs), newer atypical molecules and the older tricyclic antidepressants. All have the capacity to relieve depression and to potentially help the suicide requester when motivated out of despair.

How anxiety and depression influence pain intensity is a complicated issue. Anxiety and depression may be the consequences of unrelieved pain. Pain produces considerable distress for patients, causing anxiety, depression, and hostility interfering with the quality of life. Anxious or depressed patients who are in pain should initially be treated with analgesics to reduce their pain. If anxiety and depression persist after their pain is substantially relieved, more traditional mental health interventions are indicated.

Since the late 1980s we have assumed that cancer patients could not participate in rehabilitation programs and so we have provided cancer pain sufferers with a wide range of therapeutic options from high dose opioid analgesics to anesthetic blocks to neuro-destructive lesioning. As long as the patients were determined by their physicians to be terminally ill, with less than a year of life expected, a "no holds barred" approach to controlling their pain was taken. In doing so, a great many Americans died far better in the last decade than in previous modern decades. The addition of hospice to end-of-life care permitted the exploration of the role of anticipatory bereavement, spiritual needs and psychosocial support for the terminally ill and their family members.

To control pain we might initially consider anti-inflammatory agents and opioid analgesics. To take the edge off of any underlying inflammatory process anti-inflammatory agents would prove very useful, whether non-steroidal or steroidal in their composition. The use of these medications would allow us to control the toxic chemical events leading to the sensitization of the nervous system and the further experience of pain in response to disease or illness. Opioid analgesics could then be added upon this base of inflammation control to maximize comfort.

What about opioid analgesics? They can be used in any setting, and their benefits generally outweigh their few significant risks such as sedation, constipation, nausea and vomiting, itching and respiratory depression. Providing opioid analgesics is the standard of care for end-of-life pain management. We must be aware that the optimal analgesic dose varies widely among patients.

The factors that limit our use of these opioid medications usually involve patient and professional barriers. Patients are concerned that they might get "hooked" on the medication, or might appear weak if they cannot handle the pain that others can. Practitioners, especially those who prescribe opioid analgesics, worry that too much medication could cause respiratory arrest, that controlling the pain might mask emerging problems, or that patients might not want the side effects associated with starting opioid medications. Due to knowledge deficits about opioids there is still an erroneous belief that a very narrow continuum exists between prescribing opioids for pain, obtaining pain relief, inducing sedation, creating respiratory depression and eventually the death of the patient.

Why not focus on pain management near the end of life? Why not utilize every medication available, including opioid analgesics, to reduce or eliminate pain? How many elderly cancer patients do we hear about stealing money from the church collection plates to buy drugs? Where is the runaway drug problem we hear about that allegedly comes from giving prescription medications to people in pain? Why do we ever ration opioid analgesics for terminally ill patients?

Making cancer patients comfortable is not difficult. It is clear that cancer patients are going to eventually die from their underlying disease, not because of the analgesics we offer. Our task with palliative care is not to necessarily prolong life at any cost, but to improve the quality of the days remaining. We are not withdrawing all support, only changing the focus of the care provided. When our intent is the relief of pain and suffering, then we are justified in offering whatever analgesic medications, in whatever doses, are necessary to modify the pain. Giving enough medication to make patients comfortable is not passive euthanasia. Giving enough medication to relieve pain is the physician's duty.

Many physicians believe that they could risk disciplinary action if they use high doses of opioid analgesics or other controlled substances to manage pain. They believe that if they under treat pain they face no risk of professional consequences. They fail to understand that patients have the right to adequate pain medication. Physicians have successfully defended the withholding of pain medication by claiming that no clear guidelines existed about how to provide adequate pain care. With the emergence of national, state and medical board guidelines concerning the relief of pain, physicians cannot make such claims any longer.

We have to do a better job managing pain in America if we want to help our patients to not feel they must die to get pain relief. We must get past any barriers preventing us from making patients comfortable. We must aggressively eliminate physical suffering before we can ever consider assisting any suicide. We must educate our patients and their families to demand adequate pain management services, to utilize these techniques and services without fear, shame or guilt, and work with health care educators and policy makers to set aside the 90-year experiment in unnecessary opioid regulation.

We can control physical symptoms with the assistance of physical and occupational therapies, access to pastoral care services, and adequate amounts of medication to control pain, breathlessness, nausea and vomiting. Without the help of a minister, priest, rabbi or other pastoral representative there can be no exploration of the meaning of the suffering, the purpose of life and the preparatory work to close one's life.

WHAT MUST BE DONE TO HELP PEOPLE
PREPARE FOR A NATURAL DEATH?

It is so unfair to deprive people of their final opportunity for gift giving and establishing a legacy by ending their lives prematurely. The final aspects of life may provide the greatest opportunities for personal growth, the settling of old scores, and the passing on of traditions. If we can make the ill physically and psychologically comfortable why would we need to kill them?

We must address the fears of the seriously ill about their loss of control. We must explore areas of their lives dealing with efficacy, accomplishment and independence. We must accept that patients ultimately have legal rights concerning their own medical care, and as such may accept or refuse any medical intervention, including those intended for life prolongation. Those with serious illnesses who are not wishing to continue life-sustaining therapies may "opt out" at any time by forgoing further treatment (dialysis, intravenous fluids and nutrition, or receiving antibiotics with bouts of serious infections). By doing so, these people may select comfort care over curative care when cure is no longer possible.

To make this outcome likely each of us must select personal advocates and proxies for making health care decisions when we are no longer able to decide for ourselves. We must prepare written advance directives and face the inevitability of our own deaths. We must make a commitment to aid patients and loved ones as much as possible to maintain control. We must control pain and other bothersome symptoms.

Knowledge is power and patients deserve full explanations about their diseases, the techniques used to control bothersome symptoms, and the expected course with or without treatment. Those wishing to be sedated to help manage intractable symptoms may be sedated. Sedation is not the same as euthanasia or passive assisted suicide; it is merely the ability to sleep through difficult periods.

If practitioners commit to managing symptoms and addressing their patients' fears of being burdensome to caregivers and loved ones, would any prematurely end their lives? If financial problems could be solved would these people still believe themselves to be "burdens" upon their families. Perhaps social workers, lawyers and insurance agents could clarify the reality of these situations and diminish the desire of our patients to die. Allowing the ill to make medical decisions for as long as they are capable, and to not be embarrassed about their illness, would do much to promote the well being needed to avert the suicidal drive. Dignity and control are easily available upon a moment of reflection.

Reassuring patients that we are going to stay with them for the duration does much to address their fears of abandonment. We must provide appropriate assurances that we will continue to be involved in their care regardless of the direction their condition takes. There will be continuity of care for the seriously ill if caregivers commit to its importance. Palliative care is not abandonment. It is not the absence of care. Palliative care is a highly evolved and different type of health care entirely dedicated to the relief of bothersome symptoms and the improvement in the quality of remaining life.

CAN WE PROVIDE LEGAL ALTERNATIVES FOR SUICIDE?

We certainly can provide information about the likely outcome and expected course of the disease. We can assure patients that we will respect their right to refuse any and all treatments. We can honor requests for discontinuation and withdrawal of burdensome therapies. We can elect to not replace declining oral intake with other routes. We can stop feeding people who are dying and we can prevent misguided forced-feedings that only increase misery, but do not change the inevitable outcome. We can redirect caregivers to still feel they are important even when they are prevented from forcing fluids and nutrition. In doing so we can shorten the time to naturally die without actively accelerating the process.

To facilitate the withdrawal of treatment or to manage uncontrollable physical symptoms we may offer sedation. Sedation may be continuous or intermittent. Ultimately, patients die from their underlying diseases, not from the methods routinely used to provide terminal comfort. Analgesics, sedatives and anesthetics all make the final days of life more tolerable.

When faced with difficult situations, health care professionals do not need to panic and reach for poison. They need to talk with their patients. They need to seek support from trusted colleagues. They need to allow consultations with pain control specialists and biomedical ethicists. Together, pain and suffering can be lessened. Together, misery can be resolved and patients can naturally die supported, appreciated and appropriately cared for without resorting to acts of terminal violence.

According to the Institute of Medicine in 1998, palliative care seeks to prevent, relieve, reduce or soothe the symptoms of disease or disorder without achieving a cure. Palliative care is not restricted to only those who are dying or those enrolled in hospice programs. Palliative care attends closely to the emotional, spiritual, and practical needs and goals of patients and those close to them. The World Health Organization sees palliative care as the active total care of patients whose disease is not responsive to curative treatment. This includes the control of pain, of other symptoms, and of psychological, social and spiritual problems. The goal of palliative care is achievement of the best quality of life for patients and their families.

To do the best job for the terminally ill we must develop centers of excellence for palliative care. These may be hospice programs, panels of traveling experts or downloadable resources from the Internet. While not every member of the American Academy of Pain Management is an end-of-life care expert, most are predisposed to team work and know how to obtain additional resources for their patients. Information about the American Academy of Pain Management, credentialed pain practitioners, accredited pain management programs, and the EPEC curriculum is available on the Website of the Academy (www.aapainmanage.org).

Care for the terminally ill affirms life and regards dying as one part of the normal life process. Doing the right thing for our patients requires that health care practitioners neither hasten nor postpone death. Practitioners are challenged to provide relief from pain, other symptoms, and to integrate psychological and spiritual care into everyday practice rather than passing out poisons. Using an interdisciplinary team to provide a support system for the entire family does much to diminish the drive for premature demise.

17

◆

Choosing the Time and Manner of Your Death

by Cynthia St. John
Executive Director
Dying With Dignity

I
N LIFE, THERE ARE SOME DECISIONS and actions that we have
control over and there are others that we do not. As society slowly recognizes that we do have control over many of the choices we make in
life, we must also recognize that one of those choices must be the ability to choose the time and manner of our death.

For this reason, Dying With Dignity (DWD), a Canadian Society concerned with the quality of dying, was formed in 1980. It is a charitable society that strives to improve the quality of dying for every Canadian. It is also
a member of the World Federation of Right To Die Societies.

DWD recognizes that every terminally ill, mentally competent adult has
his or her own definition of dying with dignity. Because medical advances in
the last 50 years have enabled the body to live longer and prolong death,
there is a need to recognize that not everyone wishes to prolong the
inevitable. DWD advocates and educates about the importance of making

choices at the end of life including the ability to hasten one's death via safe, legal, physician assisted dying or voluntary euthanasia. DWD recognizes that specific safeguards would need to be implemented to avoid abuse of a law that permits physician assisted dying.

It seems incomprehensible that we are a society that is not looking after the dying and a society that condones death without dignity. Our health care system requires more extensive training for professionals working in end of life care. Better access to hospice and palliative care programs must be addressed. It is not okay to have any individual suffer at the end of life.

For some individuals, death with dignity implies letting "nature take its course" and not hastening the dying process. For others, self-control and autonomy are critical and therefore, a hastened death is desirable. Whatever the choice is, we have a fundamental right to make that choice. Many terminally ill individuals can currently choose to withdraw from treatment. Why then, can we not choose when and how we die? Current cases all over the world indicate that the issues of choice in dying are not going to fade. It is time for our governments to recognize that dying with dignity is of paramount importance to so many of us and that we will not tolerate politicians making laws that inhibit us from having a good death.

At the end of the day, what really matters is that our dying loved one leaves this world free of pain, suffering, and on their own terms. Isn't that really what it's all about?

18

◆

Lorraine's Story
She Took the Road Less Traveled to Make All the Difference

By The Rev. George D. Exoo, Ph.D.

I, the Lord of sea and sky,
I have heard my people cry.
All who dwell in dark and pain
My hand will save.
I who made the stars at night,
I will make their darkness bright.
Who will bear my light to them?
Whom shall I send?
Here I am, Lord. Is it I, Lord?
I have heard you calling in the night.
I will go, Lord, if you need me.
I will hold your people in my heart.

Never before have so many people packed the Unitarian-Universalist Church of Sarasota for a memorial service. They had come from as far away as New York to honor the life of Lorraine Bate Orr. They rose to sing a contemporary setting of Isaiah 6:1-9 by Roman Catholic bard, Marty Haugen.

233

Their friend, Lorraine, often cited that very text "Here I am, send me." as the words impelling her fifteen year crusade to secure the legal right to a death with dignity for the terminally and hopelessly ill. The feisty 79 year old Ottawa native successfully fought first for passage of living will legislation in South Carolina. Then, with her own death, she drew public attention to a case now before the Florida Supreme Court to legalize physician assisted suicide and beyond that, voluntary euthanasia.

Chaplain of the Hemlock of Western Pennsylvania and West Virginia and long-time friend, I was at Orr's side as she "self-delivered" with barbiturates, scotch, and finally a plastic bag.

Simply put, Lorraine Orr did not want to become a vegetable. In February she had been hit by a stroke that left her temporarily weakened. That event heralded further problems. She phoned me, and we agreed that, whenever she directed, I would be at her side to guide her as her soul departed to the Light.

The call came just five months later, much sooner than any of her many friends and I would have hoped. The afternoon of Monday, July 8, my phone in Pittsburgh rang. It was Lorraine.

"You must come now, dear. Now is the time I need you."

"Can I come on Wednesday?" I insisted.

"No! That will be too late. Come right away."

"What's wrong?" I questioned.

"The gah baw. The gah baw."

She could not remember the name of the Hemlock Society, nor that of close Hemlock friends who were scheduled to have dinner with her later that evening.

Three hours later the next available flight for Tampa departed Pittsburgh. I was aboard. Just after one in the morning I entered Lorraine's elegant condominium. She sat on the couch basked in lamplight. As usual, stacks of good books surrounded her. This time, however, a scrapbook of articles documenting her years in theater and in radio sat next to her last will and testament on the coffee table. Soft strains of Mozart brushed the air.

Back to her usual articulate self, she quickly told me of the events that had prompted her phone call. That morning she had been on the phone when she suddenly lost her ability to speak. It was a second stroke.

"Next time I might not be so lucky. I don't want to be a nursing home vegetable."

There was nothing I could say. She was right. Once a vegetable, she would have been in a prison of paralysis: fully able to think, fully able to live without life supports, skidding into poverty, a helpless lump of flesh, beyond the penumbra of any advanced directive or the ability to end her own life, save through starvation and dehydration. Anyone who might have assisted her with euthanasia would have faced swift murder charges.

There was something surreal about the night. Here I was a thousand miles from home planning to witness the suicide of revered soul mate, yet acting like it was all just an ordinary, friendly visit. She wanted to involve the press, she told me. Hemlock's suit in the Florida courts to secure the right to physician aid in dying was predicated on a unique privacy statute. "The court seems to be dragging. We need to generate some publicity to get our case moving. The paper said they'll run a story if we can supply a local angle, so I said, 'Use me!'"

Before retiring she casually announced, "If it's OK with you, I'd like to get started just after lunch tomorrow."

*****

Lorraine's ever cheery disposition hearkened back to the noblesse oblige of Canadian aristocracy. Sir Henry Bate, her grandfather, built much of Ottawa's late nineteenth century infrastructure. Despite thirteen children, the Bates were rich. Lewellyn, the last of Sir Henry's children, sired four daughters, Lorraine among them. She arrived in August of 1916.

Character counted, Lewellyn taught his children, even when financial mismanagement by his business staff forced him into bankruptcy. Through hard times she learned to keep up good appearances, even if things backstage lay in shambles. Her practice in dissembling paid off. When the New York stage beckoned, she left for Manhattan. She was then but 19.

To support herself, Lorraine took odd jobs at Lord & Taylor and Saks Fifth Avenue. Lodging at the protective Rehearsal Club ran $13 a week. "None of us were in it for the money," she said. "One year I made $5,000. That was an astounding salary for a young actress."

The movie Stage Door with Katherine Hepburn and Ginger Rogers, recounted life at the Rehearsal Club. Lorraine was in it, a memory she treasured always. Soon her clever way with words landed her in advertising Agency work who eventually brought her into radio where for twenty years, starting in 1959, she produced with her husband, John, a syndicated talk feature called "Good Living."

In 1979 the couple retired to Charleston, South Carolina and quickly joined the Unitarian Church where I was minister.

Two years later doctors diagnosed John with cancer of the throat. In the surgery that followed, he lost much of his lower jaw and larynx. No longer able to speak, a Harvard graduate who had made his living with words, now elephantine in appearance, surgery had robbed John of all dignity and life quality. Soon it was clear he was dying. A second operation followed, then the demand for prostate surgery. John wanted no part of it; neither did Lorraine. To both of them it was patently clear that John was a hunk of flesh attached to an insurance policy through which Charleston doctors, John Hawk and Fleetwood Hassell, could fatten their already plump wallets. Questioning why her dying husband should undergo prostate surgery, Hawk and Hassell merely patronized Lorraine.

My entreaties also fell on deaf ears.

A young doctor in the congregation promised to assist the Orrs, but acquiesced for fear of losing hospital privileges, should he counter Hawk's judgment. Then a nurse, now dead, confided in Lorraine the doctors' intention to consign her to the State Mental Hospital in Columbia if she persisted in defying them.

There was little she could do, we felt, but sneak John out of state. Back in New York City the Orrs had connections to a Catholic hospice via their beloved family physician and friend, Bry Benjamin. Despite John's critical condition, they boarded a Pullman heading north. Once at Penn Station, arriving in the middle of the night, no red cap was in sight. Alone, Lorraine pushed John's wheel chair and dragged their luggage through the connecting corridor to Grand Central Station and transportation to the hospice. John died six weeks later.

For a decade living will legislation had stalled in Columbia. Had it been in place, Hawk and Hassell would not have been able so easily to plunder John's dying flesh. Soon after Lorraine's return, thanks to a sympathetic

[Unitarian] contact inside the Governor's office, Lorraine became chair of the South Carolina Citizens' Committee for the Right to Die. She collared legislators, addressed committees. Sometimes I was able to be at her side. At length the bill passed. That was in February 1986.

By the time Governor Richard Riley signed the bill, Lorraine had already relocated to her native Ottawa. I drove her car there and expected she would live out her days on Canadian soil.

In 1992 she found me in Pittsburgh, reporting that she had two years earlier moved to Sarasota. She was, she said, heavily involved in Hemlock as publicity chair, sharing the story of John, and urging Floridians to support physician aid in dying.

I visited her mid November 1993 for a whirlwind week of trips to the Poetry Society, the Jungian Society, a church bazaar, and Hemlock. She told me of a Hemlock chapter starting in Pittsburgh and launched me into an innovative chaplaincy of spiritually preparing the terminally ill to die, then guiding them through the self-delivery process. During my stay, *The New York Times Sunday Magazine* published the account of the work of my Unitarian colleague, Ralph Mero and his assistance with self-delivery of a terminally ill Seattle Roman Catholic. For me the appearance of this article was a Celestine coincidence, an arrangement of Spirit I now believe focused my own birth vision and life's mission.

With those who seek Compassionate Chaplaincy's aid, we share the near death experiences of my South Carolina friend, Danion Brinkley, dead twenty-eight minutes after a lightning strike. We tell also the even more dramatic story of Soviet medical doctor, George Rodonaia, dead fully three days before returning to life. Near death experience research started by Dr. Raymond Moody back in the late sixties shapes for me a science of death preparation nascent in Buddhist literature for two millennia. We begin our work with the dying by showing Moody's video, *Life After Life* [1992]. The film quiets anxiety, offering evidence of a gentle, orderly process of life review and self-judgment sometime immediately after death. With this road map as our guide we train people until they reflexively look for the Light, rather than attending to discomforts that may temporarily attend the dying process.

They spend their final hour of consciousness in an autobiographical review. Together we laugh, sometimes cry, but always there is great affirmation of gifts given and received. Consciousness fades to the sound of favorite music, poetry, psalmody, and prayers — never to the sterile clatter of hospital high tech.

People fear dying alone; self-deliverers fear failure. Our presence wipes away both anxieties.

We ask for evidence (in the form of a pre-arranged sign) that people have reached the Other Side. Uncommon scents offer excellent confirmation, especially when others, not clued in, also notice them. The verification has never failed to appear. We take this as a metaphysical attestation that those we have assisted have received no condemnation for their act. Those who profit financially from protracted dying are quick to make pious claims that assisting a suicide is wrong. We do not care what the AMA, the Supreme Court, or the Pope think on this subject. If we thought those we assist would receive eternal condemnation for cutting short their earthly sojourn, we would cease this work. What the Universe says is quite another matter, and from that Source, affirmation continues to be strong.

*****

The Sarasota morning dawned, casual and lazy. I showered as Lorraine carried out her usual routine, minus care for Victoria, her beloved Chihuahua. A dog-lover friend had whisked Victoria off to a new home the night before. It had been a terrifying day for the tiny dog, who knew something was wrong with her mistress.

Lorraine ran to the drugstore for Dramamine and to the bank. I took the opportunity to study the scrapbook and her CD library to prepare music to accompany the day's later events.

As she handed me an envelope with a check to cover my travel expenses, she explained that she wanted her one surviving sister to get the bulk of her estate, not her sister's children. They had drained their mother's assets to the nub, gobbling up a $300,000 estate from another sister in just two years.

Only one thing might have delayed the schedule — a return call from Tom Lyons of the **Sarasota Herald-Tribune**. The popular columnist had written about Lorraine's work with Hemlock. Now she wanted to use him to tell the story of her own death to underscore the need for legalized physician assisted suicide and beyond that voluntary euthanasia for the helplessly ill. She would not be acting now, she insisted, had she some assurance that, were she to become a vegetable, she could then get the help with euthanasia she had directed in her living will.

Lyons did return the call about eleven. I left the room as she spoke, but could hear her hearty laugh and what sounded like an ordinary, pleasant conversation with any old friend.

"It's time for me to go," she began. Lyons asked her, she told me after hanging up, how old she was. When she said "I'll be 80 next month," he had quipped, "no, it doesn't look like you will." They had laughed, and so did we. The woman possessed magnanimous spiritual poise. How dare any human worm of lesser mettle and character condemn her, as some have tried.

People must decide for themselves when quality of life has ended. For some it may be when they're hours from a natural death. For others when illness forces a loss of independence. For others when money falls below a threshold they find comfortable. We encourage independence in all areas of life. End of life decisions should be no different. The ebb of life is no time to surrender personal sovereignty to medical doctors, psychologists, social workers, clerics, or family. Lorraine chose the time that was right for her to act.

*****

Noontime came soon enough. Lorraine fixed herself the lunch of tea and toast recommended by her Hemlock friend, Derek Humphry, in his instructional manual, **Final Exit**. On the bestseller list for months, the book continues to be the manual of choice for the terminally ill and physicians alike.

Soon several prescription bottles, with identifying sources effaced, appeared on the kitchen counter. "Derek says this should be one and a half times a lethal dose." She poured the contents into apple sauce, then mashed and stirred them into a thick decoction.

I tasted the goop and found it sharply bitter. "Better add some sweetener."

She produced a jar of honey and added a tablespoon or so, finally chuckling "It's OK. I can manage it." I snapped her picture with a Polaroid.

"Let me get a picture of Julia Child at work," I chimed. Her prep completed, she began rinsing dishes and popping them in the dish washer.

"Lorraine, whatever are you doing?" I asked.

"Got to tidy up, you know. I wouldn't want anyone to find this kitchen a mess. That wouldn't be fair!"

For dessert Lorraine took a pair of Dramamine tablets to settle her stomach, lest the onslaught of apple sauce and scotch should trigger reflux. She retired to the den and we spoke more about her life. I got the scoop on husband number one and stories of her career in New York. We did the whole sweep. Then it was time for that apple sauce. She consumed the bowlful as though it were a gourmet flambe.

For some reason we had forgotten until this tight moment to fiddle with a large plastic bag and neck collar she had secured from the Right to Die Society in Vancouver. The concept of the bag is that one slips it over the head just at the moment of passing out. Theoretically, the bag should contain enough air to allow its user to fall deeply into a coma before the no-fail death by asphyxiation.

Lorraine donned the bag, hatlike, but with its humongous size, the thing simply flopped over, offering only a small reservoir of air. I lifted it off and scooped it full of air as best I could. Once the pills are down, sleep follows in just ten minutes. I had planned to use this precious time for spiritual centering. Here we were, fussing with technical stuff, while those pills began their inexorable absorption into her system.

"OK," I finally said. "It's not perfect, but let's make do. Have some scotch."

Lorraine began sipping her scotch as though she had all afternoon to nurse it.

"Come on, bottoms up," I ordered.

I would have preferred she drank half a bottle of Cutty Sark, not half a glass. She slipped into unconsciousness, forgetting the bag entirely. It remained on her forehead, a grossly oversize shower cap.

Out came the books: Emerson's **Self-Reliance**, Byron, Henley's **Invictus**, **psalms**. Two hours into her sleep, her breathing gradually slowing, the phone rang — a loud bell a few feet from her head. The answering machine started. A woman blithered something about her grandchildren.

To my horror, Lorraine half opened her eyes.

"Hi," I said. "How are you doing?"

"Fine," she mumbled and with both hands reached up, pulled down the bag, and fastened it.

My heart sank. For all its efficiency, the bag portends a struggle, not a gentle drift into nothingness. No Sarasota physician would quietly write script to aid her. With proper pharmacological assistance, rather than willy-nilly stockpiling of whatever drugs she could find, that horrible bag would have been unnecessary. This is why legalization of assistance is absolutely necessary.

For perhaps twenty minutes I held Lorraine's hands and fervently prayed with her.

"Go to the Light. Look for the Light," I instructed.

When the end came, I continued to read psalms, though by that time, through tears. Those who have had near death experiences report that they float above and look down on their still body. Thus I continue my counsel after death comes. For Lorraine I read a meditation from Steven Levine's book, Who Dies?

I called Tom Lyons to report the end and left to join Walt and Nan Billings, Lorraine's close friends from Hemlock. After dinner, we returned to her house and called the police. I told my story over the next five hours. In doing so, I honored Lorraine. I cooperated fully with their questioning. Not to do so would have been unfaithful to Lorraine's wish to publicize her death. Police finger printed me and read me Miranda rights, but in the end, Tom Lyons tells me, recommended the State Attorney General take no further action.

Lorraine and I had agreed on a sign she would send me once she safely reached the Other Side. She would use a small child to let me know she had arrived safely in God's arms. I don't normally attend to children, and they ignore me. Any contact would be out of the ordinary, I reasoned. I pressed her to be more specific, but she desisted.

The next afternoon flying home, a boy about five seated in front of me one position to the right, suddenly turned around, "Are you wearing your seat belt?" "Yes," I replied. "See?" he said to his father. Could this be the small child? Possibly, but the question about my seat belt didn't exactly smack me in the soul.

An hour later a second incident proved more potent. An East Indian mother sat next to me while I awaited connections. Her little boy, three or four, kept staring at me with penetrating dark eyes. It was Lorraine, I am certain. Not the strongest discarnate confirmation I have received, but precisely the one she specified.

Lorraine visited me one more time. She appeared during a walk of the medieval labyrinth now a tool for spiritual contemplation at the Trinity Episcopal Cathedral in Cleveland. Within twenty feet of entering that sacred space, I was again in tears. She was there in the upper air of the stone apse among the carved faces of angels that looked down on the congregation of peripatetic pilgrims.

"O Lorraine, did I do the right thing?" I asked her.

Once in the center of the labyrinth, a place reserved for contemplation, I sat down. There she spoke to me in words from George O'dell. "All our lives we are in need of others...and at the hour of our death, would have gentle hands to guide us...." The exit walk took thirty minutes. Lorraine's presence had been healing to my soul. I was at peace.

Would John Orr have chosen the same course, had Derek Humphry's instructions been available to him in 1983? I'm convinced of it. Knowing John as I did, I'd venture he has been nudging Lorraine from the Other Side. She reported several post-mortem appearances from him. Near death experience researcher, Melvin Morse, calls these appearances "parting visions." He reports they are quite common.

The stroke victim Lorraine might have become suffers the cruelest of loopholes in proposed physician-aid-in-dying legislation. Model legislation offers no option for people needing assistance with administration of whatever hemlock they take. This fine line distinguishes assisted suicide from voluntary euthanasia. Alzheimer patients face the same problem because of their advancing mental incompetence. It may take some years for the legal penumbra to guarantee equal protection for the stroke victim Lorraine Orr might have become or for those hopelessly afflicted with Alzheimer's Disease. Compassionate caregivers will ignore the distinction. Jesus, after all, healed on the Sabbath.

Only one form of euthanasia, removal of artificial life support systems, is now legal. Those asking for this help can still encounter real obstacles.

Recently an ALS victim in the North Hills of Pittsburgh sought my assistance in removing her feeding tube. We had been in dialogue for months. Her old-timey Catholic husband, out of tune with recent enabling pronouncements from the American Council of Bishops, insisted on prolonging her suffering and dying. The Council no longer requires Catholics to go to the mat to keep dying patients alive. Extraordinary means (feeding tubes and artificial respiration) are no longer required. Removal is tantamount to not starting their use.

My North Hills friend assigned her durable power of attorney for health care to me and executed an aggressive living will. The result? Her physician, a native of the Indian subcontinent, refused to honor these documents. He did not return my calls. Forty-eight hours later a palliative care doctor phoned him. "It is the right of the husband to say what will happen to the wife," he said. "If you try to enforce the living will, I will have the patient declared mentally incompetent." I shuddered at his arrogant (not to mention chauvinistic) hubris, recalling the Hawk-Hassell conspiracy to consign Lorraine to an insane asylum.

*****

Connections into Tampa Airport were tight the night of Lorraine's memorial service. A vicious flash thunder storm precluded a hasty drive to the church. I arrived ten minutes after the start, walking to the chancel in my clerical collar as though the entrance had been planned that way for weeks.

Before I spoke, the presiding minister, the Revd. Richard Benner, played a tape of Lorraine speaking several years ago. These are her words: As a naturalist, I believe there is some long range plan. This doesn't mean I'm going to sit back in resignation and accept whatever happens to come along. My very religion, my rebellion, may be essential to the success of that plan, and when the time comes that I find the quality of mylife unacceptable, I will treat myself with the same compassion that I treated my 18 year old cat, Bibo, who suffered from kidney and liver failure. I had him released last summer.

I shared Lorraine's story, urging the audience to tell and retell it until law guarantees every adult the right to a dignified death. In the end, we all stood to sing the Canadian national anthem: "O Canada! Glorious and free!...We stand on guard for thee." In life and in death, Lorraine Bate Orr stood on guard for more than her native Canada. She stood on guard for us all.

Section Seven

19

♦

Reality Sitting Down

by Marilyn Cooper

ULLSHIT", I REPLIED TO THE DOCTORS sitting around the table. They had just told me I had Amyotrophic Lateral Sclerosis (ALS) and would be on life support in two years and dead within three. I had three babies and a husband who couldn't boil water. My initial response to the diagnosis was that I needed to take care of my young children and run my home. I had no space in my life for this thing called ALS. I had a job to do and they had no right to give me a time frame.

That was the beginning of what evolved into my way of looking at life and coping with my disability. I am calling it a disability and NOT an illness. An illness to me is a cold, the flu, or even cancer. I do not feel ill. Maybe some would call this denial, but a little denial never hurts. I am a realist and I deal with ALS every day of my life. The way I chose to cope with my ALS is to just get on with my life. When we are home with the flu for instance, we lay in bed and obsess on how awful we feel. I can not do this every day. Twenty-five years later I have proven the doctors wrong.

IN THE BEGINNING...

I was born in 1944 to Jewish parents living in England. We emigrated to sunny California in 1948. My parents and I lived a quiet life in Los Angeles. I am an only child, and I was very close to both of them. My father was a man of few words with a wonderful sense of humor. My mother was very artistic and I grew up in the warmth of a traditional Jewish home. I attended Hamilton High School in West Los Angeles and then majored in History at the University of California Los Angeles (UCLA). During my freshman year I met my husband. We knew immediately we would be married, but waited until he finished law school in 1965. I became pregnant while working on my senior thesis and Andrew was born shortly after my graduation from UCLA in 1966. Heather followed in 1969, and Steven was born in 1972. My husband became a successful attorney and is a partner in his law firm.

1973 was a difficult year. On my 29th birthday, my father suddenly died. Three months later my mother had an emergency hysterectomy. Three months after that we almost lost our daughter to a severe asthma attack. A series of relatives died and problems were compounded with personal financial difficulties. Through it all I kept everything going , raising the three children with no help in the house and little family support. The following year I developed a pain in my hip and severe cramps in my legs and hands. Twice when I sneezed, I lost my balance and fell.

My family physician in Northridge recommended I see a neurologist, but I refused. A few months later I visited a top Beverly Hills physician who prescribed vitamin therapy and said to put the baby in a stroller and run. I tried running but collapsed on my neighbor's lawn. I returned to my family physician and, this time, allowed him to refer me to a neurologist, whom I promptly visited. The neurologist placed me in the UCLA Neuro-Psychiatric Institute where I was put through a battery of tests over a two-week period. In April of 1975, he told me I had Amyotrophic Lateral Sclerosis (ALS) but did not explain it to me. I had never heard of it, and he did not refer to it by its common name, "Lou Gehrig's Disease". He did, however, explain it to my husband. I left the hospital in total denial while my poor husband went into mourning. A short while later, a few doctors told me exactly what was going on.

Friends disappeared. My mother told me how difficult it was for her. We were left to cope with little support. My husband was so shocked he escaped into his work. About nine months later it all hit me and I plunged into a deep depression. I was referred to a psychiatrist, whom I saw every day for one week, and then every-other-day the next week. In the safe environment of the psychiatrist's office I allowed myself to feel for the first time the loss I was suffering. I talked and talked, and felt I had permission to grieve for the future I had planned but feared I would not experience. This was the beginning of learning to cope with ALS.

My husband and I continued to struggle without support until our Rabbi, Michael Menitoff, called us and came to visit. He arrived at four in the afternoon, stayed for dinner, and finally left at two in the morning. He helped us communicate with one another and gave us the support we needed. Soon we became very involved in our synagogue, Temple Ramat Zion, and developed a wonderful support network. We also became involved in the Jewish community in Los Angeles.

DISABLED BUT ABLE

In 1978, I had progressed to the point of walking with a cane but was still driving. Our insurance agent was a neighbor of ours and his wife was a personal friend. When the agent heard I was walking with a cane, he cancelled my car insurance, feeling it wasn't safe for me to drive. I was furious and felt betrayed. I went to another insurance company and continued driving for another four years.

In 1980, we moved from a two-story home into our current one-story home near California State University of Northridge. I had always been extremely active and independent which carried over into the years of physical disability. When I did finally have to give up driving, it was difficult emotionally because it meant giving in to the disease. However, I was fortunate to live near the University and hired a student who worked for me throughout her four years of college. She did my marketing, drove car pool, and helped me to continue with the daily tasks of raising a family.

When I made the transition from a cane to a walker I was uncomfortable using the walker in public. I was vain. Instead, I used a small traveling wheelchair. Eventually I realized that I needed a regular wheelchair, which I used for five years. In 1987, I bought a powered wheelchair, which opened up a whole new world. I had my independence back. I went anywhere I wanted.

Finally, in 1999 I got the ultimate in power wheelchairs. It's a rolling arm-chair with comfort deluxe. It reclines, tilts and does everything except sing and dance.

My husband and I love to travel and have not stopped. Traveling in a wheelchair has prevented us getting to all the places we'd like, but it has occasionally allowed us unique opportunities.

On a trip to St. Petersburg, Russia, we noticed a complete absence of dis-abled people in public. When we walked in the gardens of the Hermitage museum, people stared at me as if they had never seen a person in a wheel-chair. And yet, when we entered the museum itself, and found there was no elevator, other tourists and a couple of local men rushed to help carry me up the grand staircase.

Because I was unable to board the tourist coach, we were provided a driver and a "guide" for a day. This gave us a certain freedom to travel the city and see sites that were technically off-limits to tourists. We convinced the guide to take us to a synagogue. With some hesitation, he agreed and had us driven to a very old synagogue. Our reluctant guide and driver then had to carry me up the steps to the entrance. We knew they weren't supposed to take us there, let alone facilitate our entry. We met teachers and children studying Hebrew with the hope of leaving Russia and going to Israel. It was an amazing emotional experience and we felt we had triumphed over Russian rules.

Traveling by airplane is a nightmare. I sit in a regular seat during the flight, but in order to get to it I have to transfer from my wheelchair to an aisle chair, which is wheeled down the narrow aisle of the plane. Sometimes the attendants are careful and well trained, but there are those who bump me around and are insensitive to how they move me. When I travel I use a light-weight wheelchair which folds up easily for storage. With the help of my hus-band, I am able to walk about six to eight steps. This gets us to the bathroom, where we imitate two sardines doing the *Tango* in the incredibly tight space. Of course this is difficult on both of us so I try not to drink during the flight. This causes dehydration and I depart the plane like a limp rag. But it hasn't stopped me from traveling. This year we are going to Tahiti, an eight hour flight, followed by a ten day cruise in the Tahitian Islands.

Two years ago we shared a wonderful trip to Ireland with dear friends whom we've known since college, Carol and Marty Klein. We drove around the country, staying in bed and breakfasts and exploring the back roads and villages. Everywhere we went we asked the locals to tell us where we could enjoy live Irish music and we'd end up in smoky pubs. The Irish people were wonderful. They called me "Dearie", put my wheelchair right up front near the musicians, and brought me beer. *A fine ol' time it was!* In our travels, we have encountered so many welcoming people who go out of their way to make a disabled traveler comfortable. I have found that when I greet people with a smile and look them directly in the eye, they respond and are friendly — except in New York!

While no one would ever assert that being in a wheelchair is a good thing, there are benefits that my family and close friends have been able to gain by spending time with me. The day the movie *ET* was released, our good friends the Binders and our family went to stand in line. Due to my inability to wait outside for so long or compete with a crowd of mobile people, my husband and I were allowed to enter the theater ahead of the crowd. Our friends and the six children continued to wait in line appropriately. By the time they got inside, the theater was almost full and all the good seats taken. Except the ten seats in one row smack in the center of the theater which my husband had draped with our coats. We sat together as families and had the best seats in the house.

STAYING PRODUCTIVE

As one who loves to learn, I've continued to take classes, on and off, over the years. When my youngest son started high school, I felt I was ready to go back to school full-time. I applied to a paraprofessional counseling program at the University of Judaism in 1985 and was rejected because of my disability. I was devastated to be rejected in that manner. I reapplied two years later and immediately told them I would not tolerate any discrimination. Despite this warning, during the interview they asked me, "If we let you in our program, how will you go to the bathroom?" I responded by letting them know I felt their remarks were discriminatory. They rejected my notion of discrimination and asserted that I see reality differently than the rest of the world. To which I replied, "You're right. I see it sitting down." This time, they accepted me and I completed the two year program.

My experience during the program at the University of Judaism was mostly positive, but I did encounter occasional challenges. While classes were readily accessible for my wheelchair, the social events were not. Frequently, parties were held at sites inaccessible to me. And when it came time for graduation, I was told I would have to sit in the audience as there was no access to the stage. However, I knew there was a ramp backstage and I told them I would be on the stage with the rest of my class. They were horrified. When my name was called at the graduation, I received a standing ovation from my classmates and the audience as I wheeled across the stage.

Next, I applied to California State University, Northridge and was accepted into their counseling program. Dr. Robert Docter initially interviewed me and later became my mentor. The instructors as well as my classmates were very supportive and I was elated to be in this stimulating atmosphere. The facilities for the handicapped on campus were amazingly advanced. I was given proctors and extra time in order to write my exams long hand in blue books. When it came time for my senior thesis, Dr. Doctor and Dr. Sarah Moskowitz were my examiners. They made it a really pleasant experience and I graduated with a Master's of Science in Counseling.

I am very proud of the fact that even though I have lived so much of my adult life in a wheelchair, I have accomplished things and entered into situations that most "normal" people would not ever consider. Following my graduation from CSUN, I interned at the Salvation Army's adult rehabilitation program. I counseled alcoholic and drug dependent men who were now in recovery. Most of my clients were ex-cons and were in the program by court mandate. I had a heavy case load and led a support group. I also taught a class about reentering society (i.e., opening bank accounts, healthy eating habits, how to rent an apartment, etc.) to thirty-five men. Imagine a room full of ethnically diverse tough guys and me, a little Jewish woman in a wheelchair. They saw me as a role model; if I could overcome obstacles in my life and be productive, so could they.

My counseling degree has allowed me opportunities to continue to grow as a professional and as an individual. I have met wonderful people who have shown me acceptance and respect. Only occasionally have I been stuck in an uncomfortable situation where I have felt discrimination. I take what I learn from each experience and each person with whom I encounter and apply it to each new experience. I try very hard, despite exhaustion that comes quickly, to stretch myself intellectually and professionally. I now lead a twice-monthly support group for middle-aged people with elderly parents. Having lost both my parents as well as my husband's parents, I am, unfortunately, quite experienced in this area.

I also feel it is important to give back some of what I receive in support and assistance. For this reason, I volunteer my services at UCLA's Muscular Dystrophy Clinic for ALS. I sit on the board of the Muscular Dystrophy Association Los Angeles Area Chapter, as well as on the National Task Force on Public Awareness. They both involve community outreach and working with the media.

LIFE TODAY

The evolution of the way I look at life and cope with my disability goes back to my refusal to listen to the doctors' dire predictions. For twenty-five years I have fought that decree with every breath.

However, I have had to make space in my life for my disability. I have had to learn how to ask for help, and I have had to learn how to accept help. I am fortunate to be surrounded by people who seem to anticipate when and how I need help. My husband and my three children have grown with me in this process. The children were told right away I was not well and as they became older their understanding deepened. They always helped when I became tired. One day the washing machine overflowed and water and suds were everywhere. When I called for help, Andy and Heather came running with towels to mop up the mess. Steven, who was four at the time, ran upstairs and returned with his two toy boats, helping to make the best of the situation.

My husband, Dick. To say he is one-of-a-kind would be an understatement of huge magnitude. His enthusiasm and his ability to never accept the doctors' verdicts have made our lives together one hell of an exciting roller-coaster ride — which is better than a merry-go-round. One story from early in my years of disability epitomizes Dick's ability to make each day an adventure. In 1977, I participated in a clinical study at the National Institutes of Health in Bethesda, Maryland. Over the course of two weeks I as hooked to an I.V. that either pumped some new experimental drug or a placebo into my veins. It was a debilitating experience. The nurses on my floor never quite knew what to do when Dick would show up each morning to visit. His unbounded energy and devotion to me took them aback. He did everything possible in his power to make this horrendous experience a little more tolerable.

On one occasion in particular, Dick even did something beyond belief to make me feel better and provide a brief ray of sunlight in a very gloomy episode. My good friend, Farla Binder, was flying into Bethesda to surprise me, and Dick decided to turn the tables on her. I still don't know how he did it, but he convinced the doctors, using all of his lawyerly persuasion, to allow me to leave the hospital. They taped my arm to a board, leaving the I.V. needle in my vein, and lent us a wheelchair. The look on Farla's face when she came off the plane and saw me sitting there waiting for her was priceless. The three of us spent the day sight-seeing in Washington, D.C. — much better than sitting in the hospital with all three of us feeling sorry for ourselves.

I also am very fortunate to have a housekeeper and companion who anticipates my needs, sometimes before I even know it. Carmen Gomez has taught me Spanish and I taught her Kosher cooking. Occasionally in the afternoon, I find myself thinking about having a cookie and Carmen will walk in with one in her hand.

I have had to learn how to be patient and how to handle disappointments. I have to wait for people to show up, to drive me, to help me, even to feed me. Eventually, most of my needs are met, although not always exactly as I would like. Disappointments are hard to take, even when one is fully functional. It is doubly disappointing when I look forward to a party or special event and then, for any number of reasons, am not able to get there. I say to myself, if only I were not dependent. I am fortunate in that between Carmen, my husband, my children, and a few friends, 90% of my needs are being met.

I still find it extremely hard to ask for help, especially outside my dependable circle of people. I think this is mainly because I fear rejection and disappointment. I still have a vivid memory from about ten years ago of a friend sitting in my kitchen, enjoying a cup of tea and casually announcing that I could never call on her again for help because she had too much to do. I felt as if I had been slapped in the face. I never again asked her for anything. And yet, there are so many people who say to me, "Call me if you need help." The trick is figuring out who is sincere and which person to ask for different needs.

My feelings of dependency were heightened during the Northridge Earthquake. "Normal people" felt vulnerable. I felt ten times more vulnerable. When the quake started, my husband rolled over on me in bed, pulled the covers over himself — covering me at the same time — and we just held on to each other until the earth calmed down enough for us to get out of our house. I still don't know how he managed to get me into the wheelchair and outside to safety because I was so disoriented. In fact, he was truly my hero.

One has to learn new coping skills for each new phase of disability. Giving up driving was a major disappointment for me. The solution was to teach Carmen how to drive. As each child in turn learned to drive, he or she also took on additional responsibilities such as contributing to the errands. Going into a wheelchair presented another obstacle to daily life because I had to wait to be pushed anywhere I wanted to go. I remember when Andy was packing to go away for college. It was gut-wrenching to think about him moving out. He pushed my wheelchair into his room, forcing me to watch him pack. As I was unable to leave, I was stuck watching my child grow up.

My disability has affected each of my children in a different but positive way. Very early on, I made a conscious effort not to be a burden or an intrusion on their lives, and I made sure they had normal school lives. My boys were involved in basketball leagues and my daughter took ballet at a school that fed into professional companies. My kids grew up knowing their mother could die early, but instead of causing them pain, they learned to appreciate every day. My husband and I turned the situation around to make them more sensitive to the needs of others. I remember once having a visitor to our home who had a broken leg. Heather made sure the guest had a stool to prop her leg on and then offered her a cup of tea. The visitor was amazed that a nine year old girl would be so considerate. Now that the children are adults, this "caretaker" tendency has continued.

My disability has also affected my marriage. On top of all the normal stresses in any marriage, we have the added stress of a wife who needs help to bathe, dress, eat, and so on. My husband has done more than most men would do. Indeed, many men would have left wives in my position. Thankfully, we have the financial resources to hire caretakers so that Richard can be my husband and not my nurse.

When my daughter was in high school, her biology teacher asked if I would consider speaking to his class. I told him I had no idea what I would talk about. He looked at me in amazement and said, "About yourself, of course." Up until that minute I had never thought I had done anything special. He made me reevaluate the circumstances of my life. For the first time, I realized I had something to say; I had a philosophy. I agreed to talk to the class and after I told the students about ALS, I talked to them about how life is made up of choices. You can either lie down in the street and let the truck run over you or you can get up and walk away. I chose to get up.

Over the years people have told me how I am an inspiration to them. I hate that with a passion! I have lived my life, day-by-day, doing what I need to do for those I love and for myself. I now see that viewing myself as disabled and not ill is a frame around this picture. Recently, a childhood friend of Andy's was diagnosed with a malignant brain tumor. He is thirty-three years old, brilliant, with a beautiful wife and a new baby daughter. He told me I was one of his role models. I was touched and humbled. This young man is fighting his way through his illness and I am very honored to be part of his support system.

My work at the Salvation Army helped me put words to my feelings. The 12 step program applies not only to alcoholics but also to anyone who needs support in overcoming a hurdle. "One day at a time" has became my motto. However, I would like to offer a slight modification, because I fully believe in planning for the future. I feel I have set goals to energize myself for the future. When I was first diagnosed, I set the goal to be at Andrew's Bar Mitzvah which was five years away. I accomplished that goal and then went on to plan Heather's Bat Mitzvah. Three years later I was planning Steven's Bar Mitzvah. Then I looked forward to my children's graduations from high school and college. Now we're looking forward to weddings and grandchildren. Andy married Julie in 1997 and they just had their first child — and our first grandchild — Michael Oliver. Needless to say, we are thrilled to be Grandma Mar and Grandpa Dick. Now my goal is to watch Michael grow up and share in the joys of his life.

My daughter Heather and I are very close. I remember my grandmother Hinda, for whom she is named, said, "Every woman needs to have one daughter to keep her young." We have a great time together, vacationing, shopping, going to the theater, and doing all the things that mothers and daughters share. She also is my back-up support when caretakers do not show up. She is always gracious and giving. Heather is currently the Associate Director for the American Israel Public Affairs Committee (AIPAC), the organization which lobbies Congress on behalf of pro-Israel issues. I am very proud of her, especially when I hear Congresspeople and Senators calling her by her first name in conversation.

My boys keep me involved in sports. I love basketball and football and I have season tickets to UCLA basketball. Andrew holds the position of Associate Vice President for American Express Financial Services overseeing the financial planners in central California. My daughter-in-law, Julie, is a recent graduate of the University of Minnesota majoring in architecture. She graduated Phi Beta Kappa, putting the rest of us to shame. My younger son, Steven, lives in San Francisco and works for the stock brokerage, Charles Schwab. He is a project manager and works on very complicated matters behind the scenes. I still do not comprehend what his responsibilities really are. We are thankful our children are all healthy, happy and productive adults.

I am an avid reader. At this moment I have fourteen books by my bedside waiting to be read. So many books, so little time. My sister-in-law, Stephanie Cooper, and I started a book club about two-and-a-half years ago and it has grown to a group of twelve bright women. We meet once a month and have intelligent and animated discussions about the book we have just read and how we relate to it as women. The club meets at my house in order that I don't have to worry about getting a ride or being able to make it up someone else's front steps.

I keep myself busy and yet I pace myself. I try not to plan too much in one day but I plan something for every day, even if I plan to simply stay home and read. Keeping busy, staying involved, and planning for the future is the key to my well-being.

"TO LIFE, L'CHAIM!"

My opinion about the "Right to Die" has evolved over the last twenty-five years since my diagnosis. The miracles of modern technology in prolonging life have influenced my opinion. I have also been heavily influenced by my conservative Judaism, which has taught me to respect and revere life.

When I was diagnosed with ALS, I was told I would be on life support in two years and dead at three. Twenty-five years ago I made a living will that said I would prefer never to be placed on life support if it meant being a vegetable. Since then, with a new generation of electronics, life support has a different meaning. Ventilators and feeding machines now are portable and enable the patient to lead a more normal life. And so my feeling of continuing life has new dimensions. Where once I would never allow myself to be attached to a machine, now, if I could keep my present quality of life, I would allow it. However, since I have high cholesterol and a family history of heart disease, I am sure a heart attack will get me before the ALS does. And then I will not have this decision to make.

According to Rabbi Elliot Dorff in his book, **Matters of Life and Death: A Jewish Approach to Modern Medical Ethics**, "whereas Judaism justifies homicides in cases of self-defense and war, it prohibits murder, including one's own (suicide)."[1] Dorff also had an amazing few lines on disability. "The Jewish tradition, in contrast, calls upon us to evaluate life from God's perspective. That means that the value of life does not depend on the level of one's abilities; it derives from the image of God imbedded in us. The tradition thus strongly affirms the divine quality of the life of disabled people, even though everyone would undoubtedly prefer not to be disabled. Indeed, our tradition demands that, upon seeing a disabled person, we bless God for making people different, thus boldly reasserting the divine quality of such lives."[2] He goes on to discuss assisted suicide. This again is considered against Jewish tradition and tantamount to murder. In the past, people would die of acute illnesses. However, now many of these same illnesses, if not cured, are controlled by medication and/or machines. Rabbi Dorff feels this is preferable as long as the patient has support from family, friends, or even a hospice. He feels that the worst part of dying is being alone. And it is a Mitzvah (a good deed) to support an ill person. In fact we are commanded to do so. "...even when life is not ideal and we question a divine dignity and its character as a gift, we lack the authority to destroy it because our bodies belong to God, who alone has the right to terminate life."[3]

My personal feeling is that any individual with such an illness has a choice how to live and how to die. And we must respect an individual's choice. Indeed, American law does not prohibit suicide. My choice is to live my life to the fullest for as long as God grants me. Maybe this is part of the reason that the doctors' original prediction has not come to pass. I refuse to give in. Every day is an adventure. I learn from every person I meet. My family and my friends are my enjoyment. There is not a chance that I would end this life.

In conclusion, My grandmother always said, "The first hundred years are the hardest."

She was right.

REFERENCES

[1]   Dorff, Elliot N. *Matters of Life and Death: A Jewish Approach to Modern Medical Ethics*. Philadelphia. The Jewish Publication Society, 1998. P.177

[2]   Ibid.

[3]   Ibid

20

♦

Life's Final Chapter
Questions and Answers

by Samira K. Beckwith, C.H.E., L.C.S.W.
President and CEO, Hope Hospice and Palliative Care
Past Chairperson, National Hospice Organization
Past President, Florida Hospices and Palliative Care

S OME PEOPLE DENY IT, some plot ways to cheat it, some joke about it and most avoid talking about it. Death is still a taboo subject in our society. Fewer than 25% of Americans have thought about how they'd like to be cared for at the end of life and even fewer put it in writing.

An example of this reluctance is the finding of a recent survey conducted by the National Hospice Foundation that more than one out of every four adults were not likely to discuss issues related to their parent's death with them. Surprisingly this was even true if the parent was terminally ill and had less than six months to live. They were more likely to talk to their children about such sensitive topics as drugs and sex.

No matter how much we seek to avoid this difficult subject, eventually we must come to accept the fact that Death, like birth is a natural part of Life. There are obvious differences but yet some important similarities. Both are more than just medical or physical events. Both require preparation, education, and support as well as special attention to the needs of the family.

For over 20 years, I have had both the personal and professional opportunity to care for people during the final chapter of their life. My interest in how people live and are cared for during this mostly difficult time began when I was being treated for Hodgkin's disease. During those long and difficult years, I had the opportunity to talk to many patients and families while sitting in hospitals and clinics. It was through this personal experience and hundreds of discussions that I realized that a better way to care for people with serious illnesses and at the end of life needed to be developed.

Medical advances have increased life expectancy. Fortunately, many diseases can be cured, organs transplanted and quality of life has been greatly improved. At the same time the healthcare system has developed in a manner that does little to respect the right of the individual and treat the person as a whole being instead of a disease. Additionally the recent emphasis on cost and productivity has resulted in a neglect of the caring roles of comfort and support that had been an important health care value. People have become simply patients and diseases are treated without attention to the impact on the person and their family.

Throughout this period of increased technology and rapid medical advances, the end of life has become primarily a medical event handled in the hospital and treated as a failure. Numerous groups including the Medicare Payment Advisory Commission have documented the crisis that exists at the end of life. According to the commission, "the gap between the care now given to dying beneficiaries and ideal care is wider than in probably any other area of medicine. Closing this gap should be one of the highest priorities of the Medicare program. There has been too little thought (given) to how to care for chronically ill individuals and even less about how to provide care when people have reached a terminal point in their life." A recent review of medical textbooks showed that only 2% contained information about caring for people at the end of life. Nearly 40% of neurologists thought they needed to call a lawyer in order to stop a ventilator and 25% of oncologists' state that they did not want to take care of dying patients because it made them feel bad.

An important question for us as a society is how should we treat people at the end of life.

Hubert Humphrey once wrote that "the moral test of government is how it treats those who are at the dawn of life, the children: those who are in the twilight of life, the aged and those who are in the shadow of life, the sick, the needy and the handicapped."

This was the basis for the development of the modern day hospices. Hospices really developed in response to the unmet needs of people at the end of life. Hospice is a program of care that provides the specialized skills and services that people need to meet the complex physical, psychosocial, spiritual, emotional and practical issues that confront a patient and family at the end of life. The goal of hospice care is to assist the patient to live each day as fully as possible with their pain and symptoms managed as well as to help the family cope with their grief and loss. The focus of care is the patient and the family with an aim of making each day count, allowing the person to live as fully as possible. Hospice cannot extend the amount of time a person lives but can add more life to each day.

The choices at the end of life should not be between living in pain or suicide. Through hospice, the health care community never has to say to a person, "there is nothing more we can do for you." With hospice, the focus of care shifts from cure to comfort and although we cannot extend a person's life we can enhance the quality.

Even with all the progress we've made in end of life care, too many Americans still die alone or in pain, often enduring costly and ineffective treatments and being referred to hospice very late or not at all.

There are multiple reasons for this ongoing crisis. Dealing with the final stage of life is difficult. Difficult for health care providers because their goal is to cure and too often they have not received the training needed in palliative care. It is also difficult for them to predict prognosis with the certainty that is required by misplaced regulatory efforts.

Since 1982 when the Medicare Hospice Benefit was enacted there have been great advances in the methods and medications available to provide pain management and symptom control. However, this information has not been widely accepted outside of the hospice community. Affirmation of the appropriate use of controlled substances to alleviate pain and symptoms is needed. Education of health care professionals and research, which will increase the competencies of those providing care, is critical to improving care. And finally, we must recognize that palliative care includes more than treatment of pain and symptoms, that it also includes the "enhancement of quality of life."

This increased awareness will help to break down the barriers that keep people from being able to access hospice care. It will also facilitate earlier referrals to hospice. Patients are too often referred at the brink of death. Currently, over half of our patients are admitted to hospice within 3 weeks of their death. Many of these patients have suffered needlessly and the most common question we hear from the families is "Why?" The son of a man who was cared for by our hospice for only 5 hours talked with me about the relief that he and his family experienced once their father was under hospice care. Even with such a short length of stay he was able to see the difference in his father's care.

An additional barrier to people receiving adequate pain management is that of cost. The reimbursement mechanism for hospice has not been reviewed since it was first enacted in 1982 and needs to be updated to account for the real costs associated with compassionate and modern approaches to care for the dying. A recent example in our hospice is a woman who needed 800 mg every 12 hours of an oral pain medication. The cost for this one medication was $95 per day and our reimbursement rate is only $93 per day. This per diem reimbursement needs to cover all care and services.

A teacher was curled in a fetal position when the nurse and social worker went to his home to admit him to hospice service. He talked about his pain and asked for help to end his life. Within hours, his pain was controlled. He spent his final months visiting with friends and family. Good pain control is not difficult. What is difficult is to correct the misunderstandings that exist and make it available to those in need.

During a recent conversation, a woman talked with me about her mother who lives in our community. Her mother wanted a stash of pills to keep "just in case." She feared the suffering she anticipated having to suffer in the final stage of her Parkinson's. After visiting our Hospice House, she told her daughter that she wouldn't need the "stash" after all. She felt safe knowing that she would have the care she needed when her time came.

We, in hospice have hundreds of thousands of stories about making people's final days warm and memorable. Helping a couple to celebrate their anniversary, allowing a terminally ill wife and husband to live together until their deaths, which occurred within days of each other; a woman who wanted to see her granddaughter born before she died was able to see her in an ultrasound picture; a young mother who was able to write letters for her children to read as they grew up are just a few of those stories.

The end of life is not an easy time but we can make it less difficult for people as they complete the final portion on their journey on the road of life. Hospices can easily and competently care for many more people in need of good end of life care. People of all ages with any end stage disease must have access to the healing that is possible at the end of life.

Due to a demand from the people, birthing has become an intimate family time that is a celebration of life. As a nation, it is time that we recognize that no one is more vulnerable than a person at the end of life and that it is a moral outrage that each person does not have the same loving care, support and specialized skills needed at the end of life as we provide at the beginning. Our response as a community must be to look for ways to care for this most vulnerable population of which most of us will belong to unless we die suddenly.

As Harley-Davidson says, "it's not the destination, but how you get there."

21

♦

A Spiritual Perspective

by Dr. Bill Bright

MANY ARE CONCERNED that our culture is increasingly a culture of death. We live in a violent world. I believe it is "as in the days of Noah," as our Lord Jesus referred to it, and it tells us in Genesis 6:11 that in Noah's day, "the earth was filled with violence."

The present violent trend in America began in 1962 when violent crime began to skyrocket, the very same year the U.S. Supreme Court banned God from our public schools. In 1973, the killing of unborn babies was officially legalized by our federal government through the Roe v. Wade decision of the U.S. Supreme Court. Since then the blood of close to 40 million babies cries out from the ground from the holocaust of abortion. Someday, in eternity or before, many people will be gripped by sudden and stark remorse and terror of what we have done.

The culture of death is now spreading further in our society through the practice of doctor-assisted suicide, or euthanasia. We have reason to be greatly concerned not just for individual lives affected but the implications for the future, and where this will lead. For example, in the Netherlands a survey showed that of 11,800 patients euthanized in Holland, nearly 6,000 were performed without the patient's consent! An additional 13,506 patients were denied critical medical treatment with the specific aim of terminating life— a process the Dutch call "euthanasia by omission." Fully 64 percent of the patients give no permission for their fate.

With both abortion and euthanasia, the choice of death is often determined not by those affected but by an elitist group who try to assume God-like power, reminding us of Hitler's Germany. Unless the trend is reversed, with the burgeoning population and increase in the elderly and infirm, society may be entering a Draconian stage, the sheer horror of which is unimaginable.

Of course, many hurting and seemingly hopeless people may want mercy and the right to choose death. Who cannot sympathize with their desire to end their pain? However, no one is more merciful than God, who is repeatedly revealed in the Jewish and Christian Scriptures as the God of all mercy. What does He have to say about it?

Everything we do in life should be guided by the laws and precepts of the One who created us, the almighty God of the universe who created 100 billion or more galaxies, and who gave us His holy Word, the Bible, as the revelation of Himself, His plan of redemption for humanity, and our guidebook.

Nowhere in God's Word does He authorize the merciful taking of one's own life or the life of someone else. He leaves that to His own discretion, wisdom and timing, and for His own purposes.

On the contrary, the Scriptures are full of promises of physical healing. Jesus healed all who came to Him. After Jesus ascended, the ministry of healing was given to the church (James 5:14-15, 1 Corinthians 12:9, etc.). Of course, I fully realize that for different reasons many people who pray for healing are not healed, but an amazing number are healed. But I have wondered if as much time spent trying to justify euthanasia was spent in fervent prayer to the Lord Jesus for healing, the idea of the mercy killing or suicide for many people might become irrelevant. For example, a friend had a 12-year-old niece who had been in a coma for several weeks due to brain encephalitis. The attending doctors tried everything but finally gave up all hope. They recommended to the parents that life support be removed so she could die. But the parents were strong Christian believers who knew God's Word and power, and instead enlisted an army of prayer warriors, using the Internet. One day about 2-3 weeks later the little girl suddenly opened her eyes, asked for her daddy, and exclaimed, "I'm hungry!" The doctors agreed that it was a miracle, defying medical explanation. The little girl went back home and to school.

The Bible does not say, "Is any one of you sick? He should call Dr. Kevorkian." Really, it does not even say "Call the doctor." Instead, it says:

> *"Is any one of you sick? He should call the elders of the church to pray over him and anoint him with oil in the name of the Lord. And the prayer offered in faith will make the sick person well; the Lord will raise him up"* (James 5:14-15), NIV).

My point is that as long as there is life, we have the right and obligation to pray for the continuation of that life, and also for comfort and mercy— God's mercy. In seemingly hopeless situations, many people have asked the Lord that if He was not going to heal a person to go ahead and take them peaceably and quickly, and He did! But that was His choice, not ours.

Because of God's sovereignty over life, I do not believe we have a right to die at our own discretion, or a right to help someone else die. Instead, we do have an obligation to trust God and His love, wisdom, providence and plan for our lives, from the first breath to the last.

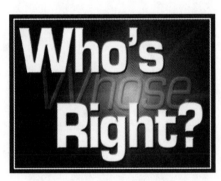

Section Eight

22

◆

A Love Story

by Hillary Parsons

*(I dedicate this story to my mother, Gloria Rose Greenwood,
who gave me the confidence, the strength of character
and the love to last a lifetime)*

I WAS ASKED TO WRITE A CHAPTER for this book based upon our family's experiences. Our experiences are unique but the story is not an uncommon one. My best wishes go out to those families who are suffering. It is my hope that our story will be helpful to others who face their own health crisis and have to make the extraordinarily difficult decisions necessary with more understanding, dignity and compassion for those we love who depend on us.

My husband Kevin is a medical doctor, boarded in Internal Medicine and Geriatrics and I have worked as a registered nurse for twenty-five years. We have both struggled with the concept of death and dying for many years — Kevin, as both a geriatric physician and a patient, and I as a critical care and oncology nurse. In past decades euthanasia existed in the hospital and was not uncommon at all. I first experienced euthanasia in nursing school, working as a nurse's aide during the summer. One evening the nurse in charge asked me to sit at the bedside of a patient to take her vital signs (blood pressure, pulse and breathing rate) every fifteen minutes. The patient was an elderly lady in the final stages of terminal cancer and she was no longer alert. I took her vital signs every ten minutes. It made me very nervous as her pulse was slow, her breathing rate was slow and I didn't understand why I was sitting with her for four hours. The charge nurse came by frequently to administer increasing doses of morphine which acts to relieve pain but will slowly stop a patient's breathing completely. I asked the charge nurse what she was doing and why it was necessary to monitor her so closely. She told me very clearly that the increasing doses of morphine would gradually cause this lady to go from taking slow breaths to taking no breaths. I was "helping" this lady to die. At age nineteen, I had absolutely no idea that this went on in hospitals all the time. It continues today, although sometimes not as obvious.

As a critical care nurse and later as a nursing supervisor, I saw decisions made, often without much discussion but definitely with the patient in mind. More recently euthanasia has come to the forefront of medical ethics and while the discussions have continued and the associated paperwork has grown, no useful "rules" have emerged. My husband and I have no formal legal training or degrees in medical ethics; we can only provide a viewpoint with experience both as medical care providers and as a family facing a slow, seemingly inexorable path towards death. Experience is sometimes the best teacher but some questions have no right answer.

Kevin and I met when he was a medical intern at Harbor/UCLA Medical Center near Los Angeles. We were married and lived a typically busy lifestyle until moving to Dallas, Texas for Kevin's first real medical position. We had never lived outside of southern California and we worked long hours. We both developed a serious influenza illness during the first winter in Texas. Kevin was bedridden with pneumonia which became the first step down a long road of chronic illness to a point moments from death.

Soon after the pneumonia Kevin accepted a position at Scripps Clinic in San Diego and I started working as a supervisor in the Intensive Care Unit nearby. Kevin was never really the same; he tired easily and could no longer play tennis or enjoy skiing. There were frequent lung and skin infections and the onset of new and severe asthma that required the use of a breathing machine to administer medication several times through the night. While working Kevin collapsed in his office and was hospitalized next door to one of his own patients. They told me that Kevin had no white blood cells to fight infections; any infection could be deadly. The chief of Oncology at the hospital felt that Kevin had leukemia. A bone marrow biopsy was scheduled but the results would not be available until the next day. Of course we were all terribly worried and anxious. Kevin's father turned to the window in the room. I'm sure that he was crying and didn't want anyone to see — a rare moment for that man.

A young female resident walked in and was silent for a long moment obviously considering her words carefully. Finally, she broke the silence: "I hate to disagree with my chief of service, but I don't think you have leukemia. You just don't look like it to me and if you don't mind, I'd like to do another bone marrow biopsy and look at every slide myself." The painful biopsy was repeated and we continued to wait hour after hour as the resident looked at many, many slides to see if there were any leukemic cells. After looking at over forty slides, not one leukemic cell was found. We breathed a huge sigh of relief but only for a moment. The question came rushing in, "If Kevin doesn't have leukemia, what does he have?" This became the continuing question and the saga of our lives.

Kevin left the hospital with the infections cured but his blood counts were still low and he developed a host of new symptoms. The worst of these new symptoms was vertigo, a sensation similar to that spinning sensation you get if you drink way too much alcohol, but his spinning never subsided. The vertigo was so severe that Kevin was unable to turn his head in any direction without immediately vomiting. He kept a bucket or trash can by the side of the bed and vomited during the night three, four or five times. He threw up so much he felt it was keeping me awake at night and he began sleeping out in the family room or the living room so that he wouldn't bother me. All this vomiting caused Kevin to lose a great deal of weight. He went from a trim 165 pounds down to 130 pounds in a few months. Kevin was beginning to look like a man who was dying from an aggressive cancer.

I had a friend who was an Oncologist, so I asked him to evaluate Kevin but still nothing was found. Mysteriously, over several months the vertigo began to diminish and Kevin started to feel better. He wasn't well enough to work as a physician so he went to work for his father who owned a company in Los Angeles. Kevin could contribute but come and go as he pleased depending upon his health. We had to move back to Los Angeles and live on less than half our previous income.

The job was not nearly as demanding as the previous medical jobs and Kevin continued to improve and gain weight. The healthier Kevin became the more he talked about returning to medicine. Eventually, he felt he was ready to go back to being a physician and took a nine to five position as an academic and teaching physician at the Long Beach Veterans Hospital. Since Kevin was well enough to go back to work I also went back to nursing at Kaiser Hospital in Los Angeles.

We were in our thirties and our children, Jesse and Sarah, were six and two years old. Things went well for a time and Kevin seemed happy being a physician again. But when I found about thirty parking tickets in his car I knew something was wrong again. The physicians at the Veterans Hospital have their own parking lot but it is quite far away in order that the patients can park close. Kevin was parking in the closer patients' lot and was getting frequent parking tickets. He purchased a folding camping cot and was sleeping in his office during lunch or whenever he had time. Kevin never mentioned any of this to me but I noticed he was losing weight again and deteriorating, although not dramatically. It was not as obvious as the last time. It was also obvious that Kevin was trying to ignore this recent onset of illness.

The truth came out when Kevin collapsed and was admitted to the Intensive Care Unit in critical condition. Again, his blood counts were low and he had a serious infection but there was still no underlying reason discovered for his problems. There seemed to be no one who could help and no place left to go. After three weeks in the hospital Kevin came home only slightly improved, unable to even sit up for more than a few minutes. As he lay in bed all day, Kevin read what medicine he could, trying to help himself discover what was happening to his body. He was a physician and he thought he could figure out what all the others could not. That did not happen.

Since I was working at Kaiser, we were both covered and could receive free care there. I decided to see what they could do to help. Kevin was an inpatient at Kaiser for about three weeks and they did all the tests but Kevin went home in a wheelchair with no diagnosis. We were now a couple of years into this situation and Kevin again weighed 130 pounds, deteriorating and dying slowly. We just did not know what to do; we did the best we could day by day. Kevin couldn't work and I had to.

One night after work I just silently watched Kevin — I knew that my husband was dying and nobody knew why. I sat silently for a long while. In a flash of an instant I started moving. I put both children in the car and started driving until I thought of a friend nearby. I dropped Jesse and Sarah there and went back to get Kevin. I finally was able to help Kevin into the car and had to keep the seat reclined as far as it would go; otherwise Kevin would start to vomit again. I was driving in desperation, to the only place I could think of that might still help — UCLA Medical Center.

Kevin and I showed up in the Emergency Room and while he looked chronically ill, thin and weak they could not find any reason for this and wanted to send him home. Despite the low blood pressure, vomiting and weakness the resident just said: "I'm sorry, there's nothing we can do, you'll have to take him home." I replied, "No". "No, I am not taking him home, this is the last place I am taking him and you are going to figure out what is wrong with him." I asked them who was the attending physician on call and if they could call him. That night we got to meet a very remarkable physician, Dr. Shapiro. He listened to the story and told the resident to admit Kevin. Kevin was in the hospital for 28 days. During that time so much happened it's hard to relate and much of it is, I think, purposely forgotten as a necessity of self-preservation during such stress.

Kevin was placed in strict isolation because both his white and red blood cell counts were very low. I had to put on a surgical gown and mask just to walk into his room. I was working at Kaiser from 7:00 am to 3:30 p.m. and would then drive to the hospital to be with Kevin from 4:00 p.m. until I went home around midnight. I did not just sit and visit; I performed much of Kevin's nursing care because the nursing staff is always short-staffed, as they are now in all hospitals. I realized that I wanted to be there and might as well help with Kevin's care. I turned and cleaned him; he was so weak.

Because Kevin's blood counts were very low and he was at such risk of deadly infection, they decided to remove his spleen both to bring up his blood counts and to look again for cancer. It turned out not to be a good decision. This whole time Kevin was suffering from a disease that only about 300 people in the entire world had. It is called Eaton-Lambert Myasthenic Syndrome or LEMS for short and it is an "autoimmune" disorder where the body's own immune system attacks itself. In this case antibodies are made that attack the nerve cells which signal muscles to move. This was why

Kevin was so weak. The only thing that most physicians knew about LEMS was that only old men who smoked and had lung cancer got it and then only rarely. Kevin was not old and did not smoke but the doctors still thought some cancer must be present for him to have LEMS. This was one of the main reasons to do the exploratory surgery — to look for that elusive cancer. What the doctors did not realize was that the medications given to put Kevin asleep for the surgery would make the LEMS problem a hundred times worse.

After the surgery I went to the recovery room to see him and he was on a ventilator which was breathing for him. He had been in the recovery room for probably about four hours, awake and alert but not breathing on his own. I said to him, "try to breathe" but I could tell from watching the ventilator that he wasn't breathing at all. I repeated myself and urged him to try and breathe but again, nothing. I gave him a piece of paper and pen to write since he could not talk with a tube down his trachea and he could barely write: "I can't". I thought, my God, now he's on a ventilator permanently.

The doctors had no idea how long Kevin would be unable to breathe for himself but after several days he slowly developed enough strength to get off the ventilator. Of course, no cancer was found and I thought maybe the worst was over — it wasn't. It was inevitable Kevin would get pneumonia after spending such a long time on the ventilator. With Kevin's impaired immune system there was every chance that a severe pneumonia would be deadly. I was scared, frustrated and angry.

There was one point I shall never forget. Kevin was in a great deal of pain and on a morphine drip which he could dose himself by pushing a button. One evening when Kevin's mother was in the room with us Kevin whispered to me, "Get her out of here." I did not understand what Kevin was doing because he was being harsh and he is not like that ever. He repeated, this time saying: "Please get my mother out of the room, I have to tell you something." I asked Kevin's mother if she wouldn't mind leaving us alone for a little while. After a long silence Kevin spoke. He didn't have the forcefulness of breath to allow him to speak normally so I got close to him and he whispered to me: "Say good-bye, I'm dying." Being a nurse I held his hand but also was feeling his pulse. I knew he was not dying — at least not at that instant. I got really, really angry. Others would have cried or been upset but I just got mad. The children were young, I was young, it was so unfair, and besides, Kevin promised me he would be with me to raise the children, live life together and grow old together — not to leave me alone. Immediately I responded: "You're not going to die on me". I called for the nurse and the morphine drip was decreased and after a few minutes Kevin actually felt better. Besides having just too much morphine I think Kevin had just had enough and wanted out. He had surgery, test after test, he just felt terrible and maybe did not really want to live anymore, but I could feel that it was not his time and I was just not going to let him go. I was terribly sad but I just kept coming and staying with Kevin every night. Although I almost never saw Jesse or Sarah, I was lucky enough to have a wonderful lady, Pat Ragona, who watched them every night while I was gone. Pat never asked anything of me, not even money, and was a good friend. I came home each night, sent Pat home, looked in on the sleeping children and sat alone. We had a small stoop in the front of the house and I sat there in the night and cried. I cried in frustration, I cried in fear and I cried because I felt so alone. One night Jesse, who was six years old, came outside in his pajamas. It was about 2:30 am. He put his arm around me and asked me what was wrong. I told him: "Daddy is very sick." The children had not been to the hospital to see Kevin as he just did not look good and we agreed it was not a good idea. Jesse just left his arm around me and did not say anything. He was comforting me and he was only six; he was an incredible child and now a wonderful young man.

Kevin was not getting better; instead, he developed a severe pneumonia and was suddenly at eminent risk, again. I called Dr. Shapiro and he came immediately and caught up with Kevin on the way to radiology. They needed a good standing chest x-ray but Kevin was becoming incoherent and much too weak to stand. Dr. Shapiro put on one of the lead aprons, lifted Kevin up and held him long enough to get the x-ray. This was an act of commitment and kindness that lifts my spirits now every time I think about it. Thank you Dr. Shapiro.

With aggressive three-antibiotic therapy, Kevin slowly recovered. Then a most amazing thing happened — Kevin quickly got stronger, not quite normal but almost. I had not seen him walk quickly or even move much for so long — he was like a new person. It was as though he was cured; it was so incredible. Somehow I was just not that surprised when the weakness returned just a few days later and Kevin was again weak and bedridden. Apparently, taking out the spleen also temporarily removed the majority of the antibodies which were causing the disease; however, other cells just took over making the antibodies and we were right back where we started before the surgery.

Finally, with a diagnosis this time, Kevin came home from the hospital. He could get to the bathroom and feed himself, but he was still deteriorating slowly. We knew what to call the disease, but we didn't know what to do about it or how to treat it. Kevin was bedridden most of the time. I do not know how much time went by, probably about three months, and I just got fed up with the whole thing. I was trying to work and do the childcare and care for Kevin and it was just too much. Again, I became angry, frustrated and tired.

I put Kevin in a wheelchair and took him to a busy shopping mall. I parked him next to the rail on the third floor and I said, "Look around you. Everyone is living and you're not. You are just willing yourself to die and just lying there but it is not going to work". I continued telling him that he had a choice. Even though his body was of little or no use anymore, his brain was still good and he could still do so much with it if he wanted. I told him if he didn't try to help himself and live again, I would put him in a nursing home or let his mother take care of him.

Kevin knew me well enough to be horrified I would do it. Even my mother was horrified when I told her. Kevin is a wonderful man and a kind person; but, I just — I was thirty-six years old with two children and I thought — no way. I have to get on with my life but I had a husband who could not help me, would not help himself and was not a partner anymore.

Within a few weeks Kevin was tooling around in the wheelchair, then to a walker and then with a cane. Months later he walked slowly without any assistance. Kevin went to work; on himself. He worked nearly every waking moment, on the telephone, on the Internet and at the library, investigating this rare disease, LEMS. There were a few doing some research, mainly in Oxford, England. They were using an experimental medication not available in the United States called DAP. DAP is an abbreviation for the chemical name, 3,4 diaminopyradine. Kevin found that DAP had been reported to cause seizures and so it was not used much anymore. Seizures did not worry Kevin; he was more concerned about his muscles being so weak that at times he could hardly breathe. Because Kevin was a physician, he convinced the doctors at Oxford to send him some DAP to try. It was amazing. Without question, Kevin was now out of bed. The medication allowed Kevin to function again. He was driving again and he was definitely on his way. He was better. He was gaining weight. I was not seeing the deterioration anymore, I was now seeing progress. Kevin continues to take the DAP and he has helped every patient he knows to get the medication. Kevin was building a network of LEMS patients which would help them all. He follows every patient himself and many of them telephone him at home with questions and concerns. He talks to them and their physicians frequently. They are all a family now. When one dies they are profiled in the LEMS newsletter and the family is consoled by the other patients.

One of the many wonderful patients, a young girl about 30, lives in our area. Her husband knew she had this disease when he married her. Because she is so weak, he has to physically turn her several times per night just so she can get enough sleep. I am not strong enough to turn Kevin at night so he wakes frequently and has to keep his DAP and water by the bed to take if he gets too weak.

A couple of years passed and Kevin asked me once if I thought it was possible for him to do medical research at a center to learn more about LEMS. We wondered if it would be too exhausting, if anyone would let someone with almost no research experience begin such a project as a part-timer and if he could work effectively in a research laboratory. In retrospect it was a big request of him and me but I thought he could do it. Kevin approached Jerry Nepom who is the director at the Virginia Mason Research Center in Seattle. Jerry agreed to give Kevin the chance to try and provided the necessary research space and seed money. Kevin started going into the lab, when he could, without any pay but with new hope for the future.

Kevin has been in the laboratory now for nearly two years; he goes in three to four days per week for about four hours at a time. While he cannot physically spend more time working, he also reads several hours per day right up until he turns off the lights and goes to sleep. Kevin is a professional learner; it is one of his best skills and this is a wonderful challenge and a personal quest to eventually contribute to curing his disease. Other researchers in the lab give Kevin support, advise and help him learn all the basics he needs. He is publishing his first medical paper and he hopes to get grant funding in order to get a research assistant who could get more done in the lab and also start studies involving LEMS patients and treatments. Kevin is dedicated to his new work and it has played an important part is giving him renewed purpose and a new life.

Kevin and I have been the subject recently of several newspaper articles and a television segment on **NBC Nightly News**. Kevin is a private person and does not like notoriety or a spot-light shining on our family. It was something we agreed to do reluctantly to help boost the public relations for Virginia Mason Research and a way to help pay back Jerry Nepom for his kindness by supporting the research foundation's attempts to gather donations. I do not think Kevin will ever stop his research efforts as long as he is able to think. Right now he is medically stable. He has gained back most of the weight but he is not heavy by any means. He can walk without a cane but is slow. He has a particular kind of walk that is distinctive to LEMS patients. My daughter Sarah calls it his "penguin walk"; she has never seen him walk normally but it doesn't seem to bother her.

In a strange way that is apparently common to families in our situation, we are a very close and happy family. The ordeal has worked to bring us together almost as a single force; we have a marriage that we know will endure. The children have an attentive father who is home most of the time. We live for today and enjoy our simple family moments, not getting concerned about "the small stuff". I guess life has never been better.

But what does this story have to do with euthanasia? We are not experts on medical ethics. We have no credentials from which to offer judgment. All we have is the experience to see the issue from several viewpoints — as a Geriatrician and a critical care/cancer nurse, as parents with a newborn son who needed major surgery at birth and nearly died, as children trying to do what is right for the health care of our parents, and as people who care. What can we add to what has already been said? I think we look at the issue from a practical viewpoint. First, if we do not have the answers, certainly lawyers and lawmakers do not and should not be involved in the process. This should not be a legal issue. It is one of patients' rights to be unencumbered by strangers and in a simple world the patient should decide his or her own destiny. A human life is "sacred" only if it is living. This is not a religious issue and I do not even think it is really a moral issue. The goal for all is to live a fruitful, happy life and then die with no period of disability or suffering. The question involves quality of life that can only be defined by the individual involved. We favor informed decisions made between physician and patient prior to illness. In the absence of predirectives it must be a decision reached among caring family with the counsel of the concerned health care team. If the patient's wishes are unknown, the family should appoint a spokesperson to help advise the health care team. Many hospitals now have ethics committees that help with these matters. Health care givers should be involved, offering their experience and guarding against situations where improper motives, depression or other psychiatric illness is involved. The role of the physician is as a consultant to advise and relieve suffering whenever possible, not as a prolonger of a life of suffering. As medical technology advances, questions of what is death and what defines euthanasia change. Easy answers may not ever be possible; however, these tough decisions should be made at a level as close to the patient as possible. This method may not be "clean" or easy but it provides the best flexibility possible to address this complicated problem. Kevin and I have discussed the issue of our death. We both do not want prolonged life under conditions that we both understand. Our choices are our own — each person should have the right and the responsibility to discuss the issue with both physicians and family members.

Finally, ours is a love story. It is a story of one man, Kevin, who to me is a hero. He's not famous, he's not athletic, he's not a rock star and he's not a movie star, but he is a bigger hero than any. Every single day of every single week of every single year, Kevin tries to do his best both for his family and for the patients with LEMS. I believe in his lifetime, he will cure this disease and so does he. Wish us luck!

23

◆

The Case for Physician Aid in Dying

by Faye J. Girsh
Executive Director, Hemlock Society, USA.

O
N JUNE 26, 1997, the U.S. Supreme Court issued a unanimously ambivalent opinion saying that there is no right to physician-assisted dying under the 14th Amendment, but that it is a matter to be left to state legislatures.[1-2]

Rather than putting a stop to the debate, the decision has raised the volume of dialogue, which will increase as citizens vote on ballot initiatives and legislators introduce bills permitting physician aid in dying. Especially for the past five years, the American public has been deluged with journal and newspaper articles, TV coverage, books, court decisions, jury verdicts, surveys, referenda, legislation — more than the average person can follow. One fortunate fallout of the controversy has been greater attention to the care of the terminally ill.

The right-to-die issue rivals the abortion controversy in capturing public attention, after enabling legislation is passed, the divisiveness about the issue will not disappear since there is a strong, religiously dominated minority who see both issues as a threat to the sanctity of life and who will continue to rail against choice in these areas.

As with most other strongly held beliefs, there are advocacy organizations for both sides. The Hemlock Society was founded in 1980, shortly after the first "living will law" was passed in California in 1976; since then other organizations have developed. The mission of the Hemlock Society is to maximize the options for a dignified death, including voluntary physician aid in dying for terminally ill, mentally competent adults.

When the Hemlock Society was founded, "passive euthanasia" was just becoming acceptable, i.e., letting a patient die by refusal or removal of life support. It was a decade later that the Supreme Court, albeit weakly, affirmed the right of all Americans to refuse or withdraw unwanted medical treatment, including food and hydration, and to have an agent speak for them if they were incompetent.[3] But that is not enough, since many patients who stop treatment die a prolonged and agonizing death and others do not have treatment to remove and so have no way to hasten their deaths.

Although there had been perfunctory legislation unsuccessfully introduced in the first half of this century, it was in 1988 that the recent attempts to pass laws permitting physician aid in dying began. In California the Humane and Dignified Death Act was proposed but did not get enough signatures to get on the ballot.[4] In 1991, 46% of the voters in Washington supported Proposition 119.[5] The following year a similar ballot measure, Proposition 161, was placed before the people of California and also received 46% of the vote.[6] Both campaigns were expensive and heated; advocates of physician aid in dying were outspent three to one, with the money for opposing physician aid in dying coming primarily from Catholic sources.

The issue is not one which affects just Americans. Since 1984 the Dutch have permitted physician-assisted suicide under strict judicial guidelines although no law has been passed. In Switzerland about 120 people on average have died each year with the help of physicians and members of the Exit Society following a law passed there 60 years ago allowing euthanasia if the intent is benign.[8] The Northern Territory of Australia, under the Rights of the Terminally Ill Act, permitted four people with cancer to die with the help of a doctor from July, 1996 to December, 1996 before the law was repealed by the federal parliament.[9] This year in Colombia, a Catholic country, the Constitutional Court ruled that mercy killing should be decriminalized. (10)

Why the growing consensus? Below I will list the reasons the Hemlock Society — and the majority of Americans polled — believe that providing physician-assisted dying for a terminally ill, mentally incompetent adult who requests it is a humane, compassionate, safe and effective option which should be made legal.

EIGHTEEN REASONS FOR LEGALIZATION

1. It is inhumane, cruel and even barbaric to make a suffering person, whose death is inevitable, live longer than he or she wishes. It is the final decision a person makes; there must be autonomy at that time of life if at no other. To quote legal philosopher Ronald Sworkin: "Making someone die in a way that others approve, but he believes is a horrifying contradiction of his life, is a devastating, odious form of tyranny".[11-12]

2. It is necessary for physicians to be the agents of death if the person wants to die quickly, safely, peacefully and non-violently since the best means to accomplish this is medication that only doctors can prescribe. There is no prohibition against a person killing oneself. In a civilized society a person should be able to die quickly with dignity and certainty in the company of loved ones, if that is her wish. Methods at the individual's disposal, however, are usually violent and uncertain, as well as traumatizing to the patient and the family.

   Ironically, the moral and ethical objections to hastening death do not concern self-deliverance. There is little concern in the dialogues about the fact that people choose to hasten their deaths. It is about the role of the doctor and the ethics and legality of providing assistance. There is little dialogue about a person who is not a doctor providing help, although this too is illegal since it is still assisted suicide.

3. A dying person who wishes to hasten her inevitable death does not cause the same repercussions as someone who is committing suicide, as we know it. Suicide, as we think of it, occurs in a person who is emotionally unstable and has a problem that will go

away with time and/or intervention. It has been called a permanent solution to a temporary problem. Suicide traumatizes survivors because of the guilt they feel that they could have helped,
that they were not able to talk about it, that the death was sudden and often violent and that there would have been a long, fulfilling life ahead if the person had changed his or her mind. With
a terminally ill person, if physician-assisted dying were legal, the
family could be present, good-byes could be said, and the death
could be, as some family members who have openly participated
describe it, a "wonderful" experience. And there would be no
guilt that the person could have lived a full life had the hastened
death not occurred since it would be at the patient's request, usually with the consultation of the family, and in the context of terminal illness.

4. A significant majority of Americans favor legalizing physician aid
in dying for terminally ill people who request it and this number
has increased steadily.

In a democratic society it is the case that laws follow the will of
the people. In this case, lawmakers have been intimidated by the
force of the religious objections and have ducked the issue thus
far.

5. Disabled, poor, elderly and minority people also want to die a
good death. Polls of disabled individuals show a majority in support. A 1994 Harris Poll found 66% of people with disabilities
surveyed support a right to assisted dying.[13] Between 63% and
90% of people with AIDS want this option and 55% have considered it for themselves. [14, 15] Two articles by influential disabled
individuals indicate their reasoning in favoring legal physician
aid in dying.[16, 17]

Support is also strong from older Americans. A 1996 survey by
RxRemedy Magazine of more than 30,000 people over 55
showed that 65% agreed that terminally ill people had a right to
commit suicide with a doctor's assistance.[18]

In the guise of protecting these groups, opponents argue that they
would be hurt by an assisted dying law since they would be vul-

nerable. This "protection" not only deprives people who are not in these categories of choice and dignity in dying, it robs those very groups of this option with no evidence that this is a choice they would not want. In fact, evidence suggests that all people want this option, regardless of their status.

6. It is consistent with a doctor's role to relieve suffering and to do no harm. Few doctors now take the actual Hippocratic Oath, which is irrelevant in many respects to modern medicine. Relief of suffering is the major objective of medicine; in the final extremes of a patient's life, the only way to relieve suffering may be to comply with a patient's wish for death. Many patients would trust a doctor more who would offer them all alternatives at life's end than those who would stop short of granting them their wish. What is likely is that patients and doctors do not have a dialogue about this and that physician aid in dying would actually enhance the doctor-patient relationship.[19]

7. Physicians are helping patients die now with no monitoring or controls. They cannot contact consultants or openly discuss their choices. A recent study of physicians in San Francisco who work with AIDS patients showed that 53% provided help in dying.[20]

   Surveys of doctors also show support for legalization. Fifty-four percent of Washington State physicians surveyed agreed physician aid in dying should be legal under some conditions.[21] In Oregon, 60% of physicians agreed and 66% agreed in Michigan.[22, 23]

8. Religious opinions about the sanctity of life would be respected. People who do not want a hastened death would not have to have one. However, there are many ways of hastening death, or at least not extending life, which are approved by religious groups including refusal of treatment including food and hydration, hospice, and the double effect (providing enough pain medication to end suffering without the direct intention of causing death, even if death is a result). Even groups most passionately concerned about the sanctity of life, which at one time raised concerns about refusal of treatment, have come to a position that quantity

of life considerations must be balanced against quality of life realities.[24] Surveys which have analyzed their results by religious preference show that at least 50% of Catholics favor this; one survey finds up to 72% of Catholics endorse the idea.[18, 25]

9. Palliative care would not be precluded. Most of us do not want to make the choice between compassionate hospice care, which could provide excellent pain relief, and the option of asking for a hastened death if pain and suffering were unbearable. Nobody seems to argue that all dying patients should have the option to refuse heroic measures, should receive the best pain relief available, and should have access to hospice services. The debate is whether there also must be a choice between hospice and assisted dying. Janet Good, former president of the Hemlock Society of Michigan, died recently of pancreatic cancer while under the excellent care of the Angela Hospice and apparently with the help of Dr. Kevorkian. It seems logical, in fact, for some non-religious hospices to provide the help desired by a small percentage of their patients.

10. There would be no progression beyond what public policy dictated. Terminally ill, mentally competent adults is the category of individuals we are generally talking about now, although some proposals have included people with hopeless illnesses. We have not had a chance to see how this model of physician aid in dying will work; it is premature to consider expanding the law at this point. Slippery slopes are neither predictable or preventable; it is pointless to argue that allowing this limited model of help for dying, competent adults will inevitably lead to other consequences which are undesirable for the society.

11. Refusal of treatment is not enough and is morally equivalent to asking for help in dying. Many people feel that they are protected because they have an advance directive. This only permits refusal or termination of treatment. It will not assure that death will not be prolonged and agonizing. In the situation of refusal of treatment the wish of the patient is to end life. It is often the fortunate patient who can "pull the plug"; for those who do not have

a plug, assisted dying is the humane and ethically equivalent solution.

12. People would live longer and better knowing there is help if the suffering becomes unbearable. The anxiety of not knowing how much longer one would have to suffer and watch the family suffer adds to the burden of terminal illness. Many people must end their lives prematurely through suicide while they are still able. Life could be extended if they knew help would be available from a physician.

13. Not all pain can be controlled. Even taking the best estimate from hospice, that 97% of pain is controllable, that still leaves 3% of dying people whose pain is unrelievable. What help is there for them? And, not all suffering is caused by physical pain. Surveys of patients in Holland who request aid in dying show that pain is fifth on the list of reasons why they ask for a hastened death. It is "senseless suffering" and the indignities of dependency, incontinence, and poor quality of life which lead them to request a hastened death.[26] In addition, not all patients want the consequences of adequate pain control, which include diminution of cognitive function and severe constipation.

14. Physician aid in dying is commonly practiced today in the United States. Doctors have always helped their patients end their suffering. If we are concerned about abuse of this practice, there should be controls and monitoring. In addition, it is a disservice to those people who cannot get help because they lack a personal relationship to their doctor, or have a doctor who is unwilling to risk legal action and loss of license. Aid in dying must be regulated, legalized and above board so that doctors, families and patients can discuss it as part of the continuum of care. The process and criteria should be regulated and the outcomes reported. This is the way to prevent abuses and stop the slippery slope — not by driving it underground.

15. The issue will not go away. Increasingly, people are dying of chronic, debilitating illnesses such as cancer, neurological diseases, AIDS, and heart disease. This means longer periods of suf-

fering and a prolongation of the dying process. People fear this extended dependency and want to know there is an end about which they can make a determination.

16. Physician aid in dying is not a significant cost-cutting measure. What we know from Holland is that life is reduced by a matter of days when physician intervention occurs. It is more of a cost-saving when treatment is refused, so there would be an incentive for managed care organizations to encourage patients to refuse or terminate life-saving treatments or even to refer them prematurely for hospice care. There is no hue and cry about this and certainly no suggestion that we should rescind the right to refuse treatment or hospice because of the possible coercion that people might be experiencing from the physician or the insurance carrier.

17. The abuses of not permitting lawful aid in dying far outweigh any that would arise if a carefully safeguarded law were in place. What we have now are botched attempts, trauma to the family, needless suffering on the part of patients and their loved ones, doctors who are helping without any type of oversight, and juries who acquit physicians and loved ones who help. Above all, there is injustice to a dying individual who is denied the ultimate choice of deciding the time and manner of her death.

18. A mockery is made of the existing law. Juries routinely acquit physicians and loved ones who provide compassionate help and most cases are not even charged or brought to trial. The principle of double effect is used as a "don't ask, don't tell" situation where medication is given to hasten death but the "intention" is only to relieve suffering. This means doctors and patients cannot discuss it; patients who would like help are wary of putting their doctors in a criminal situation.

WHAT'S NEXT?

There is no question that physician aid in dying will eventually be an option for people who live in developed countries where chronic diseases are the major cause of death. People want this, doctors want it; it can be regulated, and individuals in a free world must be able to decide this ultimate question about their lives.

REFERENCES:

1. *Washington v. Glucksberg*, 117 S. Ct. 2258; 1997.

2. *Vacco v. Quill*, 117 S. Ct. 2293; 1997.

3. *Cruzan v. Director*, Missouri Department of Health, U.S. Supreme Court, No. 2841, 1990.

4. Risley, RL. *Death with Dignity: A New Law Permitting Physician Aid-In-Dying*. Eugene, Oregon: The Hemlock Society, 1989.

5. Washington Death with Dignity Act, 1991.

6. California Death with Dignity Act, 1992.

7. Oregon Death with Dignity Act, 1994.

8. Shar M. "Assisted Suicide in Switzerland: When Is It Permitted?" 1997 *Hawaii Medical Journal* 56:3:63-7.

9. Northern Territory of Australia REPR009. Rights of the Terminally Ill Act. 1996.

10. Sequera V. "Columbian High Court OK's Euthanasia." *Rocky Mountain News*, p. 52A, May 22, 1997.

11. Dworkin, R. Life's Dominion: *An Argument about Abortion, Euthanasia, and Individual Freedom*. New York: Vintage Books/Random House, 1994.

12. The Polling Report, July 28, 1997.

13. Public Opinion Online. Question 004 NEW06090. New York: Louis Harris and Associates, 1995.

14. Breitbart W, Rosenfeld BD, Passik SD. 1996. "Interest in Physician-Assisted Suicide among Ambulatory HIV-infected patients." *Amer Journal Psychiatry* 153:238-42.

15. Tindall B., Forde S, Carr A, Barker S, Cooper DA, "Attitudes to Euthanasia and Assisted Suicide in a Group of Homosexual Men with Advanced HIV Disease." 1993. J. *Acquir Immune Def. Syndr* 6:1069-70.

16. Batavia A. 1997. "Disability and Physician-Assisted Suicide." *New Engl J. Medicine* 336:1671-1673.

17. Corbet B. 1997. "Closet Talk" *New Mobility* 8:3.

18. Cataldi S. and Case C. "Rx-Remedy survey of 30,000 Americans age 55 and over indicates strong support for the right to die." 1997; *Hawaii Medical Journal* 56:74.

19. Girsh FJ. "Physician aid-in dying: What physicians say, what patients say." August, 1992, *Western Journal of Medicine* 157:188-189.

20. Slome LR et al. "Physician-assisted suicide and patients with human immunodeficiency virus disease." 1997; *New England Journal of Medicine* 36:6:417-421.

21. Back AL, Wallace JI, Starks HE, and Pearlman RA. "Physician-assisted suicide and euthanasia in Washington State: Patient requests and physician responses". JAMA 275(12):919-25.

22. Lee MA et al. "Legalizing assisted suicide: views of physicians in Oregon." 1996; *New England Journal of Medicine* 334:310-5.

23. Bachman JG, Alcser KH, Doukas DJ, Lichtenstein RL, Corning AD, and Brody H. "Attitudes of Michigan physicians and the public toward legalizing physician-assisted suicide and voluntary euthanasia." 1996; *New England Journal of Medicine* 334(5):303-309.

24. Girsh FJ. "The case for physician assisted dying." 1997; Paper presented to the International Catholic Press Association Conference; Denver, CO.

25. Blendon RJ and Szalay US. 1992. "Should Physicians Aid Their Patients in Dying?" JAMA 267:2658-2662.

26. Van der Wal G, et al. 1991. "Euthanasia and assisted suicide by general practitioners." Translated from the Dutch, copyright The Hemlock Society. The survey originally appeared in *Mediseh Contact*, the weekly journal of the Royal Dutch Medical Association.

24

◆

One Woman's Story

by Josephine M. Koss
President of the Compassionate Chaplaincy Foundation

I REMEMBER ONLY TOO CLEARLY the moment in May 1995 when George made that final decision. We were eating dinner one Friday and he said, "It's getting difficult for me to lift the fork to my mouth and my hands are weakening so that I can hardly hold the silverware. I won't be able to eat much longer." George had decided as soon as his illness was diagnosed that he would NEVER be fed by anyone else or by a feeding tube. So as crushing as this news was, it came as no surprise when George said, "I think I'd better plan to do it on Monday night."

"Do it" meant intentional deathing. Several years before this, after two close family members had been in nursing homes, we decided that we did not want that kind of existence for ourselves; nor did we want to put each other through the anguish of seeing our loved one live out the rest of his days in an institution. We had talked about this a few years before George's illness and we made our wills, living wills and burial plans many years before. We talked about this part of life when we were healthy, happy and very active.

George and I did everything together. We did not need other couples to be able to enjoy life. We were so very close. Our activities included gardening, working out at the spa, dance lessons, ballroom dancing, travelling and more.

So when George first started limping when rising from a sitting position, his solution was to check through books and do recommended back and leg strengthening exercises. He would say there was no pain; it was more like a weakness in his back. That weakness started about ten years priors to his diagnosis. Yes, he had seen doctors, undergone physical therapy regimens and many tests. But mercifully, the physicians could not find the cause of his problem.

Then during George's final summer, his back worsened and he underwent physical therapy again. His back continued to get worse. We always went to the shore in September and walked miles along the shore in the morning and miles on the boardwalk in the evening. This summer of 1994 George could not walk much at all.

The Saturday after Thanksgiving, we departed for our two-week cruise in the Caribbean. George fell several times and found that he lacked the stamina to dance the night away. George was losing the physical ability to do the things that gave him the greatest joy.

On Christmas evening, George who had a beautiful, deep voice and for years sang in the choirs of the Corpus Christi Church and the Barbershoppers could not sing. Another part of him had died. A few days later, George tried to throw one of our cat's plastic bell balls and it traveled only a few feet. He, a former mathematics teacher, began to slur his words.

We immediately called our internist for an appointment. On January 9, 1995, the doctor examined George and ordered an MRI, saying if this test did not indicate what the problem was, he would send George to a neurologist. The look on the doctor's face when he looked into George's mouth told me he had a horrible suspicion of just what the illness was.

On January 31, the neurologist gave George and EMG, followed by a series of other tests. The diagnosis — ALS. Amyotrophic Lateral Sclerosis. A DEATH SENTENCE.

We had wonderful support from our family doctor, his nurses the visiting nurse and the aid. Our physician sent the latter two though George insisted these support personnel would not be necessary. How very wrong he was.

The ALS was progressing rapidly. George was using a quad cane by mid-February 1995 and getting weaker all the time. Lying down after breakfast, lunch and dinner and using a walker before the end of March, George attempted to commit suicide when I was away from home for a doctor's appointment. When I returned, he was in the garage with the door closed and the car's engine was running. A suicide note was on the front seat. That attempt was unsuccessful and I implored my husband to wait before he tried again. I'm so glad he did not die alone. I wanted to be with him at that time.

By now, we needed a hospital bed downstairs, because the steps were too difficult for George to negotiate more than once a day, even with my help or the help of an aid. George was falling more often now and he usually needed my support in addition to the walker. The one part of him, besides his brain which was not deteriorating was his pulmonary function, probably due in part to his strong lungs and his knowing how to breathe properly after all his years of singing. This frightened him. He knew it extended his life.

Meanwhile, we read an article in the newspaper referring to Derek Humphry's book. George had me buy **Final Exit** immediately. We both read the book and joined the Hemlock Society. Their ONLY recommendation was to read **Final Exit**. We had. Then we called the Pittsburgh chapter. We were put in touch with their chaplain who offered to visit us. When the Rev. George Exoo visited, he saw how my husband's muscles had atrophied, how weak he was and how determined to die he was. For all this time George kept saying he was not afraid to die, he was afraid to live. So at George's request, the Chaplain George Exoo promised he would be with us on the night my husband would choose to die. We knew this man could provide no drugs, but my husband wanted someone with me on that night.

I called the minister when George made his decision. The reason for choosing that particular date, May 22, 1995, was that George Koss knew he must be able to get the medicines, prepare them and take them himself. If I were to help, I could be arrested. My dear husband did not want to leave with that thought.

Unknown to me, George had a cache of drugs that had been prescribed for various illnesses in previous years. As difficult as it was, he prepared these drugs early Monday, to be taken that evening with vodka. George made his preparations before The Rev. Exoo arrived so this good man would not be implicated.

When George Exoo came, he had George spend his final hour of consciousness giving an autobiographical sketch. There was much laughter as the evening progressed, for George, fearing that this attempt may fail, decided to drink a fairly large amount of vodka that he had previously mixed with orange juice. In his weakened state, he was a very happy, though somewhat inebriated man.

But he did die happy. Not as a completely physically deteriorated person with a good brain trapped inside his body. ALS does not affect the brain. George's suffering had finally ended.

However, if George could have had the assurance of physician assisted death when he felt he could no longer tolerate his illness, he would have waited. Perhaps only several weeks. Perhaps a month. Perhaps longer. No one will ever know.

I believe assisted dying should be a private matter among the terminally or incurably ill patient, his close family and his physician. If not, more and more people will choose to die earlier in their illness so they can do what is necessary not to implicate their loved ones. Assurance of help from our doctors would, at the very least, result in peace during our last days.

We as family, friends and neighbors must listen to those who are terminally or incurably ill. We MUST respect each individual's very personal decision that only he can decide when the quality of life is nonexistent for him.

Section Nine

25

◆

An MS Patient

The following article was written and submitted

by an Anonymous MS Patient

WHEN I WAS FIRST ASKED TO CONSIDER sharing my story with the people putting this book together, I was enthusiastic about the possibilities that the invitation presented. I'd be able to tell others what it is like to be healthy all of your life, experience the benefits of a good education and a good job, how it feels to know that you've got the world by the shorthairs, and then to have it all destroyed by a single diagnosis. But as time has passed, I've become unsure about sharing my story with anyone — especially my position on issues such as assisted suicide. That is why I opted for anonymity and was appreciative of the promise from the publisher that my name and location would be kept a secret.

But as time went by and my condition has gotten worse, I vacillated back and forth, unsure if I really wanted to leave myself open to possible exposure. This project has taken me many months to write, tear up, rewrite, tear up, and finish. What you read here was painful to put on paper, but it is my sincere hope that those of you who read it will allow yourselves to open your minds, as well as your hearts, and ask what you would truly do if you were in my shoes.

WHEN IT ALL BEGAN...

Some will tell you that according to the textbooks, you are a better candidate for multiple sclerosis in your twenties and less so latter in life. Typically you will hear that an MS diagnosis is usually made on people between the ages of 20 and 40. Well, my body forgot to read the textbooks. My diagnosis came in my mid-forties. I'm sure it wouldn't have mattered if I were twenty-five or eighty-five; just hearing the words, "you have what appears to be MS" will just took my breath away. Being somewhat athletic (a little golf now and then, a random pickup tennis match, and a regular time to play racket ball twice weekly), I assumed that my fair physical condition would enable me to ward off the impact of the disease. Boy was I wrong.

Before I was officially diagnosed, I was getting many of the warning signs — some of which I denied as signs of illness and attributed to laziness or getting older: tripping when merely walking down a city street, misjudging the height of curbs, stumbling over little bumps in sidewalks or when entering doorways. There was increased numbness (you know, the old pins and needles feeling you get when you leg "falls asleep" and is waking up) in my left leg above the knee. As time went by I realized that I wasn't accurately judging distances the way I used to. In the old days I go shag a fly ball while running full out; now I was reaching for a pen and overshooting it by a few inches or nearly braking coffee cups when placing them back on tables or counters. Headaches appeared to be more frequent, but I attributed them to stress on the job. Dizziness was something that I began to take for granted. My vision was in and out — clear then blurred. There was an increased feeling that I had to urinate and when I did, I seemed unable to stop the flow or complete the act without some small degree of embarrassing leakage. And periodically a nausea overtook me that made me want to lie down and roll up in a ball. When I would get myself really fatigued or emotionally upset over what was happening to me, one relief, which had always worked in the past, now seemed to work against me — hot baths. In the old days I would soak away my stress or tension in the hottest bath I could stand. Those baths were wonderful and their therapeutic effect very positive. Now, those very same baths turned me into a limp image of my former self. No longer did they invigorate me and sooth my tension; now they became one of my worst ene-mies. The whole thing was beginning to overtake my ability to shrug things off and it is fair to say that I was beginning a long and debilitating bout with depression.

The small tripping incidents increased. The stumbling seemed to increase. The headaches and dizziness grew more frequent. My wife was no dummy and saw what was going on. She questioned me often about why I was appearing to slur my words and what was causing me to be so absentminded. Finally, out of a combination of wanting to satisfy my wife's concerns and to sooth my own fears, which were increasing, I made an appointment to see the family physician.

This was the beginning of the end for me. The first thing I learned was that there are exact tests for detecting MS. First there were the routine ques-tions and denials. Then there was apparently too much information pointing in one direction to ignore, so I was given an MRI. My brain was scanned in a search for evidence of scarring caused by the presence of MS; this is also known as plaques. At the same time I was given a CT scan — more for com-parison purposes than anything else, since the MRI is a more definitive tool in locating plaques. Before I heard any confirmation or denial of MS, I was told that the MRI, while a great tool, cannot be the only means of diagnosis. And it was important that I understand that some things spotted (lesions) may be more a part of the aging process than the onset of disease.

So additional tests were conducted: blood workups, urine tests, vision tests, tests where I had to walk up and down lines painted on a hospital floor, balance and coordination tests. A series of evoked potential tests were con-ducted by another technician to see if electrical messages were being received properly by my brain. I was asked about my family's medical, emotional, and social history. Then there were the spinal taps (two of them) that provided spinal fluid for observation and testing. These tests weren't as horrible as friends and relatives had suggested, but they were scary.

No definitive tests! That's what they told me. Blood tests alone won't do it. The MRI is a good indicator, but not conclusive. Neurological exams will point out various symptoms, but are not in and of themselves conclusive.

I also found out that the majority of physicians are very insecure about making that initial diagnosis and will put it off as long as possible — in the event that some other diagnosis can be made. Apparently medical professionals are concerned about the impact the phrase "you have multiple sclerosis" has on a person and avoid it like the plague. Boy, I quickly found out that they were right. My physician said that I had "probable MS" and promised that we'd do testing on a regular basis to confirm or dismiss the "probable" part. Hearing the diagnosis is similar to being kicked in the groin by someone wearing shoes the size Shaquille O'Neal wears — only more painful and longer lasting. "Probable" seemed chicken to me. Is being sued the most important thing a doctor has on his mind?

The one thing that stands out in my mind was the physician who said to me, "Remember, MS isn't fatal."

I don't know what you might think, but I've always been impressed with statistics. However, when you become a statistic, the love seems to go out of it. I have read one series of numbers after another and have concluded that I'm a winner in most examples. First off, MS supposedly is found with greater frequency in higher latitudes above 40 degrees latitude from the equator. In the U.S. the median is the 37th parallel. I qualify there. But still the odds are low for contracting MS: somewhere between 57-140 cases per 100,000 people (the average is nearly 1 chance in 1,000). I guess I beat the odds here — which wasn't what I'd want to do if I had a choice. MS is more common among Caucasians (those with northern European ancestry) than other races. I fit that description. MS is almost twice as prevalent among women as men. Now here is one that I beat again and didn't have a choice in the matter.

Well, "probable" or real, whatever I had was beginning to show itself more and more. The attacks came more frequently. Since I traveled in my business, the attacks often took place in hotel rooms in strange cities. I often found myself facing long hours of numbness and tingling and nausea and little strength to phone home and pretend to be okay. Right in the middle of a business meeting, I'd find my words coming slower and often more slurred; I'd rise from a chair and trip over the leg and into the arms of the person whose hand I was attempting to shake. And all of this seemed to lower my ability to shake things off. My attitude got more negative and my mouth more foul. I didn't want to curse at things; I would have preferred to laugh them off. But for reasons that I didn't seem able to control, I was pissed off much of the time. And when I came home from a trip, it wasn't long before my wife became the person I took it out on. How unfair that was.

I would go for what seemed weeks without an attack — what I called my dry periods. But then, sure as the sun rises, I'd get hit with one attack after another. One relapse after another with slower recovery became common. This routine became the standard and this is how I lived for years. And with each attack, it seemed that the flair up and the recovery period lasted longer and longer. On some of my trips, I'd actually find myself spending the entire day in bed, unable to get up. My energy levels decreased to a point that some who observed me thought I was hung over or worse yet, drunk.

The worst part of this entire disease is what it did to the thing I loved most in life: my wife. It killed her. It killed her love for me. It destroyed our marriage. And with all that I can muster, I want it known that she put up with as much as I did. She suffered. She was disabled by what I was going through. Everything I experienced slopped over onto her. And eventually, she couldn't take it any more. I don't hate her for being honest. It sure hurts to think about what was and know that it can never be again. After eighteen years, we separated and divorced. She wasn't weak or uncaring. She was beaten down by MS just as much as I have been.

Today I find myself in a situation where I am in constant pain. There are days when I cannot get move. I have spent as many as three days in bed, struggling to crawl to the toilet, unable to do more than drink some liquid, and unable to think straight. I'm not completely bedfast, but I'm getting close. The wheelchair that I use around my home helps me keep somewhat mobile, but it doesn't allow me any real freedom outdoors. My days of hiking are long gone. My love for writing is virtually at an end (it took me months to get all of this onto paper). In fact, this would not have made it to paper if a close friend hadn't taken my statement down and typed this article for me.

Over the past couple of years, the combination of constant pain, nausea, inability to stand and walk without devices, and that dizziness that I'm suspended in most of the day (and this day is not one of those, otherwise I could not have kept a crystallized thought) has made life pure hell. The drugs that I've taken and still take aren't making life as user friendly as we all had hoped. I've tried Avonex and Betaseron was considered. The Avonex (Interferon) made me more depressed and more apt to have to urinate more frequently.

I've used Copaxone and the self-injected solution didn't do much to curb or ward off attacks and the side effects were not fun.

Over the years I've been spared the attempts of quacks to provide me with remedies and cures. I'm aware of others who have been plagued by these demons. Luckily I avoided them and they didn't find me. The wheelchair has become my friend and my enemy. It helps me do things I no longer have the strength to do for myself, but it keeps me a prisoner. The exercise I tried in the early stages became impossible to maintain. Fatigue took over and that coupled with the constant pain prohibited me from continuing. There are wonderful people who have cared for me and keep more than a watchful eye on my every move (as few as there are these days). Without the caregivers that have devoted themselves to my daily existence, I don't think I'd be around to share this much with you.

I don't believe in what some call spontaneous remission. At least, I haven't seen it. I do support alternative therapies and have participated in a few test situations myself without success. There was Chelation. Tried that. Didn't work for me. May work for others. I've been a gatherer of information all my life. I like to read and study and seek answers. However, when this disease put its arms around me, I had no idea that I'd find so little in the way of concrete information that I can hold on to. This lack of information on the disease has added to my already enlarged state of depression. (And I don't want you as a reader to automatically conclude that my decisions are solely based on depression. I've spent a bunch of time investigating my attitudes, beliefs, knowledge along with my depression and have concluded that much of my thinking is clear. It may not be clear in another person's opinion, but that is also what my Democrat friends say about my Republican leanings.) There was a period when T'ai Chi was a great friend and benefactor for me. I enjoyed it and found the meditative aspects most positive. But the truth be known, it didn't do anything for me physically — and that is where the real disintegration has taken place.

The nights are longer than ever. The days can be bright and sunny, but they aren't part of my routine any longer. What is my routine? Slowness to get started, ever-present pain, dizziness that prevents me from standing erect (when I can get up), inability to dress myself, tie shoes, navigate hallways and sidewalks, days spent sitting in a wheelchair — unable to move the wheels, blurred vision, no appetite, loss of bladder control, frequent memory lapses: these are my days. These are my nights. These are my weeks…months.

The things I loved are gone. The person that I was is gone. My mind was once sharp as a tack and now hangs limp at my side. The friends that once laughed and drank with me are largely invisible and absent; I am the disease I have. What was once life to me is now a burden to be faced and fought. I've lost the will to fight. I want to rest. I want to return to the person I once was. He awaits me somewhere in the distance. He doesn't taunt me, but he knows that I'd be happier with him, as I was, even if it is only a dream.

That is why, when the next big attack puts me down, I will use the time of recovery to make the final plans for my death. I've got too much respect for others to argue the issues any longer and attempt to justify my position or what I'm about to do. That's not for others to decide or judge. It's my body that has been ravaged. It is my mind that has been stolen from me. Those few lucid days I have periodically are not sufficient to sustain me. It is those crazed days of pain and torment that have proven to me that my decision to take my life to another plane isn't wrong. It's not a matter of right or wrong. It's a matter of human dignity. I've lost mine. Where do you suggest I find it? In a book; on TV; in a church; in a nursing home; in a VA hospital; in drugs? My future exists in my death. That will provide me the release I need from these years of attempting to do the "right thing." For all my beliefs and trust, there has been release. I've played the game fairly and honestly. I've been a good patient. I respect my doctors — I don't understand them much of the time (as I believe they fail to understand me or my disease). The clergy I've known are good people for whom I hold respect; but they don't have the answers I need. They have the answers they need. But that isn't good enough for me any longer. The answer is within me.

I asked the publisher to not print my name and address. I am concerned that well meaning people will judge this article as inappropriate and the decision I've made as one based on depression and confusion. I am concerned that they will attempt to stop me from following through on my decision. That cannot happen. I'm not a supporter of Dr. K and the methods he has employed (and I don't want to even have him enter this discussion). And I don't want people confusing my death with his definition of assisted suicide. It is my hope that any of you reading this don't make the judgment that I am going to seek the assistance of someone like him. I must leave this life in control — not out of control and controlled by others. So therefore, shortly after recovery from my next relapse, I will leave this wonderful life that I've experienced. My friends and loved ones are fewer these days than a decade ago, but that goes with the disease. To those who have stood by me and supported my decisions, I thank you all. My fondest memories during the worst days of pain and disability have been your shining faces. Friends are and have been my best drug.

26

♦

A Deadly
"Medical Treatment"

By Rita L. Marker

This is information [about assisted suicide and euthanasia] that will come as a shock to the many members of the public — including legislators and even some physicians — who have never considered that the procedures involved in physician-assisted suicide and euthanasia might sometimes add to the suffering they are meant to alleviate and might also preclude the tranquil death being sought.[1]

I N MID-FEBRUARY THE **New England Journal of Medicine** published an article that marked the first time in which a major U.S. medical journal revealed the problems, complications and difficulties encountered when euthanasia and assisted suicide are carried out.[2]

Yet the ongoing debate over legalization of euthanasia and assisted suicide continues to be characterized by euphemisms. "Death with dignity," "aid-in-dying," "helping someone die," and "letting someone die" are the soft phrases used to mask harsh realities.

Many people are still under the mistaken impression that hapless patients can be involuntarily tethered to machines to keep them alive and that laws need to be changed so patients can be "allowed to die." However the law makes it very clear that people cannot be subjected to medical treatments that they do not want.

The current debate is about one issue, and one issue only. It can be expressed in the form of a question: Should the crime of assisted suicide be transformed into a "medical treatment?"

Those who believe that the answer to that question should be "yes" have constantly portrayed assisted suicide as a means of achieving a peaceful gentle death in which a person "slips peacefully away."

At the time this commentary is being written, Oregon remains the only place in the United States where assisted suicide has become an acceptable medical treatment.

There, it not only is permitted but is paid for with private insurance and with state Medicaid funds under the part of the Oregon Health Plan called "comfort care."[3]

The Oregon experience provides an opportunity to examine how such a law could pass and how it is implemented.

SELLING ASSISTED SUICIDE

Whether the "product" is a soft drink or death, a television ad is the most efficient method to sell large numbers of people on the idea that they need what is being advertised.

The centerpiece of the campaign to pass Oregon's "Death with Dignity Act" was a 60-second television commercial, featuring Patty A. Rosen, a former nurse who had been director of an Oregon Hemlock chapter since 1989. (Her affiliation with Hemlock was not acknowledged in the ad.) The commercial played on voters' fears of uncontrollable pain and offered peaceful-dignified-death-with-pills as the solution.

Wearing a purple sweater and a long skirt, Rosen strolled through a wooded area. As slow, sad music played in the background, she said:

"I am a criminal. My 25-year-old daughter, Jody, was dying of bone cancer. The pain was so great that she couldn't bear to be touched, and drugs didn't help. Jody only had a few weeks to live when she decided she wanted to end her life. But it wasn't legally possible.

"So I broke the law and got her the pills necessary. And as she slipped peacefully away, I climbed into her bed and took her in my arms (Rosen's voice cracked with emotion at this point) for the first time in months.

"When did we give up our right to run our own lives? Doesn't government have better things to do than make criminals out of law-abiding citizens? Are we going to let one church make the rules for all of us?

"Measure 16 would have allowed my daughter to die with dignity. It has safeguards against abuse. I was a registered nurse. I know. Vote yes on 16. We should all have the right to live every minute of our lives with dignity."

The ad was powerful, compelling. Rosen followed up on it by traveling throughout the state speaking on behalf of Measure 16. When she was interviewed for articles about the proposal, she repeated the story of how she gave Jody the pills and "she slipped peacefully away."

It was a good story. But it wasn't true.

Two years earlier, during a campaign in California[4] to legalize euthanasia by lethal injection as well as assisted suicide, Rosen told an audience she had given her daughter pills but they hadn't worked and it had been necessary to give her a lethal injection.

First, Rosen said, she gave her daughter the pills, then she described what happened next:

So she went to sleep. I didn't know about plastic bags. I wish I had. [I]t seemed to be backfiring. And I was fortunate enough at the very last to be able to hit a vein right and say "Bye, Jody. See you later."[5]

During the Measure 16 campaign, the public didn't know about the discrepancy between the pills-only and the lethal injection versions of Rosen's story until three days before the actual voting took place. At that time, in an article appeared in an inside section of the Oregonian in which Rosen admitted her daughter had, indeed, died of a lethal injection. She explained that, after giving her daughter the pills, she gave her a suppository so she wouldn't vomit up the pills. Then, fearing that the pills would not do the job, she had injected her daughter with a lethal amount of morphine. Nevertheless, Rosen defended the campaign ad, saying, "I OK'd the script and it came from my heart."[6]

Measure 16 spokespersons played down the importance of the article, claiming there was nothing wrong with leaving out the part about the lethal injection since Rosen's daughter would have died from the pills alone if Rosen had only waited a little longer and not panicked.[7]

Three days after the lethal injection story broke, voters went to the polls and approved Measure 16, the Oregon "Death with Dignity Act." With its passage, Oregon became the only place where an intentionally prescribed drug overdose is considered a "medical treatment" under the law. Because of legal challenges to the Oregon law's constitutionality,[8] it was not implemented until late 1997, just weeks prior to a failed attempt to repeal it.[9]

INSIDE THE PACKAGE

Oregon voters bought the assisted suicide package that had been wrapped in soothing words and commercial hype. But few Oregonians knew the actual contents of the law. For example:

Oregon's assisted suicide law has no safeguards for the patient at the time the drug overdose is taken.

> The Oregon law's safeguards, illusory though they may be, only cover behavior up through the time the doctor writes the prescription for lethal drugs. The law contains no provisions dealing with what happens after the patient receives the prescription. The prescribed drugs could be stored over time, with no concern for public safety or for protecting the vulnerable patient from those who might benefit from the patient's early demise.

> Furthermore, even the requirement that the patient's judgment not be impaired refers only to the time between the requests for assisted

suicide and the time of prescribing. Nothing in the law requires that the patient be competent at the time the deadly overdose is taken.

A 1997 Oregon Bar Association publication about Oregon's "Death with Dignity" law, noted that "The Act merely regulates the conduct of all parties up to the point of the drug prescription."[10]

Under the Oregon assisted suicide law, family members don't have to be notified when a doctor is going to help a loved one commit suicide.

Family notification is *not required*, only recommended.[11] The patient's family doesn't need to be notified until after the patient is dead.

Under Oregon's assisted suicide law, government health programs, managed care programs, HMOs and other health insurance companies can cut costs by approving and paying for inexpensive prescriptions for suicide.

Under the Oregon Health Plan, the state maintains a priority list of medical services. The list includes 743 line items, of which 574 are funded. Assisted suicide is funded under line item number 263, "comfort care."[12]

Non-governmental health insurance plans also pay for coverage of assisted suicide. Company spokespersons have explained that the lethal prescription is "no different than any other covered prescription."[13] Drugs for assisted suicide cost about $35 to $45, making them far less expensive than providing palliative care.

Oregon's assisted suicide law gives insurance companies, health providers, HMOs and others the opportunity to suggest assisted suicide or encourage a patient to request a lethal prescription.

The law does not allow anyone to "coerce" or use "undue influence" to obtain a request for assisted suicide.[14] However, this does not prevent subjecting a vulnerable patient to subtle pressure or other forms of manipulation.

Oregon's assisted suicide law permits doctors to help mentally ill or depressed patients commit suicide.

Mental illness and depression do not bar a prescription for assisted suicide, nor do they require that the suicidal patient receive counseling. A referral for counseling is only necessary if, in the "opinion" of the attending physician, the patient requesting death has a "psychiatric or psychological disorder, including depression, *causing impaired judgment.*"[15]

Even then, the law does not preclude people who are depressed or who have psychiatric or psychological disorders from obtaining a prescription for lethal drugs as long as a mental health professional determines that the person's judgment is not impaired.

Furthermore, neither early dementia nor other cognitive problems automatically prevents a patient from being "qualified" for assisted suicide.[16] Practice guidelines for implementing the Oregon law indicate that a person for whom the court has appointed a guardian or conservator can still qualify for assisted suicide. The guidelines merely suggest that doctors notify (not obtain permission from) the guardian or conservator regarding the request for lethal drugs.[17]

If one health professional finds the patient unqualified for assisted suicide, "shopping" can take place until the request is approved.

Even if a patient is found to have "impaired judgment," Oregon's law does not prohibit a health provider, family member or others from arranging for the patient to be evaluated by other health professionals until one is found who declares that the patient is capable of choosing assisted suicide.

Mail order drug overdoses are permitted under Oregon's assisted suicide law.

Nothing in the Oregon law requires that the patient obtain the lethal drugs in person. In one reported assisted suicide under the state's new law, the patient received them via Federal Express.[18]

Prescriptions by mail are commonplace, particularly for the elderly, for people with disabilities and for individuals who live in rural areas.

Mail order pharmacies are growing and, as managed care programs attempt to cut back on costs and increase profits, some have employed practices to drive enrollees to use mail order pharmacies owned by the HMO itself.

Under Oregon's assisted suicide law, requests for assisted suicide do not need to be made in person.

Oregon's law requires that a patient make two oral requests and one written request for assisted suicide within a time span of no less than fifteen days.[19] However, there is no requirement that any of these be made in person. The two oral requests could be made by phone and the witnessed, written request could be sent by mail to the doctor, who could then prescribe the drugs for assisted suicide.

Soothing words and images of loving family members surrounding the deathbed made for good promotional material. But there is no way to know what is really taking place at death scenes in Oregon now that doctors have been given the power to prescribe assisted suicide.

"JUST A COCK AND BULL STORY"

Proponents of assisted suicide have claimed that Oregon's assisted suicide law can be carefully monitored to prevent any abuse. They have pointed to the two official reports[20] that have been issued by the Oregon Health Division (OHD) on Oregon's assisted suicide law, claiming that the reports prove that the law is working well.

Indeed, Dr. Katrina Hedberg, co-author of both official reports has explicitly denied that there have been any problems in connection with assisted suicide. Referring to prior warnings from opponents of assisted suicide about potential complications, Hedberg stated, "Those things have not materialized."[21]

But Hedberg's reassurances are hollow and reliance on the OHD's official reports for an accurate picture of legalized assisted suicide is misplaced.

Under careful scrutiny, the Oregon assisted suicide law's reporting procedures are weak, at best.

All actual requirements for reporting are directed only at the OHD which must make rules to facilitate information collection, review a sample of records and issue an annual statistical report.[22] Doctors who prescribe drugs for assisted suicide need only maintain documentation of the process in patients' medical records.[23] And, although the OHD has the mandate of requiring health care providers to file a copy of dispensing records,[24] there are no penalties in the law for health care providers who fail to provide any reports. Additionally, Hedberg has acknowledged that the OHD has no regulatory authority or resources to ensure compliance with reporting requirements.[25]

The OHD admits that information on which its official reports are based may be incomplete and inaccurate. Only prescribing physicians were interviewed for either report. The first report stated that among its limitations was the fact that "the possibility of physician bias must be considered."[26] In addition, it conceded, "[W]e cannot detect or collect data on issues of noncompliance with any accuracy"[27] and "We do not know if covert physician-assisted continued to be practiced in Oregon in 1998."[28]

The second report noted similar problems. "Underreporting cannot be assessed, and noncompliance is difficult to assess because of the possible repercussions for non-compliant physicians reporting data to the division."[29]

The OHD even admitted that reporting physicians may have fabricated their versions of the circumstances surrounding the prescriptions written for patients: "For that matter, the entire account could have been a cock-and-bull story. We assume, however that physicians were their usual careful and accurate selves."[30]

Since information in official reports is limited to that which assisted suicide advocates choose to report, there is no way to know how many, or under what circumstances, patients have died from assisted suicide in Oregon.

Thus, statements that 43 is the number of deaths that occurred during the first two years of legal physician-assisted suicide in Oregon must be viewed with great skepticism. Other unreported deaths may well have occurred.

Nonetheless, even the selectively reported information appearing in the Oregon reports raises as many questions as it answers. For example, one patient was reported to have taken the lethal dose more than eight months after receiving the prescription.[31] But lethal prescriptions under Oregon's

"Death with Dignity Act" are supposed to be limited to patients who have a life expectancy of six months or less.

How many other patients would have lived months or years had they not taken the lethal overdose?

Again, there is no way to know.

The OHD is not authorized to investigate how physicians determine their patients' diagnoses or life expectancies[32] so the actual life expectancy of those who died after taking prescriptions for assisted suicide is unknown.

Official reports from Oregon also contain figures indicating that sixty-one percent of patients did not receive their lethal drug prescriptions from the first physician they asked.[33] Since the refusing physicians were not interviewed by the OHD for the official reports there is no way to know why these doctors refused to prescribe or why they determined that the patient was not qualified for an assisted suicide death under the Oregon law.

Was it because the patient was not terminally ill? Was it because the patient was not competent? Was it because the physician was opposed to assisted suicide?

Answers to these questions are not known, because the physicians were never asked.

The OHD's figures also indicate that some patients knew their doctors for only two weeks before the lethal dose was prescribed.[34]

Because at least two weeks must elapse between the first and last requests for the lethal dose, it appears that, in these cases, the physician-patient relationship was established for the specific purpose of obtaining the drugs for assisted suicide.

The reports state that none of those who died from assisted suicide did so because of financial pressures. This is somewhat questionable given the fact that more that 14% of the deaths reported were those of Medicaid patients, who are among the poorest Oregonians.[35]

Yet, advocates of assisted suicide claim that the Oregon law assures that patients will be informed of "all options." This is often interpreted as meaning that assisted suicide would be freely chosen after one has rejected those options.

But, on closer examination, it is clear that the Oregon law only requires the doctor to inform the patient of the "feasible alternatives, including, but not limited to, comfort care, hospice care and pain control."[36] Since hospice and other types of necessary support and care would not be a "feasible alternative" for patients who do not have the financial resources to obtain them, there is even some question as to whether the physician would have to inform a patient about such services.

In fact, in the absence of the ability to afford such services, being "informed" about them is not only futile. It is cruel.

It is also cruel to hide the fact that assisted suicide does not ensure the peaceful death so persuasively (and deceptively) described in the "and-she-slipped-peacefully-away" commercials that ushered in the Oregon "Death with Dignity Act."

NEWS REPORTS CONTRADICT OFFICIAL REPORTS

Overdoses of barbiturates, which are the most commonly used drugs for assisted suicide, are known to cause distressing — even excruciating — symptoms. Extreme gasping can take place. Muscle spasms can occur. As he loses consciousness, a person may vomit and then inhale the vomit. Panic can set in. Feelings of terror and even physical lashing out can happen due to drug-induced confusion. Other problems — difficulty in taking the drugs, failure of the drugs to induce unconsciousness and a number of days elapsing before death occurs — have also been noted.[37]

As previously noted, the absence of *reported* problems in the implementation of Oregon's assisted suicide law is used as proof that no problems have occurred.

But published information, describing the very real problems with assisted suicide in the Netherlands, strongly suggests that similar difficulties may be taking place in Oregon.

In the Netherlands, the Royal Dutch Association of Pharmacy has formulated guidelines intended to prevent problems and to increase the efficiency of assisted suicide. Yet, even with such guidance, there are still problems with reported physician-assisted suicide:

Muscle spasms, extreme gasping and vomiting occurred in 7% of assisted suicide cases.[38]

Because of other problems, doctors decided to administer a lethal injection in 18% of attempted assisted suicides.[39]

In 14% of assisted suicides, patients did not become unconscious, or they awoke or lingered far longer than expected.[40]

And, even in the Netherlands, problems may have been underreported since "it seems likely that the physicians whose patients experienced the worst complications would be most reluctant to answer questions about untoward events."[41]

Dr. Sherwin Nuland of Yale University School of Medicine (who, incidentally, favors assisted suicide) pointed to the Dutch figures and to the lack of any reported problems in Oregon. "The Dutch findings seem more credible," he wrote.

In addition to the conclusions that can be drawn by comparing the Dutch experience and the *reported* Oregon experience, there is actual information from Oregon showing that the rosy picture painted in Oregon's official reports cannot be believed.

News reports from Oregon have revealed troubling information about two assisted suicide cases in Oregon — information that was conspicuous for its absence from the official Oregon reports.

Patrick Matheny received his lethal dose of drugs from the Oregon Health Sciences University via Federal Express. Four months later, on the day of his death, he experienced difficulty and had to be "helped" to die by his brother-in-law, Joe Hayes. Hayes said, "It doesn't go smoothly for everyone. For Pat, it was a huge problem. It would not have worked without help."[42]

Another assisted suicide in which problems were encountered was described by attorney Cynthia Barrett in December 1999 during a class at Portland Community College titled, "Physician-Assisted Suicide: Counseling Patients/Clients."

"The man was at home. There was no doctor there," Barrett said. "After he took it [the drug overdose], he began to have some physical symptoms. The symptoms were hard for his wife to handle. Well, she [the wife] called 911. The guy ended up being taken by 911 to a local Portland hospital. Revived. In the middle of it. And taken to a local nursing facility. I don't know if he went back home. He died shortly — some period of time after that time."[43]

George Eighmey, director of the Oregon chapter of Compassion in Dying (an assisted suicide advocacy group), who was also present at the workshop told those in attendance that the man "wasn't one of our patients."[44]

Barrett's remarks may never have been reported if Catherine Hamilton, a nurse who opposes assisted suicide, had not been at the workshop. According to Hamilton, Eighmey approached her after the session and told her that the information was confidential and should not be discussed with the media. His invocation of confidentiality was without merit, given the fact that Barrett hadn't given any identifying information. There was only one reason to keep the story "confidential." It was to keep information about the "botched suicide" away from the public.

But Hamilton's account of the event appeared in an article published by **Brainstorm**, an Internet magazine.[45]

It led to an interview on Portland's KXL radio in which Eighmey was asked if he was familiar with the case that Hamilton had described. Eighmey accused Hamilton of "irresponsible, unsubstantiated reporting" and said that neither he nor two other workshop participants had heard Barrett say anything about such a case. "So whether Mrs. Hamilton is hearing things or not we don't know," he said.[46]

His suggestion that Hamilton had been imagining things might have prevailed. But, apparently unnoticed by Eighmey, the workshop had been recorded and the talk show host was aware of this. When he told Eighmey that both Barrett's remarks and Eighmey's statement (that the patient wasn't Compassion in Dying's) were on tape, Eighmey chose to end the interview.[47]

Are the Matheny death and the case described by Cynthia Barrett the only times that complications have arisen in conjunction with the Oregon assisted suicide law? There is no way to know.

CONCLUSION

The Oregon experience demonstrates that the selling of assisted suicide can be done with soothing words and images. But, once legal, the "medical treatment" of death-by-lethal-prescription is shrouded in secrecy.

Whether other states will eventually embrace Oregon-style "comfort care" will depend upon a willingness of all to carefully examine what is truly at stake in this debate. It will also depend upon a recognition that assisted suicide, if legal, may be a "choice" for some. But for others, it may become the only "medical treatment" they can afford.

Indeed, it is true that assisted suicide is inexpensive in terms of dollars spent for a lethal overdose. But it is far too costly in terms of danger to individuals and to society.

This is one "medical treatment" that should be rejected.

Rita L. Marker is an attorney and executive director of the International Anti-Euthanasia Task Force. She is the author of *Deadly Compassion* (William Morrow & Co., 1993).

REFERENCES

1   Sherwin Nuland, "Physician-Assisted Suicide and Euthanasia in Practice," 342 *New England Journal of Medicine* (February 24, 2000) p.583.

2   Johanna H. Groenwoud, M.D., et al., "Clinical Problems with the Performance of Euthanasia and Physician-Assisted Suicide in the Netherlands," 342 *The New England Journal of Medicine* (February 24, 2000) pp. 551-556.

3   Dan Postrel, "State could cover assisted suicide," *Statesman Journal* (Salem, OR), December 1, 1994, p. A1.

4   California's Proposition 161, the 1992 ballot initiative to legalize "aid-in-dying," failed to pass.

5   Transcript of audio tape of panel discussion, "Grief, Guilt and Assisted Suicide," at the Hemlock Society's 6th National Conference at the Hyatt Regency Hotel in Long Beach, CA on Sept. 25, 1992. Tape and transcript on file with author. In both the 1994 campaign ad and the 1992 Hemlock presentation, Ms. Rosen claimed that her daughter's pain was uncontrollable. However, according to the death certificate for Jody Grape (Patty Rosen's daughter), Ms. Grape's attending physician for the five months prior to her death was Dr. William Swartz, an obstetri-

cian-gynecologist. Jody Grape had thyroid cancer that had metastasized. Swartz (who also signed her death certificate) would have been poorly equipped to provide adequate palliative care for her condition. Death certificate on file with author.

6 O'Keefe, Mark, "TV ad on assisted suicide leaves out part of story," *The Oregonian*, Nov. 4, 1994, p. C1.

7 Ibid.

8 *Lee v. Harcleroad*, 1997 USAPLEX 7578.

9 Measure 16, the Oregon "Death with Dignity Act," passed in 1994. Measure 51, an attempt to repeal the "Death with Dignity Act," failed in 1997.

10 Barbara Coombs Lee, Eli D. Stutsman, Kelly T. Hagen, "Physician Assisted Suicide," *Oregon Health Law Manual*, Volume 2: Life and Death Decisions, (Oregon State Bar, 1997), Chapter 8, p. 13. (emphasis added)

11 ORS 127.835 §3.05.

12 Erin Barnett, "Suicide coverage passes review," *Oregonian*, April 26, 1999.

13 Dan Postrel, "State could cover assisted suicide," *Statesman Journal*, Salem, OR), December 6, 1994.

14 ORS 127.890 §4.02 (2).

15 ORS 127.825 §3.03 (emphasis added).

16 Erin Barnett, "A family struggle: Is Mom capable of choosing to die?" *The Oregonian*, October, 17, 1999.

17 Barbara Coombs Lee, Eli D. Stutsman, Kelly T. Hagen, "Physician Assisted Suicide," *Oregon Health Law Manual*, Volume 2: Life and Death Decisions (Oregon State Bar Association, 1997), Chapter 8, p.12.

18 Erin Barnett, "Dilemma of Assisted Suicide: When?" *Oregonian*, January 17, 1999.

19 ORS 127.840 §3.06.

20 "Oregon's Death with Dignity Act: The First Year's Experience," Department of Human Resources, Oregon Health Division,

Center for Disease Prevention and Epidemiology (February 18, 1999). Hereafter referred to as "OHD Report 1." The entire official first year report is available on line at:

http://www.ohd.hr.state.or.us/chs/pas/year1/ar-index.htm.

"Oregon's Death with Dignity Act: The Second Year's Experience," Department of Human Services, Oregon Health Division, Center for Disease Prevention and Epidemiology (February 23, 2000).s Hereafter referred to as "OHD Report 2." The entire official second year report is available at: http://www.ohd.hr.state.or.us/chs/pas/ar-index.htm.

21 Joe Rojas-Burke, "Suicide critics say lack of problems in Oregon is odd," The Oregonian, February 24, 2000.

22 ORS 127.865 § 3.11.

23 ORS 127.855 § 3.09.

24 ORS 127.865 § 3.11 (b).

25 Linda Prager, "Details emerge on Oregon's first assisted suicides," American Medical News, September 7, 1998.

26 OHD Report 1, p. 9.

27 Ibid.

28 Ibid.

29 Ann Sullivan, Katrina Hedberg, and David Fleming, "Legalized Physician-Assisted Suicide in Oregon — The Second Year," 342 New England Journal of Medicine (February 24, 2000) p. 603 and OHD Report 2, p. 12.

30 Oregon Health Division, CD Summary, (March 16, 1999), p. 2. The OHD's CD Summary is available at: http://www.ohd.hr.state.or.us/chs/pas/pascdsm2.htm.

31 Ann Sullivan, Katrina Hedberg, and David Fleming, "Legalized Physician-Assisted Suicide in Oregon — The Second Year," 342 New England Journal of Medicine (February 24, 2000) p. 599.

32 Katrina Hedberg et al., Letter to the Editor, Hastings Center Report (Jan.-Feb. 2000) p. 4.

33 Ann Sullivan, Katrina Hedberg, and David Fleming, "Legalized Physician-Assisted Suicide in Oregon — The Second Year," 342 *New England Journal of Medicine* (February 24, 2000) p. 603.

34 Ibid., p. 601, Table 2 and OHD Report 2, Table 2.

35 Amy Sullivan, Katrina Hedberg, and David Fleming, "Legalized Physician-Assisted Suicide in Oregon — The Second Year," 342 *New England Journal of Medicine* (February 24, 2000) p. 600.

36 ORS 127.815 § 301 (2)(E).

37 Johanna H. Groenwoud, M.D., et al., "Clinical Problems with the Performance of Euthanasia and Physician-Assisted Suicide in the Netherlands," 342 The *New England Journal of Medicine* (February 24, 2000) p. 553-555 and David Reinhard, "The pills don't kill: The case," *The Oregonian*, March 23, 2000.

38 Johanna H. Groenwoud, M.D., et al., "Clinical Problems with the Performance of Euthanasia and Physician-Assisted Suicide in the Netherlands," 342 The *New England Journal of Medicine* (February 24, 2000) p. 553-555.

39 Ibid., p. 554.

40 Ibid., p. 555.

41 Sherwin Nuland, "Physician-Assisted Suicide and Euthanasia in Practice," 342 *New England Journal of Medicine* (February 24, 2000) p.583.

42 Erin Barnett, "Dilemma of assisted suicide: When?" Oregonian, January 17, 1999 and Erin Barnett, "Man with ALS makes up his mind to die," *The Oregonian*, March 11, 1999.

43 Catherine Hamilton, "The Oregon Report: What's Hiding behind the Numbers?" *Brainstorm*, March 2000, www.brainstormnw.com

44 Ibid.

45 Ibid.

46 David Reinhard, "The pills don't kill: The case, First of two parts," *The Oregonian*, March 23, 2000 and Reinhard, "The pills

don't kill: The cover-up, Second of two parts," *The Oregonian*, March 26, 2000.

47 Ibid.

27

---◆---

Beyond Physician-assisted Suicide

The Art and Science of Dying Well

by John Hofsess

John Hofsess is the founder of the Right to Die Society of Canada in 1991 and the originator of DeathNET, the first web site devoted to "end of life" issues and problems. (http://www.rights.org/deathnet), DeathNET came on-line January 1995 and has recorded nearly one million accesses to its homepage.

PROLOGUE

My acquaintance with Bob Horn began with an article he wrote for the **Los Angeles Times** ("Choosing Life: Even on a Ventilator"; May 16, 1996).

He got right to the point in his opening paragraph:

"In the national debate on doctor-assisted suicide, we have heard from judges and lawyers, doctors and clergymen, ethicists and editorial writers, politicians and pundits. The one group conspicuously absent so far from the discussion is the one most affected by its outcome: the terminally ill."

Bob had no illusions about his illness or his prospects: "ALS is a terminal illness. It is progressive, unrelenting, merciless." Despite being offered, on two occasions, help to die by his doctors, Bob chose to live. But, unlike some people who believe that because they live in a certain manner every one else should do the same, Bob did not elevate his personal choice (living on a ventilator) to a doctrinaire position.

He wrote: "Although I made the right decision for me, that is not to say that my choice would be appropriate for everyone. The personal struggles of people against life-threatening illnesses do not lend themselves to facile judgments. These are highly individual battles that depend on many factors, from personal outlook and philosophy to the specific circumstances and, significantly, to the nature of the illness itself. For instance, in ALS, the symptoms vary dramatically from patient to patient; one person's experience is no guide to someone else's."

In his book, **How Will They Know if I'm Dead?** (1997) Bob says that his favorite passage in the Bible is from First Corinthians: "If I speak in tongues of men and of angels, but have not love, I am a noisy gong or a clanging cymbal." When a person is imbued with compassion and respect for others, he or she will — like Bob Horn — honor the choices that other people make.

Bob's book deepened my appreciation for his wisdom. All too often where "right to die" issues are concerned, public debate is little more than the clanging of gongs and cymbals. Consider Bill White of Rochester, NY. (August, 1999). His life had been sustained by a ventilator for 32 years. White had spent more than half of his life in a hospital, following an accident in his late teens which left him a quadriplegic. Now his health was deteriorating below a level that was acceptable to him. He requested that hospital officials disconnect him from the respirator and let him die.

Bill White wanted his wishes to be kept private. He wanted the hospital to act with discretion. But, as it happened, he had a friend, Mike McBride, who had other ideas and values. McBride made White's plight public and turned his request into a public controversy. Thus White had to spend his last weeks on earth as the subject of a clamorous court action in which "disability activists" argued that he should be prevented from having his respirator disconnected. Members of a group called Not Dead Yet staged a vigil outside the hospital proclaiming their "love" for a man they had never met and did not know. And the media — which thrive on divisiveness — rewarded the protesters with the publicity they sought.

Fortunately, for Bill White, case law in New York State protected his right to refuse medical treatment. "What gives you the right to come in here and make decisions for Mr. White?" U.S. District Judge Charles S. Siragusa asked a lawyer for the Center for Disability Rights. "Is there any indication that Mr. White, even though his body is disabled, can't make a decision for himself?"

Ironically, the Center for Disability Rights argued in court that Bill White had no "rights" because he was not of sound mind. Lawyers argued that White was "depressed" and should be transferred to another facility of *their* recommendation against his wishes. After several days of listening to arguments based on politics and legal technicalities, the judge ruled in White's favor.

All this gratuitous turmoil is far removed from the philosophy of respecting personal choice articulated by Bob Horn. We rarely hear Bob's thoughtful views conveyed by the media. Whereas we often see the "confrontational" antics of activists determined to impose their views upon everyone else. Not Dead Yet claims to speak for everyone who is disabled — but it doesn't speak for Bob Horn. (Nor does it speak for at least six other disabled individuals who publicly fought for the right to have an assisted death — ranging from the late Noel Earley of Rhode Island to the late Austin Bastable of Windsor, Ontario). It obviously didn't speak for Bill White. Perhaps the truth is that Not Dead Yet doesn't speak for any disabled person who believes in having a choice.*

---

*NOTE: **Not Dead Yet** claims to be motivated by the belief that legalized forms of euthanasia and assisted suicide will inevitably be used against society's disenfranchised groups. They apparently believe, based upon certain historical records from Nazi Germany, that the disabled will be first in line for mass extermination if *voluntary* assisted death is permitted for the terminally ill. It would make more sense if **Not Dead Yet** lobbied for assisted suicide laws that specifically exclude the disabled rather than trying to prevent everyone else from having a choice on the basis of little more than paranoia. It is worth noting, I believe, that we do not find similarly hysterical fears among Jewish people or homosexuals, groups victimized by the Nazis in far greater numbers than the disabled. In fact, support for assisted suicide is quite strong in those social groups. If **Not Dead Yet** lobbied for the disabled to be excluded from proposed assisted suicide laws it would also have the effect of determining the size of their constituency. Such a law would permit the terminally ill to have assistance in dying but not if they were also disabled. The disabled would be forced to live, whether they wanted to or not, and die only through the approved methods of palliative care. Such a law might not be constitutional but it does appear to be the legislative position of **Not Dead Yet**, so why not pursue it openly?

Choice is what my work is all about. I am not prejudicially pro-euthanasia and I certainly do not favor physician-assisted suicide. But I passionately believe in empowering individuals with the freedom to make decisions about where, when, how, and with whom they will die. That means that I work on a practical level to extend the range of end-of-life choices.

Because there are already plenty of people working in the well-funded field of palliative care, I have become a specialist in suicide methodology. That doesn't mean that I believe that suicide is preferable to the ways of palliative care. Rather, I believe that suicide needs resourceful researchers to ensure that it is *as well-developed a field as palliative care*. If I were terminally ill, I would want to know what my options are in dying well. If someone said to me: "well we can offer you palliative care or we can offer you palliative care" — I wouldn't think that was much of a choice.

On the other hand, I *would* have a meaningful choice if someone with expertise in suicide methods were to say: "you can either die painlessly but slowly, over the course of several weeks, under standard procedures of palliative care, or you can have a quick and pleasant death with the use of inert gas".

I would want to know more about these options — among others. *Ideally, I would make an informed decision in a calm environment without pressure from outside groups.* I would be free to have the best death that I can afford and which is consistent with my values.

It is because I believe in certain fundamental human rights — paramount among which is a person's freedom to choose in all matters affecting his or her final days — that I engage in the work I do. I try to make *choice* a meaningful word.

THE ART AND SCIENCE OF SUICIDE

June 25, 1998: One of those days when history is made offstage. After two years of effort and an accumulative investment of more than $12,000, the Last Rights research team had its first working model of a "debreather."

I placed a soft, pliable silicone mask over my nose and mouth. I continued to breathe normally. There was no odor. The air seemed exactly the same (including its temperature) as that which I was accustomed to breathing. *But it wasn't the same.* A sensor connected to the mask measured the amount of oxygen in the system. Within minutes, the oxygen level declined sharply from 21% (normal air) to less than 12%. And with each new breath, the oxygen level continued to decline. There was no discomfort. I had no awareness (apart from watching the oxygen sensor-readout) of any significant change going on. I did not, on this occasion, push the system to the extent that our chief engineer had — that is, actually blacking out due to lack of oxygen. I felt momentarily light-headed but quickly recovered when the mask was removed.

Had I continued breathing with the mask on, I would have passed out in another couple of minutes. I would have died a few minutes after becoming unconscious. The Debreather is a means of gently inducing death that requires *no restricted medications, no poisons and no compressed gases*. The debreather processes ordinary air in such a way as to painlessly cause death in approximately 20 minutes. Needless to say, no doctor is required. With the advent of the debreather, it may be said that *physician-assisted suicide* is a concept that has come and gone without ever coming to fruition

Most right-to-die organizations tend to support the *medicalization* of death, a process that subordinates individual freedom to the policies and practices of doctors, psychiatrists, pharmacists, medical ethicists, and a wide range of medical associations. Right-to-die organizations do this because they base their political policies on extremely conservative "death science": methods of causing death that depend crucially on a doctor's prescription.

Needless to say, if the sole method of suicide of which you approve is a massive overdose of a restricted medication that only a doctor may prescribe, inevitably you are led *to (and confined to)* the concept of physician-assisted suicide.

But what if there are methods superior to the ingestion of six to ten grams of barbiturate? *Faster* methods that might take only a few minutes to work, instead of hours or days. *Safer* methods that do not give rise to vomiting or pose a risk of having a person discovered in a comatose state and revived. And, most liberating of all, methods that do not depend upon a physician's patronizing involvement. Is it likely that, with all the resourcefulness for which mankind is renowned, there are no better ways of committing suicide than overdosing on "class one" drugs?

As it happens, the debreather is merely one form of new technology which the Last Rights research team has developed for the purpose of extending the range of end-of-life options.

Another suicide method that we have developed involves the use of helium. (Other inert gas systems we have devised use nitrogen or argon). Helium is easily obtained in the form of a "party balloon kit" from outlets such as K-Mart or Toys'R'Us. The non-refillable, non-returnable cylinder of helium is then connected to a special mask. Death occurs in two or three minutes. Helium is odorless, non-inflammable, and quickly disperses posing no threat to others. Our research is described in a series of publications known as The Art and Science of Suicide series (see mailing address below). Again, no doctor is involved. No doctor is necessary. One is more likely to obtain a good death with the help of a compassionate *engineer* than one is with a doctor: no one is going to quote the Hippocratic oath in a welding supply shop.

Anyone who complains about wanting to die but not having the means is clearly someone who has not given much thought to the use of helium. *Helium is not the poor man's substitute for not having barbiturates; death by helium represents a progressive step beyond barbiturates.* For years, terminally ill people have been lamenting that they cannot get a prescription from a doctor for a lethal dose of "sleeping pills" and therefore have no choice but to die in a hospice or a hospital. But their imprisonment is strictly that of being trapped in a mindset. For approximately $100, a person may have a first-class death with helium anytime they choose: quick, safe and painless.

We do not generally find hospice advocates willing to match us in honesty and candor. Hospice is almost-always talked about in lofty or sentimental abstractions. What is it *actually* like to die in hospice? What is the average length of stay? How much does it cost? Is the price worth it? Are all or most hospices alike? Do they vary in quality like hotels — from four-star caregiving down to one-star accommodation? In other words, what is the *reality* of the hospice care you are likely to receive? What, if anything, are you *guar-*

anteed by accepting hospice care? Freedom from pain? Relief from all other miseries? Can you leave at any time? Can you change your mind — if you want to die some other way?

According to a wire story issued by United Press International (September 16, 1999) hospice professionals are said to be worried about "decreasing lengths of stay" and the economic impact upon their industry. The article went on to state that hospice pros are devising ways of making more money from their "clients" — such as admitting them earlier than usual and extending the length of stay. None of this sounded as if it was motivated by what is in the best interests of the dying patients.

On the subject of money: it may not be in the best interests of someone to spend his or her last cent on medical care that is clearly not going to result in a cure or yield much benefit of any kind. In fact, a great deal of medical care seems designed only to make doctors and hospitals richer. *One reason for choosing suicide, in the face of a life-threatening illness, is that it conserves money for possibly better use by others who are healthy.* I do not know if financial considerations played a role in Bill White's decision to "pull the plug" but it is a fact that it cost $200,000 annually to keep him hospitalized. His bills were paid by Medicaid i.e. taxpayers. I do know that if I were kept barely alive for years at such huge expense, and I was not paying the bills from my own pocket, I would feel that ending my dependence on society was in the best interests of all concerned I am not saying that no one should be sustained indefinitely at public expense but it does seem to me a strange form of selfishness for anyone to want to consume large sums of public funds without giving anything back. When I think of all the positive things that could be done with $200,000 a year, and of all the worthy causes that suffer from lack of funds, I, for one, could not elevate my ego above the greater good of those who pay the bills.

A good death through new technology (i.e. such as the debreather) can be had for approximately $400. We do not sell debreathers. But we make our devices available to specialized agencies such as Compassionate Chaplaincy in the United States or Dr. Philip Nitschke in Australia. Chaplaincy representatives are willing to travel to any point in the U.S. to make sure that the equipment is used with proper training and supervision. Dr. Nitschke does the same in Australia. No longer does a seriously ill person contemplating rational suicide *have* to be furtive or alone. No longer is a terminally ill person condemned to attempt suicide as a bungling amateur.

FACING DEATH

As I write this, an estimated 15,000 people have died as a result of an earthquake in Turkey.

Some died instantly. Under the circumstances, they were the lucky ones. Others died horrible deaths, drawn out for days. The **Turkish Daily News** reported one such instance

August 27, 1999; "Euthanasia under the rubble":

> "On the eighth day after the quake Dr. P. Gula, head of a Polish rescue team, made the hardest decision of his life in the depths of a collapsed building in Cinarcik, Yalova. In that dark and cold place the Russian, German, Israeli and Polish rescue teams tried in vain to rescue a young man named Murat who was trapped under concrete pylons from the waist down. He agreed to have his legs amputated but the pylons could not be removed. In great pain and speaking with difficulty he begged for euthanasia. Dr. Gula injected him with a high dose of narcotics. We are not publishing the quake victim's picture because it is a heartbreaking one."

Often when euthanasia is discussed, the frame of reference includes a hospital, a terminally ill patient and a doctor. The subject is debated in a clinical setting from a legal and moral perspective. But it appears that euthanasia is more likely to be practiced in catastrophic situations about which moralists say little or nothing.

Perhaps a "pro-life" doctor would have insisted on making the young man suffer for several more days before "God" took his life. There obviously was no possibility of state of the art palliative care teams tending to every person who was severely wounded and dying. The search and rescue teams had to help who they could and move on.

War is another situation in which euthanasia of the mortally wounded may be commonly practiced. In an interview I conducted in 1992 with Sir

Dirk Bogarde, he recounted a wartime instance in which he prepared to shoot a fellow soldier who was horribly wounded:

My views were formulated as a 24-year old officer in Normandy. Not everybody's privileged (or unprivileged) to go through a six-year war. After that war nothing could frighten me anymore. On one occasion the jeep ahead hit a mine; ours skidded into a ditch. Next thing I knew: there was this chap in the long grass beside me. A bloody bundle, shrapnel-ripped, legless, one arm only. The one arm reached out to me, white eyeballs wide, unseeing, in the bloody mask that had been a face. A gurgling voice said, "Help. Kill me." With shaking hands I reached for my small pouch to load my revolver. In those days officers were not allowed to have their revolver loaded for some unknown reason and so I had to look for my bullets-by which time somebody else had already taken care of him. I heard the shot. I still remember that gurgling sound. A voice pleading for death. That was the first time. I have, regrettably, heard it since.

During the war I saw more wounded men being "taken care of" than I saw being rescued. Because sometimes you were too far from a dressing station, sometimes you couldn't get them out. And they were pumping-blood, or whatever; they were in such a wreck, the only thing to do was to shoot them.

And they were, so don't think they weren't. That hardens you: you get used to the fact that it can happen. And that it is the only sensible thing to do.

Some people might say, well, that is war, or a terrible natural disaster, and normal healthcare rules don't apply in extreme situations. But it seems odd that a society should concern itself with comparatively rare events (such as the number of people assisted in their dying by Dr. Jack Kevorkian during a ten-year period) if considerably more acts of euthanasia are committed during catastrophic events and accepted .

The crucial difference between Dr. Gula in Turkey and Dr. Kevorkian in America is that the former is perceived by himself and others to be acting in an emergency in which his actions may be regrettable but necessary; whereas the latter is seen as acting gratuitously, on the basis of personal *choice*.

Yet, if I understand the views and behavior of Dr. Kevorkian correctly, it is that he too believed he was acting in an *emergency* in which his actions may be regrettable but necessary. Kevorkian saw certain forms of human suffering as shocking and intolerable — even though it was not the sort of suffering that caught the eye of a TV camera. The people he helped were not buried under a pile of bricks and twisted pylons but they were, nevertheless, pinned down, trapped, and they longed to be free.

There was a time in the history of America when to most Southerners the purchase and ownership of slaves was a normal and unremarkable aspect of their lives. But there were some individuals who saw slavery in a different light: *an affront to the rights of man.*

We live in an era in which the political establishment, the medical establishment, and the religious establishment see nothing wrong with depriving dying people of control and choice, making them, in effect, the slaves of tradition and social convention . There is no other area of modern life in which people are denied a fundamental right to make decisions affecting their livelihood. Imagine being told that you cannot marry or have children; imagine being told that you are not free to choose your religion, your vocation, or your politics. Or, worse, imagine being told all your life that you are free to choose in all such matters but have no freedom of choice during your last phase of life when it really counts.

The everyday world we live in only appears normal because we have so effectively concealed the fact that many people are suffering greatly and *want* to die. When catastrophe becomes the norm it is no longer seen to be tragic.

The media (and by extension, society at large) does not perceive human suffering *in a medical setting* to be much of a story. People are ill, they suffer, so journalists turn away — rather than turn their cameras *on*. Nothing remarkable about people having tubes connected to every orifice sometimes for months or years, even if the person is in a persistent vegetative state and warehoused in some facility along with dozens of other "veggies". We have standardized human torture in the name of medicine to such a degree that few see anything remarkable, let alone scandalous, about extending a creature's existence against its will and calling it "life".

HOW WE DIE:

Have you ever imagined about how you might *like* to die? If you have given the matter much thought, chances are you favor "passing away" unexpectedly during sleep — as the result of heart failure. That is what is said to have happened to film director, Stanley Kubrick, at age 70, four days after completing his last film *Eyes Wide Shut*.

According to this model, you enjoy reasonably good health until the very last day — and then, phfft, you are gone. No pain. No forewarning. No planning on your part.

The reason that this manner of death is attractive is threefold: it involves no protracted suffering due to illness; it is painless; *and it involves no personal responsibility.* Unlike death-by-suicide, no one has to choose; no one is accountable. Philosopher Jean-Paul Sartre made personal choice and responsibility the cornerstone of an "authentic life" — but he also drew attention to the fact that many people will go to great lengths to avoid making crucial decisions and accepting responsibility. If this is true, then one may expect death-by-suicide to be a far less popular option than those means of dying in which responsibility is borne by someone else.*

*NOTE: I recently met with a famous Canadian poet who was stricken with cancer. His mind was made up, he said, he wanted to end his life rather than go on suffering. But his wife, without actually expressing any opposition to suicide, kept encouraging him to "consider alternate therapies" and also to have one more surgical procedure. Out of love for his wife, this 90-year-old man went back to the hospital. Doctors opened him up and found that his cancer had spread beyond what they had anticipated. They now advised radiation for short-term symptom-relief. Once again the man expressed the wish "to wrap things up and die". But his wife persuaded him to hang on to see if the alternate therapies might work.

(One of these methods includes massive daily doses of vitamins) At last report, this man was barely clinging to life and having a miserable time. Whatever is going on in his home, one thing seems clear: if this man had died on the operating table, it would have been acceptable to the wife as an inadvertent side-effect of the practice of medicine. Even though this man is revered for the clarity of his intellect, he is not allowed to die as he wishes. He will be kept going apparently until he finally dies in a manner that his wife feels is socially acceptable — although it is not clear whether she is conscious of how much she is making her husband suffer in the meantime. In meeting this gentleman I was struck by the importance of not only having a choice, but of having supportive loved ones who allow one to exercise your best judgment.

Heart failure (and its somewhat more painful variation, the "heart attack") is often taken to be an "act of God". That is because there is no *obvious* connection between the act of dying and the behavior of the individual. There is, however, such a thing as committing suicide in installments through a series of choices. A person may, through an unhealthy diet, sedentary life-style, or addictions such as smoking, chop years from his or her life just as surely as the suicide does. Any behavior that shortens life significantly is "suicidal" in the broadest sense. Such behavior may not lead to a consciously self-willed death but it is a *self-caused* death nevertheless and that is the critical factor. The fact that someone may claim that he or she was simply indulging in pleasures and had no *intention* of shortening life is a case of adding one delusion on top of another. Hardly anyone nowadays can claim to be — unaware of the effects of lifestyle-choices. But even the blatant health warnings on packages of cigarettes do not prevent some people from being hypocrites. Rita Marker, a Roman Catholic teacher and Executive Director of the International Anti-Euthanasia Task Force (based in Ohio), is by her own admission a *chain-smoker*. Yet she crusades against the "immorality" of terminally ill people shortening *their* lives by suicide*.

* **NOTE:** Marker's hypocrisy is institutionalized by her Church. There has never been a Papal Encyclical condemning life-shortening activities such as smoking — but there have been numerous condemnations of suicide and euthanasia. So someone like the late Sue Rodriguez, a woman well known in Canada for her struggle with ALS., is a "sinner" for shortening her life by a few months, whereas a smoker who may shorten his or her life by 15 years or more is considered quite normal by the Catholic Church. Anyone who thinks that I am exaggerating the effects of lifestyle-choices on longevity should examine the files available at the web-site for the Centers for Disease Control under "risk factors".
(http://www.cdc.gov/nccdphp/risk.htm)

Most people discuss suicide and assisted suicide in moral or theological terms but I am interested primarily in the technological aspects. To me, it makes quite a difference whether a man shoots himself or hangs himself (i.e. dies by an act of violence committed against his person) or whether he dies peacefully with the aid of a specialized "death control" device such as the "debreather". A choice between suicide or "hospicide" is basically a choice between a quick death or a slow death. It is also a choice between determining the timing of one's death or following the indifferent course of an illness. Ultimately, suicide is or can be a choice for a certain *quality* of death.

The ideal time and way to die, in my view, is when a person is still sentient and can act calmly, without the pressure of pain and other miseries. Such a person is then in a position to celebrate their living even as they prepare to die. I would like to sit in a splendid garden for several hours before my death. Perhaps sipping champagne and listening to some Beethoven or Mozart. Or I would look out on to a seashore at sunrise or sunset, gradually becoming one with the elements. Or perhaps I would choose a comfortable lounging chair in front of a fireplace. The last place I would want to die is in a hospital bed or in some other clinical setting, gasping my last well beyond my expiry date. I still have enough aesthetic sensibility to care about the *artistic* side of dying. We have not even begun to consider the possibility of making death *pleasant* for people. By and large, the human race is unimaginative when it comes to death. People cower in fear before their religious idols and statues and pretend they are doing God's will by docilely accepting the consequences of viruses and cell mutations.

THE FUTURE OF DEATH

The Last Rights Research Project is a chronically under-funded shoestring operation that has none of the "respectability" of hospice care. Yet we provide something which hospice is loathe to offer: a *choice*, an alternative; and, in practical terms, a way for a terminally ill person to conserve money and bring an end to pointless suffering. It is sometimes considered vulgar to bring up the subject of money as a consideration for those who are dying, but the fact is, I have never heard of an economic plan by "pro-lifers" on how society is going to pay for *optimum health care for all from the cradle to the grave*. We are told we must uphold the "sanctity of life" at all costs — without anyone addressing who *pays* the bills. I find such religiosity to be tyrannical and hypocritical. Any end-of-life plan that does not give people a *choice* stands much of a chance in today's world. I have seen too many seniors, particularly women, who have little in the way of pensions or savings, eking out an impoverished existence for years, to have much faith in *compelling* people to go on existing against their wishes.

The problem for many elderly people is not that they have nothing to live for but that they so little to live with. Economic reasons are yet another reason why older people choose suicide; there's no quick fix to improve their lot in life. Everywhere we look there are cutbacks in health care and in social services. There is no "pro-life" economic plan on the table; no real help of a practical nature coming from any of the right-wing groups that oppose assisted suicide and euthanasia.

Moral abstractions in a social vacuum do not help anyone.

We recognize the realities of modern life and we are honest about peoples' prospects.

That is why we continue to develop suicide as an option in a society that is filled with end-of-life hypocrisies. The religious establishment, the political establishment, the medical establishment and the media establishment exhort people to live, spend and consume as long as possible. We tell people: the most important human right is the right to say: No more!

For more information on the Art and Science of Suicide publications and related research projects, send $2US (check or cash) to:

Last Rights Publications
P.O. Box 39018
Victoria, British Columbia V8V 4X8
Canada

An InfoPAK will be sent by return airmail.

Section Ten

28

♦

Mind Games

by *Thomas S. French, M.D.*

There is no cure for birth or death save to enjoy the interval.

— George Santayana

W HEN THREATENED, life takes on new meaning and priorities change. Job promotions, bigger paychecks, more luxurious homes and other materialistic things become less important. It's a shame we travel so far before seeing all of life's blossoms and begin to understand the meaningful priorities of life. I wish I could say that I was different. It took 34 years and a catastrophic illness before I began to see the light.

Live as if you were to die tomorrow. Learn as if you were to live forever.

—Gandhi

I don't profess to be an expert in the areas of living or dying. What I do have is nearly four years of experience wearing the label "terminally ill." With that label comes a host of emotions and the need to readjust my priorities and change my perspective of the world around me. In essence, I've been trying to be an optimistic survivor with a catastrophic, "terminal illness."

Were it offered to my choice, I should have no objection to a repetition of the same life from its beginning, only asking the advantages authors have in a second edition to correct some faults in the first.

—Benjamin Franklin

I was 34 years-old when diagnosed with Amyotrophic Lateral Sclerosis (ALS or Lou Gehrig's Disease) in January of 1996. Since then, this insidious disease has literally turned my physical body into a human train wreck. I am unable to move my legs, arms, torso and head. I require a ventilator to breathe via a tube that has been surgically placed in my trachea. I am unable to speak and can only make clicking noises. I am unable to swallow and therefore cannot eat or drink. I receive all of my nutrition through a tube that has been placed in my stomach. That's the bad news. The good news, from a physical standpoint is I have normal sensation, complete bowel and bladder control, my "equipment" is working well, I can see and hear normally and my intellect is better than ever. The even better news is I have a gem of a wife, an adorable1-year-old daughter and loving, supportive parents, siblings and in-laws. The bottom line is despite ALS, I am one lucky guy.

How ridiculous and unrealistic is the man, who is astonished at anything that happens in life.

— Marcus Aurelius
(Man Plans, God Laughs)

At the age of 14, I knew I wanted to be a physician, specifically, a plastic surgeon. It seems like yesterday when I was 14; yet, when I think of everything that has happened between then and now, it seems like a lifetime. After high school, I spent four years in college, four years in medical school, five years as an intern, resident and chief resident in General Surgery and finally, two years as a resident in Plastic Surgery. I then joined a large, hospital-based multispecialty group practice at the hospital where I was born, spent years as a volunteer and countless days and nights on medical school and surgical residency rotations. Were all of those years of training worth only three years of practice? You bet. But, it was a long way from my anticipated path which was to include practicing surgery until the age of 65 or 70, followed by 20+ years of fun. Around the age of ninety, after a day of golf, cocktails and dinner, and several hours of vigorous lovemaking, I would die peacefully in my sleep

During the residency years, I was a witness to many devastating and disabling illnesses as well as deaths of every imaginable cause. No longer was I immortal. The "it can't happen to me" phase of my life was coming to an end. Despite this realization, it was still difficult to accept that something "bad" could happen to me. This was especially true when I encountered patients with severe burns, quadriplegia, severe head injuries and progressive, disabling neurological diseases such as ALS. Surprise, surprise!

It is not in the stars to hold our destiny but in ourselves.

—William Shakespeare

When I was told I had ALS, it was like a death sentence. I scoured the medical literature looking for a ray of hope. It was not to be found. Every article and text ended with the same conclusion: progressive loss of motor control leading to paralysis and ultimately death within 3 - 5 years. Not exactly the news I was looking for.

Having been trained in traditional science-based medicine didn't help matters. I saw things as either black or white but no grays. At that point, my options were straight forward:

1. Go with the disease until it kills me.

2. Live with the disease and use any or all life sustaining measures, or

3. Exit this life on my terms — the decision of where, when and how would be mine.

My only symptom early on was slight weakness of my left thumb and it was exceedingly difficult to imagine the devastating toll that this disease would have on my body. Despite such minimal physical loss, I frequently reviewed my options. I was most comfortable with my third option - suicide. I could never imagine myself living with severe disabilities and eventually ending up on life support. So, I began setting deadlines (no pun intended) as to when I would end my life. My most humorous deadline, in retrospect, was after an incident on the island of Martinique at the end of a month long bare boat sailing trip through the Windward Islands of the Caribbean. At the time, I was still quite functional with only left-hand weakness. One night, a lone mosquito buzzed me throughout the night. I would hear the buzzing near my ear, then silence. I'd jump out of bed, turn the light on, do a little jig then look around for the beast. This routine continued all night. The next morning, I vowed it would be time to move on when I became helpless against a mosquito in the middle of the night. I've seen quite a few self-imposed deadlines come and go. I haven't set any parameters for well over a year and despite my ongoing physical losses, I am very happy to be alive. But, I still leave all my options open.

Be happy while you're living, for you're a long time dead.

— Scottish Proverb

What makes a person with ALS feel the need to hold an option as extreme as suicide? The underlying core, I believe, is FEAR. For me, it was the fear of becoming paralyzed, unable to breathe or eat on my own, being a physical and financial burden on my family, fear of loss of dignity and control over my life and basically fear of the unknown future. Death would seem to be an easy out.

Historically, I started circling the drain in August 1998. I had been having trouble breathing and had been choking on food for quite some time, although I had been eating a regular, unrestricted diet. My first ALS related trip to the emergency room was at 3:00 A.M. after choking for 12 hours on a burger and fries. It didn't take long for them to confirm my greatest fears. My ability to breathe and swallow were both severely compromised by failing muscles. This was no big surprise to me. I just didn't want to face it. My original plan was to let nature take its course. I wanted it to be known that I was not to be resuscitated if I crashed (do not resuscitate or DNR). My condition worsened later that day. I thought long and hard about my situation. Jacquie, my wife, remained optimistic about our future, despite the gruesome prognosis. She always had little rays of hope which would conquer any pessimistic thinking. I thought about my daughter, Lauren, who was born ten days earlier with me attempting to coach in an almost unintelligible voice from another hospital bed adjacent to Jacquie's. For the first time, I was thinking about the good things in my life, and less about the negatives. It was a real turning point. I changed my mind about the DNR status, not because of a fear of death but because I wanted more out of life. Death is permanent — bottom line. The doctors tuned me up & I went home. Four days later I was back in the intensive care unit (ICU). My decision was a no none-sense one. I didn't want to linger. I wanted to get the necessary procedures done and get on with my life. I had a tracheotomy and feeding tube placed and six days later I was off to a rehabilitation hospital for a month and then home. Dorothy had it right. There's no place like home.

But, home was different. It was now necessary to have nurses and nursing aides with me around the clock. Jacquie's life changed as much if not more than mine. In addition to having the responsibilities of a new baby and running a household, she continued to play the major role in my care. It was chaotic to the point that I openly questioned whether I had made the right decision. I put my trust in Jacquie, myself and God, and stopped trying to second guess our mutual decision. It was a new situation, a new life. It would get better

> *No matter where you go or what you do, you live your entire life within*
> *the confines of your head.*

> **—Terry Josephson**

Another major turning point in my struggle with ALS was when I finally stopped looking solely at the physical destruction that was taking place and shifted my thoughts to the psychological impact of the disease. ALS is a mind game — the ultimate mind game. This revelation allowed me to try new strategies. First, I became pro active. I told the "beast" that although it had wreaked havoc on me physically, in no uncertain terms would it ever conquer my mind. I became more optimistic, not necessarily about being cured, but with accepting my co-host/parasite and setting limits. It was psychological warfare and I intended to win.

The secret of health for both body & mind is not to mourn for the past,
not to worry about the future, or not to anticipate troubles, but to live in
the present moment wisely and earnestly.

—Buddha

Since traditional medicine didn't have anything to offer, I turned to alternative or complementary medicine, which was completely new to me. The topic of the mind-body connection is complex and there tends to be a significant overlap among its different modalities. There is no definitive nomenclature that I am aware of, which tends to add confusion to the subject. Despite my traditional science background, I have always believed in, but have had limited knowledge about the mind-body connection. I have tried various relaxation techniques and meditations in the past. I bought the books, listened to the tapes, etc. I was always expecting to reach some definable state that would be awesomely overwhelming. I tried and tried but nothing ever happened. Why? I was trying too hard and expecting too much.

Shortly after I was diagnosed, I started having weekly sessions of Reiki, a natural healing method that uses the hands of a healer to channel energy to another person through chakras or energy centers. It has been practiced for thousands of years and was reintroduced in the 1800's by Mikado Usui in Japan. Three Reiki masters worked on me for two to three hours a week. I learned to reach a meditative state during these sessions. It was a feeling that was as close to nirvana as I could imagine. I was aware of my surroundings but had no reaction to them. Jumbled thoughts, which consciously may have ranged from elation to deep depression or fear, would calmly percolate in and out of my unconscious mind and somehow become processed into a rational form. It is in this state of mindfulness that the unconscious mind becomes unlocked and accessible for either "work," i.e. solving complex issues or as just a calm place to hang out. Our conscious mind is too irrational and too emotional to really do anything with complex issues other than to temporarily patch them. The unconscious mind is the real work horse.

I have realized that the past and future are real illusions, that they exist
in the present, which is what there is and all there is.

—Alan Watts

During the past four years, I have processed a great deal of information. It was necessary to accept the fact that I could no longer do the things that I used to take for granted such as walking, eating, talking, skiing, sailing, playing the piano etc. In a sense, my conscious physical world has become smaller. I can remember a lot of "last times" such as my last time on skis, which by the way, was not a pretty sight. Two years ago, I would have mourned the loss of many of these activities. Today, I actually enjoy closing my eyes and reliving some of the hobbies that I used to love so much. There are times when I can actually put myself on skis or on a sailboat and write the script from there. These are incredible experiences. While most people have to pay for similar experiences, I can enjoy them anytime, with my eyes closed, free of charge.

There remain some issues which I have not fully processed or come to terms with. On a conscious level, thoughts of these incompletely processed issues are unsettling and anxiety producing. I deal with this type of situation by automatically telling myself, "WE DON'T GO THERE." What I'm actually telling myself is "you're not ready to confront this issue on a conscious level." It's not conflict avoidance but what I consider to be a "transition in progress." The biggest issue involves eating. This is a difficult obstacle for me to hurdle with any grace, perhaps because Jacquie has such a talent for cooking and with or without guests, mealtime was always an event for the two of us. I can still enjoy a morning coffee and a happy hour cocktail. The only difference is the entry point of the beverage. After that, it's all the same.

Some days you're the dog, some days you're the hydrant.

— Anonymous

Technological advances have made it possible for me to fully access my computer with my eyes. At one point about six months ago, I was working on the computer when I suddenly stopped. Tears started rolling down my cheeks. I had been writing away on the computer using only my eyes and it felt completely normal, as if I had been doing it all my life. My feelings were totally mixed. Was I giving in to the "beast" or was I unconsciously coming to terms with and acceptance of the technology that would ultimately improve my daily life? I slept on it and it resolved itself. Change, even for the better, could still be difficult. But, I realize that now. It is just another small step toward accepting not only my physical limitations but also toward accepting those advances that will ultimately allow me more independence and a better quality of life.

The best thing about the future is that it comes one day at a time

— **Abraham Lincoln**

"One day at a time." This is everyday advice handed out freely for everything from a minor headache to the loss of a loved one. How many people have thought about the true the meaning of this phrase? How many actually live life one day at a time? My guess would be, not many. I know I was great at giving out this advice but had never sat down and pondered the true meaning of it, let alone lived it. I've thought about it a lot in recent years and it makes a lot of sense. Living in the present eliminates negative comparisons between the past and present as well as anxieties about the future. So, I join the ranks of people everywhere who have made this a motto to overcome addictions or to simply get more out of life.

In theory one is aware that the earth revolves but in practice one does not perceive it, the ground on which one treads seems not to move, and one can live undisturbed.

So it is with Time in one's life.

— **Marcel Proust, In Search of Lost Time: Within a Budding Grove**

The concept of time has taken on new meaning to me. In the past, it meant you had to be in Surgery or the office in 10 minutes. It meant that fractures take six weeks to heal, if all goes well, then things go back to normal. It meant that most things could be measured or interpreted as a function of time. Now, time has a new meaning. In some ways, it doesn't seem to exist. I don't have a broken leg or appendicitis, things that get better, usually, in a defined amount of time. I have a condition with no time parameters but with complex needs. Living with ALS under my previous time parameters would be impossible. There were so many changes including structural changes to our home to make it more accessible, the need for complex medical equipment and a well-trained staff that it was unrealistic of me to expect to have everything in place, & all the loopholes worked out in a short period of time. Put a health insurance company in the middle of everything, and you might as well go hibernate for six months or so. Slowing down and having no control over it was one of the most frustrating parts of my journey, thus far. On the upside, it sure went a long way toward developing patience and resetting my levels of tolerance. Patience and tolerance go a long way when you are dependent on others for all of your needs. Unfortunately, in the working world, time is usually money, and therefore, patience is not necessarily a virtue. But, in my situation, patience or the lack thereof, can make or break you. I am at the point where virtually no amount of time alone with absolutely nothing to do, is too much. These are the times that I do "mind work," or simply watch the happenings around me. I no longer expect things to happen overnight, but I do expect them to happen in a reasonable amount of time. I have been known to write and send some unforgiving e-mails which leave little doubt about my interpretation of the given situation. I no longer say "when will such and such improve etc." I now tell myself that "it" will happen with time.

> *For a long time it had seemed to me that life was about to begin — real*
> *life. But there was always some obstacle in the way. Something to be got*
> *through first, some unfinished business, time still to be served, a debt*
> *to be paid. Then life would begin. At last it dawned on me that these*
> *obstacles were my life.*

—Fr. Alfred D'Souza

At some point, we all think that things can't get any worse in our lives and tomorrow, the next month or even next year will be better. Unfortunately, the problems that generate these thoughts and comments are all part of life's obstacles. We cannot make them disappear but we have options in how we face and overcome them. These obstacles, which seem so unfair, are simply bumps on our chosen paths in life. They are there for a purpose, for us to learn, to develop skills to allow us to cope with future problems down the road. If I think that I am immune from future problems because I have the physical and psychological burdens of ALS, then I'm in for a big surprise. These "bumps" are not bargaining chips for the future. They are simply today's lessons to help us in an unknowing way, prepare for future "bumps." This is life folks. We have to take the good with the bad. But, again, we do have options — options involving our attitude and reactions to a given situation.

The game of life is not so much in holding a good hand as playing a poor hand well.

—H.T. Leslie

With a disease such as ALS, it is very easy to compare oneself to others and drown in self pity. My mother has said on multiple occasions over the years that "ALS is the worst disease there is." I have felt the same way at times. Many people believe and live as if "the grass is greener on the other side," I believe that the grass only APPEARS greener on the other side. We all carry our burdens, some of which are more visible and heavier than others. When I would hear people complaining about this or that, I would think, "you think you have problems." It didn't take me long to lose that attitude. Someone's problem(s) may seem minor to me but to the other person, they may be overwhelming. When I watched Dr. Kevorkian euthanize the gentleman with ALS on national television, I remember thinking, why? Here was a man who was in physically better shape than I, determined to die. For a fleeting moment I thought the man was a wimp. But then I felt sorry for him, for the conflict and fear he must have had inside to make him not only want to be "put to sleep," but to have it done on camera by Dr. Death himself. God forbid I ever feel the necessity to consider taking such drastic measures.

To put my life with ALS into positive perspective, all I have to do is read the paper, watch the news and go back through history. There have been countless atrocities during the last century alone, causing human suffering at levels that are unfathomable to me. I'm not a cold, scared teenager on a battle field in a foreign land or a prisoner of the Holocaust. I am not living a tormented life surrounded by adversity and I do not carry the burden of deeply buried emotional scars. I am simply a man with a malfunctioning neuromuscular system. I do not lack shelter or food and I am surrounded by love. This is an opportunity. Although some days it's hard to see it as such, it is an opportunity to learn valuable lessons about life that very few people ever have the opportunity to learn.

Suicide (the real unassisted kind that is most familiar) is LEGAL in most states. Perhaps it's legal because the responsible party is dead and therefore cannot be held accountable. Whatever the reason, it's very clear that when you start involving other people, the terminology and the laws change. There is physician-assisted suicide, active euthanasia, passive euthanasia and involuntary euthanasia, all variations of a central theme. There are many arguments, pro and con, in the debate on physician assisted suicide. It's a no win situation, no matter which side of the fence you are on. I am pro-choice and am of the opinion that the potential for abuse with strict regulation is extremely low. My dependence on artificial life support puts me in a unique position. Without the ventilator, I would be unable to survive. Therefore, if with my consent, a physician took me off the ventilator and allowed nature to take its course, it would not be considered physician-assisted suicide. It would be an example of passive euthanasia. On the other hand, if I were able to breathe on my own, I would not be a candidate for passive euthanasia. In order to end my life, I would have to go the route of physician-assisted suicide which is only legal in Oregon. It is an option that I would want available to me if I were in a situation where physician-assisted suicide was my only choice. Whether or not I would use it doesn't matter. I like options.

In 1998, Oregon became the first, & remains the only state to legalize physician assisted suicide. Contrary to what was expected, only 23 individuals took advantage of the new law. Fifteen of these individuals committed suicide, usually within a day of receiving their prescription, 6 died of their illness without using the medication, and 2 were still alive at the end of 1998. These numbers don't suggest people lining up and knocking down their doctor's door to get a prescription for a lethal dose of drugs. They suggest to me, that people don't necessarily want to die. Rather, they want options, a way out if their worst nightmares come true.

Realists know that adequate pain relief sometimes requires dosages of narcotics in the lethal range. If you have a cancer-ridden patient in severe pain, uncontrolled by high doses of morphine, are the doctors thinking "you'll just have to suffer until your time has come?". I very much doubt it. There are groups who feel suffering is a necessary part of the dying process — "through suffering comes insight." There is truth to that statement, but not as a generalization. If the suffering comes in the form of uncontrollable pain, I'm not sure how much insight I would gain.

Can a physician morally, ethically and legally administer or prescribe such dosages? Or is this perceived as an intent to kill or assist suicide rather than an attempt to minimize human suffering? I don't know a single physician who gets any satisfaction from seeing a patient suffer. I do know doctors who will not give "off the chart doses" of narcotics in order to control pain for fear of prosecution. I have never heard a patient say "The pain is unbearable but don't give me any more pain medication." If you could really know what those patients with unrelenting pain and anti-physician assisted suicide beliefs are thinking, my guess is they would want the extra pain medication and the hastening of death, as long as it was termed "pain control" and not assisted suicide or euthanasia. For those healthy individuals who deny this is all semantics, I recommend they spend some time in a hypothetical "dying simulator." Like a flight simulator this device would simulate real-life dying with the ability to control different parameters such as the underlying disease symptoms including pain, and the ability to monitor the "patient's" responses and decisions. I'll bet the results would show that, at a certain point, the vast majority of "patients" would welcome pain relief and death, no matter what it's called.

Various studies have found undiagnosed and untreated depression as a leading cause of suicidal ideation in the terminally ill. I don't think that adding Prozac to terminal patients' coffee every morning, will necessarily eradicate the problem. But, treating the depression may lift a significant number of individuals up to a more functional level where they can think more rationally and hopefully discover ways to enjoy life, despite their illness.

Sometimes even to live is an act of courage.

—Lucius Annaeus Seneca

I am sure. depression plays a major role in individuals with ALS as well as their families and close friends. Is fear the result of depression or is depression the result of fear? I'm not sure but my gut tells me they feed each other. If we look at the major physical and psychological issues confronting individuals with ALS, it is overwhelming, depressing and frightening. By breaking "fear" down into individual components, although still depressing and scary, they are more manageable. Earlier, I mentioned the things I feared most about ALS including paralysis, the inability to breathe and eat; the fear of becoming a physical and financial burden; the fear of losing dignity and independence; and the overall fear of what the future held. To address these fears, I've found some successful strategies.

Recognizing my fears and how they affected me was step one. An important realization for me was to trust myself and listen to my "gut." Then I had to reexamine my concept of time and to realize that living with ALS is an evolving process. It cannot be rushed. Sometimes I fared better if I allowed my mind to go on cruise control and let the schizophrenic parts hash things out.

Conquering these fears requires taking control of your mind and learning to stay centered in the present. If you let your mind run free and under the control of ALS, you will only remain in a state of raw panic. It does not have to be that way. Do whatever it takes " mind work," counseling, alternative therapies etc. — anything to allow yourself to develop a new way of thinking, a new perception of life. One-day-at-a-time.

Being quadriplegic and on a ventilator requires around the clock nurses and/or aides. In addition, our families, especially our spouse or significant other, will have to take on a good deal of both physical and emotional responsibility. This leads to a very heavy load of guilt or at least it did for me. Am I being selfish and destroying their lives so I can continue my life and all the needs that go with it? These are real concerns that have to be brought into the open and discussed. Fortunately, Jacquie stood by my side, frightened and knowing what the future could bring, but not immobilized. We have similar beliefs and philosophies which have helped immensely. Yet, I still can't help but feel guilty when I see her physically and emotionally exhausted.

A good friend of ours who has many virtuous qualities, not the least of which is wisdom, once explained the situation simply: Jacquie owes me big time from a past life. I wonder what that means for me in our next life. The best I can do right now is to show her love, patience and a strong will. I can listen to her needs and allow her to vent, even if it is something to do with me. I can help her with her struggles just as she helps me. Despite my limitations, to Jacquie and Lauren, I am a husband and father first, and a person with ALS last. It is equally important that I keep in mind the fact that even though she plays a significant role in my care, first and foremost, she is my wife.

ALS is a very expensive disease, especially if you receive your care at home as I do. I estimate around the clock nurse or aide and durable medical equipment and supplies, including the ventilator, to average about $180,000 per year. Where is all that money going to come from when my Cobra period ends? I don't know and unfortunately, it remains one of the few problems I have to solve. It is a very real concern. Do I want to financially ruin my family, in order to be medicaid eligible? Absolutely not. Do I want to physically burn out my family by shifting my care to them? Absolutely not. I'm letting this problem percolate. I suspect part of the solution will involve my returning to work. Unfortunately, a hands-on medical career is not possible, right now. Another solution would be to have a philanthropist set up a trust fund and allow me to pay my home care expenses from the interest generated by the fund. I am not above soliciting funds and let there be no doubt — that was definitely a solicitation! Actually, the best way to solve all of these problems would be to find a cure and a reversal process. Hopefully, sooner than later.

While I am on the financial end of things, I would like to sidetrack and make a few personal remarks about how our government reacts to these types of medical and financial issues. It seems that every four years, the politicians have a new plan for solving all the woes of our health care system. Then, nothing happens until another four years go by, and then the cycle repeats itself. Eventually, something will have to break this bureaucratic cycle. Medicare and Social Security funding also get tossed into the campaign melting pot. Home health care was supposed to have a significant effect in reducing the total health care budget. What happened to the advocated practice of keeping patients at home rather than in institutions? I thought this was a time of greatly expanding home health care. From where I sit, it ain't happening. Is it possible that our government has its priorities screwed up?

None but a mule denies his own family

—Anonymous

Let's take a hypothetical situation. I have a child who needs a kidney transplant and a child in the next town needs a kidney transplant. I just happen to be a compatible donor for both. Who should receive my kidney? Would it be selfish if I decided to donate my kidney to my child? I wouldn't think so. I would certainly empathize with the other family and hope and pray the other child would soon get a kidney. This sounds somewhat harsh, but realistically and instinctively, we take care of our own first and help others whenever we can.

Every year, our government sends billions of dollars in aid to countries all over the world. I can certainly understand the need for outside help after a massive natural disaster, but I don't see how or why we have to get politically, financially or militarily involved in solving the rest of the planet's problems. I am a U.S. citizen sitting on American soil hoping that someday, the U.S. government will think enough of us to increase research funding and provide more help for those of us with this debilitating disease. The problem is there are ONLY 30,000 of us in this country. Thirty thousand individual catastrophes. Thirty thousand people may not seem like many, but to those of us and our families who are living with the disease, it is an astronomical figure. If you put 30,000 of eus under one roof and added a major catastrophic event, then we would possibly see some government action. There are many, many people who have generously given of their time and money in an effort to help those with ALS. But, the private sector can't do it alone. To our government, all that I can say is please, help us put ALS in the category of "diseases of the past."

Being the world's major super power cannot be easy. We live in a great nation but with all of its responsibilities, many "smaller" issues get swept under the rug. Politicians are looking for issues that attract the numbers and will not only receive a big round of applause, but a standing ovation. They give the public what they want to hear, especially during election years.

The incestuous relationship between government and big business thrives in the dark."

— Jack Anderson

One example is the pharmaceutical industry. Why do our own senior citizens have to cross the border into Canada to buy their prescription drugs? These are drugs that are identical to those sold in the U.S. but for half the cost. This is only my opinion, but I believe that the answer very simple. If you lower the price, you lower the profits. If you lower the profits, you lower the top dogs exuberant salaries and bonuses down to a still exuberant level.

At some point, the lower profits would trickle down to the politicians as a decrease in political contributions. The pharmaceutical industry tries to have us believe that research and development would suffer. If that is where they choose to make their budgetary cuts, then R and D will suffer. If they trim fat in other areas, then there would be plenty of money to go around. It's just another example of money, power and selfishness at the expense of the American public.

Tobacco. This one takes the cake. We now have billions of dollars going to individuals, their families and state governments from the tobacco industry, as compensation for smoking related illnesses. Are we to believe that smokers did not know smoking was bad for them? I knew it was bad when I first lit a cigarette at age 13 or so. To a teenager, the taboo and mystery of smoking, and the fact that adults are smoking everywhere, makes smoking even more intriguing. Nobody held a gun to my head when I lit up, and I would assume the same is true for the other millions of smokers worldwide. I really don't understand it.

I am glad I do not have to explain to a man from Mars why each day I set fire to dozens of little pieces of paper, and then put them in my mouth

— Michael McLaughlin

It is common knowledge today that smoking causes a multitude of serious health problems and in many cases, kills. The tobacco industry has blatantly lied in court regarding the addictive potential of cigarettes and their ability to cause serious health problems and death. They also tried to cover up the fact that they even put additives in the tobacco to increase their addictiveness. These are criminal acts. In addition, the tobacco industry is guilty of assisted suicide on a grand scale.

So, how does our government, judicial system and tobacco industry resolve this problem? Money, of course. The tobacco industry is now shelling out billions of dollars to state governments as compensation for smoking-related illnesses. They have lost lawsuits brought by smokers and their families for smoking-related illnesses and wrongful death with juries awarding multimillion dollar settlements. People who chose to smoke and then lost the coin toss are now getting millions because they were stupid enough to smoke in the first place. I'm sure a sizeable number of these people had their smoking related illnesses covered by medicare. Tobacco companies are spending millions on advertising campaigns that target teenagers and children, promoting their efforts to keep kids from starting smoking. Unless they have a more subtle, self-serving agenda, I would consider this corporate castration. This industry's ability to remain solvent despite the money they are spending on anti-smoking campaigns etc., can only mean one thing: they are still making a shitload of money.

Why is a product that has proven to be responsible for a great number of serious illnesses and deaths, still legal? Again, money. These giant billion dollar industries have tremendous power on Capital Hill. I don't see how there could be any other reason. Since we have potential problems with medicare funding in the not-too-distant future why not pump all of this "tobacco" money right back into health care? Better yet, have the tobacco industry self-insure health benefits for all smokers. That would solve a lot of problems. As for the consumer, you have options. Either quit or take full responsibility for your actions when you face a smoking related illness.

Although I've gone astray, there is still some relevancy to these issues. The cure for ALS is out there, probably right under our noses. To get it uncovered and to the point where it can help those of us with ALS, takes time and money. To see money squandered for political gain is a darn shame. It's high time our country reexamines its priorities and acts on campaign promises instead of trying to pacify us with lip service.

> *Lord, grant me the serenity to accept the things I cannot change,*
> *the courage to change the things I can, and the wisdom to know*
> *the difference.*

—St. Francis of Assisi

Loss of dignity and independence play heavily on those of us with ALS. No doubt, ALS robs us of varying degrees of dignity, depending on our individual perceptions and interpretations of what constitutes dignity. We have some control over how much or how little dignity we maintain but we have to let others know what is important to us. A few of my quirks include having a shave and getting fully dressed everyday. I don't like hanging out in sweats or pajamas. I like doors closed when using the bathroom, or getting dressed or undressed. For some reason, people act as if I don't need privacy and even a closed door is an invitation to walk right into my space. Knock. I am no different from anyone else. I like my privacy too. Some people also feel that they can look over my shoulder and read whatever I'm doing on the computer. To those who feel like my work on the computer is open to the public, think again. Take control and speak up about those things which would make you more comfortable and those that make you uncomfortable. As for those indignities that we can't seem to get over, accept them with dignity.

While physical independence is not easy to maintain or regain, intellectual independence remains, with few exceptions, fully intact. We can take advantage of that and continue to be involved in family and household decisions. The computer has been a life saver for me. Using Eye Gaze technology on my desktop computer and GUS software with switch scanning on my laptop, I handle a chunk of the household paperwork and correspondence via e-mail, fax and the Internet. It gives me independence and allows me to contribute to the household.

> *When you come to the end of everything you know And are faced with the darkness of the unknown,* **Faith** *is knowing one of two things will happen. Either there will be something solid for you to stand on, Or you will be taught how to fly."*

> **—Barbara J. Winter**

During the past four years, I have reinvented the wheel more times than I like to think; I have learned a great deal from these experiences.. I have developed a much greater understanding of who I am and what makes me who I am. I have answers which are satisfactory to me as why I have ALS and why am I still alive. It all hinges on a strong faith in God, Jacquie and myself. When I first was diagnosed with ALS, I prayed it wasn't true or would disappear. Nothing happened. Next, I prayed it would at least progress slowly. Nothing happened. Finally, I prayed for the strength to keep myself, Jacquie and others going and for the ability to continue on with a happy, fulfilling life. I believe that my prayers have been answered... not exactly the way I had hoped, but answered, nonetheless. The reason I am still here is two-fold. First, I'm tough and am not about to let this beast break my spirit, take away my hope and faith, or that of those around me. Secondly, God has other plans for me, of which I am not yet privy. There are other lessons for me to learn, lessons that can only be learned through my experiences with ALS. Faith in God and myself allows me to take the next step without knowing where it goes. Faith allows me to live in the "now," one day at a time, without worrying about tomorrow.

Hope is the last thing that dies in a man, and although it be exceedingly deceitful, yet it is of good use to us, that while we are traveling through life it conducts us in an easier and more pleasant way to our journey's end.

—Francois de La Rochefoucaul

"No hope is better than false hope." I've heard this line used with relative frequency and I couldn't disagree more. Hope, amongst other things, has helped me bridge the times when I have been in a ditch. It is a distant gleam when everything else seems to be in complete darkness. In addition to Jacquie and Lauren, who are hope in and of themselves, I sought hope in everything and everyone. I tried Reiki with the hope that the ALS would disappear. Is that false hope? No. At the time, that was truly hope. Although it didn't eradicate the disease, it brought me many tools and taught me many skills, which I've put to good use since then. My hope swelled when I was chosen by lottery to be on the experimental drug, Myotrophin. Despite the drug, my symptoms continued to progress, but it was another bridge of hope. I tried Acupuncture and Chinese herbs with the hope they would slow down the disease. They didn't, but they helped my shoulder pain and again, bridged a gap. I've tried reflexology, craniosacral therapy, therapeutic massage, Trager, and combinations of the different alternative therapies. I didn't have to spend a fortune and although they didn't seem to have much of an effect on the ALS, they did more than conventional medicine. They all gave me hope when I needed a charge and taught me little lessons to get me to where I am today — alive and thriving.

I like living. I have sometimes been wildly, despairingly, acutely miser-
able, racked with sorrow, but through it all I still know quite certainly
that just to be alive is a grand thing.

— **Agatha Christie**

One of the problems with ALS is that from day one, there are no written or spoken words that convey any hope. The only thing you read or hear about ALS is that Lou Gehrig had it and that it is "uniformly fatal within 3 to 5 years," along with all the nasty things that happen to your body before you die. Finally, there was good news. The FDA had approved the first drug ever to treat ALS-Rilutek. When I finally read about it, I had to laugh. This new landmark drug which was being sold for $600 +a month, was shown to pro- long tracheotomy free survival for 90 days. In other words, it bought you 3 more months of life before you needed a trach. My 90 days are long gone, but I wonder if I would have had my trach done in May 1998 instead of August 1998, if I hadn't taken Rilutek. Despite my bit of sarcasm, I am still taking the drug. Why? I suppose it offers a glimmer of hope and a first step towards treating and curing a disease which everyone associates with disability and death.

Q: Do you know what the death rate around here is?
A: One per person.

—**Anonymous**

According to most information written about ALS, I'm smack in the middle of the death zone — three to five years. What most literature doesn't mention anything about are the numerous people who have survived beyond 5 years. That's the category I'm shooting for and hope to stay there for years to come.

I wonder if we would see any changes in the progression of ALS if patients were told they have an 80% chance of living more than 5 years with minimal to moderate disability — a kind of psychological placebo. I'm not suggesting lying to patients, but to me, it's an interesting question in stark contrast to " bang, bang, in 3-5 years your dead." I don't put a lot of weight or faith in statistics. Let's face it, a 80% survival rate for disease X is great if you are one of the 80 out of 100 who survive. But it really stinks for the 20 out of 100 that die. It's aggravating data with little relevance to the individual.

I wonder where the number crunchers would put me in their ALS statistics. Am I considered dead because I require an electrical outlet or battery to stay alive? Do I really care? No! It took me awhile to reach this point where I can calmly say, I die when I die. Numbers are only numbers and in no way do they seal our fate. There is hope everywhere. Grab it and run with it.

Omnia vincit Amor. Love conquers all.

— Virgil

Jacquie and I met in high school but didn't start dating until several years later. We actually double-dated in high school but with our own separate dates. On July 3rd 1983, during the summer between college graduation and medical school matriculation, Jacquie and I were married. Between my schooling and her working, life was chaotic at times. After about five years of marriage, we tried to start a family. No luck. Over a period of about 4 years, Jacquie underwent a myriad of tests, multiple laparoscopic surgeries and series of treatments with fertility drugs. Still no luck. More frustrating were the positive pregnancy tests followed in several weeks by miscarriages on two occasions and a tubal pregnancy. It was a tough time for both of us.

During this time, I was in the hospital more than at home — a 100+ hours a week. Many nights off were spent moonlighting to supplement our incomes. These jobs included being the physician on the medical center's helicopter, covering the emergency room at a small local hospital and a walk-in clinic on weekends and finally, covering the open heart surgery unit at a local teaching hospital. My life and our marriage belonged to the hospital.

In 1992, several months after moving to Virginia to start my Plastic Surgery residency, the marriage came to a screeching halt. I was the initiator. We separated and eventually divorced, but remained friends throughout. In many ways, it was an amusing relationship. We lived separate lives but were best friends We shared our ups and downs and confided in each other about such unlikely subjects as our relationships. There was never any love lost.

"Falling in love with someone isn't always going to be easy... Anger...
tears... laughter.. It's when you want to be together despite it all.
That's when you truly love another. I'm sure of it."

—Keiichi Morisata

Jacquie was the first person I called after learning the possible diagnosis. She reacted by showing up at my door within the hour and told me she would be by my side through thick and thin. Those words were music to my ears, spoken by the only voice that could give them any meaning..

Nearly nine months later, I was putting away my shingle as a plastic surgeon. I was thirty-five. It was a difficult decision but I knew it was coming. On a whim, we decided that the city no longer needed us and we no longer needed it. We wanted someplace rural but not so far off the beaten path that we would be isolated from family and friends. Within 24 hours we were headed for New Hampshire and Vermont searching for the perfect spot to call home. We landed in central Vermont where my sister and her family live. The next day we went for a drive. It was a perfect, cool, crisp fall day. We fell in love with one particular road. It had several farms, unbelievable views and a quaint little town center located on a small lake called Silver Lake. We both agreed that we would somehow make our home on this road, the North Road in Barnard, Vermont. There were several properties for sale including one with overgrown fields, and a long driveway leading to a rustic looking cottage-like house. My sister checked it out and we returned the following weekend. The size of the house was deceiving from the front. It was rustic inside but had beautiful wide oak floors throughout and two huge stone fireplaces, a beautiful large spring fed pond behind the house and spectacular views to the west. The whole package included the house, and 89 acres of land of which about 5 acres was fields and the remainder was woods with hiking trail. We both saw potential in it but it would need a lot of work. We bought it and the demolition began. Tearing down the attached two car garage, a deck and the ensuing bonfire was a family affair. We gutted the entire house, added a sizeable living room, dining room, master bedroom/bathroom suite/loft. We replaced bathrooms, stairways, kitchen, decks, garage, all wiring and plumbing, siding, roofing and a whole lot more. It was our over-budget, behind schedule dream house.

The following spring, Jacquie and I were remarried in our living room and in late November of 1997, we held our breath as we watched a home pregnancy test turn positive. It was unbelievable, no fertility drugs, no medical intervention of any kind. On August 3rd 1998, after nearly a decade of trying to conceive, our 7 lb.7oz. miracle baby girl was born. We named her Lauren — "crown of laurel." The timing of our having a child seemed to be more than just a random event. Lauren was born about 10 days before I had to make the decision of life or death. I'm still alive. Coincidence? I doubt it. A perfectly timed gift from God? Undoubtedly!

I don't need to be king of the world, as long as I'm the hero of this little girl.

—Jani Lane

Where do I go from here? I'm really not sure. New doors are continually opening as I try to meet the challenges of ALS. I see the world in a completely different light. No longer am I a member of the overachiever's club. The only areas that I have any ambition in being the best, are as a father, as a husband and as a person. My niche in the world has yet to be carved out and as far as I'm concerned, it can wait. For the time being, I'm enjoying the ride — despite ALS.

Still round the corner there may wait, A new road or a secret gate

— J. R. R. Tolkien

It is impossible for me to close this chapter without a few words of gratitude to the many individuals that have helped me during these challenging years.

To Jacquie, Lauren and both of our families:

"If I could reach up and hold a star for every time you've made me smile, the entire evening sky would be in th palm of my hand."

—Unknown

To the congregation of the First Congregational Church of Woodstock,

To Con and Terri

To Dan, Gene, Beth, Sarah and Annette,

To Scott and Karen

To Lynn and Bud

To Terri, Lisa and the rest of the gang

To Austin and Trudi

To the physicians, nurses and Priscilla at
Dartmouth-Hitchcock Medical Center

To Mala

To my patients

*Thanks to all of you and the many more whose simple words and acts of
kindness have kept my spirit alive.*

La Vita e Belle — Life is Beautiful

29

◆

They Shoot Horses

by Anonymous

T HEY SHOOT HORSES, DON'T THEY?" a wise adage tells us. And they should. All living things deserve the right not to suffer physically when medical science offers no hope for cure of disability or pain, and when death is the only release. No compassionate person would consider it morally wrong to euthanize an animal with an incurable disease that causes intense suffering. Horse, dog, turtle, or snail, the beasts of the land, air, and sea can count on human kindness to liberate them from suffering.

Yet the reverse is true when it comes to human suffering. As writer Isaac Asimov has noted: "No decent human being would allow an animal to suffer without putting it out of its misery. It is only to human beings that human beings are so cruel as to allow them [indeed force them] to live on in pain, in hopelessness, in living death without moving a muscle to help them...."

Why is it that so many people, who recognize the right of a suffering animal, deny human beings, the life form capable of articulating the desire not to linger on in pain, the only creature able verbally to express anguish and misery, the same compassion given a squirrel?

Opponents of assisted suicide argue that, above all living things, human life stands supreme. Thus, the argument goes, human life is superior to animal life and therefore should not be ended, irrespective of medical conditions, as one would terminate the life of an animal.

To supporters of the right-to-die human beings are indeed the most important of living things. Precisely for this reason we should be more willing to end the life of an incurably ill person, requesting help. Thus can we provide relief from affliction in when the body becomes an instrument, not of pleasure, but of pain.

In all areas of medical ethics, human life is given priority over animal life. Scientists experiment on animals to find cures for human illnesses. They do not use human beings as experimentation subjects to find cures for animals. If a family had a blind dog and a blind person, but only enough money for surgery on one, clearly the sight of the person must come first. The dog would stay blind. On these points advocates and opponents of self deliverance agree.

The point of radical departure between the two arises when human illness has no cure and human living is reduced to misery.

Undoubtedly organized religion (and by this I refer not to any one specific religion, but to most of the current world religions) is the single most important factor in spreading the belief that self-deliverance is wrong. After all, what could be worse than suffering here and now for our limited life times than spending an eternity in suffering (as belief systems of the West teach) or (as Eastern systems teach) being reincarnated with even more suffering than one had in the life that forced suicide?

Thus, rather than being a source of comfort, religion becomes another source of pain. We are put into this life, not of our own choice, subjected to incurable disease. Then we are told that a force — call it God, karma, or fate, etc.—will not only hurt us in this lifetime, it will punish us with even greater suffering in another dimension or lifetime.

The issue is not this simplistic, of course, Biblical heroes, among them Saul and Samson, committed suicide. The Bible honors them. So do we. In fact the Code of Jewish Law (Shulchan Aruch) uses the example of Saul's suicide as the basis to say that those who commit suicide are acting under extreme duress, be it emotional or physical, and are thus not sinners, but victims of unbearable circumstances.

Other faiths have also offered a more reasonable approach in recent years. In 1961 the Roman Catholic Church revised its ancient ban on allowing suicides to be buried in consecrated ground. The hierarchy announced that those who take their own life can enter heaven.

This more compassionate side of religion said and done, by in large religious professionals still oppose self-deliverance. Their influence is widespread, touching not only civil government, but secular disciples, such as psychology and sociology, as well. What rational argument could an atheistic psychologist offer against suicide for the incurable ill, save that the therapist has unwittingly been influenced by religious attitudes predominant in culture?

There are those, both secular and religious, who feel life is worth living at any cost. Should they become trapped in a diseased body their attitude can offer comfort. If Christian, they may look to the death of Jesus and exalt in their pain as imitation Christi (the imitation of Christ). But for those of us who feel life with pain and disability is a form of torture and not worth living, these non-medical standards seem delusional.

For the most part American citizens appreciate the freedoms accorded them by law. Quality living requires people be able to exercise those liberties. Simply holding American citizenship is not enough. Voting, speaking freely, assembling and freely traveling — these and more are what makes being an American worthwhile, not merely holding an American passport.

Viewing life in this light, simply being alive is not enough for advocates of self-delivery. The ability to see, hear, walk, live without pain, all this and more the able-bodied take for granted. These abilities are considered basics that make life worth living. Without them life is torture.

Life is to be lived and enjoyed, not merely endured, as one endures a painful dental visit. Especially for the hopelessly ill, life is a never-ending dental visit.

The current struggle for physical aid-in-dying should be expanded to include not only the terminally ill (as under current Oregon law), but the hopelessly or chronically ill as well. Every human being will at some point ponder his own death and no doubt almost all will hope for a quick death rather than one that drags on for years and years of suffering and disability. Yet this is exactly the situation the incurably (but not terminally) ill find themselves in on a daily basis.

The quadriplegic frustrated beyond words because of her body is now in prison, a blind person whose life has changed from the great colors and beauty of this world to one of never-ending darkness, the amputee who must undergo years of therapy to learn use of legs in place of arms that are no longer there at the same time enduring the cruelty of "phantom pains" in limbs forever lost. To those who suffer and for those to whom medicine can offer no cure, death is the cure.

The argument offered that the incurably ill are merely depressed and in need of psychiatric counseling after which they can all live very worthwhile lives is a hollow argument and one not offered to individuals suffering curable illness. If one man were blind from cataracts, he would be referred to an eye surgeon, not to a psychiatrist. If a second man were blind from incurable retinitis and did not wish to live, he would be sent to a psychiatrist. Is the contradiction between curable and incurable illness not clear?

Psychiatry is a wonderful thing, but it has its limitations when dealing with problems that are physical. I speak from experience as a person with incurable illness. Whatever insights and coping techniques a good therapist can provide the basic fact is the physical problem. In the absence of medical cure, self-delivery is the cure.

As medicine evolves, so do medical ethics. In this day of high-tech medicine we take for granted how far we have come in a very short time. Until the 1840s anesthesia did not exist. Operations were performed on people who were fully conscious throughout the procedure. Then ether, a substance known for centuries, was shown to render insensible the most painful surgery. This modern medical marvel was hailed but with one exception—obstetrics. Leading Christian physicians and theologians seriously debated the ethics of allowing women to give birth in a pain-free manner. Conservatives based their arguments on the Biblical curse God placed on Eve for eating the forbidden fruit. Not just Eve, but all women, they argued, must endure physical suffering during childbirth.

Dr. Charles Meigs, a prominent obstetrician of the day, summed up the Christian argument when he described the agony of childbirth pains as being "of those natural and physiological forces the Divinity has ordained us to enjoy and suffer." Today no medical doctor or Christian theologian holds such views. Yet until Queen Victoria gave birth to her eighth child in 1853 using chloroform the use of anesthesia during childbirth was hotly debated among Christians.

Let us hope that soon the issue of self-deliverance will be handled more intelligently. Not only for those of us who suffer physically now, but for the rest of humanity who are but one accident away from hopeless crippling and unending pain cry out for such use of reason.

I began by asking why so many would deny human beings the same right to die afforded animals. I addressed the issue in which both sides share agreement: that human beings are superior creatures. I went on to argue that this capacity forces humans to suffer in ways other creatures never could. A cat with an amputated leg will never know the pain of a teen-aged girl just coming into adulthood and seeing her friends with boy friends, while she is rejected because most men are not turned on by women with one leg. Career blockage, poverty, social discrimination—all these incurably ill animals will never know, while their human counterparts deal with them daily.

I would like to close by sharing a little personal history. Among the various incurable ailments I suffer, some are more severe than others. The two most life-altering are a vertigo problem which began in the 1980s. It has come and gone through the years and has lasted for years at a time.

More recently I have a disease affecting my bones and muscles which doctors best guess is fibromyalgia. Little is known of the disease, but since first developing it two and a half years ago my health has declined rapidly. Every day is pain. It is difficult and painful for me to walk. I need a cane to do what little walking I can do. Sitting is painful. Typing this article has been murder on my back. My bones from my face to my toes feel as if they are breaking.

Back in time, when I was a teen-ager, I had a parakeet. He developed a condition that rendered him unable to fly. He would flap his wings, squawking in frustration until exhausted. Yet, other than when he tried to fly, he was a very happy, very contented little bird. He had the same personality he had before he lost his ability to fly. With his limited intelligence he could not ponder his terrible plight.

In fact, so limited was his attention span that, if while flapping his useless wings, I offered him something like lettuce or crackers he enjoyed eating, he would forget about flying. In contrast, I have far more ability to walk than the bird had to fly, yet I will never be happy with my current quality of life, while my bird was unhappy only when attempting to fly.

I agree with those who oppose self-deliverance that human life is worth more than animal life. The preciousness of human life is such that no person should be forced to live a life of pain and work disability if he desires to exit the mortal coil. Thus I support the right of self-delivery.

The innate intellectual superiority of humankind is the second reason I support this right. This intelligence means we suffer on levels animals never could.

Despite whatever religious leaders, poets, or tormented writers might preach, there is nothing noble about suffering. Not in horses. We shoot them to spare them suffering. Not in men and women either.

30

◆

Unfinished Thoughts on "The Right to Die"

by Richard H.Cox, Ph.D., M.D., D.Min.
President Emeritus, Forest Institute of Professional Psychology
Springfield, Missouri

T HIS IS UNDOUBTEDLY the most difficult writing assignment I have experienced since preparing a "Comprehensive Statement of Faith" paper for my ordination on January 23, 1950. Like all other statements of faith, it is much easier to talk about one's beliefs than it is to put those beliefs into writing. In verbal discussion one can use many qualifiers, "waffle" a bit here and there, and even debate both sides out-loud, and most of all end the conversation with a non-answer that can be revisited in the future, or never. I am quite certain that I have succeeded in using those same techniques in writing this discourse.

Due to the diverse nature of my professional life, I have been forced to visit the topic of "right to die" many times and in varying professional roles; clergyman, psychologist, physician. Throughout my life, and by virtue of these different professional roles, I have been part of the "death decision" process many times. Of course, it is not the "right to die" that we discuss,

373

since we will all die. It is the when, how, where, and by whom that we discuss the hotly debated points of view in regard to death.

I have certainly concluded that without doubt, at least for myself, there is no single, easy answer. There is no single answer that is right for everyone. God has endowed us with wisdom, but not infinite wisdom. Our carefully thought through decisions are at best human guesses. The myriad of variables and factors involved in any single decision are infinite, therefore our finite minds cannot assume to have arrived at "the answer". We all look for "black" and "white" when dealing with value issues, but regardless of how carefully I think or look, all I can seem to see are shades of gray. Further, I have found that it is easier (if there is an "easier") to decide from a single philosophical, theological or medical point of view than it is when one attempts to integrate the thinking derived from these and other disciplines.

As pastor of a church for several years I watched decisions being made primarily by doctors, sometimes including families, but mostly not. In those days mostly everyone including the doctors watched as people died. In the early fifties the extraordinary means of life support as we know them today were not available and were not part of the equation, nor was euthanasia as we now conceive of it. I recall very clearly my brother's death following neurosurgery for a malignant brain tumor. It was not for anyone to determine the moment of his death. When there was no blood pressure, no heartbeat, and no breath, physical death occurred. There were no machines keeping flesh responding to artificial physiological stimuli. Although I was close, very close to the whole situation, (I was monitoring the blood pressure and pulse much of the time), the surgeon, my sister-in-law and I accepted death when it occurred. There was no question as to whether we should have intervened in the death process or whether we should have prolonged life. We were not forced to decide whether machines should keep working; there were none in operation.

Later, by the time I added clinical psychology and pastoral counseling to my professional life, "life support" systems were becoming part of standard protocol. I was forced to observe and participate in the actual process of making the decision regarding the process of dying. I could no longer be the parish minister and simply stand by as others made the decisions or as the inevitable occurred. The healing team was beginning to add pastoral care and psychology to its forces, hence, participation from the clergy and psychologists in life and death decisions was expected.

Discussions were no longer only theoretical for anyone. Technology had started a production of machines that would inevitably confuse the issues and demand practical answers. It was no longer possible to know if the person was "dead". The time of death was when the machines were turned off. We started talking about "brain death" as a measure of when death occurred. Brain death occurred when there were three successive EEG's (electroencephalograms) that were "flat line", i.e., showed no brain activity. However, many were not willing to accept that definition of death and were convinced that some persons with "flat line" EEG's could "come back". The medical world started to keep patients "alive" with "flat EEG's", on respirators, tubes emerging from every orifice, and calling "code blue" when the electrocardiograph wailed its ominous sound and showed a "straight line" on the monitor. The medical and religious world was forced to get serious about the rapidly emerging technology of life support systems. It seemed that new methods and machines were being introduced almost daily to keep the heart beating and the lungs moving air. It was, however, clear that the heart was not beating by virtue of its own energy and that the lungs were only moving air like mechanical bellows. The decisions became very complex. Conferences were beginning to be held on the subject of "right to die", medical ethicists came on board as professional colleagues, doctors and ministers dialogued on the subject. Each profession tried to pass the proverbial buck to the next profession to make the decision about when to "pull the plug". It seemed that technology had surpassed our theology and that practicality was superceding our value systems.

In the quest to put the body, mind, and soul together, I entered the field of medicine, completing a residency in family medicine at a fine church-related hospital. There I was in the midst of those who literally had the power with the aid of technology both to fend off death and to produce death. I witnessed patients who because of "code blue" procedures lived to speak reconciling words to their families. I also witnessed those who it seemed died "too soon" before technology had a chance to work. I saw families who seemed to benefit spiritually while attending a dying patient. I saw others who were traumatized by it. I saw children who were afraid of it. I saw children who were fascinated by it. I saw patients who themselves seemed to "radiate" as they died. I saw patients who were clearly in agony. I saw families welded back together in the presence of a dying relative. I saw other families stretched and torn apart. There was more to the experience of dying than the death of a physical body.

It was (and still is) impossible for me to separate God's will, man's wisdom, and medical mechanics. I have never considered myself as changing professions but simply adding additional knowledge to a basic calling to minister to humans in suffering and need. As confusing as this often was, it also forced the beginning of an integration of theology and science that I readily admit is still far from complete. Although I could understand, to a small degree, where each of the professions of theology, psychology and medicine "were coming from", none of them offered the help that the sorrowful eyes of families surrounding the dying sought. The one thing I know for certain, from those experiences, is that being in the situation of decision making is far more difficult than only being a discussant.

Ultimately families that were usually quite unable to integrate or even understand the plethora of medical, theological, technological and psychological information were given the job to make their "own decision". Sometimes they were fortunate in that the patient ceased to respond even to life support while their family wrestled with a decision. However, most of the time "things just happened" with semi-decision making such as, "we'll put her on the respirator and see how things are in the morning". Morning came with no change as did each subsequent morning thereafter until money, technology, or both failed and the decision was made by default. More times than anyone will ever know, nurses, physicians or technical support persons made private decisions that effected drug dosages, supplemental volume adjustments, and other technological factors that made the inevitable decision unnecessary. There was nothing new with decisions of this sort. Physicians and families have since the beginning of time made decisions of this nature. The difference is in our rapidly emerging technology that allows doctors, patients, and families far greater control than ever before over the living and dying process.

When I was first asked to write my response to the debate on "right to die", I was certain that I knew my position and, as writing goes, that it would be a relatively easy task. After all, I had been part of that decision scenario as a brother, minister, psychologist and physician. Certainly I should have arrived at a personal decision by now. As I began to put it on paper it became painfully obvious that I didn't have the slightest idea of a position that was firm enough to put into print. As providence would have it I was at the same time writing a chapter for another book on spirituality which required a similar kind of soul searching. I completed the chapter and when reading it aloud (as is my usual custom) for syntactical and grammatical errors, I realized that I had not only written that chapter, but that if I believed what I had written, I had also in a large measure addressed my position on euthanasia. This was a surprise and relief to me, yet I had many doubts that I could justify and document what I had written. Just as in this writing, when I thought I had a singular frame of mind on a given topic, I thought of some variable that called everything I had written into doubt.

Much of my position is based upon the teachings of Paul Tillich regarding the reality and life of the human Spirit. Tillich states that the word spirit should be capitalized. He states, "The term 'spiritual' (with lower case s) must be sharply distinguished from 'Spiritual' (with a capital S). The latter refers to activities of the divine Spirit in man; the former, to the dynamic-creative-nature of man's personal and communal life", (Tillich, 1951). I find it inescapable that the Spirit is present at conception and continues to live beyond physical death. Once one accepts this premise, the only way to discuss euthanasia is to separate the body and the Spirit. It is necessary to believe that the physical body can be destroyed voluntarily without disturbing the Spirit. Further, it is necessary to believe that the Spirit becomes part of the physical body at birth and stops at death. We must return to a Cartesian mind-body separation in our thinking to support this view.

We can postulate that since God is control of Spirit before, during, and after physical life, He can and does take control of it regardless of what we do to ourselves or what others do to us physically. The Spirit is therefore part of the physical human while he/she is on earth and in the care of God when the physical person is not in the flesh. This is not a difficult position to accept. It is however equally as difficult to discuss as is any other position regarding the human spirit. It is beyond my ability to understand, let alone, put into words from which anyone, including myself, could make responsible decisions. To believe that God imparts Spirit, supports it, and receives it back is not an unacceptable point of view to me. As a matter of fact this argument is entirely compatible with the view of nearly all religions. Although I accept the eternal nature of the Spirit, it is simply not possible for me to discover my individual responsibility in regard to Spirit with God's omniscience and omnipotence. We are left to act in accord with our best human wisdom, medical knowledge, unique circumstances in each situation, and the "small still voice" inside each of us.

Recently a person in our community committed suicide. When my friend told me about it, he said, "he killed his self". I immediately in my mind corrected his grammar to "himself". Then I started to think about it and it occurred to me that there is much more included in this statement than correct grammar. Is the "self" something that one can kill? If he killed his body how did he impact his "self", i.e., Spirit. I am reminded of Martin Luther's hymn, "A Mighty Fortress Is Our God" which states, "The body they may kill; God's truth abideth still; His kingdom is forever". From a theological perspective, that which Luther calls the "truth" and "kingdom" (Spirit) which cannot be killed, is undoubtedly contrasted to the opposite, the body, which can be killed. So one must ask, when one commits suicide, or another performs euthanasia, what does one kill? In modern literature we tend not to use the word "kill". That word sounds primitive, cruel and criminal. Yet, euthanasia was first discussed in literature as "mercy *killing*". The modern trend is an attempt to view euthanasia as a process that should be normalized, therefore, eliminating the negative connotations.

This becomes a very serious discussion because most persons when discussing euthanasia speak of it as having to do only with the physical body. They tend to deny or otherwise pretend that the Spirit is something that either does not exist or can be ignored. One physician is quoted as saying that "we take care of the body and let God take care of the spirit". This position allows the physician to treat the body as a separate entity and to escape any responsibility for the spirit. Interestingly enough, we cannot deny that Biblical theology, and the theology of most religions would assert that regardless of what we do to ourselves or others that God will take care of the Spirit. Or sometimes, we hear, "he is already dead", indicating that there is no need to attempt life support. Physicians could not function if they did not make decisions of this sort. However, they are nonetheless very serious decisions that may prolong or end a person's life. Nothing in this discussion is meant to imply that medical decisions are easy, and I have never seen them entered into lightly.

However, since the presence, absence, or condition of the Spirit cannot be known, sometimes it is assumed that such does not exist or that it must be ignored. Mercy killing can only deal with the body. We do not know whether the Spirit is suffering or not. We may not need to worry about the Spirit. It may be that the Giver of Spirit manages its entrance and departure quite apart from human intervention on either end of life.

There abound stories of persons who report "seeing the spirit" leave the body. Others state that they could physically "feel" when the spirit left a loved one in the dying moment. Others will maintain that they observed the spirit leave the body before the body took its last breath. We could get into a discussion as to whether the Spirit gives up the body or whether the body gives up the Spirit. We would doubtless end up in a deadlock since we don't know and can't find out. However, New Testament scripture indicates that when Jesus was crucified He "gave up the Spirit". In either case, we have admitted that the Spirit has a life that extends beyond the human body. The importance of this to our discussion is that the Spirit is real and cannot be dismissed as being imagination or immaterial to our considerations in permitting life or in determining the moment of death.

Judeo-Christian theology does not allow us to separate the body and spirit. New Testament theology makes it very clear that the body and mind are both gifts of God and are intended for the glory of God. (I Corinthians 6: 19-20 RSV). Yet by the same token, when the body dies, as in the case of Jesus' crucifixion, the Scriptures state, "…and Jesus cried again with a loud voice and yielded up his spirit" (Matthew 27:50 RSV), indicating that the Spirit is a separate entity and continues after the body dies.

Theology, philosophy, and medicine, all become part of the discussion, but each in very different ways. The debate only includes philosophy if we see the issue as being intellectual and theoretical. Philosophy as a "reasoned theory" is in truth not a part of the discussion for most people. When people speak of their "philosophy" of death and dying, they are mostly talking about their "theology". For those who believe that life is from God, in order to be theologically consistent, they must believe that death is also from God as well. The discussion is a deeply spiritual one. Medicine becomes part of the discussion because medical technology has the where-with-all to continue physiological functioning and to end life. Medicine as a discipline does not take a position regarding Spirit. The practice of medicine must go on in a real world while the philosophers continue to debate issues that we surely will not settle soon.

However, the spiritual issue is not usually why medicine becomes part of the discussion. Medical interventions become part of the debate because of their ability to deal with pain. Pain and suffering have led to the debate on euthanasia. Euthanasia and life support must be seen as separate issues. Euthanasia, is in my opinion, a different issue than life support in terminal illness. Life support, is a continuation of physiological mechanisms when spontaneous function has ceased. When the body no longer has the ability to function without machines and the brain fails to register any activity, most medical and theological persons are willing to consider the patient "dead". We need not view discontinuing the machines as the withdrawing of "life support", but rather the discontinuation of mechanized physical function. "Life support" is for that purpose, namely, to support a viable life and offer assistance to the body to restore itself. Mechanized life continuation after viability is lost is not life support but mechanical physiology. Euthanasia deals with stopping life. Usually this is when the inevitable is known and when that which we perceive as the quality of life no longer exists. Sometimes the decision is made to end life because there is excruciating pain and at other times it is because there is "no known medical hope". Life support and euthanasia are therefore very different issues. Life support deals with the mechanical *continuation* of life in the hope that the body will regain health and independently assume those functions once again. Euthanasia deals with the artificial *discontinuation* of life and eliminates any hope of restoration.

To deal with the issue of euthanasia from the theological perspective is difficult because of the profound differences between theoretical and practical theology. Practical theology inevitably follows social dictum. In order to survive, the body of organized theologians — the church — develops rationalizations, symbols and rituals to accept and integrate societal demands. Throughout history the church has changed its mind many times as to what constitutes unacceptable behavior. Inevitably social pressure is victorious over all but the most theoretical of religious practices. Therefore we have the discrepancy between what is called "systematic theology" and "practical theology". "Ivory tower" theologians and the pulpit preachers may agree in theoretical theology but major differences are abundantly apparent in applied theology. Philosophical theologians will continue the debate over euthanasia and right to die issues long after the parish ministers have decided how to deal with it on a practical, daily basis, just as they have with numerous other controversial subjects such as abortion, suicide, and homosexuality.

Because we have also been given intelligence and wisdom by the same God who has given us our body and Spirit, we must use all of these gifts in a sacred fashion. Decisions as to what we believe can only be made when considering the body and mind as one, and when allowing for divine intervention. However, prolonging physical existence when life has ended, and precipitating death before life has ended are both acts of assumed omnipotence. Omnipotence is not ours to assume, in my opinion, however, it is not possible to live without at times assuming some of it. Assuming to make a decision for self or another may be an act of omnipotence, however, negligence is no different. To neglect to use our God-given knowledge is no less an act of assumed omnipotence. To muddy the waters even further, we may out of the negligent form of omnipotence fail to recognize when life is over and allow the body to die. In the final analysis, the moment we presume to take any action on behalf of another person or ourselves, we assume a posture of omnipotence. Some segments of many religions, including Christianity, would argue that the body and soul are on loan to us from God, and therefore we cannot make those decisions even for ourselves. Most would emphasize the importance of human responsibility while being led by the composite of our best knowledge, past experience, and inner Spirit.

Such decisions seem to become more difficult with every new technological invention. What are we to do with the plethora of emerging medical and scientific knowledge that surely must come from God? If the Scriptures of any religion were written today would they not include these new gifts from God? Are not the Scriptures dynamic in relation to life rather than statically bound in theoretical theology? Theology as a theory is a human invention just as are the technologies.

Certainly death is the one item in our experience that we cannot overcome so we develop theories to ignore it and methods to avoid knowing it is happening. The dissonance between religious views and technological developments has produced the problem. In a simplistic society the answers were easier because the choices were fewer. If we could find ways that technology and theology could better serve each other there would be less to debate. It is only the theological value we give to technology and the technological value we give to theology that allows us to debate at all. As a result, mechanistic medicine takes on theological purpose and theology constantly redefines itself in order to attempt to make theology relevant. By giving such status to each position, we can debate the experience of dying while denying death itself.

Technology is not responsible for our efforts to end life or even to end it painlessly. Hemlock and other potions have been around for centuries. Long before Socrates potions and other methods were used to end life. The larger issue may not be ending one's own life, as arguable as that may be, but in presuming to end someone else's.

Most persons do not fear death nearly as much as they fear the process of dying. Woody Allen is reputed to have said, "I don't mind dying, I just don't want to be there when it happens". It may well be that we do not fear death nearly as much as the experience of dying. It is not dying that we debate. It is the when, how, and where that we debate. That is why many attempt to escape the process by a quicker and less painful means. All religions have attempted to find ways of dealing with the end of life. Becker in **The Denial of Death**, recounts the anthropologically and historically documented accounts of the human race needing a hero who could go into the spirit world of the dead and return alive. Christianity added to this literature with the death and resurrection of Jesus. Becker further states that, "when philosophy took over from religion it also took over religion's central problem, and death became the real 'muse of philosophy' from it's beginnings in Greece right through Heidegger and modern existentialism", (Becker 1973).

In order to wrestle with the problem of euthanasia one must determine for him/herself a starting point. If that point is philosophy there are more degrees of freedom. That freedom can come from combining acceptable parts from multiple philosophical points of view and be mixtures of differing cultures, theologies and personal preferences. If the starting point for euthanasia is to end pain and suffering, nearly always the decision must be a shared one with the enabler of the final act. If the enabler does not share the conviction, it would have to be seen murder rather than assisted suicide. If the starting point is religious there are fewer degrees of freedom in that most religions have a sacred literature, i.e., the Bible, Koran, etc., and their doctrines prescribe and proscribe guidelines for the end of life. Of course, there are extremely varying points of view and interpretation of those Scriptures regarding what might be thought of as guidelines. Certainly there are persons of profound religious belief that differ sharply on euthanasia. If the starting point is spiritual (as differentiated from religious), there are even fewer degrees of freedom in that belief in the Spirit, according to many, rules out any control we might have over its entrance or exit from the human body. It is at this point that we wrestle with our knowledge of Spirit, what is Spirit, and whether we have anything to say at anytime about the entrance, exit, or destiny of Spirit. Or, whether we are willing to accept the life of the Spirit apart from the body both before life and after death.

While writing this article, Paul Harvey, the noted radio journalist, told of a lady who had gone into a coma at the birth of her child and on Christmas day sixteen years later awoke, started writing letters, and the next day was shopping in the mall! One cannot help but to ask what if someone had determined years ago that the "plug" should have been pulled. I am reminded of the Psalmist who wrote, "But I trust in thee, O Lord, I say Thou art my God. My times are in thy hand... be strong, and let your heart take courage, all you who wait for the Lord!"(Psalm 31: 14-15, 24 RSV).

The first action that that would help those present when we die is to transmit our wishes via writing. At least this makes the decision ours, although it does not necessarily avoid implicating the conscience and behavior of others. This is not only the "easiest" but probably also the most personally responsible action on our part. The decision then does not need to be whether to discontinue life support, for we may have made the decision not to start it in the first place. A decision regarding this circumstance of death does not however, answer the question regarding "physician assisted suicide" i.e., euthanasia. Euthanasia cannot be a solo decision. It must be a joint decision between the individual and whomever he/she assumes will help them with their suicide.

There are several decision possibilities to be considered in the "right to die" debate. Each decision results from one's belief system. Those that require participation must of necessity involve other's belief systems as well. These are only a few:

- The decision not to begin life support systems at all.
- The decision to withdraw only mechanical life support systems (respirators, etc. but continue tube feeding and hydration).

- The decision to withdraw all life support systems including feeding tubes.

- The decision to pre-empt death due to pain and quality of life issues (euthanasia).

- The decision to allow death to come naturally with maximum pain relief.

- The decision to allow death to come naturally with palliative pain relief.

- The decision to allow death to come naturally without medical intervention.

The Anglican theologian, John S. Pobee, in writing on a quite different matter suggests that in order to deal with a serious problem, "we need four Hs: Honesty, Humanity, Humility, and Honor" (Pobee, 1995). I would suggest that all of these attributes are necessary if we are to make any headway in looking at a human situation so serious as death and our human ability to intervene in that process. Theology, psychology, and medicine all approach life and death based on different premises. Theology is based in faith, discernment and discipline. Psychology is based on culture and human behavior. Medicine is based on "do no harm" and scientific insights. Hopefully theology can lead the way in finding the truth, i.e., honesty. Hopefully psychology can lead the way in understanding human behavior, i.e., humanity. Hopefully medicine will continue to acknowledge inadequacy when dealing with life and death, i.e., humility. The common denominator of these three fields is that each is attempting to promote the ultimate good for every human being. The major difference is between those who must have personal participation and those who assume to deal only with the philosophy and theory of life and death. Perhaps through meaningful interdisciplinary dialogue these three and other professions can help us to move toward honor when we (as we must) assume to be God's agents on earth.

It would interesting to know what Paul Tillich, Ernest Becker and some of our other great thinkers would be writing if they were alive today. They both saw unbelievable medical technology, but both preceded the awesome technology and scientific knowledge available today. They, nor any of us, can foresee the even more incredible advances in medical technology that will be available tomorrow. We will most certainly have to face other questions such as "since my liver is failing should I clone a kidney or some other body part and store it in deep-freeze for later use?" We will need to ask what is the maximum point of physical degeneration when "spare body parts" should not be used? We already must answer questions as to who should receive the limited number of organ transplants. We will also face the utilization of other than human organ transplants and other than human cloned organs. The "right to die" issue will be confounded by questions such as, "have we exhausted all extremities to prolong life?" And questions such as, "how many body parts can one have and still be 'her/himself'?" We will ask, "when a person receives another person's body part, does that person also receive some of the emotion, personality, etc. of the donor?" Do different organ transplants bring differing amounts and kinds of personality factors from the donor? The questions will doubtless cause even greater debates as to the relation between DNA and the human Spirit. Is the Spirit in the DNA? If so, does that not mean that the human Spirit is present at sperm/egg fertilization? There are many other and far more profound questions than these that will emerge.

Recently a wind disaster of historical proportions occurred in France resulting in electrical failure in many hospitals. Life support systems were disrupted. In talking with a health care professional while riding on the airplane, with tremendous pain in his eyes he told me about having to decide which machines they would keep running on generators and batteries and which ones they could not accommodate. After a period of silence, he turned to me and said, "Of course, you know, we were not discontinuing machines, we were discontinuing people". In forced situations such as this, how does one, regardless of theological, philosophical or medical knowledge make a "wise" decision? We cannot live in a real world without knowing that at times we are "God's hands" and that if there is such a thing as human omnipotence, we are the instruments of it in those situations.

I am certain that Paul Tillich would continue to support the Spirit as the essence of God in man, and in so doing, declare our individual right and responsibility to act accordingly. I am not sure how he would handle the myriad of technologically driven decisions we must handle as we attempt to meet God's perfection in an imperfect world. I believe that he would include all of God's revelations to us whether through theological, psychological or medical insight. I am certain that he would not assume to know what we all must believe, neither would he claim to have the whole truth. I would consider it a privilege to stand with him should these be his statements, and I feel certain that Tillich would find agreement, as do I, with the last paragraph Becker wrote in his **The Denial of Death** may have stated it best of all: "We can conclude that a project as grand as the scientific-mythical construction of victory over human limitation is not something that can be programmed by science. Even more, it comes from the vital energies of masses of men sweating within the nightmare of creation — and it is not even in man's hands to program. Who knows what form the forward momentum of life will take in the time ahead or what use it will make of our anguished searching. The most that any one of us can seem to do is to fashion something — an object or ourselves — and drop it into the confusion, make an offering of it, so to speak, to the life force" (Becker, 1973).

REFERENCES

Tillich, Paul, *Systematic Theology*, Vol. 1, University of Chicago Press, Chicago, 1951, p.15

The Hymnal, Presbyterian Board of Christian Education, Philadelphia, 1933, p.266

Becker, Ernest, *The Denial of Death*, Free Press, 1973, p.12

Ibid, p. 285

Pobee, John S., Afro-Anglicanism: Quo Vadimus, *Anglican Theological Review*, Fall 1995, Vol. 77, Issue 4, p. 502.

The Holy Bible, Revised Standard Version, Thomas Nelson & Sons, NY, 1952

31

♦

A Christian Theology of the Right to Die

by *The Rev. Dr. David Richardson*

District Superintendent, California-Pacific Conference

of the United States Methodist Church

T
HE CHRISTIAN DISCUSSION of the "right to die" cannot be addressed without an appeal to experience. This is equally true when the issue is framed differently as the "right to life," the "sanctity of life," or "physician assisted suicide." Too often we reach conclusions about these issues based entirely on principles, reason or tradition, without taking into consideration the real life dilemmas faced by persons for whom a decision to live or die is imminent. Families who anguish over the suffering of a loved one or who are facing a moment in a hospital when life support systems are about to be withdrawn are not easily swayed or comforted by abstract arguments which do not consider their situations.

Anthony DeMello tells the story of a dervish who was sitting peacefully by a river, yielding a bare neck to a passerby who succumbed to the temptation to give it a whack. The dervish got up in pain wanting to hit him back, but the aggressor said, "Wait a minute, you can hit me if you wish. But first you must answer this question: Was the sound of the whack produced by my hand or by the back of your neck?" To this the dervish said, "Answer that yourself. My pain won't allow me to theorize. You can afford to do so, because you don't feel what I feel."[1]

We can afford to theorize about death when it is not immediately before us. Suffering is one thing when it is an abstraction but quite another when it is our own. Few people have illustrated this better than C.S. Lewis who wrote his book **The Problem of Pain** when he was reflecting on theodicy as a rational theological thinker. It is a very thoughtful book which provided many answers to the problem of suffering, but those answers provided little solace to him when his wife was dying with cancer. Her dying brought a very different view of the problem which is reflected in his **Grief Observed**. The neatly packaged answers of his first book provided Lewis with no more comfort than Job got from the advice of his friends. Death looks different when we are face to face with it.

Any wisdom that the Christian might add to the discussion of the right to die must be informed by experience. The Old Testament scholar Rolf P. Knierim identifies "wisdom" and "heart" as two of the signs of the Spirit of God. Wisdom is spirituality in the Old Testament. The opposite of wisdom is "folly." Wisdom is not equated with intelligence or the human mind alone, which can at times be very foolish. Wisdom must be in touch with the world and have practical application. Wisdom must be set within the context of life, it must be experiential. Our very being is given vitality when the mind and heart are connected. The ancient Hebrews did not understand the controlling nature of the brain as modern physiology presents it. The heart was the center of feeling, and it was understood as the source of life. When the heart stopped beating there was no life.[2]

A Christian discussion of the right to die must consider issues of the heart as well as the mind. Any wisdom we bring to the questions before us must touch human feelings as well as values and principles. Mark Twain said the one possession each person is born too which outvalues all his others is his last breath. Thus, when it comes to life and death, we are dealing with the highest principles, with ultimate values, but these are mere abstractions until we discuss them in the context of our life and our death. This is a very personal discussion, and thus it is about right, our rights.

An individual should have a say in the decisions related to his/her own life and death. Certainly the state also has a say in this as the courts have been so clear to uphold. Doctors also have a say. Family members and our community are very important in matters of life and death, but ultimately it is a very personal matter. Life and death have always been the substance of religious sentiment. Paleontologists have looked for funerary evidence as a sign of religion in ancient cultures. The earliest records of early civilization beyond tools have been steles or petrogliphs instructing humans in religious matters, about how to live their lives. Life and death are religious matters.

Christian theology places a high priority on experience for its wisdom. In addition, however, it also values reason, tradition and scripture. The four have been called the "quadrilateral" in Wesleyan thinking. While John Wesley did not actually use the word, Albert Outler coined the phrase to understand the four-sided method of Wesley's theology. Wesley was a man of skilled reasoning capacity, a man of philosophy who was at the same time very practically grounded in experience. He also valued the traditions of the church and searched the scriptures diligently for answers to life's questions.

The many differences of opinion in Christian theology about the substantive issues of life can be attributed to the weight an individual or denomination gives to one or more of these four criteria for decision making. Martin Luther is often misunderstood in his emphasis upon *sola scriptura*, "only scripture," in his argument with the Roman Catholic Church over the place of tradition. Most Christian groups, including Lutheran and Roman Catholic, appeal to reason, scripture, tradition, and experience to some degree or another. It is the weight of one against another that determines the position taken.

The approach to the question of the right to die is not simply a philosophic one. Reason is an important part of the discussion but alone it is inadequate. Many physicians deal with life and death from the perspective of reason only, making science, based primarily on statistics from experimental data and case studies, the fundamental determination for life and death issues. Perhaps this is why Dr. Jack Kevorkian has evoked such a negative response from many persons who wish to take a serious and responsible look at the issue of the right to die. Kevorkian has written, "Any religion ought to be irrelevant to the strictly secular doctor patient relationship. After all, it is a medical problem that brings the patient to the doctor. If the patient has any religious qualms or constraints, he has consulted the wrong professional ... is it not lucicrous for a minister, priest, or rabbi to tell a doctor how, when, or where to excise a gall bladder or to treat myocardial infarction — or to help a suffering and pleading patient die ..."[3]

His "fail-safe" model does not take into consideration the issues of the heart. He tries to eliminate any reference to feelings. In his outline of the fail-safe method he is rather flip as he gives the documentation of the process. His paper trail of death distances him from those who recognize the act of living and dying as sacred. "Wanda Endittal" is the patient, her mother and father are "Flo N. Tiers" and "Justin Tiers." The doctor "Will B Reddy" seems a bit too eager, as does "Dr. Death", Kevorkian's own self-reference. The assisting physician is "Frieda Blaime, MD." The whole matter is rather sterile, but it is medical and scientific as if these disciplines were beyond morality and ethics. From the Christian perspective this is a foolish way to deal with life and death matters. Wisdom requires us to consider other things.

Law approaches life and death from an additional perspective, precedent and tradition. In *Washington v. Glucksberg*, one of the defining cases to date, Justice Rehnquist wrote, "We begin as we always do in all due-process cases, by examining our nation's history, legal traditions, and practices."[4] History and tradition are very important criteria for deciding the issue of the right to die. In upholding the state's ban on physician assisted suicide the court cited 700 years of Anglo-American common-law traditions. As one reads various appellate court decisions as well as the Supreme Court decisions, one finds reference to Greek philosophic schools and the Hippocratic Oath, as well as the traditions of the church fathers, in particular Augustine. Tradition is very important to law.

Reason and experience also are brought in to the discussion for the court, which is why there are varying concurring opinions as well as dissenting ones. While precedent has been very important to its decisions, the court has been clear that it does not want to rule out further discussion on this complicated issue of the right to die. Its decisions have been narrowly related to particular situations. Justice Stevens, in his concurring opinion to *Washington vs. Glucksberg*, wrote, "there are situations in which an interest in hastening death is legitimate. Indeed, not only is that interest sometimes legitimate, I am also convinced that there are times when it is entitled to constitutional protection."[5]

Law, philosophy, and medicine have their particular interests and methodologies for discussing the right to die. Christians as practitioners of these professions also share these interests. There is, however, the fourth criteria that is particular to the Christian discussion, scripture. Scripture is a very important authority for Christian self-understanding. It is a common source, which binds people of many differing cultures and denominations. It must be part of the discussion.

What follows is a discussion of the right to die and physician assisted suicide within the Christian context.

* * * *

There are six suicides described in the Bible. The suicides of Samson, Abimelech, Saul, Ahithophel and Zimri are reported in the Old Testament and in the New Testament we are told that Judas killed himself. In none of these cases is suicide viewed in a favorable light. They are the result of actions or inactions that put the individuals in disfavor with God. The judgment of God is witnessed to in each event.

Abimelech is a rather obscure figure in the early days when Israel and the Canaanites were still vying with one another for power. Abimelech, the bastard son of Gideon, seized power over Shechem by killing his 70 half-brothers. He ruled for three years but God "sent an evil spirit between him and the lords of Shechem"[6] (Judges 9:22), who sought to avenge his brothers. In the ensuing struggle many were killed and Abimelech raised the city and sowed it with salt. As he was about to burn a tower at Thebez, in which his enemies were hiding, he suffered the indignity of having his head crushed by a stone thrown by a woman. Rather than let people say "A woman killed him," he demanded that his sword bearer draw his sword and kill him. "Thus, God repaid Abimelech for the crime he committed against his father in killing his seventy brothers" (Judges 9:56).

Ahithophel was an advisor to Absalom in his rebellion against David. He was viewed as a wise man but David outsmarted him, putting a spy, Hushai, within the camp of Absalom. David turned the counsel of Athithopel into "foolishness" (2 Sam. 15:31). Hushai was able to cast doubt upon his advice and when Ahithophel realized that his recommendations were rejected in favor of Hushai's and that he would be implicated as a conspirator against David, he hanged himself.

Zimri was a military commander who gained his throne by assassination. He only ruled as a king of Israel for seven days. The army rose up against him and forced him to take refuge in the citadel of the palace which he burned down around him, causing his own death (I Kings 16:15ff). His death, like that of Abimeleh and Ahithopel, is seen as his just reward because he had done evil in the sight of the Lord.

The suicide of Saul is a bit more complicated. There are three reports of his death in the Old Testament. Two accounts are virtually identical (I Sam. 31:1-6 & I Chron 10:1-16). Saul had found disfavor with God, but he certainly is viewed with more compassion than the other three whom we've just discussed. Saul is a tragic figure that tries to act as God's anointed by establishing a monarchy among a people who were not accustomed to one. His mental collapse is recorded in the story, and he finally is unable to exercise much of any leadership, becoming paranoid about David. In his final battle against the Philistines he is mortally wounded. Like Abimelech he requested his armor-bearer to kill him lest he be found by his enemies and made sport of. The armor-bearer refused, and the terrified Saul fell on his own sword.

The variant account tells it differently. Here David learns from a young Amalekite that during the battle he had come upon Saul leaning on his spear. Saul beckoned the young man to come and kill him for he was near death. "So I stood over him and, killed him, for I knew that he could not live after he had fallen" (II Sam 1:10). For this mercy killing, David had the Amalekite killed. Blood was on his head because he had killed the Lord's anointed.

The death of Judas in the New Testament follows a similar theme. Matthew tells it as a suicide by hanging after he had thrown the pieces of silver in the temple. It was "blood money." As with the others we have considered, he had brought his own judgment upon himself (Matt 27:3-10). The book of Acts is not quite as clear about his death. In this story, Judas bought a field with the money and through a deadlong fall he was disemboweled. The field became known as the "Field of Blood" (Acts 1:18-20). Whether it was a suicide or an accident it is viewed in the context of judgment for his sin.

A very different perspective of suicide is connected with Samson. His suicide is viewed as heroic, for in pulling down the pillars of the temple of Dagon he not only killed himself but in his death he killed more of his enemies than he had killed in his life (Judges 16:30). Yes, Samson experienced the judgment of God for his foolishness, his selfishness and uncontrolled passions, forgetting his vow, but in the end his act of suicide was a vindication. Suicide was an act of devotion. In the end he followed God.

We can see from the suicides presented in the Bible that they have very little in common with the issues that surround physician assisted suicide as it is presently constituted in today's discussions. All of the individuals had gotten themselves into their predicaments due to some human failure, flaw or sin. Five of the suicides were viewed as God's judgment against them. Abimelech has himself killed out of chagrin, Saul to avoid torture and suffering, Ahitophel to escape David's wrath, Zimri out of desperation, Judas out of guilt. In the case of Saul the idea of a mercy killing was anathema. One account has the aide refusing the request, the other account has David killing the aide for acquiescing to Saul.

None of these suicides has much in common with the problems faced today by people whose lives have been extended by the miracles of modern medicine. The weight of God's judgment upon these individuals in the Bible cannot be applied to people who are kept alive because of artificial feeding, hydration, or mechanical respirators. We can derive no principles from these six situations that give us a definitive answer for the question of life and death in our modern technological context.

The Bible is rather indifferent to suicide. In its great wealth of sacred stories we have only these six accounts. The sins or failings of these individuals are what come under judgment, not the act of suicide itself. There are prohibitions against killing, but not against suicide. In the New Testament neither Jesus nor Paul speak against it. In fact, the New Testament presents self-sacrificial ideas, which recognize that there are higher values than physical life. "No one has greater love than this, to lay down one's life for one's friends" (John 15:13). Jesus recognized that we may lose our life for his sake and in so doing we gain it (Matt 10:39). Paul urged the Romans to "present their bodies as a living sacrifice, holy and acceptable to God, which is your worship" (Rom 12:1). No wonder the early church became so enamored with martyrdom, which is in some cases invited. The early church father, Tertullian, suggested that the martyrdom of Jesus was a kind of passive suicide for the greater cause of God's plan for salvation. Certainly many of the early martyrs of the church were enthusiastic about their deaths, and in some cases they forced it from their persecutors.

Martyrdom has been called "holy dying." Early Christians placed higher value on faithfulness to God than to the preservation of life. Their Roman persecutors tried to get them to curse or renounce Christ, but they refused. Their dying was in itself an affirmation of life, which they viewed as far greater than simple physical survival. They viewed life from the context of eternity and understood the faithful living of it to be more important than merely prolonging one's days. The quality of nature of living was of higher value than the quantity of days and years. Hence, Polycarp could say, "I must needs be burned alive."[7] Christians could give witness to their faith through martyrdom, which made them into heroes among their community, to be canonized later as "saints" of the church.

Martyrdom can be a kind of passive suicide, fitting Durkheim's classical definition of any death resulting directly or indirectly from a positive or negative act of the victim himself, which he knows will produce this result. This "despising of life" led to excesses. The Donatists invited martyrdom. Death was the way to hasten eternity. Death was a way for some to escape guilt and sin. With the development of asceticism and its emphasis upon the spiritual and its denial of the physical, some individuals literally killed themselves through self-denial.

Some commentators have suggested that Augustine's prohibitions against suicide were directly motivated by such extremists as the Donatists. Edward J. Larson & Darrel W. Amundsen have effectively refuted this theory, suggesting that if Augustine was worried about depleting the ranks of Christians through suicide or martyrdom why did he wait so long to speak out against it?

Eastern Christians also opposed suicide, and Augustine had very little influence among them.[8] Augustine confirmed the sanctity of life from the standpoint of the "image of God" (*Imago Dei*). Referring to the creation story, he recognized that human life was holy because we were made in the image of God. We are in ontological relationship to God, which has been marred by our revolt against God and against our created condition. Life is sacred and hence, should not be taken by our own hand.

What this analysis of the early church shows us is that the sanctity of life is not tied up with physical or mortal life. The spiritual being, the life lived in accordance to God, was what made human life sacred. Augustine opposed suicide because he valued our real human nature as creatures in the "image of God." Life must be treated with care and respect. But as we can see from the story of martyrdom, physical life was not the highest value. Current "sanctity of life" positions as presented in modern times are quite foreign to early Christianity. As Geoffrey Drutchas put it, Patristic theology and anthropology was guarded and circumspect in its valuation of mortal life. There is little continuity between the Patristic fathers' professed beliefs about mortal human life and the more modern theological convictions about the sacredness of human life."[9]

Physical life was not the highest value for the early church. Living faithfully in accordance to God's call was more important than preserving life. If it came to it, one might have to choose death rather than violate the life God has given us to live. Hellenistic culture looked upon suicide with neither fear nor revulsion, but as a validation of the way a person had lived. It was an extension of one's values. While early Christians were never comfortable with this view of suicide, we can conclude that their approach to martyrdom was similar. The highest value was how one lived, not the preservation of life itself. It was not "sanctity of life" at all costs.

The New Testament presents an obligation to die for Christ if it is the only alternative to denying him. The early church had its extremists but many Christians found other ways to avoid persecution. Clement of Alexandria opposed seeking martyrdom. Tertullian thought flight was legitimate. Some individuals bribed officials and others forged documents. Of course, some chose apostasy. Death was not sought by most. If martyrdom is understood in some circumstances as passive suicide, it cannot be viewed as active suicide. In other words, it is the choice of life no matter what its cost. If death comes at the hand of one's persecutors then it is the price one must pay to achieve true life in Christ. It is, to use Bonhoeffer's words, "the cost of discipleship."

With time the prohibition against suicide became law. In the 6th century the church legislated against it citing the prohibition against killing. Of course, the prohibition was against murder, and suicide was viewed as self-murder. The Hellenistic attitude toward suicide was supplanted by a new elevation of life which prohibited taking one's life for any reason. In fact, in their research of Christian tradition, Larson and Amundsen conclude that "we are confident that, in the entirety of patristic literature, there is not a single example of Christians committing suicide, asking others' assistance in doing so or requesting others to kill them directly..."[10]

Suicide was particularly stigmatized as sin. Judas' act of hanging himself, in the eyes of the church fathers, outweighed his guilt for the betrayal of Christ. Suicide prevented penitence and forgiveness, thus effectively blocking salvation. By medieval times the bodies of suicide victims could not be buried in consecrated ground. Aquinas called suicide a mortal sin. Many commentators would argue, however, that this was largely due to Hellenistic ideas rather than Biblical roots. Augustine was greatly influenced by Plato's **Phaedo**, arguing that Christians are needed in this world and should not kill themselves. Stoicism's concept of the "divine spark" in humankind helped shape the *imago Dei* in Christian theology. This gave great impetus to the Renaissance which declared human beings to be the center of the universe. The 19th century historian E.H. Lecky in his book **History of European Morals from Augustine to Charlemagne**, insisted that life's sanctity was the product of Christianity. He may also have been the first person to coin the word "euthanasia." Geoffrey Drutchas calls this book the "ground zero source for the sanctity of life."[11]

Drutchas argues that Christianity was not originally concerned with fostering an appreciation for the sacredness of physical human life. Indeed most evidence points to the contrary. The phrase sanctity of life does not appear in the Old or New Testaments. It is out of tune with scripture. Even the *imago Dei* is not a predominant theme in the Old Testament, and it certainly does not warrant support for the sacredness of life principle. It was Hellenistic philosophy which pushed Christians to the humanism of the later middle ages and the subsequent Enlightenment.

It is questionable that the sacredness of life was very persuasive in Christian circles beyond the condemnation of suicide. One only has to look at the church's pronouncements about the Crusades, about holy war, and the justification of capital punishment to realize that the sacredness of life played little role in ecclesiastical politics or civil life. Nevertheless, we can see from this examination of both scripture and tradition that suicide has not been favorably looked upon by Christians. In scripture it is portrayed in the context of judgment of sin. Physical life, however, in Biblical terms is not so important as to be cherished above other values. One might have to sacrifice life rather than lose the life to which God calls us. Glanvill Williams wrote that in the early church Christians spent more energy learning how to die than learning how to live. In Christian tradition we see that martyrs occasionally invited death but the later church fathers sought other means to avoid such extremes. Finally, suicide was condemned by the church.

What then can a Christian say about physician assisted suicide? Does it come under the indictment of the church which in the development of its traditions always seems to oppose suicide? Certainly this is the official perspective of the Roman Catholic Church. Pope Pius XI in his encyclical **Casti Connubi** (1931) wrote that no one has the power or public authority to destroy life. He was concerned about innocent life, in particular the unborn, but the prohibition extends to other innocents, those who are too ill to make decisions for themselves. More recently, Pope John Paul II issued his encyclical **The Gospel of Life**, in which he claims that neither abortion nor euthanasia can be tolerated. "I claim that euthanasia is a grave violation of the law of God."[12]

But here it is necessary to look at some fine distinctions. Even John Paul II recognized that we must distinguish euthanasia from a decision to forgo aggressive medical treatment. One can in good conscience, refuse forms of treatment which might be burdensome even though the refusal may hasten death. Most ethicists and current law recognize this right. John Paul II calls this a decision of conscience to take care of ourselves. Edward J. Larsen and Darrel W. Amundsen explain this well:

> "A distinct line exists between life-sustaining medical treatment and actively intervening with the intent to cause death. Although we recognize both that patients die and doctors allow death to happen through withholding or withdrawing life sustaining medical treatment and that some people refer to such acts as a 'passive euthanasia' we broadly distinguish them from suicide and euthanasia (or those same people tend to call 'active euthanasia')... For us the right to die implicit in acknowledging an individual's autonomy over receiving or rejecting medical treatment is fundamentally different from the duty to die and the right to kill the dying that seem to follow from the social acceptance of physician-assisted suicide and

euthanasia…the former can affirm the sanctity of life within the Christian tradition while the latter would inevitably deny it.[13]

While the distinctions made by Larson and Amundsen are good, their conclusion about what affirms the sanctity of life and what denies it is flawed. To understand this we must continue to scrutinize what is meant by the sanctity of life. Many Christian theologians deny the sanctity of life doctrine, suggesting that only God is holy. Karl Barth recognized that the sanctity of life can be idolatrous, making human life a "second God." Paul Tillich's classic definition of idolatry is that of making something ultimate which is less than ultimate. The way the "right to life" advocates define the sanctity of life does precisely this. In their arguments God is no longer ultimate but life is ultimate.

In Geoffrey Drutchas' view, theologians have drawn a line in the sand over this issue. We can find them on both sides. For instance, Paul Ramsey, Langdon Gilkey, James Wall, Pope John Paul II and many others believe the sanctity of life principle must be upheld if humankind is to have a viable future. We must unequivocally commit ourselves to support the sanctity of life. James Gustafson, Charles Hartshorn, John Cobb, Joseph Fletcher and others I've mentioned above believe that the sanctity of life is counterproductive and wrong. Only God is holy.

Perhaps the line drawn over this issue is a battle of words, an abstraction far removed from the experience of someone whose life is on the line and who faces great suffering and the loss of physical or mental control. To someone cringing with how to manage pain from one day to the next without hope of survival, the words of Geoffrey Drutchas might ring home, "the sanctity of life doctrine makes itself the handmaiden to scientific imperialism."[14] The words, however, are important, no matter what side one takes on the issue of physician-assisted suicide or euthanasia.

Perhaps the phrase "sanctity of life" is not specifically spelled out in the Bible, but it is implied. That life is a gift from God is basic from the opening pages of Genesis. Humankind created in the image of God does require us to recognize the importance of human life. All of creation is holy in that it is of God. This does not, however, pit human life against God in our allegiance or value structures. The fact that Adam and Eve sought to be "like God" in the scheme of things is identified as sin. Their idolatry was to displace god with themselves.

Another way of putting the issue is to say that life is "sacramental." In other words, God participates in human life. We are in a sacramental universe. God participates in all of creation. We must take care of creation and bring reverence to all life. This is what Pierre Teilhard de Chardin called "personalizing the universe." He wrote, "A sense of the universe, a sense of the all, the nostalgia which seizes us when confronted by nature, beauty, music — these seem to be an expectation and awareness of a Great Presence."[15]

To say that life is holy or sacred is not in itself idolatrous. It is to invest creation, life — that which is not ultimate — with the ultimate, God. This leads us to great respect for life and requires that we value life, both of which are essential to ethical decisions about life and death. As de Chardin put it, "It is easy enough to understand that God can be grasped in and through every life. But can God also be found in and through every death? This is what perplexes us deeply. And yet, this is what we must learn to acknowledge as a matter of settled habit and practice, unless we abandon all that is most characteristically Christian in the Christian outlook…"[16]

Dr. Kevorkian's denial of religion's importance in physician assisted suicide misses the most important dynamic in this profound decision. God is present in every death. Ethical decisions related to physician assisted suicide are religious decisions. Life itself is not ultimate nor is it the highest value. It must be treated with profound respect but this is not idolatry. How an individual might decide about questions of life or death for him/herself is a question of profound significance to that person. It is a decision of the heart as well as the mind. Informing that decision will be what that individual believes about scripture and what that individual values in his/her tradition. It is a very personal decision that should not be surrendered to doctors, the state, clergy, or others. The entire community of that person is important to the decision but it is finally an individual one.

Physician assisted suicide can only be justified within the Christian context if a person has ceased to possess an independent existence unsupported by dramatic costly medical intervention, such as life support systems, feeding tubes, ventilators, etc. which now contribute more to human suffering than to viable, meaningful life. A moral argument for physician assisted suicide does not include suicide simply because an individual is depressed or tired of living. Life is a gift, a sacred trust, which God requires us to live out according to God's will. In the case of one who has already lost that ability apart from artificial means, the decision is to finally acquiesce to what creation and God's wisdom have already determined. Such a decision is not inevitable and it is not required of one, for there are many individuals who have availed themselves of the wonders of modern medicine and thrived, living meaningful, loving and happy lives. But if there comes a time when that existence crosses over the barrier of toleration, they should not have to suffer more in the course of their dying. It is at such a time as this that they need the further assistance of a physician so that death will come painlessly. It would be immoral for such brave ones, who have lived so long under such difficult circumstances, if they had to decide for the passive suicide which is the only available option in most states. To decide on the removal of a respirator means they will die of suffocation, to decide on the removal of a feeding tube means they will either die of starvation of dehydration. Physician assisted suicide is really not suicide in the classic Christian understanding. For those who request death at the careful hands of a physician, life has already been taken from them. In most cases they would love to choose life, but that is no longer their choice.

This argument does not address the issue of euthanasia except as it applies to an individual who is not able to actively participate in his/her death and requires the assistance of a physician. This is only technically different than physician assisted suicide as described above and may be called passive euthanasia. A more extensive exploration of euthanasia brings in moral arguments far beyond what we have examined in this discussion. The issue of the protection of the innocent who have had no participation in the decision of their life or death is paramount to this question. The role of society and its concern for justice and the protection of its people comes into play. Euthanasia in most cases is removed from the arena of personal decision making. It is not supported by scripture or tradition. It is at this point that the line for the sanctity of life might be drawn. We have already witnessed the casuistry of several societies in this century which have made decisions for individuals and groups of people that led to death rather than life.

Ultimately, this entire discussion is a statement about life. The Christian decision is centered on life. It is a life lived according to God's purposes. It is lived to fulfillment as a wonderful gift from God. God is in our living and in our dying. Life is sacred, yet it is lived to a higher purpose than merely the preservation of physical life and the lengthening of our days. Our higher purpose, our prior value is that to which God calls us. Sometimes the "cost of discipleship," as Dietrich Bonhoeffer put it, requires that we lay down our life for that which is more important.

One of the most sensitive insights about suicide comes from Joseph Bayly who recognized that the Bible does not contain a hierarchy of sins. All sin is included in the forgiving work of Jesus Christ. Even if one should decide that physician assisted suicide is sin (which is not the viewpoint being presented here) it too as all human actions, comes under the loving forgiveness of Christ. Bayly writes that he believes that God "knows our frame, remembers that we are dust" and does not commit us to human judgment. Thank God! God knows all the factors in our total situation.[17]

We must remember the dervish who reminded the passerby that he could afford to theorize because he did not feel the dervish's pain. The discussion of right to die must consider all the factors in an individual's situation. It is a question that must look at scripture, tradition and follow reason, but it also must acknowledge the dying person's experience.

REFERENCES

1   Anthony DeMello, *The Song of the Bird* (New York:Image Books, 1984), pg. 35.

2   Rolf P. Knierim, *The Task of Old Testament Theology* (Grand Rapids: Wm. B. Eerdmans Publishing Co., 1995), pp 283ff.

3   Jack Kevorkian, "A Fail-safe Model for Justifiable Medically Assisted Suicide," in Michael Uhlmann (ed.) *Last Rights* (Grand Rapids: Eerdmans Publishing Co., 1998), pp 263-295.

4   *Washington v. Glucksberg*, United States Supreme Court, June 26, 1997" in Ibid., pp. 600-629.

5   Ibid. pg. 616.

6   Quotations Bible are from the New Revised Standard Version, (Cambridge: University Press, 1989).

7   Henry Bettenson, ed., *Documents of Christian Church* (London: Oxford University Press, 1963), pg. 12.

8   Edward J. Larson & Darrel W. Amundsen. *A Different Death* (Downers Grove, Ill: Intervarsity Press, 1998). Pp. 26-27.

9   Geoffrey Drutchas, *Is Life Sacred?* (Cleveland: The Pilgrim Press, 1998) pg. 25.

10 Larson & Amundsen, op cit. Pg. 101.

11 Drutchas, op. cit. pg. 19.

12 John Paul II., The Gospel of Life in Uhlmann, op. cit. pg 229.

13 Larson & Amundsen, op. cit. pg. 29.

14 Drutchas, op. cit. pg 147.

15 Pierre Teilhard de Chardin, *The Phenomenon of Man* (New York: Harper & Row, 1955) pg. 266.

16 Pierre Teilhard de Chardin, *The Divine Milieu* (New York: Harper & Row, 1960), pg. 80.

17 Quoted in Larson & Amundsen, op. cit. pg. 29.

Who's Right?

Section Eleven

Epilogue

◆

by Dr. Todd Michael FACOFP, FAAPM
Emergency and Trauma Medicine

THE FIRST PHYSICIAN ASSISTED DEATH I ever witnessed made the biggest impression on me. I was only a first year medical student at the time.

That one began one blustery March day in northern Iowa. It was a late spring. Snow covered the ground, packed to an icy sheen on the sidewalks. And snow continued to fall, blown nearly horizontal in the harsh wind. The windchill was nearly thirty below.

Distant in the desolate landscape, a tiny figure leaned into the gale, a spry but aged man picking his way gingerly over the ice. He had made this walk — just under a mile — hundreds of times and wasn't about to let another cold day keep him from his daily exercise. But at ninety six years of age the going was tough.

As his heart rate and blood pressure increased with the exertion, a sizeable piece of plaque in his carotid artery was suddenly dislodged. In a split second it was swept upwards into the Circle of Willis, then the left middle cerebral artery where it finally came to rest.

When they found him nearly an hour later, a jagged rut trailed behind him in the crusted snow. With the arm and leg that still moved, He had pulled himself nearly three hundred yards and was in grave condition.

But this man, who I had loved for so long, was built to last. A champion fullback in his younger days, his heart and lungs were still incredibly strong. When I finally got to his bedside, some twelve hours later, I was shocked at what I saw. His entire body was flailing back and forth in a nearly constant seizure. But he still knew me and could still speak single words with great effort.

I stayed at my grandfather's side for about two hours, just being there, saying little if anything. What was there to say except, "I love you." It was obvious that he would remain in this unspeakable state until his heart or lungs or kidneys failed him. And that could be months or even years. He was that strong. The situation seemed hopelessly nightmarish.

During this time something curious unfolded. His physician, a trusted personal and family friend for the last fifty years, came in not once but twice. Each time he took a sterile syringe and a vial of medicine from his black bag, loaded the syringe, then administered an intramuscular injection into my grandfather's arm. I had never seen a doctor do this himself. This was a nurse's task. At the time I remember thinking, "That's really great. His physician cares enough about him to actually come in to see him every few hours and actually gives him the medicine himself. He must be exceptionally diligent."

But it slowly dawned on me. As he gave the third injection, I glanced at the vial of medicine and saw that it was morphine sulfate. Judging by the amount in the syringe, I estimated the dose at about fifteen milligrams. A single dose of this would not be lethal, per se, but multiple doses, closely spaced, might conceivably… But it would be utterly impossible to say one way or the other for sure. And it would be impossible to *prove*.

With the third injection several hours later, my grandfather's horrifying flailing slowed somewhat and he began to sleep deeply, his respirations gradually lengthening and becoming shallow. He died quietly in his sleep about twelve hours later a few minutes after his only son arrived from Michigan. My mother told me the doctor had come back in several times during that period, but I didn't ask her whether he had received any more injections. There seemed to be no point talking about the matter. It would only draw attention to something that needed to remain unspoken by all.

Actually, no one did say a word. I even doubt anyone was in the room during certain critical moments.

It was all done very quietly, very compassionately, and very sentiently. No other course of action made any sense at all. The stroke was massive and agonizing but hadn't affected grandfather's brainstem in any way. If nothing else had been done he would have lived for months, perhaps for years before finally being released from his state of extremis — his terrible suffering.

Although he passed away himself many years ago, I have always looked back at that doctor with extraordinary respect and gratitude. He displayed such compassion. He had the depth, the wisdom to know what his old and dear friend needed most when the chips were finally down. And he had the courage to deliver.

My grandmother, on the other side of the family, suffered an altogether different fate. She was a nervous woman who had survived the deaths of all her relatives, most of her friends, her husband, and her only child. Life was very painful for her as she grew old, alone in her simple house with little to do. When she was in her late sixties she confided in me that she wanted more than anything in the world just to die, to "go home." She had carefully — and I mean *carefully* — signed all the appropriate documents which would prevent anyone from interfering if she became gravely ill.

But she was a strong old Iowan too. She made it all the way through her seventies, and as the quality of her life became increasingly dismal, through most of her eighties. One day, while visiting a friend on another floor of the nursing home, she suffered a massive MI or heart attack. Within seconds she went into ventricular fibrillation and began to die.

But they didn't know her on that floor. They didn't know anything about her wishes — or the papers. So they rushed the crash cart over to her, charged the paddles and administered a two hundred joule countershock across her frail chest.

One didn't do it. So they began CPR with full chest compressions, intubated her, and continued to shock her as lidocaine and epinephrine were given IV. After about ten minutes, they had her back in a rhythm that would sustain life, put her on a ventilator, and shipped her to the ICU. To keep her from pulling the tube out, she was paralyzed. My brother and I sat through the entire night at her bedside. Later we would learn that four of her tiny ribs were cracked and she was in horrible pain with each breath.

She lived as a partial vegetable for ten more years. During this time she was constantly crying and shaking as though in a nightmare. Her doctor —

a distant and unapproachable man — refused to sedate her telling me that he was concerned she would become addicted to the sedatives.

EXTREMES

These are what must be clearly understood when trying to arrive to arrive at an intelligent position on any subject. You have to understand the true end-points of the spectrum if you are to understand where to achieve a balanced stance. When looking at the issues of euthanasia and assisted suicide, this is particularly true.

Basically, one extreme is to have no concern whatsoever what other people and their physicians do. Laws and rules that would reflect this extreme would be essentially non-existent. In other words, if society decided that this was the correct way to view what people and their doctors did with their lives, there would be no laws to limit or direct anyone's actions. Physicians could hook people up to an IV and administer lethal drugs to a patient on their own judgment, or at the mere request of a patient. There would be no oversight whatsoever, no guidelines to follow, no ethics committees to answer to.

The opposite extreme would be to have *too much* concern for the way people and their doctors handled life and death issues. If society decided that this was the correct way to view what other people did, there would be extremely elaborate and restrictive laws — and draconian punishments to back them up. Such laws would forbid assisted suicide under any circumstances and for any reason. Vigilence would be acute and there would be no exceptions. Punishments for even slight violations of these laws would be extraordinarily harsh.

This kind of extreme has a name. When a person or has a pathological excess of concern over what other people do, when they seek to have extreme control over other's actions, this is referred to as *co-dependence*. The classic example of this is the husband or wife who obsesses over a spouse's alcohol problem and seeks to control every aspect of that person's life in an attempt to "help."

But individuals aren't the only ones that can be codependent. An entire society can be codependent. An entire institution — such a religion or profession — can be codependent.

The question is, where should *our* society place itself along the spectrum of possible positions that lie between the two extremes? Where is the point of balance, of sanity? Where is the point that is at once healthy, wise, and compassionate?

How should this balance point be expressed exactly. Should it be expressed through self-imposed rules within the medical profession or should society step in and legislate actual laws governing the subject?

Hopefully this book will help you arrive at an intelligent, balanced position by bringing to light the thoughts and experiences of a number of eminently qualified individuals, people who have thought about the subject, dealt with it intimately, over a period of years. You have learned what others think. Now it is time to reexamine your own attitudes to see if they need to be adjusted.

The Right to Die is not a simple subject and it is not likely to be resolved to everyone's satisfaction. At least, not in our lifetime. But as we make our way into the dawn of this great new millennium we seem increasingly unafraid to talk about the matter and to share our inner thoughts. This can only help.

The Final Word

◆

by Robert C. Horn, III

I DON'T REMEMBER WHO SPOKE THESE WORDS of wisdom to me much less where, when or under what circumstances. He or she said, "a long book deserves a short conclusion." It is difficult to resist the temptation to gas on and on. However, I will respect the advice.

The chapters and commentaries in this book remind me of an episode in the book **Ultimate High** by Goran Kropp. He was a mountaineer who climbed Mount Everest and, on principle, he did it without supplemental oxygen. On his descent from his successful climb to the summit, he was completely exhausted. As he collapsed into his tent at Camp Pour, he noticed there was an oxygen bottle next to his sleeping bag. Although he decided against using it, he gratefully acknowledged it was comforting to know it was there in case he needed it to save his life.

Judith Beay makes exactly the same point in her chapter, only in reverse. She writes that a tremendous weight had been lifted off her shoulders when she learned that she could end her life if it became unbearable. Many of the terminally or critically ill people who have shared their stories in this book agree with her. Helynn Hoffa and I certainly do, as well as many of the commentators. Of course, many of the contributors to the book disagree, some vehemently.

The contributions here present an accurate range of the diversity of points of view on this important subject. Some may argue that some opinions have been given short shrift while proponents of the opposite side can argue

411

that same thing. Or they can protest the _____ side's arguments have been given too much space. The editors wanted a manageable book rather than a multi-volume set of books.

The American Medical Association (AMA) strongly supports a bill called the Pain Relief Promotion Act which is currently in Congress. This bill would permit physicians to pursue aggressive pain management strategies, or palliative care, even if it unintentionally hastens a patient's death. The bill is seen as an antidote to physician-assisted suicide. It is high time the medical profession paid attention to end of life care because it has a poor record — or as the AMA charitably says a "less than ideal" record — especially in alleviating pain. This seems to provide an answer to the prototypical situation of a fatal illness coupled with severe pain (classic illustration: widespread cancer). It does not, however, address those people with permanent disability without much physical pain.

ALS patients are fortunate in some respects. If they are on a ventilator, they can choose to have it disconnected, as Herbert Hendin points out. (Some people with ALS die before they can get on a vent). But what about people with other illnesses such as post-polio syndrome, multiple sclerosis, severe burns or bipolar disorder? It doesn't seem right that people with pain will receive palliative care while those with permanent, severe disabilities who are also terminally ill will just have to suffer.

I think it boils down to what researchers like to call "QOL" — quality of life, to the rest of us. I firmly believe that the affected individual is the best one to judge his or her own quality of life. After all, no one can crawl into another person's skin and mind. Others should be consulted — family, friends, religious people, psychiatrists and others that the person is comfortable with.

Let me close by drawing from personal experience. I had no idea of what life would be like on a ventilator. But more than nine years later, I am still very happy I chose life. I am blessed to have a strong supportive group of family and friends. Some days are awful like the day when I realized my leg wouldn't nudge the computer foot pedal so I couldn't type. I lost another bit of my already vastly diminished independence. I am now working to gain it back by brain waves, infrared devices, or movement of my eyebrows. I'll take whatever works!

Although most readers may not believe this, I have had and currently have, a good quality of life. Being paralyzed and unable to speak are perhaps the cruelest ironies for a teacher who is used to gesturing and talking in fifty minute bursts. What good is a high school soccer coach who can't call to his girls? But I have gotten to see our children grow into young adults, two return from Japan, one got married and whose wife is expecting their first child and our first grandchild, been able to attend church, live theater, museums, movies, visits with friends and even the occasional baseball game, enjoyed managing my fantasy baseball team which has finished in first place the last two years, read and written numerous articles and two books. I am convinced that what I can do is more important than what I can't do. Overall, I don't consider myself the luckiest man on the face of the earth as Lou Gehrig said, but I do consider myself a very fortunate man.

I have bad days, mediocre days, and great days just like "normal" people do. The good days outnumber the other ones by I'd guess four or five to one. Weekends are the most difficult because I want to be like the man I used to be. I keep pretty much the same schedule on weekdays: read, study, write, and I hope, learn. Most of the time it is wonderful to be alive. That is what I would like to say to people in similar situations to mine who are contemplating physician assisted suicide or other forms of hastening their death. As my brother Tom wrote, life is reversible, death is not. I will continue to respect and support those who make the decision to end their life. I just wish they would get a chance to communicate with one or more of the heroines and heroes in this book.

Appendices

Additional Reading

◆

THE BOOKS REFERENCED BELOW were compiled by the publisher for the purpose of offering readers the broadest, most objective list of books available on the issues discussed in this publication. Books on this list represent a wide range of viewpoints and opinions. Some are strongly pro-life and anti-euthanasia; others are pro-euthanasia; and other make a concerted effort to be neutral. There is no intent on the part of the publisher to push one point of view in this book or with this list of suggested readings. It is the responsibility of the reader to uncover what is appropriate and acceptable material given one's own circumstances and needs. We recognize that there are many other titles that might appear in this list, however, every effort was made to insure that the list contain a wide mix of readily available titles.

Albom, Mitch, *Tuesdays with Morrie: An Old Man, A Young Man, and Life's Greatest Lesson*. New York: Doubleday, 1997.

Amery, Jean, *On Suicide: A Discourse on Voluntary Death*. 1999.

Anders, George, *Health Against Wealth: HMOs and the Breakdown of Medical Trust*. New York: Houghton-Mifflin, 1996.

Annas, George J., *The Rights of Patients*.
Carbondale, IL: Southern Illinois University Press, 1989.

Basta, Lofty, *Graceful Exit: Life and Death on Your Own Terms*. 1996.

Battin, Margaret P. and Lipman, Arthur G., *Drug Use in Assisted Suicide and Euthanasia*. Binghamton, N.Y.: Haworth Press, Inc., 1996.

Battin, Margaret P., Rhodes, Rosamond, and Silvers, Anita, *Physician Assisted Suicide: Expanding the Debate*. Routledge, 1998.

Beauchamp, Tom L, *Intending Death: The Ethics of Assisted Suicide and Euthanasia*. Scarborough, Ontario: Prentice Hall Canada, 1996.

Beauchamp, Tom L. and Childress, James F., *Principles of Biomedical Ethics*, 3rd ed. New York: Oxford University Press, 1989.

Bennett, William J., *The Book of Virtues: A Treasury of Great Moral Stories*. New York: Simon & Schuster, 1993.

Bennett, William J., *The Index of Leading Cultural Indicators: American Society at the End of the Twentieth Century*. Colorado Spring: WaterBrook Press, 1999.

Berger, Arthur S., *Dying and Death in Law and Medicine*. Westport, CT: Praeger Publishers, 1993.

Bernardi, Peter J., *The Truth About Physician-Assisted Suicide*. Liguori, MO: Liguori Publications, 1996.

Betzold, Michael, *Appointment with Doctor Death*. Troy, MI: Momentum Books, 1993.

Robert Bork, *Slouching Towards Gomorrah: Modern Liberalism and American Decline*. New York: Regan Books, Harper Collins, 1996.

Bright, Bill and Damoose, John N., *Red Sky in the Morning: How You Can Help Prevent America's Gathering Storms*. Orlando: NewLife Publications, 1998.

Bronfenbrenner, Urie, McClelland, Peter, Wethington, Elaine, Moen, Phyllis, and Ceci, Stephen, *The State of Americans*. New York: Free Press, 1996.

Brown, Harold O. J., *Assisted Suicide and Euthanasia: A Christian Perspective Resource Notebook*. Bannockburn, IL: Center for Bioethics and Human Dignity, 1996.

Brown, Judy, *The Choice: Seasons of Loss and Renewal After a Father's Decision to Die*. Canari Press, 1995.

Cameron, Nigel M., *The New Medicine: Life and Death after Hippocrates*. Wheaton, IL: Crossway Books, 1991.

Cason-Reiser, Gail, Reiser, G.R., Demoratz, Michael, J., and Reiser, Richard, *Dying 101: A Short Course in Living for the Terminally Ill*. Pushing the Envelope Publications: 1966.

Clark, David and Emmett, Peter, *When Someone You Love is Dying: Making Wise Decisions at the End of Life*. Minneapolis: Bethany House Publishers, 1998.

Clark, Nina, *The Politics of Physician-Assisted Suicide*. New York: Garland Publishing, 1997.

Culver, Charles M. and Gert, Bernard, *Philosophy in Medicine*. New York: Oxford University Press, 1982.

Cundiff, David, *Euthanasia Is Not the Answer: A Hospice Physician's View*. New Jersey: Humana Press, 1992.

Delury, George E., *But What If She Wants to Die? A Husband's Story*. Birch Lane Press, 1997.

Demy, Timothy J. and Stewart, Gary P, *Suicide: A Christian Response, Crucial Considerations for Choosing Life*. Grand Rapids, MI: Kregel Publications, 1998.

Despelder, Lynne Ann and Strickland, Albert Lee,
The Last Dance: Encountering Death and Dying (4th ed.).
Mountain View, CA: Mayfield Publishing Company, 1996.

Despelder, Lynne Ann and Strickland, Albert Lee,
The Path Ahead: Readings in Death and Dying.
Mountain View, CA: Mayfield Publishing Company, 1995.

Emanuel, Linda L., *Regulating How We Die: The Ethical,
Medical, and Legal Issues Surrounding Physician Assisted Suicide*.
Harvard University Press, 1998.

Furrow, B. R., Johnson, S. H., Jost, T. S., and Schwartz, R. L.,
Health Law. St. Paul, MN: West Publishing, 1991.

Field, Marilyn J. and Cassell, Christine K., ed.
Approaching Death: Improving Care at the End of Life.
Washington, D.C.: National Academy Press, 1997.

Filene, Peter, *In the Arms of Others: A Culture History of the Right to
Die in America*. Ivan R. Dee Publisher, 1998.

Geis, Saly B. and Messer, Donald E., *How Shall We Die? Helping
Christians Debate Assisted Suicide*. Abingdon Press, 1997.

Geisler, Norman and Turek, Frank, *Legislating Morality: Is It Wise? Is It
Legal? Is It Possible?* Minneapolis: Bethany House Publishers, 1998.

Gilles, John, *A Guide to Caring for & Coping with Aging Parents*.
Nashville: Thomas Nelson Publishers, 1981.

Glick, Henry R., *The Right to Die*.
New York: Columbia University Press, 1992.

Greenberg, Samuel L., *Euthanasia and Assisted Suicide: Psychosocial
Issues*. Charles C. Thomas Publishers, 1997.

Grollman, E., *Talking About Death*. Boston: Beacon Press, 1974.

Guroian, Vigen, *Life's Living Toward Dying*.
Grand Rapids, MI: Eerdmans, 1996.

Harper, George Lea, Jr., *Living with Dying: Finding Meaning in Chronic Illness*. Grand Rapids, MI: Eerdmans, 1992.

Hoefler, James M., *Deathright*. San Francisco: Westview Press, 1994.

Horan, Dennis J and Mall, David, eds., *Death, Dying and Euthanasia*. Washington, D.C.: University Publications of America, 1977.

Horn, Robert C., III, *How Will They Know If I'm Dead? Transcending Disability and Terminal Illness*. Boca Raton: GR/St. Lucie Press, 1997.

Humphry, Derek, **Final Exit**. Eugene, OR: The Hemlock Society, 1991.

Humphry, Derek and Clement, Mary, *Freedom to Die: People Politics and The Right-to-Die Movement*. New York: St. Martins Press, 1998.

Humphry, Derek, *Jean's Way*. London, UK: Quartet Books, 1978.

Humphry, Derek, *Lawful Exit*. Junction City, OR: Norris Lane Press, 1993.

Humphry, Derek, *Let Me Die Before I Wake*.
Los Angeles: Hemlock Society, 1982.

Jakobovits, Rabbi Immanuel, *Jewish Medical Ethics: A Comparative and Historical Study of the Jewish Religious Attitudes to Medicine and Its Practice*. New York: Philosophical Library, 1959.

Jamison, Stephen, *Assisted Suicide: A Decision-Making Guide for Health Professionals*. San Francisco: Jossey Bass, 1997.

Jamison, Stephen, *Final Acts of Love: Families, Friends and Assisted Dying*. J. P. Tarcher, 1997.

Johns, Fran Moreland, *Dying Unafraid*. Synergistic Press, 1999.

Jonsen, Albert R., Siegler, Mark, and Winslade, W. J., *Clinical Ethics: A Practical Approach to Ethical Decisions in Clinical Medicine*, 2nd. ed. New York: Macmillan, 1986.

Johnston, Brian P., *Death As a Salesman: What's Wrong With Assisted Suicide*. New York: New Regency Pub. 1998.

Junkerman, Charles and Schiedermayer, David, *Practical Ethics for Students, Interns, and Residents*. Frederick, MD: University Publishing, 1994.

Katz, Jay, *The Silent World of Doctor and Patient*. New York: The Free Press, 1984.

Kilner, John F., *Dignity and Dying: A Christian Appraisal*. Grand Rapids, MI: Eerdmans, 1996.

Kilner, John F., *Life on the Line*. Grand Rapids, MI: Eerdmans, 1992.

Koop, C. Everett, *Koop: The Memoirs of America's Family Doctor*. Grand Rapids, MI: Zondervan Publishing House, 1992.

Koop, Ruth, *When Someone You Love Is Dying*. Grand Rapids: Zondervan, 1980.

Kimbrell, Andrew, *The Human Body Shop: The Cloning, Engineering, and Marketing of Life*. Washington, D.C.: Regnery Publishing, Inc., 1998.

Kubler-Ross, Elisabeth, *Death: The Final Stage of Growth*. Englewood Cliffs, NJ: Prentice-Hall, 1975.

Kubler-Ross, Elisabeth, *On Death and Dying: What the Dying Have to Teach Doctors, Nurses, Clergy, and Their Own Families*. New York: The Macmillan Company, 1969.

Kushner, Harold, *When Bad Things Happen to Good People*.
New York: Schocken, 1981.

Lammers, Stephen E. and Verhey, Allen, *On Moral Medicine: Theological Perspectives in Medical Ethics*. Grand Rapids, MI: Eerdmans, 1987.

Landes, Alison, *Death and Dying — Who Decides?*
ISBN: 1573020273, 1996.

Larue, Gerald, *Playing God: Fifty Religious Views on Your Right to Die*.
Wakefield, RI: Moyer Bell, 1996.

Lifton, R. J. and Olson, E., *Living and Dying*. New York: Bantam, 1975.

Longacre, Christine, *Facing Death and Finding Hope: A Guide to the Emotional and Spiritual Care of the Dying*.
New York: Doubleday, 1998.

Loving, Carol, *My Son, My Sorrow: A Mother's Pleas to Dr. Kevorkian*.
New Horizon Press, 1998.

Lucado, Max, *Tell Me the Secrets: Treasures for Eternity*.
Wheaton: Crossway, 1993.

Lynn, Joanne, ed., *By No Extraordinary Means: The Choice to Forgo Life-Sustaining Food and Water*. Indiana University Press, 1986

Lynn, Joanne, ed., **Handbook for Mortals: Guidance for People Facing Serious Illness**. New York: Oxford University Press, 1999.

Mace, Nancy L. and Robins, Peter V., *The 36-Hour Day: A Family Guide to Caring for Parents with Alzheimer's Disease, Related Dementing Illnesses and Memory Loss Later in Life*.
Baltimore: Johns Hopkins University Press, 1981.

Marker, Rita, *Deadly Compassion: The Death of Ann Humphry and the Truth About Euthanasia*. New York: William Morrow, 1993.

Maxwell, Jane, *Getting Away With Murder: A True Story of Love and Death*. 1994.

May, William F., *The Physician's Covenant*. Philadelphia: Westminster Press, 1983.

McKhann, Charles, *A Time to Die: The Place for Physician Assistance*, New Haven, CN: Yale University Press, 1999.

McNees, Pat, *Dying: A Book of Comfort*. New York: Warner Books,1996.

Meisel, Alan, *The Right to Die*. New York: John Wiley & Sons, Inc., 1989-Present (Update annually).

Meyer, Charles, *A Good Death: Challenges, Choices and Care Options*. Twenty Third Publications, 1998.

Mitford, Jessica, *The American Way of Death*. New York: Crest Books, 1963.

Moreno, Jonathan D., *Arguing Euthanasia: The Controversy over Mercy Killing, Assisted Suicide, and the Right to Die*. New York: Simon & Schuster, 1995.

Morgan, Ernest, *Dealing Creatively With Death*, 13th ed. Barclay House Books, 1998.

Morris, Jennifer, *Pride Against Prejudice: Transforming Attitudes to Disability*. Philadelphia: New Society Press, 1991.

Neils, Rob, *Death With Dignity: Frequently Asked Questions*. Kendall/Hunt Publishing Company, 1997.

Nuland, Sherwin B., *How We Die: Reflections on Life's Final Chapter*. New York: Alfred A. Knopf, Inc., 1995.

Orr, Robert, Biebel, David, and Schiedermayer, David,
More Life and Death Decisions: Help in Making Tough Choices About Care for the Elderly, Euthanasia, and Medical Treatment Options.
Grand Rapids: MI: Baker Books, 1997.

Phipps, William E., *Death: Confronting the Reality*.
Atlanta: John Knox Press, 1987.

Prado, C. G. and Taylor, S.J, *Assisted Suicide: Theory and Practice in Elective Death*. Humanity Books, 1999.

President's Commission, *Defining Death:*
Medical, Legal and Ethical Issues in the Determination of Death.
Washington, D.C.: U.S. Government Printing Office, 1981.

Quill, T.E., *A Midwife Through the Dying Process*.
Baltimore: Johns Hopkins, 1996.

Quill, T.E., *Death and Dignity: Making Choices and Taking Charge*.
New York: Norton, 1993.

Quinlan, Joseph and Julia with Battelle, Phyllis, *Karen Ann: The Quinlans Tell Their Story*. Garden City: Doubleday & Co., Inc., 1977.

Rachels, James, *The End of Life*. Oxford: Oxford University Press, 1986.

Ramsey, Paul, *Ethics at the Edges of Life: Medical and Legal Intersections*. New Haven: Yale University Press, 1978.

Ramsey, Paul, *The Patient as a Person*.
New Haven: Yale University Press, 1970.

Ray, M. Catherine, *I'm Here to Help: A Guide for Caregivers, Hospice Workers, and Volunteers*. New York: Bantam Books, 1997.

Richards, Lawrence O. and Johnson, Paul, *Death & the Caring Community*. Portland, OR: Multnomah Press, 1980.

Rollin, Betty, *Last Wish*. Public Affairs, 1998.

Rothman, David J., *Strangers at the Beside*. New York: Basic Books, 1991.

Rubin, Susan B., *When Doctors Say No: The Battleground of Medical Futility*. Indiana University Press, 1998.

Samuelson, Robert J., *The Good Life and Its Discontents*.
New York: Times Books, 1995.

Schneiderman, Lawrence J. and Jecker, Nancy S., *Wrong Medicine*.
Baltimore: Johns Hopkins University Press, 1995.

Schiedermayer, David L., *Putting the Soul Back in Medicine*.
Grand Rapids, MI: Baker Book House, 1994.

Schneidman, E.S., *Definition of Suicide*. New York: Wiley, 1985.

Seale, C. and Cartwright, A., *The Year Before Death*.
Hants, UK: Avebury, 1994.

Sequin, Marilynne and Smith, Cheryl K., *A Gentle Death*.
Key Porter Books, 1996.

Savelson, Lonny, *A Chosen Death: The Dying Confront Assisted Suicide*.
University of California Press, 1998.

Shepard, M., *Someone You Love is Dying*. New York: Harmony, 1976.

Singer, Peter, *Rethinking Life and Death*.
New York: St. Martin's Press, 1994.

Smith, Douglas C. and Smith, Doug, *Caregiving: Hospice-Proven Techniques for Healing Body and Soul*. IDG Books, 1997.

Smith, Wesley J., *Forced Exit: The Slippery Slope from Assisted Suicide to Legalized Murder*. New York: Times Books, 1997.

Spiro, Howard M., Curnen Mary G. McCrea, and Wandel, Lee Palmer, *Facing Death*. 1996.

Stewart, Gary P., Cutrer, William, R., Demy, Timothy J., O'Mathuna, Donal P., Cunnigham, Paige C., Kilner, John, and Bevington, Linda K., *Basic Questions on End of Life Decisions: How Do We Know What's Right?* Grand Rapids, MI: Kregel Publications, 1998.

Stewart, Gary P., Cutrer, William, R., Demy, Timothy J., O'Mathuna, Donal P., Cunnigham, Paige C., Kilner, John, and Bevington, Linda K., *Basic Questions on Suicide and Euthanasia: Are They Ever Right?* Grand Rapids, MI: Kregel Publications, 1998.

Stillion, Judith M. and McDowell, Eugene E., *Suicide Across the Life Span: Premature Exits* (2nd ed.). Washington, D.C.: Taylor and Friends, 1996.

Stone, Geo, *Suicide and Attempted Suicide: Methods and Consequences.* Carroll and Graf, 1999

Tomer, Adrian, ed., *Death Attitudes and the Other Adult: Theories, Concepts and Applications*. Philadelphia: Taylor-Francis Publishers, 1999.

Vatican, *The Vatican's Declaration on Euthanasia*. Rome: Vatican, 1980.

Veatch, Robert M., *Death, Dying, and the Biological Revolution*. New Haven: Yale University Press, 1976.

Vitez, Michael, *Final Choices: Seeking the Good Death*. Philadelphia: Camino Books, Inc., 1998.

Webb, Marilyn, *The Good Death: The New American Search to Reshape the End of Life*. New York: Bantam, Doubleday, Dell Publishers, 1997.

Weenolsen, P, *The Art of Dying: How to Leave This World with Dignity and Grace, at Peace with Yourself and Your Loved Ones*. New York: St. Martin's Press, 1996.

Weir, Robert F., *Abating Treatment with Critically Ill Patients*.
New York: Oxford University Press, 1989.

Weir, Robert F., ed., *Ethical issues in Death and Dying*, 2nd. Ed.
New York: Columbia University Press, 1986.

Werth, James L., *Rational Suicide? Implications for Mental Health
Professionals*. Washington, D.C.: Taylor & Francis, 1996.

Westley, Dick, *When It's Right to Die: Conflicting Voices, Difficult
Choices*. Twenty Third Publications, 1995.

White, J., *A Practical Guide to Death and Dying*.
Wheaton, IL: Guest Books, 1980.

Whitehead, John, *The Stealing of America*.
Westchester, IL: Crossway Books, 1983.

Wong, P.T. and Stiller, C., *End of Life Issues:
Interdisciplinary and Multidimensional Perspectives*.
New York: Springer, 1999.

Woodman, Sue, Last Rights: *The Struggle Over the Right to Die*.
Perseus Press, 1998.

Yancy, Philip, *Disappointment With God: Three Questions
No One Asks Aloud*. Grand Rapids: Zondervan, 1988.

PERIODICALS:

Personal recommendations of Robert Horn

"Clinical Problems with the Performance of Euthanasia and Physician-Assisted Suicide in the Netherlands." Groenewould, van der Heide, et al. The New England Journal of Medicine – February 24, 2000, Vol. 342, No. 8

"Physician-Assisted Suicide and Euthanasia in Practice." Editorial. The New England Journal of Medicine – February 24, 2000. Vol. 342, No. 8

"Legalized Physician-Assisted Suicide in Oregon – The Second Year." Sullivan, et al. The New England Journal of Medicine – February 24, 2000. Vol. 342, No. 8

Organizations, Societies, Self-Help Groups, Websites, and Independent Resources
When Seeking Additional Information...

◆

TOO MANY TIMES, people pick up reading material in hopes of getting insights into places and people who might be able to provide face-to-face, hands-on assistance or highly informative reality checks on issues of importance. In the case of death and dying issues, the publisher feels that it is critical that users of this book have an objective list of resources that can be contacted. To those ends, the following is a list of organizations, societies and self-help groups that represent pro-choice, anti-euthanasia, as well as neutral positions on the issues at hand. They are listed alphabetically. We've made every attempt to provide current addresses, telephone and fax numbers, as well as Websites and e-mail addresses.

It is recommended that when using an online site that offers a search engine (such as WebMD or DrKoop.com) that the following words might be entered when searching for information:

Death • End of life • Palliative care • End of life
Last acts • Euthanasia • Specific illness, disease, condition

The following list is arranged alphabetical to assist you in finding organizations, groups, and Internet sites that might prove valuable.

Alliance for Aging Research
2021 K Street, N.W.
Suite 305
Washington, D.C. 20006
202-293-2856

ALS Association
27001 Agoura Rd.
Suite 150
Calabasas Hills, CA 9130-5104
www.als.org/

ALS Society of Canada
265 Yorkland Blvd.
Ste. 300
Toronto, Ontario
Canada M2J 1S5
800-267-4257 (in Canada0
416-497-2267
416-497-1256 Fax
www.als.ca/
alscanada@als.ca

American Academy of Hospice and Palliative Medicine
4700 W. Lake Ave.
Chicago, IL 60025-1485
847-375-4712
847-375-6312 fax
www.aahpm.org/
aahpm@aaphm.org

American Academy of Neurology
1080 Montreal Ave.
St. Paul, MN 55116
651-695-1940
www.aan.com
web@aan.com

American Brain Tumor Association
2720 River Road
Des Plaines, IL 60018
847-827-9910
847-827-9918 Fax
800-886-2282 Patient Line
www.abta.org
info@abta.org

American Dietetic Association
216 W. Jackson Blvd.
Chicago, IL 60606-6995
312-889-0040
www.eatright.org/
webmaster@eatright.org

AMERICAN FOUNDATION FOR SUICIDE PREVENTION
Main Office
120 Wall Street
22nd Floor
New York, NY 10005
888-333-AFSP
212-363-3500
inquiry@afsp.org

Florida Chapter
12360 Wiles Rd.
Coral Springs, FL 33076
954-227-9740

Midwestern Chapter
Rush-Presbyterian-St. Luke's Medical Center
Suite 955
1725 W. Harrison St.
Chicago, IL 60555
312-942-2177
312-942-2177 Fax
jlarson491@aol.com

New England Chapter
56 Broad St.
Boston, MA 02109
617-439-0338
617-439-0338 Fax
asfne@worldnet.att.net

New York Chapter
120 Wall St.
22nd Floor
New York, NY 10005
212-363-3500

Northeastern Ohio Chapter
30195 Chagrin Blvd.
210N
Cleveland, OH 44124
216-464-3471
216-831-0928

Greater Philadelphia Chapter
The Pennsylvania Hospital
800 Spruce St.
Philadelphia, PA 19107
215-829-7314
215-829-7315 Fax
hosuda@pahosp.com

Pittsburgh Chapter
3811 O'Hara St.
Room E833
Pittsburgh, PA 15213
412-624-0331
412-624-4962
haasgl@msx.upms.edu

Southeastern Chapter
459 Blanton Rd., NW
Atlanta, GA 30342-3651
404-257-9415
404-843-2386

Southwestern Chapter
UTMSH Psychiatry
1300 Mourund Ave.
Suite 270
Houston, TX 77030
713-500-2555
713-500-2557 Fax

Western Chapter
10565 Civic Center Dr.
Suite 165
Rancho Cucamonga, CA 91730
909-987-0011
afspwd@earthlink.net

Northwestern Chapter
PO Box 25587
Portland, OR 97298-0587
360-737-2436
chet@coho.net

American Medical Association
515 North state Street
Chicago, IL 60610
312-464-4430

American Society of Law, Medicine & Ethics
765 Commonwealth Ave.
16th Floor
Boston, MA 02215
617-262-4990
617-437-7596
www.aslme.org
info@aslme.org

Americans for Better Care of the Dying (ABCD)
4125 Albemarle Street, NW
Suite 310
Washington, D.C. 20016
202-895-9485
caring1@erols.com

Americans United for Life
343 South Dearborn
Suite 1804
Chicago, IL 60604
312-786-9494

Archdiocese of Boston
Office for Health Care Ministry
St. Elizabeth's Hospital
736 Cambridge St.
Boston, MA 02035
617-789-2457
617-789-2573 Fax
www.rcab.org/pilotlaw/Column050997.html
www.rcab.org/healthcare/HealthHome.html

Association for Death Education and
Counseling
342 N. Main St.
Hartford, CN 06117-2507
860-586-7503
860-586-7550 Fax
www.adec.org/
info@adec.org

The Body (An AIDS and HIV
Information Resource)
Body Health Resources Corporation
250 West 57th Street
New York, NY 10019
www.thebody.com/index.shtml

Canadian Physicians for Life
Administration
10150 Gillanders Road
Chilliwack, BC
Canada V2P 6H4
604-794-3772
604-794-3960 Fax
www.physiciansforlife.ca/
info@physiciansforlife.ca

CBS HealthWatch
www.cbs.medscape.com/medscape

CHOICE IN DYING
National Office:
1035 30th Street, NW
Washington, D.C. 20007
202-338-9790
202-338-0242 Fax

Program Offices:
475 Riverside Drive
New York, NY 10015
800-989-9455
212-870-2003
www.choices.org./

Christian Medical and Dental Society
888-271-7637
423-844-1000
423-844-1005 Fax
www.cmds.org/
dugan@cmdsmail.org

Crohn's and Colitis Disease Foundation
of America
386 Park Ave. South
17th FLR
New York, NY 10016-8804
800-932-2423
212-685-3440
212-779-4098 Fax
www.ccfa.org/
info@ccfa.org

Crohn's and Colitis Foundation of Canada
301 - 21 St. Clair Ave. East
Toronto, Ontario
Canada M4T 1L9
800-387-1479 (in Canada)
416-920-5035
416-929-0364 Fax
www.ccfc.ca/
ccfc@netcom.ca

Crohn's Disease
www.healingwell.com/ibd/

COMPASSION IN DYING
Compassion in Dying Federation and of the state of Oregon
PMB 410, 6312 SW Capitol Hwy.
Portland, OR 97201
503-525-1956
503-228-9160 Fax
www.CompassionInDying.org
or@compassionindying.org

Compassion in Dying of Alaska
P.O. Box 233858
Anchorage, Alaska 99523-3858
970-566-7188
970-562-1577 Fax
ak@compassionindying.org

Compassion in Dying of New York
PMB 2010
244 Fifth Ave.
New York, NY 10001-7604
212-561-9175
ny@compassionindying.org

Compassion in Dying of Northern California
PMB 615
1275 4th street
Santa Rosa, CA 95404
707-544-5993
707-544-5993 (phone first, prior to faxing)
nca@compassionindying.org

Compassion in Dying of Southern California
PMB 249
1940 Westwood Blvd.
Los Angeles, CA 90025-4614
213-896-1616
sca@compassionindying.org

Compassion in Dying of Washington
410 E. Denny Way
Suite 108
Seattle, WA 98122
206-256-1636
206-256-1640 Fax
1-887-222-2816 (in Washington)
wa@compassionindying.org

Cystic Fibrosis Foundation
6931 Arlington Rd.
Bethesda, MD 20814
800-344-4823
301-951-4222
301-951-6378 Fax
www.cff.org/
info@cff.org

Death with Dignity National Center
1818 N Street, NW
Suite 450
Washington, D.C. 20036
202-530-2900
admin@deathwithdignity.org
deathwithdignity@aol.com

DrKoop.com
www.drkoop.com

Dying Well Network
www.ior.com/~robneils
Rob Neils, Ph.D.
Spokane, WA

Dying With Dignity
#705
55 Eglinton Ave. East
Toronto, Ontario
M4P 2X7 Canada
416-486-3998
416-489-9010 Fax
www.web.net/dwd
dwdca@web.apc.org

Euthanasia Research & Guidance Organization (ERGO!)
24829 Norris Lane
Junction City, OR 97448-9559
541-998-3285
541-998-1873 (voice/fax)
www.FinalExit.org
ergo@efn.org

Euthanasia Prevention Coalition
103 – 2609 Westview Dr.
Suite 126
North Vancouver, BC
Canada, V7N 4N2
604-794-3772
604-794-3960 Fax
www.epc.bc.ca/
info@epc.bc.ca

Euthanasia.com
www.euthanasia.com/index.html

Goodbye, A Choice-in-Dying Society
PO Box 79521
Kingsway RPO
Vancouver, BC
V5R 5Z6 Canada
604-451-9626

Health A to Z. Com
www.healthatoz.com

HealthCentral. Com
www.healthcentral.com

Hemlock Society U.S.A.
PO Box 101810
Denver, CO 80250
800-247-7421
303-639-1224 Fax
www.hemlock.org
hemlock@privatei.com

HOSPICE FOUNDATION OF AMERICA

2001 S St., NW
Suite 300
Washington, D.C. 20009
800-854-3402
202-638-5312 Fax
www.hospicefoundation.org/
hfa@hospicefoundation.org

Hospice Foundation of America
(Miami Offices)
777 17th St.
Suite 401
Miami, FL 33139
305-358-9272
305-358-0092 Fax
Hospice Web
Site offers links to hospice locations
nationwide
www.teleport.com/~hospice/index.html

LAST ACTS

a national coalition to improve care and caring at the end of life
www.lastacts.org/
rsilletto@rwjf.org

Consumer Outreach
Nancy Reller
1951 Kidwell dr.
Suite 205
Vienna, VA 22182
703-827-8771
nreller@bballard.com

Palliative Care
Karen Long
730 North Franklin
Suite 504
Chicago, IL 60610
312-642-8652
karenl@stewcommltd.com

Innovations in End-of-Life Care
Anna Romer, Managing Editor
Center for Applied Ethics & Professional
Practice
55 Chapel St.
Newton, MA 02458
617-969-7100
intleoljournal@edc.org

Online Discussion Groups
Shawn Taylor Zelman
1951 Kidwell Drive
Suite 205
Vienna, VA 22182
703-827-8771
szelman@bballard.com

Multiple Sclerosis Foundation
6350 North Adams Ave.
Ft. Lauderdale, FL 33309-2130
800-441-7055
954-351-0630 Fax
www.msfacts.org/
support@msfacts.org

Multiple Sclerosis Society of Canada
150 Bloor St. East
Ste. 1000
Toronto, Ontario
Canada M4W 3P9
416-922-6065
416-922-75381 Fax
www.mssoc.ca/
info@mssoc.ca

Muscular Dystrophy Association
3300 E. Sunrise Dr.
Tuscon, AZ 857189
800-572-1717
www.mdausa.org/
mda@mdausa.org

**National Hospice and
Palliative Care Organization**
1700 Diagonal Rd.
Suite 300
Alexandria, VA 22314
703-243-5900
www.nho.org/

National Hospice Organization
1901 N. Moore Street
Suite 901
Arlington, VA 22209
800-658-8898

National Institutes of Health
Solar Building
Rockville, MD
www.nih.gov/ninr/end-of-life.htm

National Multiple Sclerosis Society
733 Third Ave.
New York, NY 10017
800-344-4867
www.nmss.org/
info@nmss.org

**National Reference Center
for Bioethics Literature**
From BIOETHICSLINE, a National
Library of Medicine online bibliographic
database
Georgetown University
Washington, D.C.
www.georgetown.edu/research/nrcbl/bib-
lios/suicide.htm

National Right to Life Committee
419 Seventh Street, N.W.
Suite 500
Washington, D.C. 20004
202-828-8800

**New York State Task Force
on Life and Law**
www.health.state.ny.us/nysdoh/provider/
death.htm

**National Tay-Sachs and Allied Diseases
of Ontario**
512 Wichlow Rd.
Burlington, Ontario
Canada L7L 2H8
905-634- 4101
www3.simpatico.ca/ntsad/index.html
ntsad@sympatico.ca

Oregon Death With Dignity
818 SW. 3rd Ave.
Suite 218
Portland, OR 97204
503-228-6079
www.oregondwd.org/
info@dwd.org

Oregon Death With Dignity Law
www.rights.org/~deathnet/ergo_orlaw.html
Full text of law

Oregon Hospice Association
P.O. Box 1079
Portland, OR 97296-0796
503-228-2104
502-222-4907 Fax
info@oregonhospice.org
www.oregonhospice.org/

Pennsylvania Health Care Association
2401 Park drive
Harrisburg, PA 17110
800-990-7206

**Surrey/White Rock Choice
in Dying Society**
P.O. Box 75062
White Rock PO
Surrey, BC
V4A 9M4 Canada

**UAHC Committee on Older Adults
Committee on Bioethics
Committee on the Synagogue
as a Caring Community**
838 Fifth Avenue
New York, NY 10021
212-650-4120

WebMD
www.webmd.com

World Federation of Neurology – ALS
www.fnals.org/

If you found this book thought provoking...
If you are interested in having this author...
or other of our consulting authors
design a workshop or seminar for your
company, organization, school, or team...

Let the experienced and knowledge group of experts at *The Diogenes Consortium* go to work for you. With literally hundreds of years of combined experience in:

Human Resources • Employee Retention
Management • Pro-Active Leadership • Teams
Encouragement • Empowerment • Motivation
Energizing • Delegating Responsibility
Spirituality in the Workplace
Presentations to start-ups and Fortune 100 companies,
tax-exempt organizations and schools
(public & private, elementary through university)
religious groups and organizations

Call today for a list of our
authors/speakers/presenters/consultants

Call toll free at 866-602-1476
Or write to us at:
2445 River Tree Circle
Sanford, FL 32771